ASSESSMENT TOOLS FOR RECREATIONAL THERAPY
Second Edition

ASSESSMENT TOOLS FOR RECREATIONAL THERAPY
Second Edition

RED BOOK #1

joan burlingame, CTRS, HTR and Thomas M. Blaschko, MA
Idyll Arbor, Inc., Ravensdale, Washington

Idyll Arbor, Inc.
PO Box 720
Ravensdale, WA 98051
(206) 432-3231 (area code 425 after April 1997)

Author's Note: As it approached time for the sixth printing of this book, we decided to update the book with the most current versions of the tools. The second edition is not a major re-work of the first, only an update.

ISBN number 1-882883-31-4

Printed in the United States of America

For Alice Wessels Burlingame, founder of the field of Horticultural Therapy, and my grandmother and mentor.

jb

For my parents, Oliver T. Blaschko and Margaret MacLeod Blaschko, who always encouraged me to think and read and write, (and who probably never expected this book would be one of the results).

TMB

Contents

Acknowledgments

This book would not have been possible without the contributions of many people. Johna Peterson, CTRS has always been available to give constructive criticism with a large dose of practical insight thrown in. Julie Dunn, CTRS, and Norma Stumbo. CTRS, have been supportive and generous in answering many of our questions through the last few years. To these women we wish to express our gratitude. We also wish to thank the creative people who have generously allowed us to include their assessments in this volume and all of the therapists who have tried out the assessments contained in this book and who have given us feedback about the strengths and weaknesses of each.

Chapter 1

INTRODUCTION

The overall purpose of this book is to help the consumer of recreational therapy services receive quality care. To help accomplish this goal, this book on the assessment process was written. The process of assessing a client's needs (and the determination of the client's need for intervention from the recreational therapist) is a critical step to receiving quality care.

WHAT IS AN ASSESSMENT?

What is an 'assessment'? Stumbo and Thompson (1986) define assessment as:

> the process of gathering information about an individual in order that the most appropriate services may be provided to diminish or eliminate the individual's problems with his/her leisure (page 28).

There are many different ways and reasons to gather information. Too often the recreational therapist is confused about which type of assessment tools to use. The best way to determine which tools to use is by figuring out:

1. What the therapist needs to find out about a client's leisure knowledge, functional skills, and leisure skills, and
2. What type of assessments are required by the agency funding the client's treatment.

The first question requires that the therapist be familiar with the disabilities commonly associated with the client's diagnoses. One source of information can be seen in Table 1-1 which shows a treatment protocol which includes assessment tools to be used. Other sources of information, which are outside the scope of this book, come from professional knowledge and skills.

The second question can be answered by reading the written guidelines concerning the assessment process produced by most funding and accrediting agencies. These guidelines are used for quality control and as a way to review the appropriateness of the services delivered (utilization review). Some of the agencies which help fund the services of recreational therapist are

1. Health Care Finance Administration (HCFA) (Medicare and Medicaid)
2. Department of Education (Special Education Services)
3. Third Party Payers (Health Insurance Companies)
4. Foundations
5. Trust Funds

These agencies require all the health care professionals to use one (or more) of three distinct strategies of assessments. The three types of assessment strategies are

1. Norm-referenced
2. Criterion-referenced
3. Functional-Environmental

NORM - REFERENCED

Norm-referenced assessments are those assessment tools which have been administered to thousands of individuals for the purpose of being able to compare an individual's performance against other individuals who have been assessed. Probably the best known type of norm-referenced assessment is the Intelligent Quotient (IQ). Norm-referenced assessments are usually extremely sensitive to errors in the administration of the assessment. For that reason, norm-referenced assessments should be administered only by those individuals who have been carefully trained to follow the strict guidelines for administration of the assessment.

One of the primary reasons that a funding agency would require a norm-referenced assessment is to determine the client's eligibility for services. The Health Care Finance Administration (HCFA) requires that individuals seeking training and residential services through Medicaid be administered one of the IQ tests that have a norm-referenced scoring system. Usually an individual who has been tested as having an IQ of 80 or below can qualify for services. Most school districts require that a child have a measured IQ below 80 or above 120 before they can qualify for special services. (The funding differences for school aged children with IQ's below 80 and those who have 'normal' IQ's can be quite significant. It is not unusual for a school district to budget $25 dollars per day per student in the regular classes. The funding allocated for a student with special needs can easily be three times that -- $75 dollars, or more, a day.) The field of recreational therapy has no nationally recognized assessment tools which are used to determine baseline needs like the IQ assessments.

Two of the assessments in this book are norm-referenced assessment tools, though. The first one is the Leisure Diagnostic Battery (LDB) and the second one is the WAID (What Am I Doing). Rather than being used to determine who qualifies for services and who does not, they are used to determine the place the client fits in the continuum of possible scores. Norm-referenced assessment scores can often be misused because the score the client receives (as with an IQ score) seldom equates with actual ability. Two individuals with the same scores on the LDB may actually have significantly different levels of skill (ability) in the areas that they have mutual interests.

The primary limitation of norm-referenced assessment tools is that they seldom tell the therapist the client's actual skill level. For this reason, many of the funding agencies require that the recreational therapist (and the other team members) use criterion-referenced assessment tools.

CRITERION - REFERENCED

Criterion-referenced assessments are those assessments which help the therapist determine the client's general skills. Michael S. Chapman (1989) lists three attributes of the criterion-referenced assessment (page 130):

1. Assessment of the person in real or simulated settings
2. Assessment of a specific area of development
3. Determination of how a person learns a new concept

The structure of a criterion-referenced assessment usually starts out measuring low skill levels in a specific area and continues to measure increments of increased skill level until competency to actually perform a task has been demonstrated. The client being assessed is placed at the level of competency s/he demonstrates in the assessment.

The primary reason that a funding agency requires a criterion-referenced assessment is to ensure appropriateness of treatment rather than to determine eligibility. A criterion-referenced assessment helps the therapist determine which treatment protocol to use and/or in which treatment group to place the client. By comparing the scores of a series of clients with similar disabilities, and the achieved treatment outcomes, the professionals responsible for conducting quality assurance and utilization review audits can determine the appropriateness of services delivered. (Please see Table 1-1 for an example of how the use of specific assessment tools are integrated into treatment protocols.)

Many of the assessments in this book are criterion-referenced. The General Recreation Screening Tool (GRST), the Recreation Early Development Screening Tool (REDS), and the FOX are three examples of criterion-referenced assessment tools.

Almost all funding sources require that a criterion-referenced assessment tool be used by the therapist. However, even criterion-referenced assessment tools have their limitations. One of the most obvious limitations can be easily seen by reviewing the GRST. It, as with most criterion-referenced assessments, measures only a handful of skills at any one skill level and is therefore very likely to miss problem areas that will limit the client's overall progress.

Michael S. Chapman (1989) points out another limitation to criterion-referenced assessment tools (page 131):

> An additional limitation of criterion-referenced tests involves staff's understanding of test design. Most test items are activities used to measure underlying skill development. For example, the ability to stack blocks is used on many test to assess the underlying skills of reaching, grasping, positioning in space, and releasing an item. These skills, performed in a coordinated manner, are assessed by stacking blocks. To assume that the person needs to learn stacking blocks when this activity is failed on an assessment may be an erroneous conclusion. Staff need to understand clearly the underlying skill(s) being assessed by the test item in order to prevent training in inappropriate areas. Further assessment of the person will determine if stacking blocks was failed due to his or her inability to reach, grasp, position an object in space, or to release the object. Instruction can then focus on the appropriate skill.

One of the nice qualities of the criterion-referenced assessments is that, unlike the norm-referenced assessment, administration of the entire assessment tool is not required. The therapist can select just the section(s) that s/he needs. An example would be, if the recreational therapist worked on a rehabilitation unit with an occupational therapist and a physical therapist, s/he may choose to administer only the last three sections of the CERT — Physical Disabilities assessment (Cognition, Communication, and Behavior).

One last issue with criterion-referenced assessments (and one which some therapists see as a limitation) is that the therapist may need many criterion-referenced tools to meet his/her assessment needs.

TREATMENT PROTOCOL: DECONDITIONING

SOURCE: The information used to develop this protocol may be found in **Geriatric Rehabilitation** by Bryan Kemp, Kenneth Bremmel-Smith, and Joseph Ramsdell published in 1990 by College-Hill Press, A Division of Little, Brown, and Company, Inc., 34 Beacon Street, Boston, MA 02108.

CRITERIA:
1) Bedrest or chair rest (which produces the same EEG patterns as individuals placed in environments which promote sensory deprivation).
2) Noted decrease in cognitive ability including verbal fluency, color discrimination, reversible figures, distorted awareness of time. Also potential decrease in thermoregulation.
3) Noted increase in anxiety, irritability, depression, and possible hallucinatory experiences.
4) Decrease in balance (after 2-3 weeks on bed rest).
5) Increase in resting heart rate (by the end of 3 weeks, morning heart rate can increase by 21%, evening by 33%, or an average of 1 heart beat per 2 days of bedrest).
6) Decrease in oxygen uptake (anticipated 15-30% decrease in uptake after just 3 weeks of bedrest).

SERVICE:
1) Decrease sensory deprivation through moderate activities in bed (including some exercise) 3x day minimum. (1 - 2 hr/wk)
2) Because decrease in balance will not be overcome by in-bed activity, extra safety precautions (including a pototential increase in staffing) to reduce risk of falls during activity will be implemented by the CTRS for the first 5 days out of bed. (as needed; extra staff need not be CTRS)
3) Activities to help maintain central brain processing (e.g., pattern tracing skills). (A potential decrease of 10% in performance can be as a direct result of bedrest and not as a result of medication or the disease process.) (1 - 2 hr/wk)
4) Development/Implementation of an exercise program using client-selected leisure activities to help decrease resting heart rate and increase oxygen uptake (a minimum of 20 minutes of exercises 3x week for 6 weeeks will be required). (Time depends on degree of supervision required)
5) Assist client in leisure programming selection which will help him/her avoid polluted air for a minimum of 6 weeks after d/c of bedrest due to decreased oxygen uptake. (.5 hr. per admission)

BILLING CODES: 97114, 97139, 97145, 97240, and 97530

SOURCE OF BILLING CODES: American Medical Association, **Physycian's Current Procedural Terminology 1990**, American Medical Association, Chicago, 1990.

Depending on the type of activity utilized as the treatment modality, one or more of these billing codes may be used.

OUTCOMES:
1) Client will maintain reality orientation score and central brain processing skills through the period of bedrest as measured by the Idyll Arbor Reality Orientation Assessment and by pattern tracing skill assessments.
2) Client will remain free from injuries due to falls after an extended period of bedrest.
3) Client's resting heart rate will not increase more than 15% (morning) or 20% (evening).
4) Client's score on the Modified Beck Depression Inventory will remain relatively stable over the period of bedrest.

Idyll Arbor, Inc. Ravensdale, WA

_______Approved
_______Reviewed
_______Revised

TABLE 1-1: INCLUDING ASSESSMENT TOOLS IN TREATMENT PROTOCOLS
The recreational therapy department may want to include the use of specific assessments in its written plans of treatment (called 'Treatment Protocols'). Above is a sample treatment protocol from Idyll Arbor, Inc.'s Policy and Procedure Manual (1990).

Perhaps most important in promoting the use of criterion-referenced assessment tools is the Health Care Finance Administration's strong move toward the support of criterion-referenced assessments. An agency may be disqualified from receiving ANY Medicare or Medicaid funds if the institution's staff do not use criterion-referenced assessment tools.

FUNCTIONAL - ENVIRONMENTAL

The functional-environmental assessment is one which measures the client's skill level and abilities within the environment s/he operates. A functional-environmental assessment is a criterion-referenced assessment which measures the interaction between the client and his/her environment. The Bus Utilization Skill Assessment (BUS) is an example of a functional-environmental assessment. The BUS measures the appropriateness of the client's interactions with his/her environment (i.e., riding the bus). As the environment around riding public transportation is constantly changing, the BUS assesses the client's ability to successfully meet the challenges of the changing environment.

STRATEGIES SUMMARY

A recreational therapist may well decide to administer a norm-referenced assessment (i.e., the LDB) to obtain some general information about the client's leisure lifestyle. And the recreational therapist may also administer a criterion-referenced assessment to fine-tune his/her knowledge of the client's needs and strengths. But the 'working' assessment which will help the therapist measure the client's actual, demonstrated ability to execute a skill will be through the use of a functional-environmental assessment. Not all of these assessments need to be administered during the initial assessment process.

SELECTING ASSESSMENT TOOLS

Most recreational therapy departments will need to have a minimum of 10 assessments which the staff are trained to use. For the recreational therapy department which serves numerous populations or which serves clients with similar diagnoses but significantly different functional levels, more than 10 may be required. Most of the assessments will use either the criterion-referenced or functional-environmental strategies.

Each department should identify the primary leisure and functional needs of the populations which they serve. Once this is done, the staff can locate assessment tools which measure these needs. The department should have some criteria (in addition to what the assessment measures) to determine the appropriateness of the assessment tool. Stumbo and Rickards (1986) developed a checklist for selecting an assessment. Please refer to Table 1-2.

COSTS OF ASSESSMENT TOOLS

The cost of conducting an assessment will vary from facility to facility. The greatest portion of the cost will be staff time. A realistic amount of money should be budgeted to purchase standardized assessment tools. The cost for assessment supplies will probably cost between $1.50 to $3.00 per admission.

A department seldom saves money by developing their own standardized assessment. Even if they had staff who were well-trained in the theory and practice of developing assessment tools, the amount of staff time alone that goes into developing an assessment is prohibitive for most facilities. Idyll Arbor, Inc. has found that the real cost of developing an assessment tool is between $2,000 and $10,000. This cost does not reflect the cost of reliability or validity testing beyond the initial trials.

ASSESSMENT TOOL VERSUS ASSESSMENT REPORT

There is a difference between an assessment report and an assessment tool. An assessment tool is a set of questions grouped together in either the norm-referenced, criterion-referenced, or functional-environmental strategy. An assessment report is the document which the therapist uses to record pertinent information about the client, to interpret information about the client, and to recommend specific treatment goals. Most in-house assessments are actually assessment reports and not standardized testing tools. Normally a therapist will use an in-house assessment report in addition to standardized assessment tools. The reader will find samples of assessment reports in Chapter Eight of this book titled SAMPLE ASSESSMENT REPORTS.

ASSESSMENTS TO BE USED IN CLINICAL SETTINGS VERSUS RESEARCH SETTINGS

Most of the recreational therapists who administer assessments will be administering them in a clinical setting. The funding for these services will likely come from either the Health Care Finance Administration or a Health Insurance Policy. The primary purpose of these assessments will be to measure the client's current status and to anticipate the client's future level of involvement in leisure activities.

In some cases the information gathered will be used for the purpose of research. Because the primary purpose of assessments for research is not always just for the client's own betterment, strict regulations exist to ensure protection of the client from potential harm. Most funding sources will not approve the use of assessments for gathering data for research without a formal approval from a certified Human Research Review Board. There are approximately 150 of these boards across the United States.

The reader should review Table 1-3, CLINICAL ASSESSMENT VERSUS RESEARCH ASSESSMENT to find a contrast/comparison of the components of the two types of assessments. In

TABLE 1-2: CHECKLIST FOR SELECTING AN ASSESSMENT

Stumbo and Rickards 1986

PROGRAM CONCERNS

Does the assessment instrument/procedure:
1. Match the intent/goals/philosophy for the overall program?
2. Match the intent/goals of the specific program?
3. Align with the program documentation?
4. Yield enough information to appropriately place clients into programs?
5. Yield the right kinds of information to appropriately place clients into programs?
6. Not repeat information gathered from other sources which is readily available to the recreational therapist?
7. Allow for information for both assessment and evaluation for the clients at a later date?
8. Yield information about clients in a consistent manner?
9. Match the resources available within the recreational therapy department (including cost, staff expertise, time for administration, and scoring)?
10. Meet professional standards?
11. Meet accrediting body standards?

POPULATION CONCERNS

Does the assessment instrument/procedure:
1. Match the client's ability (if self-administered)?
    - a. Can the clients read the instrument?
    - b. Can the clients understand the instrument?
    - c. Can the clients tabulate the results?
2. Match the client's
    - a. Performance abilities?
    - b. Needs?
    - c. Characteristics?
3. Have validity for this population?
4. Have reliability for this population?

STAFF CONCERNS

Does the assessment instrument/procedure:
1. Match the staff's abilities?
    - a. Does the staff have the expertise to administer and interpret the data collected?
    - b. Will they have time to administer the assessment?
    - c. Will they have time to score and analyze the results?
    - d. Can they interpret the results in order to place clients into appropriate activities?
    - e. Will they have time to document the results?
2. Match the training level of the staff?
3. Require extensive scoring and analysis?
4. Require extensive interpretation?
5. Provide similar results or interpretations between individual staff?

ADMINISTRATIVE CONCERNS

Does the assessment instrument/procedure:
1. Have sufficient accompanying material on administration and interpretation methods?
2. Have sufficient accompanying material on validity and reliability for similar populations and programs?
3. Provide references for further reading about the instrument/procedure?
4. Have alternative forms or methods for administration?
5. Fit within the budget allowed for assessment?
6. Allow for public use (as opposed to restricted use only by select licensed professionals or under approval by author)?
7. Allow for computer use in administration and scoring?
8. Provide enough useful information to warrant its use?
9. Combine with other assessments?
10. Have a history of use by similar agencies?

(From **Journal of Expanding Horizons in Therapeutic Recreation**, No. 1, 1986 by N. J. Stumbo and W. H. Rickards. Copyright 1986 by N. J. Stumbo. Adapted by permission. **J of EH in TR** is published by the University of Missouri, Columbia, MO).

TABLE 1-3: CLINICAL ASSESSMENT VERSUS RESEARCH ASSESSMENT

The recreational therapist will find that many of the assessment tools used in our field were developed specifically for a specific hospital or unit OR developed for research purposes. Below the therapist will find some of the primary differences between the two types. The best assessments have the most positive aspects from both sides of the chart.

The attributes that make up a good assessment for research purposes do not always make good attributes for assessments used in the clinical practice of recreational therapy.

The recreational therapist in clinical practice should try to use assessments that meet both his/her practice needs as well as use assessments that have proven to be both valid and reliable in the field. Unfortunately it is hard to find assessments that easily meet the criteria for both research and clinical practice.

CLINICAL PRACTICE	RESEARCH PURPOSES
1. The assessment(s) should gather enough information about the client's leisure history, interests, and motivations and measure the client's functional ability for the therapist to develop a treatment plan.	1. The assessment(s) should measure specific functional abilities and obtain specific information in such a manner as to make cross-comparisons easy between clients. The breadth and depth of the assessment(s) used for research purposes are seldom as extensive as those used in clinical practice.
2. The assessment(s) should provide information about possible etiology of dysfunctional skills.	2. The assessment(s) should minimize the need for professional judgment and rely heavily on objective, observable actions.
3. The assessment(s) should be able to measure minute changes in ability so that even small changes can be measured by repeating the assessment at a later date.	3. The assessment(s) must be written in such a way as to minimize bias due to the therapist's previous experience and feelings about the client.
4. The assessment(s) should be written so that two different therapists will obtain the same information (inter-rater reliability).	4. The results of the assessment(s) should not be tied to eligibility or other benefits, as this could impact the client's scores and jeopardize the validity of the answers.
5. The assessment(s) should be organized in such a manner that it provides the therapist with clear levels of skill. These levels of skills (i.e., developmental milestones) should be similar to the ones used by the rest of the treatment team.	5. The frequency of data collection is determined by a pre-set schedule and is not as responsive to the client's individual needs as an assessment program based on clinically assessed needs.
6. The assessment(s) should be able to provide a justification for determining if a client is eligible for recreational therapy services to allow benefits to be applied equitably.	6. The assessment procedures should be set up so that the therapist has limited interaction with the client to ensure limited influence on the phenomenon measured.
7. The assessment(s) should help the therapist determine both the client's normally demonstrated skill level and the client's actual skill level. (It is not necessarily normal for people to perform at their 'best' ability, especially when they experience a change in health status.)	7. The assessment(s) should measure outcomes without exploring the etiology of any failure or over-achievement. An example might be the degree to which motivation, illness, or medications had an effect on the individual's score.
8. The assessment process should be an enjoyable enough experience for the client so that it does not harm the therapist/client relationship.	8. The assessment should measure items that have a stability over a period of time. One of the areas that is extremely hard to measure is the Affective Domain. Since people's moods change frequently over the normal course of a day, it would be difficult for the researcher to feel comfortable with results obtained. The client may be upset over a negative report from his doctor ten minutes before. If the researcher is measuring the client's satisfaction with his care, he may respond negatively to a questionnaire about how well he likes the services of the recreational therapy department, even if he normally felt good about the services received. During a clinical exam the therapist would have more flexibility to explore the etiology of the client's negative mood.
9. The purpose of the assessment(s) and the way in which it is interpreted must be understood by many health care and family members who do not have an extensive background in recreational therapy practice and theory.	9. The assessment(s) usually are more useful to researchers if they demonstrate a good variance between clients. For a clinical assessment this is seldom important.
10. The assessment(s) should not have a high cost per client.	
11. The assessment(s) should not require the therapist to carry around bulky or heavy equipment. All supplies which will be used by more than one client will need to be easily cleaned.	
12. The assessment(s) should be able to indicate specific skill levels that, once these are reached, the client is no longer in need of recreational therapy services.	

(The material above was drawn from **Assessing the Elderly** by Kane and Kane, Lexington Books, 1985, pages 248 - 253.)

some cases an assessment tool may be used for both clinical administration and research data.

THE ASSESSMENT PROCESS

The assessment process is the step-by-step procedure used by the therapist to obtain enough information about a client to be able to: 1) establish if there is a need for treatment and 2) establish treatment goals. The assessment process overlaps with the development of the treatment care plan. Because clients are legally guaranteed rights, the assessment cannot be completed and the treatment started until the client (or his/her legal guardian(s)) agree with the assessed needs. The six steps of the assessment process are

1. Gathering information via the chart, interview, observation, and the use of assessment tools.

2. Compiling the information gathered into useful constructs (usually listed as 'STRENGTHS' and 'AREAS OF NEED').

3. Reviewing the findings with the individual (or his/her legal guardian) and jointly agreeing on a general treatment course and priorities.

4. Writing this information up in a way that is meaningful to the CTRS, the treatment team, and the individual.

5. Reporting the findings to the treatment team and reaching a consensus in treatment priorities so that services are integrated in a whole team/whole person approach.

6. Finalizing the treatment plan with the individual, using a contract between the individual and therapist, where appropriate, which outlines client/therapist rights and responsibilities. The final treatment plan could also state which assessment tool(s) or which behavioral objectives will be used to measure the client's outcomes.

GATHERING INFORMATION

There are many ways to gather information about an individual. The recreational therapist may review the medical chart; observe the client while engaged in leisure activities; interview the client, staff, and significant others; and administer assessment tools.

The medical chart is a file which contains information about the client. The therapist should find the client's medical diagnoses, the assessments from the entire health care team, the treatment plan, and an ongoing record of the client's day-to-day status (progress notes) in the chart. Because the chart contains the basic information about the client, including precautionary orders and determination of guardianship, this is one of the first areas the recreational therapist should start his/her assessment.

Another important part of the assessment is actual observation of the client. This observation can be broken down into two different types of observation. The first type of observation, the initial observation, is usually made without the client knowing that the therapist is observing his/her interactions with the environment. The purpose of this first observation is for the therapist to determine which criterion-referenced or functional-environmental assessment tools to administer to the client. The second observation is the specific observation required by the assessment tool being administered.

COMPILING THE INFORMATION

Once the recreational therapist has read the medical chart, observed the client, completed the appropriate interviews, and administered the indicated assessment tool(s), s/he needs to compile the information. The information needs to be organized in such a manner as to clearly point out *if* the client requires recreational therapy services, and what the most likely treatment priorities could be. The compiling of information at this point of the assessment process is still in the informal stage, as the outcomes have yet to be presented to the client or the treatment team.

REVIEWING THE FINDINGS WITH THE CLIENT

The recreational therapist should review the assessment findings with the client. The primary reasons for this are: 1) very few treatment plans will be successful if they do not have the support of the client and/or his/her significant others, and 2) both HCFA and the Joint Commission have strengthened their position on client's having the right to make decisions concerning treatment each step of the way. Clients have the right to refuse treatment, including recreational therapy treatment.

To document that a client (or his/her legal guardian) has given informed consent, the facility usually has the client (or guardian) sign an Informed Consent Form. Once this form is in the chart, usually all the therapist needs to do is to inform the client (or guardian) of possible risks associated with *either* participating or *not* participating in the treatment. The therapist should then document in the progress note section of the client's chart that the conversation took place and if the client (guardian) agreed to the treatment. The therapist should also provide some information which indicates the degree to which the client (or legal guardian) understood the risks.

WRITING THE ASSESSMENT REPORT

The recreational therapist needs to write up the information obtained in his/her assessment so that it has meaning to the other team members. Not only should the scores from the assessment be written down, but what those scores mean to the client on a day-to-day basis. What does it mean if a client scores in the 3-4 year range in the area of PLAY BEHAVIOR on the GRST? For most clients it means activities which require the client to engage in competitive behavior with his/her peers are developmentally inappropriate. (For greater detail about how to write up an assessment report, the reader should look at the sample assessment reports shown in Chapter 8).

REPORTING THE FINDINGS

The best services for the client usually occur when the entire treatment team works together. The entire team should present their assessment results and then, as a group (with the client's input), prioritize treatment goals. The team meeting is also a good place to plan avenues of integrating services. An example of integrated services would be the recreational therapist and the speech therapist working together to help a client develop a meaningful signing vocabulary which fits his/her leisure time activities. The recreational therapist could help the speech therapist and the client identify important words that the client should learn, and then provide opportunities to practice the use of the signs during activities.

FINALIZING THE TREATMENT PLAN

Once the entire team has agreed on a overall treatment plan, the recreational therapist can finalize his/her treatment goals with the client. This step may include the use of a contract between the client and the therapist. The therapist could indicate to the client which assessment tool(s) or which criteria from the behavioral objectives s/he plans to use to measure the client's progress. By providing the client with this information, the client will be able to have a clearer understanding of what is expected of him/her.

ASSESSMENT CATEGORIES FOR RECREATIONAL THERAPY

In the beginning of this chapter three strategies for assessments were reviewed: norm-referenced, criterion-referenced, and functional-environmental. These three strategies are used by all health care professionals. In the field of recreation, the catagories are the same, but the names are different. Recreation assessments are usually put into one of the following four categories:

1. Leisure Aptitude and Attitude
2. Functional Skill
3. Specific Skill
4. Combination Leisure and Functional

LEISURE APTITUDE AND ATTITUDE

This category evaluates the client's aptitudes and attitudes toward leisure, his/her interests in leisure, and how those are actually demonstrated based on the client's leisure participation patterns.

The assessment tools which are in this category will most likely come from the norm-referenced strategy.

Some of the assessment tools which fall into this category are the Leisure Diagnostic Battery (LDB), the Leisurescope, the WAID (What Am I Doing), and the RPD (Recreation Participation Data Sheet). Chapter Four is concerned with assessments which fit into this category.

FUNCTIONAL SKILL

This category evaluates the client's basic abilities in the cognitive, social, emotional, and physical domains. Baselines are established in specific skills (i.e., the ability to ambulate without falling and without adapted devices for 100 feet on level ground).

The assessment tools which are in this category will most likely come from the criterion-referenced strategy.

Some of the assessment tools which are in this category are the FACTR (Functional Assessment for Characteristics in Therapeutic Recreation), the GRST (General Recreation Screening Tool), and the BANRT (Bond-Howard Assessment on Neglect in Recreational Therapy). Chapter Five is concerned with assessments which fit into this category.

SPECIFIC ACTIVITY SKILLS

This category evaluates the client's ability to successfully participate in an activity. A Specific Activity Skills Assessment measures the degree to which a client can independently engage in a particular leisure activity. An example would be musical chairs. The client may have been assessed as having all the functional skills required to successfully participate in the game, but the client may not have learned the appropriate progression of skills for the activity to be considered to be musical chairs. Other examples would be to evaluate the client's ability to:

a) play checkers
b) play basketball
c) downhill ski
d) make a slab pot
e) order from a menu
f) sew a quilt

While some of these assessment tools can be found in the criterion-referenced strategy, most of them will be found in the functional-environmental strategy.

Some examples of assessment tools in this category would be all of the assessments in the ICAN series (including the Hiking Assessment contained in this book) and the swimming progression published by the American Red Cross. Chapter Six is concerned with assessment tools in this category.

COMBINATION OF LEISURE AND FUNCTIONAL

Some assessments, especially those developed as facility-specific intake assessments (or assessment reports) combine the leisure aptitude/attitude category with one or more sections on functional ability. These assessments almost always contain a form of the criterion-referenced strategy mixed with one of the other strategies.

Two of the Combination assessment tools in this book are the TRI (Therapeutic Recreation Inventory) and the Idyll Arbor Activity Assessment. Chapter Seven is concerned with assessments in this category.

PROFESSIONAL TRAINING AND THE ADMINISTRATION OF ASSESSMENTS

For the recreational therapist to be able to complete an assessment with the quality needed to be on a par with the other health care professionals, the therapist needs extensive training. The training the recreational therapist receives makes the services that s/he delivers different from the services of the other health care providers. With that in mind, this book is written around the basic premise that:

Recreational therapy is a professional service provided by highly trained individuals who are also certified as a CTRS (Certified Therapeutic Recreation Specialist) through the National Council of Therapeutic Recreation Certification. The CTRS has specific information and skills that set him/her apart from other individuals who facilitate leisure activities for individuals with disabilities. Other disciplines which use these tools should have equivalent training and certification.

Recreational therapy uses leisure activities as a modality to achieve a desired outcome on an assessed need combined with the therapist's formal knowledge of the physiological and psychological effect of activity on individuals with various disabilities or illness.

While the recreational therapist provides services that are unique in nature, s/he is still part of an overall treatment team. As a member of that team, the therapist must conform with basic treatment expectations. One of the basic expectations in the field of health care is that all treatment provided to the client will be directly tied to his/her diagnoses. The treatment that is to be provided is determined by the therapist's assessment of the client's strengths and deficits related to the presenting diagnoses. All treatment provided by the recreational therapist must be directly tied to both the client's diagnoses and a specifically assessed need. Treatment, therefore, cannot begin until information from the assessment process has begun to be received.

The current trend in health care is for many health care services to be delivered outside health care institutions. Recreational therapy services can be clinical in nature, whether they are being delivered in a hospital, nursing home, or elsewhere.

Not all services provided by the recreational therapist need to be 'clinical' in nature. Often the recreational therapist assists clients with disabling conditions who wish to participate in leisure activities. The facilitation of this kind of leisure (non-clinical in nature) is a very normalizing part of recreation and does not always require that an assessment be administered prior to the therapist providing services.

TIME

In most short term care facilities the therapist will have only enough time to conduct a quick functional assessment and to gather some information about the client's interests, attitudes, and participation patterns.

The amount of hours a recreational therapy department should allocate to the assessment process does not depend on the number of beds but the number of admissions combined with the depth of assessment required by the funding agency. The Idyll Arbor, Inc. staff did a study to determine how much time was required to be allocated to the assessment process to pass a Health Care Finance Administration Survey. The study and the results obtained can be found in Table 1-4, HOW MUCH TIME.

No matter what combination of types of assessment tools the therapist uses, the therapist should not administer an assessment to a client just because one is required by the facility. The therapist should always have a reason for using each assessment and for asking each and every question.

Asking questions when the therapist has no idea what s/he would do with the answer, or how they might be able to use the information to help facilitate treatment borders on the unethical. Such questions waste both the client's and the therapist's time and probe unnecessarily into the client's privacy.

ETHICS AND COPYRIGHTS

Most of the assessment tools in this book are copyrighted and **MAY NOT BE COPIED OR REPRODUCED IN ANY MANNER, IN WHOLE OR IN PART, WITHOUT PRIOR, WRITTEN PERMISSION FROM THE HOLDER OF THE COPYRIGHT.** Many of the assessments are available through Idyll Arbor, Inc., P.O. Box 720, Ravensdale, WA 98051-0720 (206) 432-3231 (area code 425 after April 1997).

One aspect of being a professional is adhering to professional ethics. It is unethical to copy materials that are copyrighted. Not only is it unethical, it is also illegal. Every time a therapist steps up to a copying machine to copy a copyrighted paper, s/he is risking a $50,000 fine. It is significantly cheaper to buy the assessment than it is to be caught copying one. Besides, most of the therapists who spend the money to put out an assessment use the proceeds to develop other tools for the field, so the therapist who is illegally copying is also robbing the field of additional tools.

TABLE 1-4: HOW MUCH TIME?

How much time should be allocated to the assessment process? A decisive answer to that question is not easily obtained. Idyll Arbor, Inc. was asked to develop such an equation for Long Term Care Facilities and Intermediate Care Facilities for the Mentally Retarded (ICF-MRs) by one of the facilities we consult with. To help determine a workable equation, the following guidelines were used:

Definition of 'Assessment Process':

1. Actual administration of assessment tools, including set-up time, other prep. time, observation time, and writing (scoring) time.
2. Scoring, summarizing of assessment findings(s), and typing or writing up the assessment report.
3. Attending care plan/individual program plan meeting(s).
4. Documenting the client's progress/regress in progress notes once a quarter.

Definition of criteria to determine if an adequate amount of time was allocated to the assessment process:
A facility was found to have allocated enough time to the assessment process if, during its last HCFA survey, the facility did not receive a (negative) citation in the area of recreation/activities for any element of the assessment process.

Definition of geographic area:
All of the facilities included in the sample were within the state of Washington. All of the ICF-MRs were in the same survey region, the long term care facilities were clustered in three different survey districts, all within the state of Washington.

Size and type of facilities:
40 facilities were compared total, 18 were ICF-MR's and 22 were long term care facilities. The sizes of the facilities (in number of beds) ranged from 6 beds to 600 beds. The recreation/activity staff to client ratio (both therapists and aides) ranged from 1 staff to 10 clients (low end) to 1 staff to 80 patients (high end). There was not a clear correlation between having a low ratio of staff to clients and passing survey.

Surveyor Information:
The survey documents from the 40 facilities were written by a total of ten surveyors; 4 ICF-MR surveyors and 6 long term care surveyors. Eight of the ten surveyors were RNs.

Delineation of Staff Qualifications:
Professional Staff: CTRS (or other licensed/certified therapist) with training in clinical practice. This group of individuals seemed to hold the basic knowledge to be able to interpret data quickly, write measurable objectives on the first attempt, and could prioritize needs fairly easily.

Other: Staff without formal training (4 year degree) in a therapy field and without training in clinical practice. This group of individuals seemed to struggle more when needing to process the assessment results into a treatment plan. They also tended to be less assertive with nursing staff and spend a lot of time going various directions, depending on which nurse was leading the care conference.

Definition of the number of weeks the average employee works per year:
The average employee in the United States works 47 weeks a year. Days not directly involved in job description include: 2 weeks vacation, 1.5 weeks holiday, .5 weeks continuing education, and one week sick leave.

An equation was roughed out and then compared to the survey documents for the 40 facilities. Out of all 40 facilities, only two which met the time criteria had any citations in the assessment process. One of the two facilities challenged the survey findings and the survey team ended up modifying the findings. Only one of the facilities which spent less time received no (negative) citations in the survey document.

It was felt that staff in long term care facilities spent the same amount of time in the assessment process as the staff in ICF-MRs. There appeared to be little difference in the amount of time the therapist spent in care meetings (which are held quarterly) held in long term care facilities and the amount of time the therapist spent in IPP (individual program plan meetings, held once a year) in ICF-MRs. Overall, the difference in time spent for the assessment process was determined more by the size of the facility than the type. The larger the facility, the longer the assessment process took.

Below is the equation that was tested against the survey results:

When Using Professional Staff

$$\text{\# hours per week for the assessment process} = \frac{(\text{\# of beds in facility} + \text{\# of new admits per year}) \times 7 \text{ hours}}{47 \text{ weeks}}$$

EXAMPLE:

$$\frac{(120 + 80) \times 7 \text{ hours}}{47 \text{ weeks}} = 29.78 \text{ hours per week}$$

When Using 'Other' Staff

$$\text{\# hours per week for the assessment process} = \frac{(\text{\# of beds in facility} + \text{\# of new admits per year}) \times 10 \text{ hours}}{47 \text{ weeks}}$$

EXAMPLE:

$$\frac{(120 + 80) \times 10 \text{ hours}}{47 \text{ weeks}} = 42.55 \text{ hours per week}$$

In the above example, it would tend to take 12.77 more hours per week to complete the assessment process with a staff person who was not a trained professional.

At some point in each facility it would be cost effective to hire a professional staff person at $4.00 more an hour in pay over a staff person in the 'Other' category based on productivity.

CONCLUSION

The recreational therapist will need to use a variety of assessment strategies and assessment tools to measure a client's need for services. The therapist needs to determine two kinds of criteria to select the assessment tools to use with each individual: 1) the specific information s/he needs to ascertain about the client's leisure and functional status and 2) the assessment strategies required by the funding agency. Most recreational therapy departments will find similarities in the types of assessments required by the department on a day-to-day basis. The department will be able to budget more realistically if it has a pre-established checklist to evaluate potential assessment tools prior to purchasing them.

References

Gardner, J.F., and Chapman, M.S.(1990) **Program Issues in Developmental Disabilities** (page 129 - 143) Baltimore, MD: Paul H. Brookes,

Kane, R.A., and Kane, R.L. (1985) **Assessing the Elderly** (pages 248 - 253) Lexington, MA: Lexington Books.

Kemp, B.K., Brummel-Smith, K., and Ramsdell, J.W. (1990) **Geriatric Rehabilitation** (pages 177 - 192) Boston, MA: College-Hill Publication.

Stumbo, N.J, and Rickards, W.H. (1986) **Journal of Expanding Horizons in Therapeutic Recreation**, No. 1, Fall 1986: University of Missouri.

Stumbo, N.J., and Thompson, S.R. (1986) **Leisure Education: A Manual of Activities and Resources**. State College, PA: Venture Publishing.

Wessel, J.A. (1979) **ICAN: Sport, Leisure, and Recreation Skills**. Northbrook, IL: Hubbard.

Chapter 2

DOCUMENTATION IN MEDICAL CHARTS

The purpose of this chapter is to provide the reader with a general overview of current practices associated with writing in a medical chart. The reader may wonder why a book on assessments goes beyond the scope of documenting for assessment only. The primary reason for covering the topic in this book is that writing in the progress notes *is* a statement of assessment — the ongoing assessment of the client's status.

There are many other reasons for writing progress notes besides the assessment aspect. They include being seen as an important member of the treatment team, providing justification for billing, and contributing to the documentation required by state laws as described below.

A recreational therapist is most effective when s/he is viewed as an important member of the treatment team. Accurate, concise, useful documentation is vital in creating this perception because the way the treatment team, the facility's administration, and the accrediting agencies view the recreational therapist is influenced more by how and what s/he writes in the progress notes than any other single factor.

To justify appropriate levels of funding for his/her department the recreational therapist needs to provide quality documentation. This is true whether the therapy services being provided are being funded through the room rate (or day-treatment rate), by third party payers (Blue Cross, Blue Shield, Medicare, Medicaid, trust funds, or other sources of funds other than the client and/or his/her family), or by the client (or his/her family). The therapist will find some guidelines for documentation in this chapter. Each department will need to modify these guidelines so that they match the specific needs of its clients and institution.

In many states the health care provider and/or institution is required to keep medical records on a client for 10 years or until the client is 18 years of age, whichever is longer. This means that each health care professional needs to leave enough information in the medical chart to allow the person reviewing the record nine years later to understand the treatment given and the reasons for that treatment. (It is a good idea to put the original score sheet for any formal assessment right into the chart.)

Treatment trends change over time. The department director should keep an archives of old policies, procedures, treatment protocols, and past standards of practice for cross-referencing in the case of a malpractice suit. Many lawsuits do not reach the courts for five or more years.

For a comprehensive discussion on this subject the reader should review the chapter titled 'Documentation in Therapeutic Recreation' by Nancy Navar in **Therapeutic Recreation Program Design, Principles and Procedures** by Carol Ann Peterson and Scout Lee Gunn, 1984.

BASIC RULES WHEN WRITING IN A CHART

1. The therapist should sign and date every entry s/he makes. The therapist should also specify his/her professional title. (In some facilities the time of day that the note was written is also recorded.)

2. The therapist should always use a black, ballpoint pen, never a pencil.

3. The therapist should write legibly, avoiding abbreviations. The only abbreviations that are allowed in medical charts are those

that are already approved by the facility in which the therapist works. The medical records department should be able to provide the therapist with a set of approved abbreviations.

4. The therapist should make error corrections by drawing a single line through inaccurate material, and then date and initial it. Never obliterate material on the record by scratching out, erasing, or using 'White-Out'.

5. The therapist should keep in mind that the chart is a means of communication for the various medical personnel involved in the client's care, and a repository for objective accounting of the progress (or lack of) in resolving the client's medical problems. It should not be a place for the therapist to vent his/her anger or frustrations at the client or his/her family. Careless, unsubstantiated statements (i.e., 'client's mother appeared schizophrenic...') may haunt the therapist and his/her facility long after the client's medical problems are resolved. Candor tempered with at least a minimum of forethought should guide the therapist as s/he makes entries in the record. Remember, it is the client's right to read his/her whole chart.

6. The therapist should document frequently enough to demonstrate the continuity of client care. The seriousness of the client's condition is an important determinant in the amount and frequency of documentation.

7. The therapist should keep documentation concise and specific, but not so brief that important facts related to the client's condition or treatment are omitted. In other words, avoid long narrative when the same information could be presented in a few sentences.

8. The therapist should use descriptive words when writing in the medical chart. See Table 2-1: Documentation: Descriptive Words for a set of commonly accepted descriptive words.

DOCUMENTATION RELATED TO THE INITIATION OF SERVICES

There are three primary ways that a therapist initiates a contact with a client. The therapist may be expected to cover a whole unit, be expected to serve only those clients referred to the therapist's service, or be expected to fill prescriptions for recreational therapy services.

UNIT COVERAGE

The first way is when the recreational therapist is responsible for seeing all the clients on a unit. In this case the therapist is expected to make a basic, formal evaluation of the client's needs between the 1st and 7th day after admission. (This time line may vary depending on the facility's own policies and procedures.)

In this case the therapist will need to determine which clients require the most immediate care. These priorities are based on the results of a formal assessment combined with professional judgment. The type of assessment and the degree of recreational therapy intervention required should be placed in the progress notes section of the medical chart.

> 6/26/90 Mrs. Brown is a 39 year old female admitted on 6/21/90 with lithium toxicity. A leisure history was taken via an interview with the client and the Functional Assessment of Characteristics for Therapeutic Recreation (FACTR) was administered. Mrs. Brown's scores on the FACTR (10/11 physical, 11/11 cognitive, and 10/11 social/emotional) were within a normal range suggesting that recreational therapy services are not indicated at this time. Her leisure history showed that she prefers low risk, small group activities. Her choices of activities tends to promote a balance across the domains. The recreational therapy department will provide her with leisure activities of her choice while she is an inpatient. Unless there are new developments during this admission, no further therapy services will be provided.

In some cases the therapist will want to document that s/he will provide ongoing monitoring to evaluate the need for initiating services throughout the admission.

> 6/29/90 Mr. Chun is a 21 year old male admitted on 6/25/90 with a C-4 complete fx (fracture) due to a MVA (motor vehicle accident). A complete leisure history was taken and the Leisure Diagnostic Battery, Short Form, was administered. Mr. Chun's past leisure patterns consisted of high risk, small group activities (e.g., demolition derby driver, river rafting, down-hill skiing, and deer hunting). Mr. Chun will require extensive recreational therapy services prior to his discharge (1x day/5 days a week) to help him adapt to his new situation. In addition, recreational therapy will help evaluate equipment needs as his rehabilitation program progresses.

> 6/14/90 Tammy is a 7 year old female admitted on 6/12/90 with the diagnosis of AML Leukemia in relapse. She is well known to the recreational therapy department due to her numerous past admissions over the last 18 months. Her current stay is anticipated to be an extended one, with transfer to the ICU (Intensive Care Unit) likely. Tammy's family is not able to be here most of the time, increasing her noted stress and fear associated with the separation and hospitalization. The assessment completed on 4/23/90 (her last admit to Children's Hospital) showed a significant fear of needles. Upon her initial assessment this has been found to still be a problem. The recreational therapy department will use puppet play to help desensitize her to needles. As her health permits, the recreational therapist will help to introduce her to the ICU and its staff to decrease the trauma of her probable transfer. In addition, the recreational therapy department will provide her with age-appropriate toys and activities.

REFERRALS

The second manner in which a therapist may initiate contact with a client is through a referral. A referral is a formal request (in writing, usually documented in the medical chart) from another person who has a legitimate interest in the treatment of the client. A member of the treatment team, a legal guardian, or the insurance company or trust fund supervisor may refer a client to the therapist.

TABLE 2-1: DOCUMENTATION: DESCRIPTIVE WORDS

Ruth Herold, CTRS and Kristin Ogren, OTR/L
Overlake Hospital and Medical Center, Bellevue, WA

MOTOR				
Posture:				
tense	rigid	slouching	slumped	head down
relaxed	open/closed			
Movements:				
coordination	balance	gait	motor planning	gross motor
fine motor	dexterity	eye-hand coordination	tremor	spasm
jerking	handwriting (quality)	dyskinesia	rocking	nervous habit
self-stimulating	mannerism	gestures	hypermobile	hyper-responsive
startles	aimless	purposeless	overstimulated	repetitive
restless	pacing	perseverating	abrupt	agitated
active	spontaneous	strong	forceful	quick
retardation	fluid	slow	latent	delayed
lethargic	listless	passive	tentative	

HELPFUL WORDS TO REMEMBER				
shows	offers	appears	age-appropriate	seems
demonstrates	states	situation-appropriate	reports	observed
noted	produces	declines	refuses	resists
withdrawals	initiates	inconsistent		

COGNITIVE				
Mental State:				
concentration	comprehension	retention	hallucinations	delusions
clear	alert	attention span	aware	perceptive
insightful	memory (recent, remote)	focused	drowsy	dull
reality testing	confused	preoccupied	distractible	disoriented
Thought Process:				
tangential	pressured	rambling	racing thoughts	tracking
processing	abstracting	flight of ideas	generalizing	blocked
expansive	concrete thinking	grandiose	obsessive	disorganized
poverty of thought	scattered			

AFFECT				
flat	blunted	bland	disappointed	dazed
controlled	constricted	matter-of-fact	sober	serious
placid	self-critical	calm	composed	comfortable
self-deprecatory	staring	relaxed	nonchalant	fixed expression
depressed	hopeless	dejected	self-effacing	despondent
sad	tearful	apprehensive	subdued	unhappy
remorseful	lacking energy	guilty	overwhelmed	powerless
belligerent	tense	irritable	frustrated	anxious
puzzled	scowling	pressured	fearful	frightened
agitated	panicky	resentful	angry	sullen
hostile	indignant	cheerful	bright	smiling
enthusiastic	eager	energetic	motivated	interested
animated	happy	spontaneous	exhilarated	euphoric
elated	labile			

TABLE 2-1 (CONT.): DOCUMENTATION: DESCRIPTIVE WORDS

Ruth Herold, CTRS and Kristin Ogren, OTR/L
Overlake Hospital and Medical Center, Bellevue, WA

TASK PERFORMANCE

Following Directions:

follows written directions	follows verbal directions	follows demonstrations	needs cuing	needs clarification
needs repeated directions	needs hands-on assist	learns quickly	retains instructions	
follows (1-2- or 3) step directions				

Use of Time:

sets goals	works intermittently	utilizes time well	plans ahead	scattered
slow to get started	organized	efficient	irregular attendance	productive
works steadily	realistic planning	works slowly	hurried	skips steps

Choice of Activity:

indecisive	hesitant	takes initiative	ambivalent	resistant
quickly engages	apathetic	slow to engage	chooses familiar activity	indifferent
unrealistic choice	seeks challenging activity	decisive	selects (type of activity)	creative
detailed	short-term	repetitive		

Approach to Activity:

patient	persistent	persevering	tolerates frustration	thorough
eager	interested	follows through	orderly	neat
compulsive	tolerates delays	accurate	careful	cautious
recognizes mistakes	impulsive	reckless	careless	use of judgement
problem solving	quality of work	seeks quick results	quick gratification	disregards mistakes
unaware of mistakes				

Independence/Dependence:

responsible	seeks direction	needs reminding	competent	independent
self reliant	accepts direction	seeks reassurance	refuses direction	teaches others
debates suggestions	disregards direction	self-sufficient		

SOCIAL

expressive	joking	congenial	engaging	agreeable
tactful	articulate	gracious	talkative	warm
open	self-disclosing	assertive	spontaneous	outspoken
cooperative	considerate	sensitive	sympathetic	care-taking
doting	tolerant	supportive	concerned	indifferent
apathetic	isolating	sense of humor	solitary	superficial
reserved	self-focused	guarded	suspicious	withdrawn
argumentative	reclusive	detached	passive	engages in power struggle
shy	timid	deferring	condescending	submissive
tentative	dependent	ingratiating	distrustful	docile
compliant	watchful	aggressive	threatening	dominating
forceful	intrusive	sarcastic	critical	provocative
cynical	flippant	competitive	boastful	

Social Behaviors:

placement of seating in group (isolates, dominates, on fringe)
awareness of social/physical boundaries
body posture: open, closed, accessible
selective interactions (peers, staff, men, women, young, old)
tone of voice (monotone, inaudible, loud, soft)
role of patient in group
patient response to authority

eye contact (direct, occasional, elusive)
group skills: parallel, competitive, cooperative
verbal/nonverbal
speech patterns (rapid, forced, spontaneous, latent)
quality of grooming
response of peers to patient

A formal referral should include enough information for the recreational therapist to begin the process of admitting the client to his/her service. This would include the client's name, diagnosis, insurance coverage, complete address, and the type of services that may be required. The therapist will need to evaluate the client to determine if the referral is appropriate.

Some examples of the different situations where a referral may be used are:

1. A recreational therapist usually covers the rehabilitation unit in a general hospital. A OB-Gyn Nurse Practitioner has a woman who is pregnant who requires bedrest and hospitalization for the last four months of her pregnancy. Her client appears depressed, due in part, to boredom. The nurse practitioner is concerned about her client's mental status and its impact on her unborn child and refers the client to the recreational therapist for evaluation and treatment.

2. A group home has a 52 year old client who is mentally retarded and beginning to show possible signs of dementia. The QMRP (Qualified Mental Retardation Professional and team leader) refers the client to a recreational therapist for formal evaluation and for the development of an appropriate day treatment program in lieu of vocational training.

3. A physician has a client who is 57 years old who has a left-sided paralysis due to a CVA. The client, the Chairman of the Board for a health insurance company, played golf three times a week prior to the CVA and now has little interest in doing anything. The physician refers the client to the therapist for an evaluation for adapted golf equipment and re-training in golf.

Generally, health care standards dictate that the professional receiving a referral will provide some kind of response within 72 hours. A written note (usually in the client's medical chart) should be made, even if services cannot be provided. Many referrals are received over the telephone. Departments that receive referrals in this manner should use a referral form which has a space to indicate the date and time the referral was received and who was assigned to respond to the referral. Written referrals should also have the date and time received on the referral.

Most recreational therapists receive many more referrals then they can take. When recreational therapists are working with clients one-on-one or in small groups, the Idyll Arbor, Inc. staff recommend that the facility has the patient-to-therapist ratios shown in Table 2-2. The reader should understand that these ratios can change significantly depending on the depth of services provided by the therapist.

PRESCRIPTIONS

The third way to initiate interaction with a client is through a prescription. A prescription is a formal order from a licensed physician. A well written prescription should indicate if the therapist is to evaluate the client and/or provide specific treatment and/or instruction. Usually a prescription is also considered to be a referral (so that both are not needed).

A referral is not a prescription. Most third party payers will not pay for recreational therapy services on the strength of a referral alone. To receive third party payment a prescription is frequently required.

To help clarify the types of services that the physician wants (or that the therapist feels are needed) the therapist will need to take an active role in writing the prescription.

The director of recreational therapy should work with the medical director to establish a recommended format for referrals to the recreational therapy department. Whenever possible, avoid a blanket referral for 'recreational therapy service', especially when the recreational therapist is billing directly (e.g., third party payment) for his/her services.

At minimum the therapist should try to have 'assessment, treatment, and appropriate instruction'. The physician should include teaching/instruction in the orders to help document that instruction is an essential part of the therapy.

Many treatment units have standard interdisciplinary treatment protocols for specific diagnoses. These interdisciplinary treatment protocols outline the types of services a client could expect when being admitted. For example, if a client is admitted with a primary diagnosis of a massive, left sided stroke, s/he could expect an assessment by the following disciplines: neurology, physiatry, physical therapy, recreational therapy, occupational therapy, dietary, nursing, speech pathology, and social work. Most insurance companies will consider funding an assessment or a treatment if it is a written part of the normal treatment protocol for that diagnoses at that institution. Recreational therapy services should be listed on the institutions standardized treatment plans wherever appropriate. When this is done, it makes it easier for the physician to write the prescription.

P.T., O.T., R.T., Speech services per protocol for massive left sided CVA.

Jon Doe-Hagen, MD

TABLE 2-2: Patient-to-Therapist Ratios

Acute Care Medicine	20:1
Burns: Acute Care	10:1
Burns: Rehabilitation	15:1
Geriatrics: Long Term	30:1
Head Injury: Early Stage	10:1
Head Injury: Mid-Late	15:1
Home Health Care	6:1
Hospice	10:1
MR/DD (Consult Only)	30:1
Psych: Long Term	20:1
Psych: Acute Care	10:1
Spinal Cord: Rehab	15:1

The recreational therapist should work with the physician to list each diagnosis with as many separate diagnoses as appropriate. All treatment must be obviously tied to one or more diagnosis and, the more detailed the listed diagnoses are, the easier it is to accomplish this. The recreational therapist is not allowed to give a client a diagnosis, but s/he can work with the physician to help facilitate a better justification for needed services, especially when the services will be paid by third-party payers. The Idyll Arbor, Inc. staff usually work with the physician when s/he writes a prescription for recreational therapy services. Instead of having the physician write an order for 'assessment and tx' (treatment) related to head injury, we would recommend that the physician write (or we would write and have the physician sign):

'Assessment and tx related to: 1. head injury; 2. loss of functional ability related to judgment, safety, pathfinding, and other executive functions; 3. left upper extremity paralysis; 4. left lower extremity paralysis and fx (fracture); 5. orientation difficulties; and 6. pain on ambulation.'

As an extension of the prescription, ask the physician to co-sign the treatment plan. Many third party payers are denying portions of treatment funding because they interpret the treatment as not having been in the physician's original order. Having the physician co-sign the treatment plan should also give support to the therapist if the issue of malpractice were to come up.

At times there will be more than one physician involved in writing the therapy orders. This is especially the case when various specialists are involved in the client's care and one physician is not willing to assume responsibility for all aspects of the client's recreational therapy care/treatment. The therapist should have the treatment plan written in such a way that each physician can co-sign on his/her orders only.

In the case of the recreational therapist working as part of the treatment team in a teaching hospital who has received orders written by numerous residents in the same department, s/he may want to have the attending physician co-sign the treatment plan.

TURNING DOWN A REFERRAL

At times the therapist will receive referrals or prescriptions for services that are not within the scope of practice for the department or that may over-extend the staff coverage. It is not considered professional to document right in the client's medical chart that you do not have enough staff at the moment to provide services. Below are some examples of how to decline a referral.

> Mrs. Robinson is a 78 year old female with a primary diagnosis of CA (cancer) of the liver. She was referred to the recreational therapy department for diversional activities. The provision of diversional activities is outside the scope of practice for the recreational therapy department. The recreational therapy department would like to thank Stan Kettering, PhD for the referral and would like to suggest that the referral be sent either to the volunteer department of this hospital or to the volunteer section of the local American Cancer Society.

> Mr. Sanyes is a 36 year old male with the primary diagnosis of Post Traumatic Stress Disorder (PTSD). He was referred to the recreational therapy department for evaluation and treatment related to blunt affect secondary to PTSD. At this time the recreational therapy department is not admitting new patients to its service. Upon a basic review of Mr. Sanyes' chart it does appear that recreational therapy services are indicated. There are two companies in the area that have provided recreational therapy services to patients when the in-house recreational therapy department's patient load was full. These services may be provided either on an outpatient or inpatient basis. If the referring physician is interested, this department will help facilitate the referral.

> Ms. Thompson is a 32 year old female with a primary diagnosis of MS referred to the recreational therapy department for assessment and treatment related to decreased physical ability to get around in the community. An initial review of the chart and an interview with the client leads the therapist to feel that the client will fit into the leisure activities that are scheduled in the evenings. This will allow the therapist more time to observe and evaluate Ms. Thompson's skills. In the future Ms. Thompson will also be scheduled for 1:1 and small group therapy outings in the community.

DOCUMENTATION RELATED TO THE REFERRAL AND THE INITIAL VISIT

It is likely that the therapist will not have an entry in the progress notes prior to his/her first contact with the client. Therefore, the therapist's note should reflect information obtained during the referral process. The therapist's documentation for the initial visit should also reflect that some of the orders (referral or prescription) were carried out during the first visit.

> 5/7/90 Order received for recreation therapy services, chart reviewed, evaluation to follow.
>
> 6/13/90 Emily is a two year old female referred to recreational therapy by Pam Elly, MSW for evaluation and intervention. The two primary reasons for the referral were the maintenance of as normal of a developmental progression as possible through the bone marrow transplant process and to provide the patient with age-appropriate avenues to express her fear and anger related to hospitalization and illness.
>
> During the first visit Emily displayed an age-appropriate fear of strangers by crying and clinging to her mother. A Raggedy Ann Doll (autoclaved per protective isolation procedures) and extra face masks were left for mom and Emily to play with. Mom was shown how to play various games (i.e., peek-a-boo) with the mask and doll to help de-mystify face masks. The procedure for bringing in toys from home was also explained to mom. She was able to verbally demonstrate an understanding of the procedure and appeared to be appropriately concerned about the risk of infection.
>
> Plan: To continue to develop a rapport with Emily. Frequency of tx (treatment) will be 3x wk, plus 2x wk PRN (as needed). Duration of tx will be for the entire hospitalization. A formal

developmental assessment will be administered when Emily no longer views the therapist as a stranger. The recreational therapy department will continue to work with the family to have her favorite toys prepared for protective isolation. To help reduce some stress on the family Emily's two siblings will be allowed to attend playroom sessions as staffing permits (coordinated with the Ronald McDonald House volunteers and staff).

SOAP NOTES

Up to this point all examples of documentation have been written in the *narrative* style. When using the narrative style the therapist writes his/her note in the same manner that s/he would report the information in a team meeting. Some facilities use a style called **SOAP**. SOAP stands for: **S**ubjective, **O**bjective, **A**ssessment, and **P**lan. If the above example were written in a SOAP format, it might look like:

S: Emily cried. Her mother said, "She has no toys in here because I'm afraid that they might have germs on them." And "My other children are upset because they have not seen me for two days."

O: Emily was crying, clinging to her mom, and hiding her face from therapist in an age-appropriate manner. The room had no toys in it. Mom's facial expression showed strain and a frown. It was obvious from her red eyes and the tear stains on her face that she, too, had been crying.

A: 1) both Emily and mom appeared to be upset
2) mom did not understand protective isolation procedures related to toys, mom did not know how recreational therapy facilitates the cleaning of toys for Emily
3) mom needed some help with child care for the two siblings
4) therapist noted that Emily had stopped crying and that mom was smiling when the therapist left

P: 1) therapist questioned mom (in a supportive manner) to ensure that she understood the protective isolation procedure as it related to toys
2) therapist gave Emily a doll with extra face masks; demonstrated to mom how to play games with doll and masks to help de-mystify the face masks.
3) therapist discussed issue of siblings with Pam Elly, MSW (who stopped in during recreational therapy session). Arrangements were made to have child care for the siblings coordinated between the Ronald McDonald House and the recreational therapy playroom to facilitate a more normal family situation.
4) recreational therapy tx 3x wk plus 2x wk PRN until discharge
5) recreational therapy to clean toys for Emily PRN
6) a formal development assessment will be administered when Emily no longer views the recreational therapist as a stranger

The recreational therapy department at Providence Hospital in Everett, Washington uses a modified SOAP note. All of their notes start out with the problem listed first with the note following in a SOAP format. An example of this style was written up by Kim Lyons, CTRS.

8/28/90 PROBLEM: decreased leisure skills, decreased mobility and endurance, decrease awareness of personal care needs, decreased community skills

S: "I didn't know I had to use my timer when I'm not at the hospital."

O: Pt. participated in community integration outing to a movie theater this evening. Pt required min. to mod. assist with w/c mobility for curbcuts, doorways, carpeting, and inclines. Required verbal cues x3 to perform pressure-releases as scheduled, and also required a verbal cue to maintain his prescribed fluid intake. Pt. demonstrated difficulty in locating the w/c accessible seating area in theater. Pt.'s parents attended outing and were instructed on assistive techniques with w/c on architectural barriers. Pt. stated enjoyment of outing.

A: Pt. demonstrates decreased awareness for need to carry over skills and self care learned in hospital to the community environment. Requires increased strength and endurance to manage community mobility independently. Parents appear appropriate and safe with use of learned assistive skills. Pt. also demonstrated some decreased adjustment to disability when in public.

P: Short Term Goal: Continue participation in community outings at least 2x wk to increase skills identified above. Long Term Goal: Independent with community leisure skills and wheelchair mobility after discharge.

Because the recreational therapist is providing a therapy with the specific goal of changing a client's ability s/he must assess a client's needs prior to beginning any treatment.

The first progress note written should indicate that some type of assessment has been initiated. A review of pertinent information in the client's chart, a face-to-face interview with the client, observation of the client, or the administration of a formal assessment tool (e.g, CERT-Psych, BANRT, etc.) should be noted. By re-reading the notes on Emily, the reader will find references to 'age-appropriate' crying (an initial, informal developmental assessment) and an assessment for the need to help provide sterilized toys (observation). Both came before any intervention by the therapist.

6/10/90 Initial interview and administration of the Bond-Howard Assessment on Neglect in Recreational Therapy (BANRT) completed and placed in the 'Assessment Section" of the chart.

6/8/90 Initial interview and administration of the Leisure Diagnostic Battery (Long Form) was completed. Interpretations of assessment will be entered in the Recreational Therapy section of the medical chart after scoring is completed.

DOCUMENTATION RELATING TO THE TREATMENT PLAN

A treatment plan should be entered into the medical chart after an assessment has been administered and interpreted, after the therapist has met with the rest of the team, and after the client and/ or his/her legal guardian have agreed to the treatment plan. It is important for the overall health of the client that health care professionals work in a coordinated manner with the client's support.

The therapist should check with his/her agency on the specific requirements related to the client stating his/her goals. Some regulatory agencies require the therapist to state right in the chart that the client has stated his/her own goal.

> 6/14/90 Recreational Therapy treatment plan reviewed with tx team and client. Client expressed excitement and agreement with the plan. The tx team coordinated plans to help facilitate client progress based on a unified definition of needs.

> 6/14/90 Recreational Therapy treatment plan reviewed with guardian. Guardian expressed agreement with all parts of the plan but one; the need to be independent in the use of public transportation. The rest of the treatment plan will be implemented. The need for the independent use of public transportation will be re-assessed later, after the guardian's other concerns have been addressed.

TREATMENT GOALS TIED DIRECTLY TO THE DIAGNOSIS

Health care standards dictate that all treatment plans will be clearly and obviously tied directly to a diagnosis. If a client is admitted to the hospital for a kidney transplant and the recreational therapy treatment goal states: 'To increase the client's awareness of Alcoholics Anonymous group leisure activities' the goal would be out of line, even if that's what the client's greatest need was! If the recreational therapist feels that this is what the treatment goal needs to be, the recreational therapist should work with the physician to list each diagnosis with as many separate diagnoses as appropriate.

Admitting Diagnosis:
Kidney Transplant

versus

Admitting Diagnoses:
Kidney transplant R/T (related to) hereditary conditions and diet
High risk dietary patterns
Inadequate water intake
Physical exercising patterns incongruent with kidney health

The second example would obviously lead to greater opportunity to develop appropriate treatment goals within the scope of practice of recreational therapy.

As the treatment plan is drawn up, the goals should reflect the diagnosis or functional need of the client and not the activity.

Stay away from writing treatment goals which reflect an activity such as:

*The client will attend 3 activities a week

*The client will participate in a sewing program 2x wk for 4 wks

*The client will engage in 5 leisure activities of his/her choice each week to promote a healthy leisure lifestyle

A better way to write treatment goals, basing them on the diagnoses would be:

*The client will demonstrate the ability to independently participate in sewing activities which require following a pattern to reduce confusion and to support reality orientation by (date).

*The client will demonstrate the ability to independently engage in activities which require the integration of motor and sensory functions three out of three trials by (date).

*The client will be able to demonstrate the ability to engage in five satisfying and normalizing activities which do not exacerbate pain in his/her lower extremity by (date).

TREATMENT GOALS TIED DIRECTLY TO THE ASSESSMENT

Whenever the therapist writes a treatment goal it should also reflect the results of the assessment given. One of the easiest ways to establish treatment goals is to take a measurable need right off of a standardized assessment.

CERT (Psych/Behavioral)
II. Individual Performance; J. Strength/Endurance

The initial assessment showed that the client '(3) tires even in seated activities'. Together the therapist and the client determine that he would be more satisfied with his leisure choices if he could increase his strength and endurance. The CERT (Psych/ Behavioral) lists '(2) tires if activity requires being on feet' as the next level of endurance. The client decides to engage in a recreational therapy program of strengthening activities to achieve this goal. The treatment goal developed directly from the assessment results might read:

> Through active participation in specific recreational therapy activities the client will increase his strength and endurance for activity by increasing tolerance time for seated activities from 5 minutes to 20 minutes, and standing activities from 0 minutes to 5 minutes by 5/12/90.

CERT (Physical Disability)
VIII. Behavior; B. Social Interaction Skills

The initial assessment showed that the client '(1) interacts only to meet personal needs'. After a planning session with the client the client agrees to try to increase her skills in this area to '(3) initiates social interaction with some individuals only'. The therapist and the client sign a contract which states that the client will attend and participate in 5 group activities a week to practice the assertiveness and conversational skills she is learning during her 1:1 sessions with the recreational therapist. During these activities she will initiate a conversation with two other peers. The treatment goal developed from the assessment results might read:

> The client will demonstrate the ability to initiate social interactions with at least two peers of her choice during a 20 minute activity 9 out of 12 trials by 7/20/90. Interactions geared toward meeting her own personal needs (e.g., pushing her w/c, picking something up for her, getting food or beverages, etc.) will not be counted in this average.

FACTR
3.10 Frustration

The initial assessment of the client showed that he tended to become 'C. Easily frustrated and as a result, was functionally unable to complete an activity'. The client expressed interest in learning coping mechanisms to help improve his ability to enjoy time with his family. Working with the client and his family, the recreational therapist helped select three leisure activities that the therapist felt that the client could successfully participate in and that the family could enjoy together. The recreational therapist would work with both the client and his family to improve their cooperative skills to decrease the interruption of activities due to frustration. The long term goal was to increase the client's ability to demonstrate greater coping skills in all areas of his treatment and life, thereby decreasing the anticipated length of admission and to increase the overall effectiveness of his treatment. The treatment goal developed from the assessment results might read:

> The client will demonstrate the ability to attend to an activity (the card game 'Go Fish', a walk through the park, or reading fairy tales together) for 20 minutes five out of seven trials by 7/20/90.

The therapist should not include as one of the treatment goals: 'client will return to pre-morbid functioning' unless s/he has clear, measurable data on what that was. Funding for that service could be denied as being unreasonable because the therapist is working without a clear baseline for the goal.

DOCUMENTING OTHER NEEDS

The documentation associated with the treatment plan should also include some indication of the frequency of treatment. The frequency of treatment sessions would obviously vary depending on the type of services being delivered. In Idyll Arbor, Inc.'s recreational therapy home health care practice a typical frequency would be: 3x wk for 1-2 wks, 2x wk for 1 wk, 1x wk for 1-2 wks, 1x every 2 wks for 1-2 times. Treatment frequency should not be written just as PRN (which means 'as needed'). The therapist must be more specific, i.e., 1x wk for 5 weeks plus up to 2x wk PRN.

A well written, comprehensive treatment plan also includes a list of anticipated equipment needs. By including the equipment list in the treatment plan the therapist is providing important information both to the rest of the treatment team and to the insurance company case managers who review the chart to anticipate on-going funding needs.

If possible, the therapist should also list why the client's health is being compromised because the specialized services not been received yet.

> 7/12/90 The client has developed decubitus ulcers approximately every 6 months partly due to inactivity and isolation due to his lack of community integration skills and partly due to his in-house activities which hit the off-switch for his pressure release timer.

The one last area that should be covered during one of the therapist's first entries into the progress notes is to list the reasons why skilled services are required.

Many facilities employ both Certified Therapeutic Recreation Specialists (CTRS) and recreational therapy assistants. The therapist should clearly outline which services require the level of skills that only a CTRS is able to provide. An example would be when a client's treatment program calls for the staff to monitor for activities that could compromise the client's health. It does not take a therapist level staff person to 'observe' the client; however, it would take a therapist level staff person to 'observe and interpret'. The therapist should always include the word 'interpret' when s/he uses the word 'observe' if there is an expectation that special intervention may be required as a direct result of what is being observed. If only a CTRS's services will be given (and not those of an aide), the therapist should note in the chart that restoring the client's functional level takes the skills of a therapist to initiate a program, interpret its effectiveness, and to modify the treatment plan as needed.

DOCUMENTATION RELATING TO MEDICATIONS

Many of the medications that the client is taking will have an impact on his/her ability to successfully engage in therapy and leisure activities. The recreational therapy assessment and the treatment plan should address this issue. By working closely with a pharmacist, the recreational therapy department should be able to begin to develop protocols related to specific medications. Some medication groups that should have written treatment precautions or protocols are:

Medications that cause sensitivity to the sun:
The assessment should identify these medications and the

treatment plan should include special instructions related to how sun sensitivity will affect the client's ability to continue to engage in normal leisure activities. Will a sun block need to be ordered by the physician? Will some activities need to be avoided, and other's taught in their place?

Medications to reduce seizure activity:
Laser shows may over-stimulate the brain and decrease the effectiveness of seizure medications. Clients who are taking seizure medications may need to be educated about the need to avoid laser shows, some video games, flash bulbs, strobe lights, etc.

Medications to help treat depression:
Many of the medications prescribed for depression cause an individual to be more sensitive to the effects of alcohol. A client who will be taking anti-depression medications for any length of time should have a satisfying repertoire of leisure activities which do not promote the use of alcohol and drugs.

Medications which have a negative impact on the kidneys:
Many of the negative side effects can be decreased for medications that impact the kidneys. By increasing the rate of blood flow through the body with the use of physical activity, these side effects can frequently be lessened. Helping the client find leisure activities which s/he enjoys and which help increase the heart rate even slightly is an important component of treatment in this situation.

Medications that are sensitive to over hydration:
Many medications become less effective if the client drinks too much fluid. Frequently a client will be kept as an inpatient until his/her medication doses are worked out and balanced against his/her need. The therapist needs to use his/her leisure preference/leisure patterns assessment to anticipate a potential problem in this area. The therapist must assess whether the client is likely to engage in leisure activities (e.g., jogging in hot weather, buying large soda pops at the movies, etc.) which will significantly change his/her fluid intake patterns from those in the hospital.

As a reference, the book **Basic Guide to Physical and Phychiatric Medication for Recreational Therapy** (Skalko, Mitchell, Kaye, and Dalton, 1994) will provide the recreational therapist with a general overview of drug side effects and how they impact assessment and treatment. Of special interest is the chart which lists the recreation program considerations for anti-schizophrenic drugs and anti-depressants.

DOCUMENTATION RELATED TO ONGOING SERVICE DELIVERY

Documentation of services must continue throughout the entire time the therapist is working with a client. The primary purpose is to record the progress of the client. Other problems may arise which require special handling. The most important ones are described in this section.

PROGRESS NOTES

Whenever a therapist documents in the progress notes, s/he should re-read his/her last entry. This should be done to improve the continuity of care (and quality control) and to catch 'loose ends' which still need to be addressed.

> 6/1/90 Charlie Maystyle continues to improve in many areas of his recreational therapy tx. A memory book is being developed jointly by speech therapy and recreational therapy to help facilitate Mr. Maystyle's ability to function in the community with only moderate assist. His wife was called today and asked to bring in pictures of his immediate family and pets for the memory book. Mr. Maystyle continues to be oriented x1 (to person only) most of the time. Approximately 20% of the time he is oriented x2 (to person and place).
>
> 6/8/90 Mr. Maystyle continues to actively participate in his recreational therapy program. He is able to demonstrate an orientation x2 40% of the time. A calendar has been added to his memory book. With cueing he is able to use his memory book to be oriented to time 70% of trials run. Mrs. Maystyle was approached again about bringing photo's from home. She asked the therapist to call her tomorrow morning at 7:30 a.m. to remind her before she comes in.
>
> 6/15/90 Mr. Maystyle's functional skills related to both his recent and remote memory have remained relatively the same over this past week. This appears to be related to his having the flu and not an actual plateauing of his recovery. Mrs. Maystyle brought in family pictures on 6/9/90 which were added immediately to his memory book. The therapists noted an immediate improvement in his ability to communicate in a meaningful manner about his family and home life. At this point Mr Maystyle's cognitive impairments are still significant enough to impede his ability to function in the community with anything less than full assist. With continued recreational therapy (and the resolution of his flu) Mr Maystyle should be able to semi-independently function in the less restricted environment of his home and community versus the more restricted environment of a long term care facility. Next week (his health allowing it) 25% of his therapy sessions will be run in the community to help facilitate his eventual discharge.

To help a client continue his/her qualification for health care coverage the therapist, when appropriate, should use terms such as 'significant, pronounced, considerable, diminished, exacerbated, deteriorating, severe,' etc. when describing the client's functional limitations or reasons for treatment. These terms are good indicators that the client continues to qualify for services under his/her policy and will, more than likely, facilitate justification for therapy.

A CLIENT'S RIGHT TO REFUSE ASSESSMENT AND TREATMENT

All through the 1980's and into the 1990's the client is being seen more and more as a consumer of health care goods and services. In that light the client has the right to be non-compliant, to refuse an assessment, and to refuse treatment. The client as a consumer also has responsibilities. One of those responsibilities is to make a reasonable effort to comply with his/her treatment program. Because the client's rights allow him/her to make choices, a therapist who forces activity after noting a client's refusal or non-compliance could cause the third party payers to feel this was an unreasonable treatment and, therefore, withhold funding. It is important to document that a client is, for one reason or another, sabotaging his/her treatment. At the same time the therapist should not make entries into the chart that could cause a denial of funding.

4/29/90 The client's belligerent behavior, an expected characteristic of someone at this level of recovery from a head injury, makes treatment difficult and progress slow.

5/23/90 The client's passive, non-initiating behavior demonstrated during community outings indicates the need for further assessment to determine other causes for her inability to progress. Recreational therapy will consult with the unit's social worker to try to determine if the client has unidentified needs.

7/14/90 Little to no progress is being made on recreational therapy treatment goals despite the fact that the client agreed to them. The client's hostility toward therapy and the resulting lack of progress has been reported by the other therapy groups also. Recreational therapy treatment will be put on hold the rest of the day and alternative solutions will be brought up with the team and the client at tomorrow's meeting.

DUPLICATION OF SERVICES

Many consumers, third party payers, and even health care professionals do not understand the differences between the various therapies. To be able to provide a high quality, comprehensive program that meets the client's needs, all of the health care professionals should have some overlap in the types of services that they provide. It is acceptable in most cases to 'complement' another therapist's services, or to 'co-treat'. A recreational therapist should not refer to his/her services as 'reinforcing' the treatment of another therapy or of even 'reinforcing' recreational therapy treatment. When the therapist uses the word 'reinforcing' s/he is either reinforcing some other therapist's work thereby duplicating services, or s/he gave the client too much information the first time around. Either way, the recreational therapist does not put himself/herself in a good light. (It is okay for a therapist to reinforce positive behavior on the part of the client.)

NOTING A CHANGE IN NORMAL SERVICE DELIVERY

Whenever the frequency of recreational therapy service changes, or the nature of the service changes, the therapist should note the change *and the reason for the change* in the progress notes. If the therapist is not able to see a client due to an unexpected treatment (i.e., X-ray) or illness (i.e., the flu) the therapist should make an entry in the progress notes. The therapist should document that the need for treatment was still there but that the client was unavailable.

3/14/90 Recreational therapy services were canceled today to help facilitate client's MRI appointment over at Swedish Hospital.

Client continues to make progress on treatment goals but requires continued intervention to prepare for successful discharge. Recreational therapy services will resume tomorrow.

5/7/90 Client continues to increase his tolerance for activities. Recreational therapy services will increase from 3x wk to 5x wk to help improve client's functional ability.

2/16/90 Client's ability to engage in activities is decreasing as his CA secondary to AIDS progresses and as the doses of his pain medications increase. Reading and watching t.v. are becoming less of an option due to nausea caused by the pain medications. The client seems to be coming to a closure with many of his relationships and he demonstrates a decreased tolerance for talking with others. At this point it is appropriate for recreational therapy services to change its approach from direct care to that of being a resource for the client's significant other and direct care staff. The recreational therapist will call 2x wk to consult with the significant other and the direct care providers. In-house visits will be scheduled on a PRN basis initiated by a direct request from either the client's significant other or his direct care staff.

Changes of treatment that are a direct result of a formal care conference are usually entered into the chart by the team leader. Frequently small, informal 'care conferences' are held in the hallway, in the parking lot, or over the phone.

2/20/90 Long term goals were discussed via a phone consult with Shelley Hayes, OTR/L, from Shawn's school. A behavioral disability was identified by the school district in September of 1987. It seems that the current concerns expressed by the inpatient team are similar to his pre-morbid condition and may not be a result of his Grand Mal Seizure and anoxia on 2/13/90. Later today Ms. Hayes will drop off a copy of the school psychologist's report, Shawn's 1989 test results, and his current IEP. Ms. Hayes indicated that the school district has not been successful in developing a behavior modification program that worked for Shawn and requested that both the school psychologist and she be invited to his care conference on 2/24/90. A memo was sent to Dr. Okamoto from recreational therapy concerning this request.

8/30/90 Recreational therapist contacted (via the phone) Dr. Howard's office today concerning the client's self report of dizziness possibly related to his medication. Dr. Howard was in surgery at the time of the call but the message was relayed directly to Kris Tada, Dr. Howard's nurse practitioner.

9/9/90 Kelly's mom called the Recreational Therapy office today requesting information on summer camps for youth with Cystic Fibrosis. A camp application and scholarship application were sent out in the afternoon's mail to her home.

To help present the complex treatment picture, the therapist should document the date and topic of each consultation with the physician or other team members as it relates to the client's care.

ENABLING DOCUMENTATION

The therapist should be sensitive about the way s/he protrays clients in writing. Table 2-3 provides the therapist with basic rules for non-discriminatory charting.

TABLE 2-3: GUIDELINES FOR ENABLING DOCUMENTATION

The most important thing that we can give to our clients is respect. Any time we emphasize the disability over the person, we are showing both a lack of respect and a lack of professionalism. The general rule is to put people first, only mentioning a specific functional disability when necessary.

YES: Woman with a burn
Child with learning disabilities
Man with dementia

NO: Burned woman
Learning disabled child
Demented individual

When charting, the therapist will need to outline disabilities. Be realistic -- do not portray the client as a superhuman nor as a totally helpless individual.

YES: 34 y/o male with cognitive disabilities in the areas of problem solving, judgement concerning safety, and pathfinding due to a head injury as a result of an MVA (motor vehicle accident). No apparent physical disabilities noted except for a slight weakness in the RLE (right lower extremity).

NO: This head injured 34 y/o male needs 1:1 supervision in the community due to poor judgement. He does a great job getting around, having worked hard to overcome a right-sided weakness.

While the therapist must describe the client's disabilities, s/he should not sensationalize them.

PHRASES TO AVOID	ALTERNATIVES
1. afflicted with ...	1. has M.S.
2. crippled with ...	2. physically disabled 2. has a physical disability
3. suffers from ...	3. Charlie had a stroke
4. victim of ...	4. Shawn was in an MVA
5. stricken with ...	5. Tom has cancer
6. confined to a w/c ...	6. uses a w/c
7. w/c bound	7. uses a w/c
8. wheel-chaired	8. uses a w/c
9. special (as in specially abled)	9. patronizing, don't use
10. physically challenged 11. handi-capable 12. inconvenienced (due to a disability) 13. differently abled	10. - 13. a person has a physical, sensory, or mental disability
14. inspirational	14. patronizing
15. courageous	15. patronizing

Do not depersonalize your client when including them as part of a disability group.

YES: person with a mental disability
NO: the mentally ill

When ever possible, emphasize the client's abilities, not his/her disabilities.

YES: 65 y/o male who uses a walker for short distances (+/- 50 feet), uses a w/c for greater distances.

NO: 65 y/o partially paralyzed male who is wheelchair bound for distances longer than 50 feet.

The words 'DISABILITY' and 'HANDICAP' do not have the same definition: do not use them interchangeably. Disability refers to a functional physical, sensory, or mental limitation which interferes with a person's ability. Handicap refers to: 1) a society imposed condition or barrier, 2) a self-imposed condition or barrier, or 3) a natural condition or barrier in the environment which impedes the individuals ability to function.

DISABILITY: people who are mentally retarded
persons with cerebral palsy
individual who is visually impaired

HANDICAP: The limited availability of w/c seating is a handicap for her.
Her embarrassment over her facial scars is a handicap for her.
The fallen logs over the hiking trail were a handicap for her.

(Please note that some in some regions of the country the enabling terminology differs somewhat from what is listed above. The therapist should be sensitive to the regional trends.)

DOCUMENTING ON SENSITIVE TOPICS

An important skill related to documentation is the ability to record sensitive information in a tactful, neutral manner.

It is unlikely that any recreational therapist will be able to avoid working with clients who have been either psychologically or physically abused.

Every therapist needs to be able to document on sensitive issues in such a way as to have the documentation hold up in court.

Some of the basic guidelines to follow in this situation are:

1. Only write down observable facts.

2. Be very concrete in describing what was observed.

3. Make sure that the events written down are recorded in the exact order that they happened.

4. Avoid all mention of 'feelings'. (It is acceptable to report a quote from the client as to how they felt, i.e., "When he did that, I felt very dirty" not: The client felt dirty when he touched her in that manner.)

5. Write your note within one hour (even if it is first recorded on a scrap of paper). Do not allow the passage of time or the opinions of others to affect your note. Remember, you are writing down exactly what you saw and what you heard. You should not attempt to interpret what you saw. That is usually considered outside the scope of practice of recreational therapy.

The following is an example of documentation on a community integration outing.

> 9/19/90 This evening Tony went on a community integration outing to a restaurant with the recreational therapist and his parents. Per protocol, Tony was pre-tested using the Restaurant Module 1D of the 'Community Integration Program' by Armstrong. He was able to answer 17 out of 23 questions correctly, having the greatest difficulty in the areas of what to do in an emergency and ordering.
>
> The therapist met with Tony's mom and dad to review the ways they could assist Tony. The therapist also reviewed Tony's behavior program with his parents including reviewing some 'What if?' situations. Both mom and dad were able to verbally report back to the therapist with moderate assistance.
>
> Upon arriving at the restaurant Tony required maximum assist (using both verbal and gestural cues) to read the menu above the counter. After assisting Tony in determining his order the therapist turned around to ask Tony's parents what they were going to order.
>
> The therapist could not get the parent's attention right away due to their activity. Tony's parents were close together, engaging in an opened-mouth kiss. Mr. Smith's left hand was down the back of his wife's pants with approximately 3" of arm below his elbow still showing. Mr. Smith's right hand was under his wife's blouse and placed on her right breast. Some movements of both hands were observed.
>
> The therapist said 'Excuse me' at which point Mr. and Mrs. Smith broke their embrace. The therapist then asked the parents if they could concentrate on interacting more with their son and not with each other. They agreed to do so. The food was ordered and a table was found. The rest of the outing was uneventful.
>
> While on the outing Tony demonstrated the ability to answer only 8 of the 17 questions that he had answered correctly while in the quiet environment of his hospital room. He was very distractible in the noisy, crowded restaurant.
>
> Upon returning to the hospital the recreational therapist met with the patient's physician and the unit social worker to discuss the parent's demonstrated behavior on the outing. Recreational therapy will continue to work on Tony's ability to attend to task while in the community.

Idyll Arbor, Inc. staff have found a short booklet titled 'Teach-A-Bodies: An Effective Resource for Sex Education, Investigation, Therapy, and Courtroom Testimony' by June Harnest, M.S. helpful. While this 44 page booklet is used primarily as a guide for using anatomically correct dolls, the various chapters also contain other important information when working with clients who have been abused or clients who need to be taught about 'private parts', etc. One of the appendixes list many of the slang words used around the country for various body parts and actions related to human sexuality. (This booklet, and other supplies, may be purchased through Teach-A-Bodies, 3509 Acorn Run, Fort Worth, TX 76109, (817) 923-2380.)

There are many more topics which require extreme sensitivity on the part of the recreational therapist as s/he documents.

In cases of child abuse or suspected child abuse, find out the actual physical reason for admissions, e.g., bruises, broken arm, suspected head injury. Write this as the diagnosis rather than 'child abuse'.

In the case of Failure to Thrive, staff are often asked to make note of parent-child interaction. It is best to word this request: 'Please observe and record Robert's activities closely'. This takes the implied blame off of the parent(s) who is/are often already feeling isolated and/or incriminated. Not all cases of Failure to Thrive are caused by the client's environment.

The best general rule to use is not to write anything that the therapist would feel uncomfortable explaining to the client if s/he were to read it.

DOCUMENTATION ON DISCHARGE

Upon the client's discharge to another service or to home, the therapist will need to write up a discharge summary. The discharge summary is a short document which provides the reader with:

1. an overview of the client's history (both medical and leisure)
2. an overview of services received by the client
3. initial skills and outcomes measured as a result of therapy intervention
4. areas still needing to be addressed
5. recommendations

The information contained in the discharge summary should be very clear and concise. The therapist should strive to limit the entire recreational therapy discharge summary to just one page.

CONCLUSION

The ability to document in a professional manner is one of the most important skills that the therapist can have. It is through his/her documentation that a history of treatment is maintained and it is through the quality of his/her documentation that the therapist is judged by the rest of the extended treatment team.

The therapist must always practice the basic rules when charting, including the ability to use the facility's abbreviations without any errors. See Table 2-4: Abbreviations and Symbols. The entire therapy process should be easily followed in the client's chart, starting with the initial note, the initiation of services, the continuation of services; ending with all 'loose strings' tied up and a summary of treatment documented in the discharge summary.

References

Harnest, J. (1988) **Teach-A-Bodies: An Effective Resource for Sex Education, Investigation, Therapy and Courtroom Testimony**. Fort Worth, TX: Harnest.

Pakes and Pakes (1982) "Anti-Psychotic Drug Side Effects and Therapeutic Recreation Program Consideration" **Therapeutic Recreation Journal**, Vol. XVI, First Quarter 1982, #1: Arlington, VA: National Recreation and Parks Association.

Peterson, C.A., and Gunn, S.L. (1984) **Therapeutic Recreation Program Design: Principles and Procedures**, (Second Edition) (pages 212-266) Englewood Cliffs, NJ: Prentice-Hall.

Skalko, T.K., R.S. Mitchell, A.G. Kaye, and M.J. Dalton, **Basic Guide to Physical anf Psychiatric Medications for Recreational Therapy.** Hattiesburg, MS: American Therapeutic Recreation Association.

TABLE 2-4: ABBREVIATIONS AND SYMBOLS

To shorten the length of time it takes to write a note on a client, most institutions use abbreviations and symbols. Many of the abbreviations and symbols used are standardized throughout the United States.

A problem with client care and quality control could arise if a professional misinterprets an abbreviation or symbol used by another professional. To decrease the chance of this happening, every institution has its own set of abbreviations and symbols. Whenever a therapist starts a new job, s/he should request a copy of the approved abbreviations and symbols and memorize the material prior to writing in the client's chart.

abd	abdomen	DTR	deep tendon reflexes
a.c.	before meals	DX	diagnosis
ad lib	freely as desired	e.g.	for example
adm.	admitted; admission	E.R.	emergency room
A.I.	aortic insufficiency	ECG, EKG	electrocardiogram
ALL	acute lymphoblastic leukemia	EMG	electromyography
AML	acute myeloblastic leukemia	ENT	ear, nose, throat
amt.	amount	EOM	extraocular movements
ant.	anterior	F.H.	family history
approx.	approximately	FTT	failure to thrive
ag.	water	FUO	fever of undetermined origin
A.S.	aortic stenosis	Fx	fracture
AS	left ear	GC	gonococcus; gonorrhea
A.S.D.	atrial septal defect	GI	gastrointestinal
Atbed	At bedside	gtt.	drop (or drops)
AU	both ears	H & P	history and physical
b.i.d.	twice a day	h.s.	hour of sleep; at bedtime
B.P.	blood pressure	HA	hyperalimentation
BKA	below knee amputation	HEENT	head, eyes, ears, nose & throat
BM	bowel movement	ht.	height
c/o	complains of	Hx	history
$\bar{c}$	with	I & O	intake and output
C.C.	chief complaint	i.e.	that is
C.H.D.	congenital heart disease	I.V.C.	inferior vena cava
C.H.F.	congestive heart failure	id.	the same
C1 to C7	cervical vertebrae or nerves	IM	intramuscular
CAT	computerized axial tomography	incont.	incontinent
cath.	catheter	invol.	involuntary
cc.	cubic centimeter (or centimeters)	IQ	intelligence quotient
CHD	congenital dislocation of hip	IV	intravenous
CF	cystic fibrosis	JRA	juvenile rheumatoid arthritis
CMV	cytomegalovirus	kcal	kilocalorie
CNS	central nervous system	KUB	kidney, ureter, bladder
cont.	continue	Ⓛ; lt.	left
COPD	chronic obstructive pulmonary disease	L.A.	left atrium
CP	cerebral palsy	L1 to L5	lumbar vertebrae or nerves
CPR	cardiopulmonary resuscitation	lat.	lateral
CT	computerized axial tomography	lb.	pound
CVA	cerebrovascular accident	LLQ	left lower quadrant
D	day	LOC	level of consciousness
D.O.E.	dyspnea on exertion	LP	lumbar puncture
DC	discontinue	LUQ	left upper quadrant
diff.	differential	lytes	electrolytes
dischg	discharge	min.	minutes
dschg	discharge	misc.	miscellaneous
DM	diabetes mellitus	mod.	moderate
Dr.	doctor	MS	multiple sclerosis

N/G, NG	nasogastric
N/V	nausea, vomiting
NB	newborn
neg.	negative
neuro	neurological
no.	number
noc;noct	night
NPO	nothing by mouth
O & P	ova and parasites
O.T.	occupational therapy
OD	right eye (oculus dexter)
OPD	Outpatient Department
OS	left eye (oculus sinister)
OU	both eyes (oculi uterque)
p	after
P	pulse
p.c.	after meals
P.E.	physical examination
P.M.	12 noon to 12 midnight
p.o.	by mouth (per os)
P.R.N.	as necessary or indicated
p.r.n.	as necessary or indicated
P.T.	physical therapy
Para	multipara; primapara
per	through; by
PERRLA	pupils equal, round, react to light and accommodation
PID	pelvic inflammatory disease
PMEALS	after meals
PNP	Pediatric Nurse Practitioner
pos	positive
post-op	after operation
pre-op	before operation
prep.	preparation
PRN	as needed
Pt.	patient
q.2h.	every 2 hours
q.A.M.	every morning
q.d.	every day
q.h.	every hour
q.i.d.	4 times a day
q.o.d.	every other day
$\bar{q}$; q.	every
QIDM	four times daily with meals and at bedtime
Ⓡ, rt	right
R/O	rule out
R.A.	right atrium
R.D.	Registered Dietician
R.N.	Registered Nurse
R.T.	recreational therapy, respiratory therapy
RA	rheumatoid arthritis
RLQ	right lower quadrant
ROM	range of motion
Rx	dosage, therapy
$\bar{s}$	without
S.H.	social history
S.O.B.	shortness of breath
SIDS	sudden infant death syndrome
stat	immediately (statim)
subq	subcutaneous
T	temperature
t.i.d.	3 times a day
T.O.	telephone order
T1 to T12	thoracic vertebrae or nerves
tab.	tablet
TB	tuberculosis
Tet.	tetralogy of Fallot
TIDM	3 times daily with meals
TIW	3 times weekly
TLC	tender loving care
T.O.F.	tetralogy of Fallot
TPR	temperature, pulse, and respirations
trach	tracheostomy
U.	unit
ud	as directed
URI	upper respiratory infection
UTI	urinary tract infection
V.O.	verbal order
V.S.	vital signs
V.S.D.	ventricular septal defect
VD	venereal disease
viz.	namely
vol.	volume
w/o	without
w	with
WD	well-developed
WK	week
WNL	within normal limits
wt.	weight
X	times
>	greater than
<	less than
♀	female
♂	male
↑	up; increased; elevation
↓	down; decreased; depressed
→	causes; transfer to
+	positive
-	negative
=	equal to
≠	does not equal
2X; X2	twice
24°	24 hours
:	ratio (is to)
°	degree
'	foot
"	inch
?	question of; questionable; possible
#	number
△	change
Ø	normal

Chapter 3

QUESTIONS ABOUT ASSESSMENTS

Quite often the questions a therapist in clinical practice has about assessments cannot be answered by reading textbooks on recreational therapy or on statistics. This chapter answers frequently asked questions.

What is the difference between an assessment tool and an assessment report (or in-house assessment)?

An assessment tool is a standardized instrument which measures specific information about the client's functional ability or leisure lifestyle. Some examples of assessment tools are the Leisurescope, the General Recreation Screening Tool (GRST), the Leisure Diagnostic Battery (LDB), and the Bond-Howard Assessment on Neglect in Recreational Therapy (BANRT).

An assessment report is the form that you fill out which includes your client's history, diagnoses, and other pertinent information. It *also* includes a summary of the client's performance on assessment tools administered. Finally, it includes:

1. a summary of the information contained in the report,
2. a summary of how the client could be expected to function on a day-to-day basis, and
3. a set of recommended treatment interventions.

Include the original score sheets from all the assessment tools you administered in the report.

How can I find the one best assessment to meet the needs of my recreational therapy department?

There isn't one best assessment. In our experience most recreational therapy departments need to have at least 10 different assessments on hand in addition to their in-house assessment to meet the diversity of clients they are likely to see. Most facilities admit clients with a diversity of disabilities. For example, a rehabilitation hospital admits children and adults with spinal cord injuries, traumatic brain injury and/or CVA, burn rehabilitation, amputation, and neurological impairment. To assess a diversity of clients you need a diversity of screening tools.

Okay, how do I decide which assessments I need?

First, select initial screening tools for your clients. You may use your own in-house assessment or a standardized one. The Functional Assessment for Characteristics in Therapeutic Recreation (FACTR), Therapeutic Recreation Activity Assesment (TRAA), or the GRST are often used. Each has its strong points and weak points which are described in the assessment chapters.

After you have given the initial assessment, select secondary and/or more in-depth assessments based on your initial screening. Selecting an assessment based on the needs of your client is an important step toward meeting client's individual needs.

Let's assume, for an example, that you are a therapist working on a spinal cord unit in a rehabilitation hospital. You have two clients. One is a 27 y/o male with an L-3 incomplete fracture and a traumatic brain injury with a Rancho Los Amigos Scale level of 5. The second client is a 31 y/o male with a T-4 complete fracture, no significant brain trauma (Rancho Los Amigos level 8). You want to find out about the leisure interests of each one.

For the first client you could get the information you need by interviewing the client and the client's significant other(s), using the STILAP (using the 'M' and 'S' codes — which represent events observable by others) or the Avocational Activities Inventory and Index.

For the second client you could use the STILAP again, but you might get better results with the Leisure Interest Scale or the Leisure Diagnostic Battery. You couldn't use either of them with the first client because they require a Rancho Los Amigos Scale level of 7 or above.

Why not just use the STILAP with every client? Both the Leisure Interest Scale and the Leisure Diagnostic Battery have superior reliability and validity. You can have a higher degree of confidence in the results and be more sure of your findings. When you are selecting assessments, use the most reliable assessment you can find which matches the condition of your client.

What are the different kinds of assessments that I might use in my department?

We divide assessments into three primary categories:

1. Leisure assessments which measure some element of a client's perceived or demonstrated leisure preference, motivation, or satisfaction, e.g., LDB, Leisurescope Plus, STILAP, Leisure Motivation Scale, Recreation Participation Data Sheet (RPD), etc.

2. Functional assessments which measure functional skills, usually divided into cognitive, physical, social, and emotional domains, e.g., GRST, REDS, FOX, FACTR, OHIO, and CIP.

3. Activity assessments which measure a client's skill level in a specific activity like basketball, poker, or playing a piano, e.g., ICAN series, American Red Cross Swimming Levels.

In most cases you will want to obtain information from both the leisure and functional areas to have enough information to develop a treatment plan.

When you obtain enough information to make solid recommendations, you have done a *comprehensive assessment.*

How many different assessment tools will we want to keep in our department?

Most departments keep one or two general screening tools, then several other assessments, which may be given in part or in whole. We keep over 30. Once you read the medical chart and observe the client for a short time, you can pick the assessment tool(s) which will best answer the questions that initially popped into your head. We spend less than 45 minutes completing the chart review, observation, and the assessment tool(s).

A department which serves individuals who are developmentally disabled may need a variety of general screening tools. For clients whose general developmental level is under 12 months, they might use the REDS. For clients whose general developmental level is 1 year to 10 years, they might use the GRST. For clients whose general developmental level is over 10 years, they might use the FACTR.

How can I be sure that the results I get will fit into the categories established by the entire health care team?

Initially, you will want to review the assessment reports written by the other health care professionals on your team e.g., physician, physical therapist, occupational therapist, speech therapist, nursing, dietary, and psychology. Generally follow either domain categories (physical, cognitive, emotional, social), system categories (cardiac, neuro-muscular, skeletal, etc.), or function categories (work skills, ADL skills, etc.). Interdisciplinary coordination is promoted when you select the type of reporting format followed by your team members. Determine if you can also report client results using the same categories.

Most of the assessments in the field of recreational therapy divide skills by domain categories. If you decide to use the system or the function categories, you will have fewer assessments to choose from.

How accurate do I need to be when I estimate distances and/or time when I administer assessments?

Very. The skill to estimate measurements with accuracy is vital when you are administering assessments or providing therapy services. Please refer to Table 3-1 for a list of the basic estimation skills an entry level therapist will want to have.

How can I be sure that I will be able to use the results I get?

The greater the validity and reliability an assessment has, the better it is *as long as it measures the specific information that you want to know.* Determine: 1) the type of information you want, 2) whether to obtain it with a norm-referenced, criterion referenced, or functional-environmental tool, 3) whether or not the particular measurements obtained have any "real" meaning to the client's day-to-day ability to function, and 4) whether or not any of the assessment tools reviewed for possible use have validity and reliability information available.

How can I be sure that the assessment asks the questions that need to be asked and places the right degree of importance on each question?

When you ask if an assessment tool is measuring what it says it is measuring, you are asking whether or not the assessment is *valid.* Validity is the degree to which the assessment tool performs the task it is intended to perform. Content Validity means that the assessment tool: 1) measures what it says it is measuring, and 2) places an appropriate amount of weight on each skill measured.

The REDS, during initial testing, has demonstrated that it measures what it says it is measuring: developmental levels.

TABLE 3-1: BASIC ESTIMATION SKILLS

The recreational therapist should have some basic measurements stored in his/her head. The ability to estimate increments of distance, time, and volume correctly increases the accuracy of the therapist's assessments and increases the therapist's credibility as a member of the treatment team. The therapist should drill and practice until s/he can correctly estimate the following measures, three out of three trials, with an error rate of 5% or less. This estimation should be based solely on visual examination; stepping off distances, using the second hand on a watch, or using a measuring cup will often disrupt the flow of the assessment enough to impact the test results. Very few measurements the recreational therapist will need to make will require exact measurements (with an error rate of less than 2%). Two notable exceptions would be administering medications and taking a pulse.

DISTANCES

1. 1/8"	9. 6"	17. 2'	25. 1 cm
2. 1/4"	10. 7"	18. 3'	26. 5 cm
3. 1/2"	11. 8"	19. 4'	27. 10 cm
4. 1"	12. 9"	20. 5'	28. 1 meter
5. 2"	13. 10"	21. 10'	29. 5 meters
6. 3"	14. 11"	22. 25'	30. 10 meters
7. 4"	15. 12"	23. 50'	
8. 5"	16. 1'	24. 100'	

TIME

The recreational therapist should be able to silently count to 60 seconds (or any amount of time up to 60 seconds) with an error rate of 5% or less.

FLUID VOLUME

The recreational therapist should be able to visually determine amounts of 1 oz. - 20 oz. with an error rate of 5% or less.

SCANNING

Many assessments require the therapist to test a client's ability to visually follow an object. Without a general understanding between therapists as to scanning speed and procedures, many of the reported results will have little meaning. Below is a suggested standard for scanning:

Unless otherwise specified, the therapist should:

1. Start by moving the object from the client's left side to his/her right side, presenting the object at the client's eye level.

2. As the therapist moves the object from his/her right to left, the object should be approximately 18" to 24" from the therapist's own mid-line and approximately the same distance from the client.

3. Assume that the therapist's left side equals 9 o'clock, his/her midline equals 12 o'clock, and the therapist's right side is 3 o'clock. For scanning *slowly*, it should take the therapist 10 seconds to move the object from 3 o'clock to 9 o'clock. For scanning *at a normal (standard) speed*, it should take the therapist 8 seconds to move the object from 3 o'clock to 9 o'clock. For scanning at a *fast speed*, it should take the therapist 6 seconds to move the object from 3 o'clock to 9 o'clock.

COUNTING BEHAVIORS

One of the most important observational skills that the therapist will need to have is the ability to count the number of times a specific behavior is demonstrated during an activity. With practice, the therapist should be able to demonstrate an error rate of less than 5% on his/her behavior counts. The therapist may want to practice these skills by watching a video tape in which one or more clients are demonstrating multiple behaviors. At first the therapist will need to write down the frequency of behaviors. The skilled recreational therapist should be able to mentally count two behaviors for two separate clients who are close in proximity to each other for a minimum of 10 minutes, demonstrating an error rate less than 5%. (Example: Client A: # of non-truths (lies) spoken in a 10 minute period plus # of 'picking' incidents in a 10 minute period (Picking behaviors are those actions where the client uses his/her hands to scratch, rub, or otherwise compromise his/her skin integrity.) and Client B: # of actual contact assaults in a 10 minute period plus # of times client said "Go to Hell".)

However, the REDS lacks the appropriate weighting of skills in each domain; it does not place equal importance on all major components of each domain. Instead, it places too much emphasis on the client's ability to hear or to see. (Table # 3-2 provides the therapist with a basic list of developmental milestones. All developmental charts have decreasing accuracy as they enter the pre-adolescent years, as there is a greater variance of normal developmental skills.)

The original FACTR measured skills in three domains, with eleven questions in each. The validity of the contents were challenged because two questions seemed to be miscategorized: Question #2.11 'Purposive Interaction with Environment' was placed in the COGNITIVE DOMAIN and Question #3.11 'Decision Making Ability' was placed in the SOCIAL/EMOTIONAL DOMAIN. Most of the research associated with rehabilitation and habilitation placed 'Purposive Interaction with Environment' in the Social Domain, and 'Decision Making Ability' in the Cognitive Domain. The revised assessment tool FACTR-R (1996), shown in this book, moved the questions into the proper domains to remove these concerns.

Another assessment low on content validity is the Ohio Functional Assessment Battery (OHIO). The skills listed on the OHIO contain such a wide range of developmental ability that a client can score poorly and yet still be developmentally appropriate.

How can I be sure that what I am testing is really within the scope of practice for recreational therapy?

'Scope of Practice' refers to the services that individuals within a profession are trained to deliver. The services are tied directly to a philosophical stand which is backed by research.

In 1987 and 1996 the National Council for Therapeutic Recreation Certification (NCTRC) initiated a national job analysis to define the type of services delivered and the range of professional knowledge held by those who called themselves 'therapeutic recreation specialists'. The final results of that job analysis are available from the NCTRC, P.O. Box 479, Thiells, NY 10984-0479 (914-947-4346). When the items measured by the assessment tool fit within the areas listed on the job analysis, and also pertain to the client's ability to participate in leisure, then the assessment tool is measuring items within the scope of recreational therapy practice.

How can I tell if the client's scores are unusual?

To be able to measure that a client's scores are 'unusual', you want to first identify what is 'usual'. This information can come from either a norm-referenced or a criterion-referenced tool.

Both the Leisure Diagnostic Battery (LDB) and the What Am I Doing (WAID) have normative scales that indicate an average score for individuals in specific population groups. You may administer either of these, then compare the client's scores to tables which indicate typical scores.

Many criterion-referenced assessment tools are based on standards of ability achieved through research. Extensive research exists on developmental milestones and 'normal' gross motor and fine motor movements. When you use an assessment like the GRST or the CERT — Physical Disability, you can easily locate skill areas that are 'unusual'.

The FOX, while useful, cannot be validated. At first glance it appears to follow a developmental sequence. However, closer examination shows that the skills in any one level do not match the same developmental age. In addition, it occasionally awards a high score for behavior that is potentially maladaptive, extended eye contact which could be inappropriate staring, or touching which could be inappropriate in many situations. It is still usable, none the less, as it helps you break down social skills into distinct, very measurable elements. Use professional judgment though, when you score it.

How can I tell if individual assessment questions relate to each other?

You need adequate professional knowledge to determine if the items measured on a general assessment relate to each other in meaningful ways. Further continuing education may be useful.

Examples of assessment tools that have items which relate well to each other are the LDB, the Leisure Motivation Scale, the Leisure Attitude Scale, Leisure Satisfaction Scale, the CERT — Physical Disabilities, the CERT — Psych., and the Bus Utilization Skills Assessment (BUS).

Is it important to know if an assessment was developed for research or for clinical use?

Yes. Refer to Table 1-3. Review each assessment to determine whether or not it meets the needs of the client, prior to administering it. Many recreational therapy assessments were first developed for research and not practice.

How can I be sure that the assessment will meet the expectations of accrediting agencies?

Accrediting agencies include the Joint Commission on Accreditation of Healthcare Organizations, National Committee for Quality Assurance, Health Care Finance Administration, and the Commission on Accreditation of Rehabilitation Facilities. Each of these agencies publishes a list of minimum criteria for the content, quality, and frequency of administration of assessments. They also outline the types of functional abilities required to be measured, e.g., reality orientation. You will not find the expectations listed by professional group, e.g., assessments required by physical therapy versus recreational therapy. Instead, agencies generally outline generic standards to which all of the health care team comply. Then, each individual team decides which team

TABLE 3-2: DEVELOPMENTAL MILESTONES

1 YEAR

Beginning walking skills
Picks things up with thumb and one finger (crude pincer grasp)
Pays attention to own name
Responds to simple directions accompanied by gestures (i.e.; come, give, get)

2 YEARS

Begins to run
Builds tower of five cubes
Talks about objects or experiences with words used together (2-3 words, i.e. 'more juice')
Imitates housework

3 YEARS

Jumps in place with both feet together
Imitates circular, vertical, horizontal strokes on paper
Matches/sorts objects by shape or color or size
Plays near others, not necessarily in same activity

4 YEARS

Plays in same activity with other children, not always interacting
Imitates cross, traces diamond
Counts two objects and tells how many
Knows own sex, age, and last name

5 YEARS

Plays and interacts with other children
Can walk backwards, heel-to-toe
Draws recognizable pictures
Can separate coins by pennies, nickles, and dimes

6 YEARS

Prints some numbers, letters
Learns to distinguish left from right
Shows interest, some knowledge, of clocks and calendars
Plays simple table/board games

7 YEARS

Is in a 'for-or against' age; an age of cliques and outsiders
Begins to use elementary logic
Can count by multiples of 2, 5, and 10
Enjoys magic tricks, collecting in quantity, puzzles, and 'swapping'

8 YEARS

Gives allegiance to peers rather than to adults in case of conflict
Has collections that reflect quality as well as quantity
Finally has a combination of speed, estimating skills, and judgement skills to be able to safely cross a street which does not have a walk/don't walk light

9 YEARS

Finishes jobs s/he starts
Has strong social feelings; shows empathy and sympathy
Enjoys more complicated table games
Is less interested in money; works for service

10 YEARS

Cannot be bothered with personal hygiene; needs constant reminding, keeps room in constant disarray
Frequently oblivious to time; needs schedules; is unable to plan (becomes distracted)
Most know about sexual intercourse
Delights in physical activity: running, skating, sliding, climbing, jumping, cycling

11 YEARS

Rarely chooses to be alone; elects to be involved in family group or peer group
Argues about everything; is aware of other's fallibilities and does not hesitate to point them out
Team games are very important
'Detests' opposite sex, but girls enjoy being teased by boys

12 YEARS

Is concerned about wearing clothes that are in vogue, that fit well, and that match
Enjoys group activities involving both sexes
Enjoys collections; new dimension; mementos such as ticket stubs, clippings, photographs
Segregate into athletic and non-athletic groups

Note: The developmental information contained on this page reflects general developmental growth patterns. Cuntural and socio-economic factors may influence a child's development by as much as one year.

member will measure which required functional ability. You will want to obtain a copy to read from you administrator. Read the entire document, as some areas for which you may be responsible; e.g., temperature of food served during activities, may be found in different sections of the guidelines than the section addressing therapy services.

How can I tell if the wording of the assessment is too difficult for the client to understand?

Know your clients. Most of them will not have college degrees and may not be functional readers. It is estimated that 11% to 20% of the people in the United States are non-functional readers (World Book Encyclopedia, 1989). You may want to review the speech therapist's report, if there is one. This report may help you anticipate the client's comprehension level.

We are now working to establish problem areas associated with receptive language on all the assessments we carry. We are doing this through case studies, starting with Leisure Motivation Scale (contained in Chapter 4 of this book). Review the two case studies contained in the Leisure Motivation Scale manual to obtain the reporting format. You can help us in this process by writing up case studies related to receptive language problems and mailing them to us. If every therapist were to write up one case study a year, within a few years the assessment tools we use would be greatly enhanced.

How can I tell if an assessment will allow me to establish a baseline?

A baseline represents the status of the client before treatment. It is compared to the client's status at a future time to determine changes in the client's condition. A useful assessment measures the client's present condition and has the capacity to measure the changes you expect as a result of treatment.

Choose an assessment that has adequate detail to identify actual performance and has enough range in its questions to assess the client after the treatment is completed. For example, the Bond-Howard Assessment on Neglect in Recreational Therapy (BANRT) provides numerical values for both the client's density and scope of neglect. (See Chapter 5 of this book.)

If my client has a brain injury, which assessment tools can I use?

There are three scales used to indicate the 'level of clearing' a client has achieved from a brain injury. The Rancho Los Amigos Levels of Cognitive Functioning and the Stages of Cognitive Recovery, are behavioral recovery scales. Most rehabilitation medicine units use one or the other of these scales to track a client's progress. The assessment tools in this book indicate the minimum suggested Rancho Los Amigos Level for the administration of each assessment tool. Table #3-3 compares the two behavioral scales.

The third scale, the Glasgow Coma Scale, measures recovery during the earliest acute stages of head injury. While large amounts of data have been compiled on long-term neuropsychological disability, you will not be able to use it to determine which assessment to administer.

Will assessment results be incorrect because of scoring errors?

Yes. Always be sure to double check the scores achieved for addition or compilation errors. Also include in your department's Quality Assurance program a component which randomly checks errors on assessment tool scoring.

Some assessments are more prone to scoring errors than others. The Leisure Diagnostic Battery (written out form, not the computer form) is highly susceptible to scoring errors. So is the original STILAP. Both of these assessments are valuable nonetheless.

A tool which does not contain the measurement criteria right on the scoring sheet is also prone to scoring errors. Two examples are Parker's abbreviated versions of both the CERT — Physical Disability and the CERT — Psych. Parker's two abbreviated forms of the CERT do not list the criteria on the form (making the form a one page sheet versus the 4 page sheet of the Idyll Arbor, Inc. versions). Having the criteria on the score sheet makes it easier for the tester to score the assessment correctly. When the score sheet in put in the chart, it also is easier for other professionals to understand the individual items on the test.

If you have memorized the criteria for each functional level measured or always refers to the detailed descriptions prior to scoring, errors in scoring will be rare.

What is meant when people say that an assessment tool is 'Standardized'?

A standardized assessment tool is one which has detailed guidelines for administering the tool, observing specific behavior, and scoring the results. Standardized assessment tools have four advantages over unstandardized tools (Nunnally, 1978):

1. **Objectivity:** Standardized measures are not dependent on the personal opinions of examiners.

2. **Quantification:** Numerical precision enables finer discriminations on the dimension of interest to the assessor.

3. **Communication:** Communication among professionals is enhanced when standardized measures are used.

4. **Economy:** Standard procedures can often be administered by aides, or computer, giving professionals more time to interpret results and to plan treatment strategies.

TABLE 3-3: COMPARING SCALES FOR LEVEL OF HEAD INJURY

STAGES OF COGNITIVE RECOVERY	RANCHOS LOS AMIGOS SCALE
EARLY STAGE No evidence of problem solving No evidence of reasoning Little to no demonstration of working memory Response system (controls all output; speech, facial expression, motor planning, etc.) severely limited, often perseverative Severely decreased arousal or alertness	LEVEL ONE No response to stimuli (coma) LEVEL TWO Generalized response to stimuli (inconsistent and non-purposeful) LEVEL THREE Localized response (specific but inconsistent response to stimuli)
MIDDLE STAGE Short attention span Poor control of attention, highly distractible, inflexible Clear recognition of familiar objects Sharp deterioration with increases in rate, amount, and complexity of stimuli Disorganized search of information storage system Impulsiveness and possible perseveration Social interaction strained & often unsuccessful due to disinhibition, inappropriateness, impaired social perception Poor retention of information from day to day	LEVEL FOUR Confused — agitated (heightened state of activity with decreased ability to process information) LEVEL FIVE Confused — inappropriate, nonagitated LEVEL SIX Confused — appropriate
LATE STAGE Behavior generally goal directed, but goals may be unrealistic and social and safety judgement may be impaired Abstract thinking remains deficient	LEVEL SEVEN Automatic — appropriate LEVEL EIGHT Purposeful and appropriate (normal)
Information of the Stages of Cognitive Recovery was found in **HEAD INJURY REHABILITATION** by Mark Ylvisaker, 1985	

How can I make the assessment score sheet look professional?

A professional looking score sheet is typeset (not typed out on a typewriter) and conforms with the standards for forms outlined by the medical records profession. Some facilities require that all assessment score sheets contain an in-house number, assigned by the medical records department.

Include enough information right on the form to indicate the general information that is being measured. A professional from another discipline who is not familiar with recreational therapy assessment tools should be able to understand the information reported.

Am I stepping into occupational therapy's area if I assess the client's hand grasp?

The field of occupational therapy traditionally addresses the measurement and training of hand function. However, if you ignore the client's demonstrated skill level of hand usage, you are ignoring an important skill related to the development of a healthy leisure lifestyle. If the client is able to demonstrate only a Palmer Grasp and not a Fine Pincer Grasp, the client will not be able to successfully participate in many leisure activities. Coordinate services with your occupational therapist to determine who will address which issues surrounding hand function. (See Table #3-4 which reviews hand grasps.)

Sometimes you may hear about territorial struggles between occupational and recreational therapy. They are rarer these days because both are generally struggling to cover all the clients assigned to them. When both professions exhibit respect for each other and work together, the stress of covering all necessary services is decreased. joan worked on a team for four years (Camelot Society) where the therapists constantly consulted in order to share each other's loads. When a speech therapy service could be provided by the recreational therapist (i.e., working on signing words to be used in the community), the professional with the lightest load provided the needed service.

How can I tell if the assessment is acceptable to use with the population that I work with?

The best way to determine if an assessment is useful with your population is to contact other recreational therapists across the country to see what works for them.

Many of our assessment tools have been tested to determine if they are appropriate with different population groups. Beware of assuming, though, that just because an assessment measures functional abilities that you want to measure, that the tool is appropriate for the population.

For example, the OHIO (when it was called the OLSSON) was developed to be used with youth and adults who lived in group homes and had a primary diagnosis of mental retardation. It can also measure skills of adults with brain injuries or with dementia. However, there have been reports of clients 'insulted' when tested with some of the OHIO's age-inappropriate tools.

Another possible misuse of an assessment tool would be using the FOX with clients who are severely impaired with dementia of the Alzheimer's type. An assessment which measures the lower levels of reality orientation may be better suited.

Is it wise to use computerized assessment tools which not only score the assessment results, but also provide an interpretation?

This question can only be answered on a case-by-case (or a program-by-program) review. The computer program contains a 'library' of possible interpretations. This library is only as good as the skills of the therapist who put the interpretations into the library and the programmer who wrote the program to get the interpretations back out. Hence, these programs are seldom sensitive enough to take into consideration all factors that impact the client's quality of leisure (i.e., knowledge, physical ability, funding available, etc.). Use your own know how, too.

The field of recreational therapy is just beginning to define nationally accepted treatment protocols. Currently, the authors believe our field still lacks a reliable, valid, computer-generated interpretation of assessment scores which also meets software industry standards.

Should I avoid assessments that ask the same questions that are asked by other health care professionals?

Questions we ask measure the client's ability to successfully engage in a healthy leisure lifestyle. Human beings often perform at different skill levels depending on current mood and environment. It is okay to ask the same questions that the other team members ask as long as you have a reason for each questions you ask.

A physical therapist may measure the client's ability to walk up a 10% incline with his/her walker in the P.T. treatment room. You may also measure the client's ability to walk up a 10% incline in the community. The client's demonstrated skill in the two environments may be an important measurement to obtain, especially prior to discharge.

Do I have enough training to administer and score the assessment?

Very few of the assessment tools used in the field of recreational therapy have written guidelines or formal certification programs to ensure that only qualified people administer and interpret the scores. We recommend that the therapist administering and interpreting the assessment tools in recreational therapy be a certified therapeutic recreation specialist (CTRS). This certification gives some assurance that a recreational therapist has the basic background knowledge to understand the use of leisure as a therapy modality.

TABLE 3-4: DEVELOPMENTAL LEVELS OF HAND GRASPS

As each individual progresses through the learning process, s/he also progresses through a series of ways to hold objects with his/her hands. The recreational therapist will want to learn the developmental progression of hand grasps.

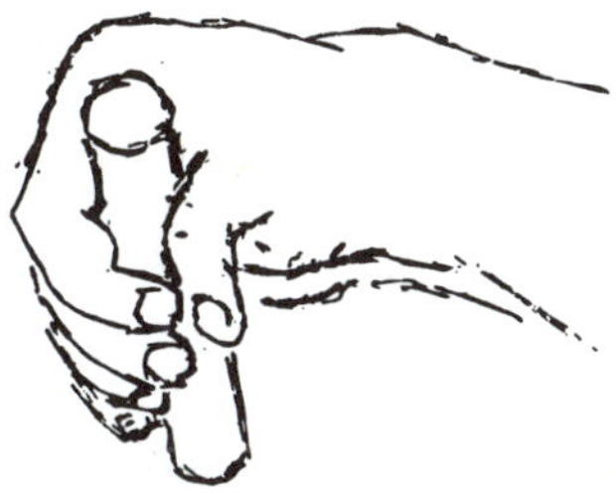

Palmer Grasp
Adducted Thumb
5 Months

Radial-Digital Grasp
Object not touching palm
8 Months

Scissor Grasp
Object held between side of finger and thumb
8 Months

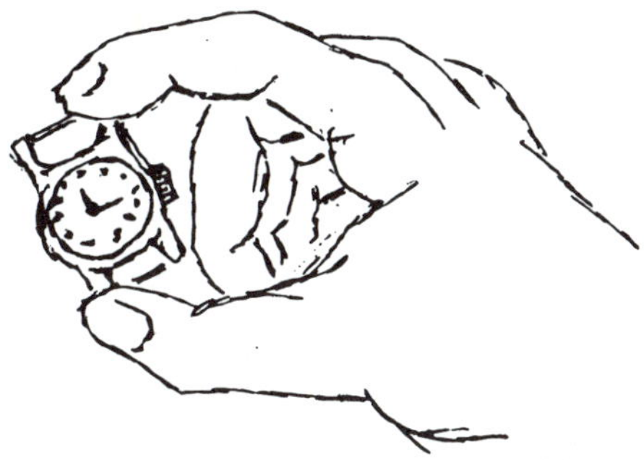

Pincer Grasp
Index finger and Thumb
10 Months

3-Jaw Chuck Grasp
Thumb and 2 fingers
10 Months

A good reference on hand grasps is **Developmental Hand Dysfunction** by Rhoda Priest Erhardt (1989) San Antonio, TX: Psychological Corporation.

Each recreational therapy department should have its own policy and procedure concerning the qualifications required to administer and interpret assessments used. One of the primary skills to be taught in course work taken by recreational therapy students, and one of the primary tasks of the student intern, is to learn how to administer and score a variety of assessment tools. If an assessment tool is administered and scored by someone who does not hold the CTRS credential, have the assessment results co-signed by a credentialed staff.

Is it okay to make copies of blank assessment tool score sheets?

No! Almost every assessment which is available to the recreational therapist which has had standardization, validity, or reliability completed is copyrighted and **MAY NOT BE COPIED OR RE-TYPED!** To use an assessment, you need to either: 1) obtain permission, in writing, from the individual or company who holds the copyright, or 2) purchase the forms.

For many years the professionals who developed assessment tools that recreational therapists used chose not to take action when copyrights were violated. However, due to the high cost of development and distribution, copyright violation is no longer being ignored. In cases where a lawyer has contacted the facility's administrator about breach of copyright, facilities have paid out of court costs for both fines and damages. Had they gone to court, there could have been a $50,000 fine for each violation.

How can I tell if an assessment will take longer to administer and score than is realistic in my setting?

How long is realistic? Most funding agencies will not pay for an assessment by a therapist (other than an IQ or similar assessment) if it takes over one hour to administer and record. Because you are part of the overall treatment team, follow the expectations outlined for all the therapies.

One assessment which has historical significance to our field is the 'Mundy' (also known as the Mundy Recreation Inventory for the Mentally Retarded or the Florida State University Diagnostic Battery of Recreation Functioning for the Trainable Mentally Retarded). The original instructions for the Mundy recommended that two therapists administer the assessment together to one client (one to present the activities and the other to record the demonstrated skill level) *and* that over an hour should be scheduled to administer the assessment! With experience you will learn how long each assessment takes.

What does it mean when a person says that an assessment is reliable?

When someone says that an assessment tool is reliable they are saying that:

1) if the same tool was administered to a client multiple times (with no intervention between administrations) there would be an underlying and consistent score obtained (estimated stability), and/or

2) if the same tool were used by two trained observers observing the same action, their scores would be similar, if not exactly the same (inter-rater reliability).

When someone indicates that an assessment tool has reliability, you will want to ask what kind of reliability.

Two of the assessments in this book report high inter-rater reliability; the OHIO and the CERT — Psych. Be aware that the inter-rater reliability determination was obtained by using individuals who were from the same group (OHIO = same T.R. class; CERT = same recreational therapy department). Both assessments *can* have strong inter-rater reliability as long as the professionals administering and scoring the assessment are well trained to use the same procedures and definitions.

References

Bolton, B. (1987) **Handbook of Measurement and Evaluation in Rehabilitation (Second Edition)**. Baltimore, MD: Paul H. Brookes Publishing Company.

Erhardt , Rhoda Priest (1989) **Developmental Hand Dysfunction**. San Antonio, TX: Psychological Corporation.

Gallo, J.J., Reichel, W., and Anderson, L. (1988) **Handbook of Geriatric Assessment**. Rockville, MD: Aspen Publication.

Gardner, J.F., and Chapman, M.S. (1989) **Program Issues in Developmental Disabilities (Second Edition)**. Baltimore, MD: Paul H. Brookes Publishing Company.

Kane, R.A., and Kane, R.L. (1985) **Assessing the Elderly**. Lexington, MA: Lexington Books.

Peterson, C.A., and Gunn, S.L. (1984) **Therapeutic Recreation Program Design: Principles and Procedures (Second Edition)**. Englewood Cliffs, NJ: Prentice-Hall.

Nunnally, J.C. (1978) **Psychometric Theory (Rev. Edition)**. New York, NY: McGraw-Hill.

Witt, P.A., and Ellis, G.D. (1989) **The Leisure Diagnostic Battery User's Manual**. State College, PA: Venture Publishing.

Ylvisaker, M. (1985) **Head Injury Rehabilitation**. Boston, MA: College-Hill Press, Inc.

Chapter 4

MEASURING LEISURE ATTRIBUTES

One of the primary differences between the field of recreational therapy and other health care fields is our emphasis on leisure as a vital component of an individual's existence. From a developmental standpoint, all the skills and attitudes that an individual acquires to be successful in a family group, in school and/or work, and, basically, to survive, are learned first through play activities. As therapists, we measure the client's leisure attributes to determine if intervention in any area will improve the client's ability to function.

The purpose of this chapter is to provide the recreational therapist with some samples of assessments which address the client's leisure attributes. We measure a client's leisure attributes, not to label a client's leisure lifestyle 'right' or 'wrong' but to determine patterns of participation (behaviors), attitudes, and interests. To help establish cultural patterns or 'norms' the leisure behaviors of many individuals are studied. The assessments in this chapter help determine how the client fits into these norms. They do not determine the client's actual, functional ability.

The therapist will be able to find a rich selection of assessments which measure a client's leisure attributes. Some of these, which are not in this chapter, are found in Table 4-1.

TABLE 4-1 Assessment Tools Measuring Leisure Attributes

Instrument/Developer	Reliability	Validity	Comments
Leisure Orientation Scale (Burdge, 1961)	unknown	unknown	historical value
Leisure Attitude Scale (Beard & Ragheb 1991)	stated	stated	useful
Leisure Ethic Scale (Slivken & Crandall 1978)	stated	stated	narrow emphasis
Study of Leisure (Neulinger 1974)	unreported	stated	historic value
Leisure Satisfaction Measure (Beard & Ragheb 1991)	stated	stated	useful
Brief Leisure Rating Scale (Ellis & Niles 1985)	stated	stated	measures helplessness
Joswiak's Leisure Counseling Assessment (Joswiak, 1975)	unreported	stated	affective domain
Mirenda Leisure Interest Finder (Mirenda 1975)	unreported	stated	historical
Leisure Activity Blank (McKechnie, 1975)	stated	stated	well-known
Avocational Activities Inventory (Overs, et al, 1980)	unreported	unreported	historical
Free Time Boredom (Ragheb and Merydith, 1995)	stated	stated	useful
Leisure Step Up (Dehn, 1995)	unknown	unknown	complete program

Table 4 - 2 Suggested Levels

The Idyll Arbor, Inc. staff reviewed the assessments contained in this book to *estimate* which groups the assessments may be given to. The determinations were based on their experience administering the assessments with the clients that they have worked with. (Idyll Arbor, Inc. has a general practice, admitting clients with all diagnoses except clients with a primary diagnosis of addiction). There has been no formal testing to establish these recommended guidelines. Each therapist will need to evaluate whether any specific assessment will work with the clients that s/he serves.

The shaded areas on the charts below indicate that the assessment is recommended for use with clients functioning at that level. To determine if an assessment is appropriate to use, determine the functional level of the client and then read the chart to determine if the assessment is appropriate for that client.

RANCHO LOS AMIGOS SCALE LEVELS

Name of Assessment	Levels: 1	2	3	4	5	6	7	8
STILAP					■	■	■	■
Leisure Motivation Scale							■	■
Leisure Diagnostic Battery							■	■
Life Satisfaction Scale							■	■
What Am I Doing?								■
Leisurescope Plus							■	■
Recreation Participation Data Sheet			■	■	■	■	■	■

DEVELOPMENTAL LEVEL

Name of Assessment	Adapted Age: Under 3	4-9	10-12	13-17	17+
STILAP			■	■	■
Leisure Motivation Scale			■	■	■
Leisure Diagnostic Battery			■	■	■
Life Satisfaction Scale			■	■	■
What Am I Doing?				■	■
Leisurescope Plus			■	■	■
Recreation Participation Data Sheet	■	■	■	■	■

REALITY ORIENTATION LEVEL

Name of Assessment	Severe to Moderate	Moderate to Mild	Mild to No Disorientation
STILAP		■	■
Leisure Motivation Scale			■
Leisure Diagnostic Battery			■
Life Satisfaction Scale			■
What Am I Doing?			■
Leisurescope Plus		■	■
Recreation Participation Data Sheet	■	■	■

STILAP

Name: State Technical Institute Leisure Activities Project

Also Known As: STILAP (1974), STILAP (1990)

Authors: The original version was a coordinated project between Nancy Navar and Carol Ann Peterson. The version that was available from 1974 through 1990 was primarily attributed to Nancy Navar. The version in this book was written by Nancy Navar and joan burlingame.

Time Needed to Administer: Administration depends a great deal on the client's speed in responding or marking activities. The therapist should allow 30 minutes for the completion of the Activity Checklist.

Time Needed to Score: Scoring the STILAP (1990) should take 15 minutes.

Recommended Disability Groups: MR/DD and adolescents and adults with physical or psychological disabilities.

Purpose of the Assessment: The main purpose of STILAP (1990) is to help the client achieve a balanced leisure lifestyle. This is done by:

1) assessing the client's leisure skill participation patterns,
2) categorizing the patterns (and, thus, assumed skills) into leisure competency areas, and
3) providing guidelines for further leisure decision making and future program involvement.

What does the Assessment Measure?: The STILAP measures:

1) the client's indicated interest in various activities,
2) indicates areas that the client is interested in learning more about, and
3) provides a systematic way for the therapist to measure the degree to which the client's leisure lifestyle is balanced.

Supplies Needed: STILAP Manual, Activity Checklist, and Scoring Sheet.

Reliability/Validity: Various publications disagree as to whether the STILAP (1974) has any stated reliability or validity. Initial validity and reliability information reported as being available for a 1980 version by Navar.

Degree of Skill Required to Administer and Score: The Activity Checklist may be administered by a recreational therapy aide; the assessment is best scored by an individual who is a Certified Therapeutic Recreation Specialist through the National Council for Therapeutic Recreation Certification (NCTRC).

Comments: The STILAP is a logical extension to the typical activity check list. The therapist is able to objectively identify areas of competencies that, once gained, could help the client achieve a healthier leisure lifestyle.

Suggested Levels: Ranchos Los Amigos Level 5 or above (may require some assistance from client's significant others). Developmental Level: The activities listed on the Activity Checklist are generally for clients over the chronological age of 10 years. A client with an adapted developmental age of 6 or above (and chronologically being an adult) may be able to answer the questions.

Distributor: Idyll Arbor, Inc., 25119 SE 262 Street, PO Box 720, Ravensdale, WA 98051-0720 (206) 432-3231 (area code 425 after April 1997).

STILAP 1990

Note: This version of the STILAP (State Technical Institute's Leisure Assessment Process) is similar to, but not identical to, the 1974 version. This version, the STILAP (1990) includes changes in scoring methods and some recategorization of activities.

THE THERAPIST SHOULD NOT COMPARE A CLIENT'S SCORES FROM THE STILAP TO THE STILAP (1990) AS THIS VERSION IS DIFFERENT!

PURPOSE: The main purpose of STILAP (1990) is to help the client achieve a balanced leisure lifestyle. This is done by:

1. assessing the client's leisure skill participation patterns,
2. categorizing these patterns (and, thus, assumed skills) into leisure competency areas, and
3. providing guidelines for further leisure decision-making and future program involvement.

INTRODUCTION AND BACKGROUND

The Certified Therapeutic Recreation Specialist (CTRS) needs assessments that are relatively easy to administer and score *and* which produce meaningful results. Like the other members of the treatment team, the CTRS must address treatment goals from the standpoint of functional abilities. A functional ability is a skill (a competency) that the client is able to demonstrate to the therapist. The uniqueness of the CTRS is that, like the dietitian, the CTRS must evaluate the client's entire 'diet' of leisure to ensure that no necessary elements are missing.

To ensure long term physical, mental, and social health, the CTRS will need to encourage a balanced leisure menu for each client. To help meet this goal, the CTRS works on a series of functional skills (competencies) as well as on the client's attitudes, knowledge, and social skills to be able to achieve the end goal of a healthy, maintainable leisure lifestyle. STILAP was designed to include a summary of leisure participation patterns to help the CTRS identify some of the elements of the client's leisure lifestyle which may need to be adjusted to promote health.

The STILAP (1974) and the STILAP (1990) have been developed as assessments to be used in actual practice (unlike assessments like the Leisure Motivation Scale and the Leisure Attitude Scale, which were first developed for research purposes and then modified for use in clinical settings). As such, the STILAP has evolved and been modified based on the clinical experience of many skilled Certified Therapeutic Recreation Specialists. As the research has not yet been completed to determine complete statistical confidence of the 14 categories (competencies), this assessment requires a professional certified at the therapeutic recreation specialist level by the National Council for Therapeutic Recreation Certification (NCTRC) to interpret the client's assessment scores.

Some basic assumptions or premises are necessary before describing the assessment process when using STILAP (1990):

1. The leisure competency statements included in STILAP (1990) are based on a 'normal' or non-disabled adult population. It is believed that this approach facilitates 'normalization' and mainstreaming efforts.

2. STILAP (1990) has been field tested and evaluated through continuous implementation (1974-1981) at State Technical Institute and Rehabilitation Center (STIRC). It was developed as a site-specific assessment. Other facilities may need to modify the activity list to better suit the needs of the clients that they serve.

3. Leisure counseling is seen as only one aspect of leisure education. Leisure education is viewed as containing the following four components: a) leisure value and attitude awareness and development, b) social interaction skills, c) leisure resources, and d) leisure activity skills.

PURPOSES OF THE LEISURE ASSESSMENT PROCESS

STILAP (1990) is basically concerned with the fourth component of leisure education, that of leisure skill acquisition. For this reason, it is important that before the CTRS attempts to utilize STILAP (1990), s/he becomes familiar with the basic concepts and techniques of leisure education. (To review the components of leisure education in greater detail the reader should read Peterson and Gunn, **Therapeutic Recreation Program Design: Principles and Procedures (Second Edition)** by Peterson and Gunn, Prentice-Hall, Inc., 1984, pages 24-44.)

One vital concept of leisure education is that the client must eventually assume personal responsibility for his/her leisure. One important technique the CTRS involved in leisure education must utilize is that of treating the client with respect (adults should be treated as adults) and dignity.

The main purpose of STILAP (1990) is to help the client achieve a balanced leisure lifestyle. This is done by assessing the client's leisure skill participation patterns; categorizing these skills into leisure competency areas; providing guidelines for further leisure decision-making and future program involvement.

STILAP (1990) will provide the CTRS with:

1. Objective data from which both staff and clients can mutually engage in responsible leisure decision making,
2. Insight into the client's leisure competency areas,
3. An interest survey tool that can be used in program planning,
4. Increased accountability in leisure counseling/education, and
5. A client-centered program evaluation tool.

While the STILAP (1990) is able to assist the CTRS in many components of the client's assessment and treatment program, it should not be used as the sole assessment tool. Depending on the services offered by the recreational therapy department, the therapist will need to select other assessment tools to measure areas that the STILAP (1990) does not measure.

ORIENTING THE CLIENTS TO LEISURE

It is vital that the client's introduction to leisure be
a) non-threatening and
b) placed into the client's individual perspective.

A. Non-threatening. Adults are often taken aghast or even defensive when a staff member speaks to them about the use of their leisure. This topic, if poorly presented, may appear to the clients as 'infringement of personal privacy'. The following statements or inferences (from client to staff) are not uncommon.

'Honey, I have handled my leisure for fifty years and no punk college graduate young enough to be my daughter is going to tell me I've got to go bowling.'

'Sonny, I was playing poker before you were born and have no interest in learning anything else.'

'Who are you to tell me I'm incompetent?'

Obviously, the preceding responses can often be avoided if an orientation session occurs. A group orientation session can incorporate several of the following topics:

1. Educational institutions are recognizing their responsibility to prepare students for responsible use of leisure.

2. Industry is recognizing the direct relationship between an employee's ability to handle his/her free time and success on the job.

3. Industry is also recognizing the direct relationship between an employee's ability to get along with co-workers and success on the job. (Many social skills are acquired through participation in leisure activities.)

4. Many students (severely disabled, past institutionalized, much past hospitalization, etc.) have not had a wide-range exposure to leisure activities. Exposure and even minimal skill development brings security. This security that 'I have done it' may encourage an individual to attempt a new leisure activity with friends, business associates, etc. in the future.

5. A client with a recently acquired disability is in a different situation than a client with a congenital disability. The former may need to relearn past activities with adaptations or seek substitute activities.

6. A person's disability may have been such a major focus in the past there was little opportunity to discover the potential abilities. Social and leisure opportunities facilitate the recognition of these personal abilities, thus enabling an individual to discover his/her full potential.

7. Free time is recognized as a problem in society today (boredom being one extreme with 'too busy' or over programming at the other extreme). Exposure to a variety of leisure opportunities and an analysis of 'What I want out of my free time' or 'What activities or social situations work for me' will aid clients in designing the use of their free time for their own satisfaction.

8. 'Enforced leisure' can be a severe problem (unemployment, retirement, and hospitalization are all enforced leisure). How to cope with this is a necessary survival skill -- for mental health, physical well-being, emotional health, and social existence.

Basically, when a client understands the importance of leisure and that leisure is a problem for many in today's society, the threat to the individual is diminished or eliminated.

It is important for the therapist to realize that the client is an individual first and foremost. The therapist will need to establish which areas of the client's leisure lifestyle can be considered within 'normal' expectations. One example would be if the client has experienced problems or difficulties with leisure (i.e., boredom, over programming), s/he possess a very 'normal' characteristic. The STILAP (1990) measures leisure patterns which are considered 'normal'. The STILAP (1990) also helps the therapist identify areas to work on to achieve a more 'normal' leisure lifestyle.

B. Placing Leisure in Perspective. Leisure improvement will probably not be a client's (or agency's) number one recognized priority. The client statements that follow are verification of this.

'I've just lost my leg and you're talking to me about skiing!'

'I'm enrolled in school to study drafting and have no time for fun and games.'

'I have enough trouble trying to quit drinking. What do I care about learning the guitar?'

Each of the preceding statements not only indicates that leisure may not be the client's number one priority, but also implies a lack of understanding of the value of leisure (first component of leisure education). A recreational therapist sensitive to both of these situations will 'prep' the client before administering an assessment tool such as STILAP (1990).

In some clinical settings other team members and third party payers may not recognize the close link between a healthy client and leisure education. In these settings the CTRS may need to call leisure education by a different name. The therapist may need to talk about 'programming or treatment to promote the client's competence to integrate functional skills in a variety of settings in such a manner as to ensure an on-going maintenance of health' (i.e., leisure education).

Leisure service, leisure counseling, or leisure education are usually ancillary or at least secondary in purpose to the major mission of an agency (i.e., physical rehabilitation unit, vocational rehabilitation trade school, alcoholism treatment center, etc.). Each of these agencies, however, probably speaks of milieu therapy, treating the total person, rehabilitating for life role competencies, etc. Until the CTRS is able to present to the treatment team and the clients the fundamental importance of treatment through the use of leisure activities, s/he may encounter some difficulty in the establishment of credibility.

ORIENTING THE CLIENTS TO STILAP (1990)

Orienting the client to the assessment and profile sheet is important to the client's understanding and appreciation of STILAP (1990). The resulting understanding and appreciation will hopefully contribute to a more valid assessment.

ACTIVITY CHECK LIST

The STILAP (1990) assessment tool comes with two forms. The first form (#150A) is an Activity Check List. The purpose of this form is to have the client indicate *if* s/he engages in any of the activities on the Check List *and* how often s/he engages in the activities on the Check List. In addition to indicating if s/he engages in any of the activities (and how often), the client also should indicate if s/he has an *interest* in developing greater skills in a specific activity.

In the front of each of the 123 activities on the Activity Check List are the letters **'M'** (for much), **'S'** (for sometimes), and **'I'** (for interest).

'MUCH' means that the client participates often in the activity and that his/her skill level is high enough for self-satisfying participation. It is evident that for different activities 'M' might have different meanings. For example, if the client is an 'M' bowler, that probably means that s/he bowls at least weekly a good portion of the year. On the other hand, the client may be an 'M' canoer and because canoeing is seasonal, s/he will not be doing it year-round.

'SOMETIMES' means that the client engages in the activity on an irregular basis, or on a seasonal basis. Examples:

'I bowl whenever my brother and sister-in-law come into town.'
'I snow ski about 10 days a year'
'I garden in the summer'

'Interested" means that the client has a definite interest in learning the skills necessary for participation is the activity or that the client is interested in increasing his/her skills in the activity.

It is possible to combine 'S' and 'I' if the client participates occasionally and is interested in learning more about the activity, or an 'M' and 'I' if s/he already participates often and is interested in learning and improving skills in the activity.

The check list does not include every possible leisure activity nor does it necessarily reflect the most desirable activities. Blanks are provided for activities not mentioned.

Clients need not complete the activity check list in the presence of the therapist. Clients able to read can take the activity check list and return it at a later date. It is important, however, for the therapist to verify the results of this check list before attempting to tabulate the information onto the profile worksheet. The therapist should take a short time to see that the client has completed the activity check list accurately (did not circle all 'M's; did understand the activities listed, etc.).

LEISURE PROFILE SCORE SHEET

The second form, the Leisure Profile Score Sheet (#150B), is the form on which the therapist tabulates and calculates the client's responses from the Activity Check List (#150A).

THEORETICAL BACKGROUND

The primary theory behind the STILAP (1990) is that an individual needs to engage in leisure activities of his/her choice in a variety of domains (or competency areas) to have a healthy leisure lifestyle. For an in depth explanation of this theory, the therapist should read the following two articles:

Navar, N. and T. Clancy. '*Leisure Skill Assessment Process in Leisure Counseling*' in Szymanski, D. J. and G. L. Hitzhusen (Eds.). **Expanding Horizons in Therapeutic Recreation VI.** University of Missouri, Columbia, 1979.

Navar, N. '*A Rationale for Leisure Skill Assessment with Handicapped Adults*', **Therapeutic Recreation Journal, XIV**, Fourth Quarter, 1980, pp. 21-28.

In these articles, Navar has listed fourteen competencies. To have a 'balanced' leisure lifestyle, it is desirable to have skills (and participate) in activities that span several different competencies. Scoring this can be complicated, since leisure competencies are not mutually exclusive. That is, several activities can be categorized into more than one competency area.

Example: Samantha, a 43 y/o female with a history of drug addition, enjoys golfing with two other women on Wednesdays. For her, golfing provides her with an opportunity to be outdoors while getting exercise and talking with her two friends. She seldom lets anything get in the way of her golfing engagement.

The client is the best source for indicating the nature of participation (i.e. Is the primary motive for golf being in the outdoors, socializing, or performing a physical skill? or Does the client engage in hiking primarily with others or mostly alone?). The intent here is to obtain a profile that fosters variety and balance in a number of different leisure activities. For this reason, during the 'prescription phase' of the assessment process, the CTRS will categorize an activity into only the primary competency area that fits a particular client.

The scoring of the STILAP is not rigid. In the preceding example, Samantha claims that golf is the physical activity she anticipates pursuing in 'later years.' This tells the CTRS to categorize Samantha's 'M' under competency F, Physical Skills With Carry Over Opportunity For Later Years. Such individualizing of the scoring of competencies has the potential to lessen reliability. For this reason, staff within one agency should agree upon scoring methods that will foster reliability.

FOURTEEN COMPETENCIES

A. PHYSICAL SKILL THAT CAN BE DONE ALONE Many people value their 'alone time' as a rewarding, peaceful or pleasant part of a day. Others dread or fear solitude and either avoid such a situation or experience it with emotions that are less than pleasant. Either outlook reaffirms the fact that many people in today's society do spend time alone. Whether or not this solitude is considered to be leisure is individually determined. Many people who are ill or disabled spend a disproportionate amount of time alone. It is logical to expect that if a person has a skill which can be utilized when no other persons are present, that person is better prepared to both handle and enjoy his/her time alone. Physical activity is documented as being beneficial to both emotional and physical health and well-being. Many people naively presume that physical leisure activities require other people. Several leisure activities can be performed by one person; i.e., jogging, exercising, yoga, billiards, relaxation techniques and so on. Often times through choice or necessity adults participate in solitary physical leisure activities.

B. PHYSICAL SKILL THAT S/HE CAN PARTICIPATE IN WITH OTHERS REGARDLESS OF SKILL LEVEL Many social physical activities (i.e., dual or team sports) contribute both to the client's social development and to physical well-being or fitness. However, social development is often frustrated or encumbered by participants or competitors who are unevenly matched. It is extremely difficult for a beginning tennis player or racquetball player to enjoy competing against an expert in these sports. On the other hand, bowlers, swimmers, or skiers of unequal ability can readily enjoy participating together. Since many physical social leisure activities are readily available to adults, it is beneficial to the therapist and to the client to assess the client's leisure participation pattern and interest in physical activities where skill level is relatively unimportant.

C. PHYSICAL SKILL THAT REQUIRES THE PARTICIPATION OF ONE OR MORE OTHERS Many common adult activities do require more than one participant. Today's society is experiencing an increased focus on lifetime sports and carry-over activities that require others. In addition, improved social interaction is a common recreational therapy goal area that can be facilitated through client involvement in leisure activities that require involvement by others. Inherent in activities such as tennis, badminton, table tennis or horseshoes is the opportunity for interaction with one or more others.

D. ACTIVITY DEPENDENT ON SOME ASPECT OF THE OUTDOOR ENVIRONMENT The ecological and environmental concerns of today are brought to focus frequently in the media, in schools, and throughout many aspects of daily life. People do not care for or protect things that they do not value. Outdoor leisure activities provide enjoyable reasons for valuing the environment. In addition, health or economic concerns often provide reasons for clients to utilize the out-of-doors. The out-of-doors provides a relatively inexpensive leisure environment for activities such as walking, gardening, bird watching, hiking, or camping.

E. PHYSICAL SKILLS NOT CONSIDERED SEASONAL Although geographic differences occur throughout the United States, each geographic region has normal or customary seasonal activities. Many persons who are very active in the summer often fail to enjoy a winter or rainy season. The 'cabin fever' occurring in snowed-in regions or 'dog days' of the south are examples of many unpleasant reactions to weather and climate. Many adults have a variety of leisure skills that upon close examination are seasonally limited. If a person is to be physically active throughout the entire year, non-seasonal activities can be pursued. Roller skating, shuffleboard, auto mechanics, hiking, and swimming are examples of leisure activities with a high probability of seasonal independence.

F. PHYSICAL SKILL WITH CARRY OVER OPPORTUNITY FOR LATER YEARS 'Later years' is often individually defined depending on one's age and life perspective. A forty-year-old male with paraplegia may consider 'later years' to be age 60 or 65, while a client who has AIDS may have the foresight and interest to plan for the 'later years' of 30 or 35. Either description implies an anticipated change in future leisure lifestyle. While there are senior citizens that play softball at age 72, they are the exception. More typical for older adults are non-team sport activities such as swimming, golf, and walking. 'Later years' implies either social or physical considerations that influence one's leisure choices. In order to prepare a client for a future leisure lifestyle that may be different from their youthful leisure participation patterns, it is important to obtain an assessment of the client's leisure competency in this area.

G. PHYSICAL SKILL WITH CARRY OVER OPPORTUNITY THAT IS VIGOROUS ENOUGH FOR CARDIOVASCULAR FITNESS Again, cardiovascular fitness can be individually defined based on an individual's age, state of fitness and physical abilities or limitations. A person with paraplegia may choose to participate in individual exercises or swimming to maintain or improve his/her cardiovascular fitness. The nineteen-year-old client who is emotionally impaired yet able-bodied obviously has different cardiovascular capacities. Jogging, racquetball, or bicycling may be of more interest or more feasible to a particular client. Whatever the level of cardiovascular fitness, it is generally accepted that leisure activities can contribute in this area. For this reason, it is important to assess whether a client has a leisure competency that has both carry over value and is vigorous enough for his/her personally defined level of cardiovascular fitness.

H. MENTAL SKILL PARTICIPATED IN ALONE So far, the leisure competencies under discussion have primarily referred to the variety of physical leisure competencies of adults. Cognitive leisure involvement is also a very common type of leisure pursuit. The unlimited opportunities to enjoy the use of the mind are frequently overlooked in traditional recreation programming. Thinking, analyzing, creating, or synthesizing are all cognitive experiences enjoyed by adults. Mental leisure activities such as solitaire, reading, writing poetry, or drawing blue print plans can provide satisfying leisure experiences. The presence of an illness or disabling condition does not negate the frequent leisure interests in solitary mental pursuits.

I. MENTAL SKILL REQUIRING ONE OR MORE OTHERS The previously mentioned social concerns of the recreational therapist apply to cognitive oriented leisure experiences. Cards, table games, current event discussion groups, and chess are examples of leisure activities that would indicate whether or not a client has a competency, leisure participation pattern or interest in pursuing social activities that are predominantly cognitive.

J. APPRECIATION SKILL OR INTEREST AREA WHICH ALLOWS FOR EMOTIONAL OR MENTAL STIMULATION THROUGH OBSERVATION OR PASSIVE RESPONSE The intent of this competency is to determine if the individual has an interest or developed skill in spectating. Spectating implies a range of activities from concerts, theater, and art appreciation to watching sporting events. The traditional categorization of recreation activities into active and passive does little toward lending either credibility or sanction to spectating and appreciation skills. Rather than lecturing that clients should be more active in their leisure pursuits, it is often in the client's and therapist's best interest to simply assess whether a client has such an appreciation skill. It is often more appropriate to acknowledge an active leisure participation pattern in an appreciation skill area than it is to say that a client is too passive. On the other hand, many clients do lack the ability or interest to actively enjoy a spectating or passive leisure activity. In this case, an assessment of competency in the appreciation skill area lends rationale for both pursuing such an interest or developing such a skill.

K. SKILL WHICH ENABLES THE CREATIVE CONSTRUCTION OR SELF-EXPRESSION THROUGH OBJECTIVE MANIPULATION, SOUND, OR VISUAL MEDIA The human need for self-expression is well documented. Leisure experiences are often presented as an enjoyable and feasible means of self-expression. When a client engages in such activities as photography, playing the guitar, painting, crafts, or 'souping up' a car engine, s/he is demonstrating leisure involvement through creative construction or self-expressive media.

L. SKILL WHICH ENABLES THE ENJOYMENT OR IMPROVEMENT OF THE HOME ENVIRONMENT If either client or staff think about a rainy, gloomy Saturday afternoon without a car, no money, and no friends available, the resulting facial expression is usually less than pleasant. 'What will I do?' is a probable question that arises from such an image. It is very important that adults be able to not only survive time at home, but enjoy such opportunities. Also, the family member may look to leisure experiences at home for social, economic, health, or mobility reasons. The area of leisure skills development in home and family activities is traditionally overlooked in institutional settings where the focus is often on group recreation activities. A comprehensive recreational therapy assessment enables the client and the recreational therapist to assess both the client's leisure interests and leisure participation pattern in home and family activities.

M. PHYSICAL OR MENTAL SKILL WHICH ENABLES PARTICIPATION IN A PREDOMINANTLY SOCIAL SITUATION Much of adult life is spent in social situations. Many of these social situations are centered around leisure activities. Conversely, leisure activities are often used as a means of meeting new people or further developing social relationships. Many of our clients need a repertoire of social leisure activity skills in order to both improve or expand their social horizons or to simply survive in social situations. When assessing a client's leisure activity skills, the recreational therapist must be concerned with the client's status in relation to leisure activities that will enable a client to successfully function in a social situation. Bowling, cards, dancing, or participation in clubs or community organizations are leisure activities that can focus on social interaction more than the actual activity skill.

N. LEADERSHIP OR INTERPERSONAL SKILL WHICH ENABLES COMMUNITY SERVICE Many clients, because of illness, disability, or institutionalization, have much practice in receiving assistance or service. Generally, adults often find service to others a pleasurable or rewarding experience. Adult clients, regardless of disability, often have a need or desire to be useful or provide service to others. Recreational therapy professionals frequently acknowledge this leadership desire of clients by enabling the client to assist in scorekeeping or by delegating canteen or equipment responsibilities to clients. Although such instances of clients providing leadership or service may be sound programming, these examples are not acknowledging that leadership can be a leisure activity skill with carry-over value for the client. Depending on the functional level of clients and the recreational therapy program resources, such activities as lifesaving, cardiopulmonary resuscitation, first aid, or leadership of youth groups can be learned by clients as a normal adult activity skill. Other types of programming to help clients acquire leadership skills as a leisure pursuit might include how to function as a committee member or what to expect from a PTA meeting.

OVERLAPPING COMPETENCY AREAS

What might be obvious now is that many of the activities within each competency may overlap into other competency areas. For instance, 'physical fitness/exercises' can be considered a 'physical skill not considered seasonal'. The overlap is not an error. Activities are listed under assigned competencies because the stated competency is inherent in the activity. The purpose of the competencies is not to rigidly categorize or stereotype activities, but to help the client become more aware of a) the different areas incorporated in his/her leisure, b) the vast leisure alternatives available, and c) the possibilities of different leisure needs that may confront the client in the future.

IMPORTANCE OF PLANNING FUTURE LEISURE

Using the client's scores from the STILAP (1990) to determine the client's competency in the various areas of leisure, the CTRS can help the client calculate future leisure needs as well as current leisure needs. A classic example of the importance of future leisure participation concerns is the high school 'jock' who eats, sleeps, and drinks team sports, never considering that s/he may not have a readily available team or that at some time s/he may not be physically able to play those sports. S/he may never have thought about the possibility of a future family and that his/her partner and children may not want to play those sports. Through the Leisure Assessment Process, it is possible to help develop the client's leisure awareness without making him/her feel inadequate.

The other classic example involved the class 'nerd'. The 'nerd' has socialization problems yet wants to make friends. His/her interests center around sedentary activities that s/he does at home: computer games, cooking, and drafting. If s/he really wants to meet other people, s/he can be guided toward leisure activities that will facilitate this.

DEFINITION OF COMPETENCY

The client may question what is meant by 'competency' and 'not meeting a competency'. Depending on the client's background these words may be threatening. For the purpose of the STILAP (1990), competency refers to one of fourteen skill areas that assist adults in responsible use of their leisure.

'Not meeting a competency' does not mean the client is inadequate; it only means that there is an area within the client's leisure that could benefit by developing a related skill. Good examples for explaining this may be:

1. An athletic person developing a sedentary skill in preparation for future physical condition, lifestyle, or new acquaintances.
2. A sedentary person developing a physical skill to aid physical condition.
3. A fairly competent person with many skills that are done alone developing new skills to help him/her meet different people.

It is important to respect each client's right to say 'no'. For instance, a client may not regularly participate in a 'mental skill that requires others'. No matter how much the client might benefit from developing such a skill, that client has the right to refuse to learn a skill that would fulfill this competency area. In this situation, the CTRS individualizes the objective STILAP (1990) results to aid in future leisure program planning and decision making.

Decisions that are written in the 'prescription choice' column are jointly made by client and therapist. A client may not have the competency 'physical skill done alone' and be interested in learning about exercise or aerobics. The decision written in the 'prescription choice' column might be 'Enroll in YMCA aerobics class to begin 8/1'.

In another instance, the client may not have the competency 'mental skill requiring others' and may not have an interest in acquiring such a skill. In this case, the 'prescription choice' column might read 'no action at this time'.

When completing the 'prescription choice' column, the CTRS considers as much information as possible to facilitate the client's leisure decision making. The individualization process should be guided not only by leisure competency information, but also by other relevant information.

INDIVIDUALIZING

Perhaps the most exciting part of the assessment process is individualizing the client's needs, abilities, and preferences. Individualizing requires flexibility, open-mindedness, empathy, the skill of a CTRS (Certified Therapeutic Recreation Specialist) and a basic belief by the practitioner in the importance of the competencies.

There are a variety of considerations to be explored when individualizing; the following exemplifies some of these considerations:

Joe is a member of a gang from the inner city of Detroit. His main leisure activity is 'hanging out on the street'. While at your facility he has the opportunity to explore a wide variety of activities; however, he wants only to participate in the leisure activities he normally does as member of his gang. The therapist may need to consider:

1. Does Joe have the ability to pursue other activities when his needs and interests change?
2. This may be Joe's first opportunity for this type of outdoor experience.
3. Will Joe be accepted by his peers upon his return to Detroit?
4. Where does Joe want to live in the future?
5. Will Joe be able to continue these activities when back in Detroit?

These considerations will be incorporated into the counseling process. Sharing thoughts and considerations with the client allows the client the opportunity to realize what outside factors may affect or influence his/her leisure in the future.

STANDARD CONSIDERATIONS

Some standard considerations should be mentioned here:

1. **TIME:** When will the client participate in the activity? Day or night, for 15 minutes or two hours, for a season or year-round, can s/he do it for 5 or 50 years?

2. **MONEY:** How much money does the activity require? Will his/her employment pay enough to afford the activity? Is the activity worth the sacrifices s/he may have to make?

3. **FAMILY AND FRIENDS:** Will participation affect any standing relationships that the client values?

4. **LOCALE:** Will the client's locale affect participation?

The objectivity of the forms utilized in the STILAP (1990) provides accuracy in assessment. The ability to take this objective information and make it meaningful to the individual is the art of Leisure Counseling.

INCORPORATING THE STILAP (1990) INTO AN EXISTING RECREATIONAL THERAPY PROGRAM

Depending on the resources (staff, facility, budget, clients, etc.) and purposes of the recreational therapy program (maintain existing knowledge, skills, and level of functioning; habilitate or bring new behaviors into existence; rehabilitate or reinstate past functional level, or hospice), implementation of STILAP (1990) can vary. Three feasible implementation strategies follow.

For someone in an Intermediate Care Facility for the Mentally Retarded (ICF-MR), STILAP (1990) is used as the foundation for determining the need for a formalized training program in leisure. Depending on the outcome of STILAP (1990), a client can a) make responsible decisions to participate in certain recreation activities, b) be prescribed (as a regular aspect of the curriculum and of the Individual Program Plan) into specific leisure skill development classes, and c) be referred to individual or group leisure counseling Ultimately, the goal is responsible use of the client's leisure.

In a community recreation setting, STILAP (1990) could be used as an educational program or as the basis for discussion in an adult leisure education group. Information secured could then help clients decide which community resources would benefit them the most.

In an alcoholism treatment center, an eight-week leisure counseling group offered to outpatients could incorporate STILAP (1990) into a group session. An alcoholism education class focusing on the role of leisure in the recovery process might utilize STILAP (1990) as a follow-up aid for interested clients.

The preceding examples indicate the diverse applicability of STILAP (1990). As mentioned previously, STILAP (1990) is a versatile yet objective tool that can be both effective and meaningful when utilized by a Certified Therapeutic Recreation Specialist.

SUGGESTED READINGS

Compton, D. and J. Goldstein. (1977) **Perspectives on Leisure Counseling.** National Recreation and Park Association: Arlington, VA.

Dehn, D. (1995) **Leisure Step Up.** Idyll Arbor, Inc.: Ravensdale, WA.

Epperson, A., P. Witt and G. Hitzhusen. (1977) **Leisure Counseling an Aspect of Leisure Education.** Charles C. Thomas: Springfield, IL.

Joswiak, Kenneth F. (1979) **Leisure Counseling Program Materials.** Hawkins and Assoc.

Mundy, Jean and L. Odum. (1979) **Leisure Education Theory and Practice.** Wiley and Sons, New York, NY.

National Recreation and Park Association. (1977) **Kangaroo Kit Leisure Education Cirriculum for Kindergarten - Grade 12.** NRPA: Arlington, VA.

Navar, N. and T. Clancy. (1979) *'Leisure Skill Assessment Process in Leisure Counseling'*, **Expanding Horizons in Therapeutic Recreation VI,** Szymanski, D.J. and Hitzhusen, G.L. (eds.). University of Missouri: Columbia, MO.

Navar, N. (1980) *'A Rationale for Leisure Skill Assessment with Handicapped Adults'*. **Therapeutic Recreation Journal,** Vol. XIV, Fourth Quarter.

Peterson, C. and S. Gunn. (1984) **Therapeutic Recreation Program Design: Principles and Procedures.** Prentice Hall, Englewood Cliffs, NJ.

Schleien, Stuart J. and M. Tipton Ray. (1988) **Community Recreation and Persons wih Disabilities**. Paul H. Brookes Publishing Co., Baltimore, MD.

STILAP (1990) ADMINISTRATIVE GUIDELINES

The new **STILAP (1990)** score sheet and competency summary sheet had limited field testing. Any suggestions that practitioners may have are welcomed by the authors.

I. Background Information

A. Development

1. STILAP (State Technical Institute's Leisure Assessment Process) was originally developed in 1974 as a joint effort between the following persons and agencies:

Nancy Navar — then employed at Leisure Services Department of State Technical Institute and Rehabilitation Center in Plainwell, Michigan.

Carol Peterson — then employed in the Field Service Unit in Physical Education and Recreation for Handicapped at Michigan State University in East Lansing, Michigan.

2. Both interview and check list versions of STILAP was field tested with several hundred adult disabled individuals. The original administrative guidelines refer to the check list version of the assessment instrument. The version included in this assessment packet is an updated version of the 1974 STILAP.

3. The chosen recreation activities are geographically oriented to Michigan. Practitioners can readily change these activities to be more geographically and culturally appropriate to their clients. When adding and deleting activities, be certain to: a. categorize the activities into the appropriate leisure competency areas, and b. alter the numbered coding system on the profile worksheet accordingly.

4. STILAP (1990) is an updated version by Nancy Navar, CTRS, and joan burlingame, CTRS. The therapist should note that changes have been made in the 1990 version. There is enough difference that a comparison of a client's scores from the 1974 to the 1990 version would be invalid.

5. The formal validation of the 1974 and the 1990 versions have not been established.

B. Leisure Competency Areas

1. The underlying philosophical structure of STILAP is the inclusion of the 14 leisure competency areas. These leisure competency areas are conceptualized for adults who are not disabled.

This 'normalization' effort implies that no specific accommodations have been made for various disabling conditions. However, the primary disability groups that the STILAP has been successfully used with clients who are

physically disabled	emotionally impaired
visually impaired	behaviorally disabled
hearing impaired	learning disabled
substance abusers	legal offenders

2. In this revision of STILAP, 'leisure competency' is used synonymously with 'leisure participation pattern'. Thus, actual skill level in a recreation activity is de-emphasized and regularity of participation is the focus.

II. Instructions for Administering the Activity Check List

A. Before the client is given the Activity Check List, the following instructions should be implemented (individually or in a group):

1. Create an environment that will help the client be comfortable and feel at ease, i.e., non-threatening, enjoyable meeting; orientation to leisure, orientation to leisure services department, orientation to function of STILAP and role of client.

2. Explain the purpose and procedure of the leisure assessment process.

3. Read the directions on the STILAP Activity Check List.

4. Emphasize the meaning of **MUCH (M)** and **SOME (S).** The client should select the 'M' if s/he can answer 'yes' to both questions:

a. Do I do this activity often?
b. Do I have adequate skills to do this activity?

The therapist should give a few examples of (M) and (S), i.e., I bowl in a league every week (M) or I bowl when my brother-in-law comes to town (S). The client should consider his/her skill level in a recreational setting, not at a highly competitive level. If the client is uncertain whether (M) or (S) is appropriate, a question mark should be placed next to that activity.

5. Describe the meaning of **'Interested' (I)**. (I) indicates an interest in learning more about the activity.

The client may circle an (S) and an (I) if participation in that activity is occasional and there is interest in learning more about the activity; or an (M) and an (I) if participation is often (regular) and there is interest in learning and improving skills in that activity. If the client has not experienced the activity but is interested in learning about the activity, s/he should mark the (I).

6. Instruct the client to not mark an activity if s/he does not participate in the activity and is not interested in learning the activity.

7. Instruct the client to place a question mark next to an activity if s/he is not sure what the activity is, or if s/he has a question about the activity.

B. Distribute the Activity Check List (if the client(s) will be filling it out himself/herself)

1. Instruct the client to print his/her name, unit, (if appropriate) bed number, and the date on the form.

2. Have the client complete the Activity Check List.

a. Some staff prefer that this be completed in the presence of a staff member, i.e., if the client has difficulty reading; if the client feels more at ease, etc.

b. Some staff prefer to have the client think about the activities overnight and complete the Activity Check List on his/her own.

3. The therapist should review the completed Activity Check List with each client individually.

a. to clarify any questions

b. to verify the validity of the responses, i.e., is (M) really a correct response?

c. to verify whether the activities marked with an (M) were primarily done alone, with others, year round, etc. (A CTRS familiar with the competency areas will be able to determine in which competency area the (M) activity should be categorized.)

C. Read the Activity Selections on the Activity Check List to the Client (if the therapist is reading the selections to the client)

1. The therapist should write in the client's name, unit, (if appropriate) bed number, and the date on the Activity Check List form.

2. Read the activities on the Activity Check List to the client one by one and wait for his/her answers. The therapist should place a question mark next to the activities that the client is not familiar with or has questions about.

3. The therapist should do 'spot checks' as s/he reads through the activities to ensure that the client understands the meaning of (M), (S), and (I).

III. Instructions for Scoring the STILAP

DIRECTIONS: The therapist will need to have the client's completed STILAP Activity Check List, The STILAP Profile Score Sheet, The STILAP Competency Summary, two different colors of Magic Marker, and a pen which has black ink.

A. Filling Out the Profile Score Sheet

The STILAP Profile Score Sheet has been designed to decrease the number of errors made by therapists when scoring the STILAP. The numbers (1-130) across the top of the graph represent the numbers for each activity (i.e., #1 = Pool/Billiards/Snooker). The letters down the left side of the graph represent the 14 Competencies (i.e., A = Physical Skill That Can be Done Alone). The letter 'O' represents 'OTHER' and will be addressed later in the scoring directions.

The therapist should notice that many of the squares in the graph have been blacked out. The white squares represent activities which are included in the competency. The black squares are not part of the competency. For example, Pool/Billiards/Snooker (number 1) belongs in the competency area Physical Skills That Can Be Done Alone (Competency A). It does not belong in the competency area Skill Which Enables Enjoyment/Improvement of the Home Environment (competency L).

There are three types of responses that need to be marked on the tabulation sheet: **M**, **S**, and **I**. One colored pen is used for the **M**'s. The other colored pen is used for the S's.

For every activity number where the client circled the **M**, the therapist should draw the **M** color down the entire column under the number with the **M** (starting at 'A' and going down to 'O').

Most of the activities cover several competencies as described earlier. There are two possible actions now, based on how well the CTRS knows the client:

If the CTRS, working with the client, can decide which competency the activity will satisfy, s/he can circle that box on the score sheet. To show that the activity has been used, the CTRS should draw a black zig zag line through the rest of the colored line. To show that the competency has been met, put an **X** in the left column next to the competency letter. (Use the top set for all of the **X**'s even if the competency was met in one of the other sets.)

If the CTRS is not sure which competency is the most important for the activity, s/he should not make any choice of competency yet.

For every number that the client circled the **S**, the therapist should draw the **S** color down the entire column under the number with the **S** (starting at 'A' and going down to 'O').

For every number that the client circled the **I**, the therapist should put an **I** in the corresponding number/box in row **O**. For every number that the client had a question about, the therapist should place a question mark in the corresponding number/box in the **O** row. This will allow the therapist to make a quick reference to the number and types of activities that the client was interested in or unsure about.

B. Finding Competencies on the Profile Score Sheet

At this point the therapist has all of the activities transferred from the client's Activity List to the Profile Score Sheet. Some competencies are already marked as met (with an **X**) and some are not. The next task is to find out how many of the rest of the competencies are being met.

To do this, place a ruler horizontally under the first line which does not have an **X** to show that the competency has been met. Reading along the line from activity #1 to activity #45 circle the first box marked with the **M** color which does not have a zig zag through it. If no **M**'s are found, go to activities #46 to #90 and then to activities #91 to #130. If an **M** is found, draw a zig zag through the the rest of the column to show that the activity has been used and put an **X** in the left column to show that the competency has been met.

Continue the process with the rest of the competency lines which do not have a marked **M** competency. Notice that sometimes the only activity which would satisfy the competency you are interested in has already been used for another competency. It is permissible to use that activity for the current competency if you can find another activity to satisfy the conflicting competency.

C. Filling Out the Competency Summary

After the client's score sheet has been marked, the totals need to be entered on the STILAP Competency Summary. This is done by totaling up the the activities which are included in each of the competency areas. Start by marking the colors used for **M** and **S** at the top of the Competency Summary form.

Score the STILAP by counting the number of times a color appears in the white squares in each row and enter the count in the appropriate column of the Competency Summary sheet. If the competency has been met, as signified by an **X** in the left column of the Profile Score Sheet, circle the number on the Competency Summary.

Take the activities which are marked with an **I** in row **O** and enter the numbers in the interest area column of the Competency Summary where they have a white box for the competency.

The CTRS may want to highlight the competencies that have not been met on the Competency Summary sheet by highlighting the competency with a yellow marker.

D. Using the results for treatment goals

The main goal of the STILAP is to determine if the client demonstrates (through participation) enough competencies to maintain a balanced leisure lifestyle. Based on the theoretical background of the STILAP, the client has a healthy leisure lifestyle if s/he has at least one circled **M** activity in each of the 14 competency areas. The more balanced the **M**'s are between the catagories, the healthier the client's leisure lifestyle is.

If the client has one or more competency areas without a circled **M**, the therapist should determine if there is a great enough need to warrant a formal treatment goal to alleviate the void. This determination should be made with the client's input.

If the competency area without an **M** has an activity with an **S**, the therapist should check for interest in that activity. Interest in an area which has some participation indicates that the therapist should put high priority on developing that activity. An **S/I** combination indicates that the client has some understanding of the activity (by having engaged in it) and a desire to increase his/her exposure.

STILAP (1990)
State Technical Institute's Leisure Assessment Process

Purpose: The purpose of the STILAP is to help assess a client's leisure participation in order to help the client achieve a balanced leisure lifestyle.

DIRECTIONS: Below is a list of various leisure activities.
Circle 'M' (much) for those activities you participate in regularly (daily, every other day, when in season, etc.).
Circle 'S' (sometimes) for those activities you have done but not on a regular basis.
Circle 'I' (interested) for those activities you would like to learn (you may or may not have done these before, but you are still interested in learning more about the activity).

M S I 1. Pool, Billiards, Snooker
M S I 2. Dieting, Nutrition
M S I 3. Bowling
M S I 4. Roller Skating
M S I 5. Archery

M S I 6. Riflery
M S I 7. Shuffleboard
M S I 8. Pin Ball/Video Games
M S I 9. Ice Skating
M S I 10. Auto Mechanics

M S I 11. Jogging, Running
M S I 12. Physical Fitness (exercises)
M S I 13. Yoga
M S I 14. Relaxation Techniques
M S I 15. Darts

M S I 16. Horse Shoes
M S I 17. Horseback Riding
M S I 18. Miniature Golf
M S I 19. Golf
M S I 20. Hunting

M S I 21. Biking
M S I 22. Motorcycling
M S I 23. Sailing
M S I 24. Canoeing
M S I 25. Boating

M S I 26. Trailer Camping
M S I 27. Tent Camping
M S I 28. Backpacking
M S I 29. Orienteering (map & compass)
M S I 30. Cross Country Skiing

M S I 31. Tobogganing
M S I 32. Snow Skiing (downhill)
M S I 33. Snow Shoeing
M S I 34. Fishing
M S I 35. Ice Fishing

M S I 36. Hiking
M S I 37. Bird Watching
M S I 38. Football
M S I 39. Softball/Baseball
M S I 40. Frizbee

M S I 41. Judo, Self-Defense
M S I 42. Table Tennis (Ping Pong)
M S I 43. Paddleball, Racquetball
M S I 44. Handball
M S I 45. Squash

M S I 46. Tennis
M S I 47. Badminton
M S I 48. Family Lawn Games
M S I 49. Volleyball
M S I 50. Basketball

M S I 51. Ice Hockey, Hockey
M S I 52. Meditation
M S I 53. Jigsaw Puzzles
M S I 54. Crossword Puzzles
M S I 55. Reading

M S I 56. Watching Football
M S I 57. Watching Baseball
M S I 58. Watching Basketball
M S I 59. Watching Other Sports
M S I 60. Watching T.V.

Client's Name	Physician	Admit #	Room/Bed

DIRECTIONS: Below is a list of various leisure activities.
Circle 'M' (much) for those activities you participate in regularly (daily, every other day, when in season, etc.).
Circle 'S' (sometimes) for those activities you have done but not on a regular basis.
Circle 'I' (interested) for those activities you would like to learn (you may or may not have done these before, but you are still interested in learning more about the activity).

M S I 61. Touring
M S I 62. Traveling
M S I 63. Listening to Music
M S I 64. Art Appreciation
M S I 65. Theater (movies or plays)

M S I 66. Party Going
M S I 67. Backgammon
M S I 68. Checkers
M S I 69. Dominos
M S I 70. Other Table Games

M S I 71. Cribbage
M S I 72. Bridge
M S I 73. Chess
M S I 74. Euchre
M S I 75. Hearts

M S I 76. Poker
M S I 77. Other Card Games
M S I 78. 'Ham' Radio Operating ('CB')
M S I 79. Writing
M S I 80. Leather Crafts

M S I 81. Jewelry Making
M S I 82. Pottery/Ceramics
M S I 83. Ceramics (molds)
M S I 84. Horn Playing
M S I 85. Guitar Playing

M S I 86. Other Musical Instruments
M S I 87. Ballroom Dancing
M S I 88. Social Dancing
M S I 89. Square Dancing
M S I 90. Drawing, Painting

M S I 91. Collecting Items (coins, stamps, etc.)
M S I 92. Singing
M S I 93. Participation in Drama Production
M S I 94. Macrame
M S I 95. Photography

M S I 96. Batik (wax fabric dyeing)
M S I 97. Lapidary (rock polishing)
M S I 98. Copper Enameling
M S I 99. String Art
M S I 100. Sewing, Needle Point, Crewel, etc.

M S I 101. Knitting, Crocheting
M S I 102. Other Crafts
M S I 103. Baking, Cooking
M S I 104. Canning
M S I 105. House Plants

M S I 106. Gardening
M S I 107. Wood Refinishing
M S I 108. Wood Working
M S I 109. Pets
M S I 110. Sweepstakes, Lottery

M S I 111. Basketball Officiating
M S I 112. Softball Officiating
M S I 113. Volleyball Officiating
M S I 114. First Aid Certification
M S I 115. Life Saving Certification

M S I 116. Member of a Church
M S I 117. Member of a School Club
M S I 118. Member of a Community Organization, Politics
M S I 119. Signing Group, Deaf Sign Language
M S I 120. Volunteer Work

M S I 121. Swimming
M S I 122. Water Skiing
M S I 123. Skin Diving, Scuba Diving
M S I 124.
M S I 125.

M S I 126.
M S I 127.
M S I 128.
M S I 129.
M S I 130.

Client's Name	Physician	Admit #	Room/Bed

STILAP (1990) COMPETENCY SUMMARY

Enter color codes here:	M	S	Interest Areas	Prescription Choice
A. Physical Skill That Can Be Done Alone				
B. Physical Skill That S/he Can Participate with Others, Regardless of Skill Level				
C. Physical Skill That Requires the Participation of One or More Others				
D. Activity Dependent on Some Aspect of the Outdoor Environment				
E. Physical Skill Not Considered Seasonal				
F. Physical Skill With Carryover Opportunity for Later Years				
G. Physical Skill With Carryover Opportunity and Vigorous Enough for Cardiovascular Fitness				
H. Mental Skill Participated in Alone				
I. Mental Skill Requiring One or More Others				
J. Appreciation Skill or Interest Area Which Allows for Emotional or Mental Stimulation Through Observation or Passive Response				
K. Skill Which Enables Creative Construction or Self-expression Through Object Manipulation, Sound, or Visual Media				
L. Skill Which Enables Enjoyment/Improvement of the Home Environment				
M. Physical or Mental Skill Which Enables Participation in a Pre-dominantly Social Situation.				
N. Leadership and/or Interpersonal Skill Which Enables Community Service				
O. Other				

ASSESSMENT SUMMARY STATEMENT:

RECOMMENDATIONS:

Client's Name	Physician	Admit #	Room/Bed

STILAP (1990) PROFILE SCORE SHEET

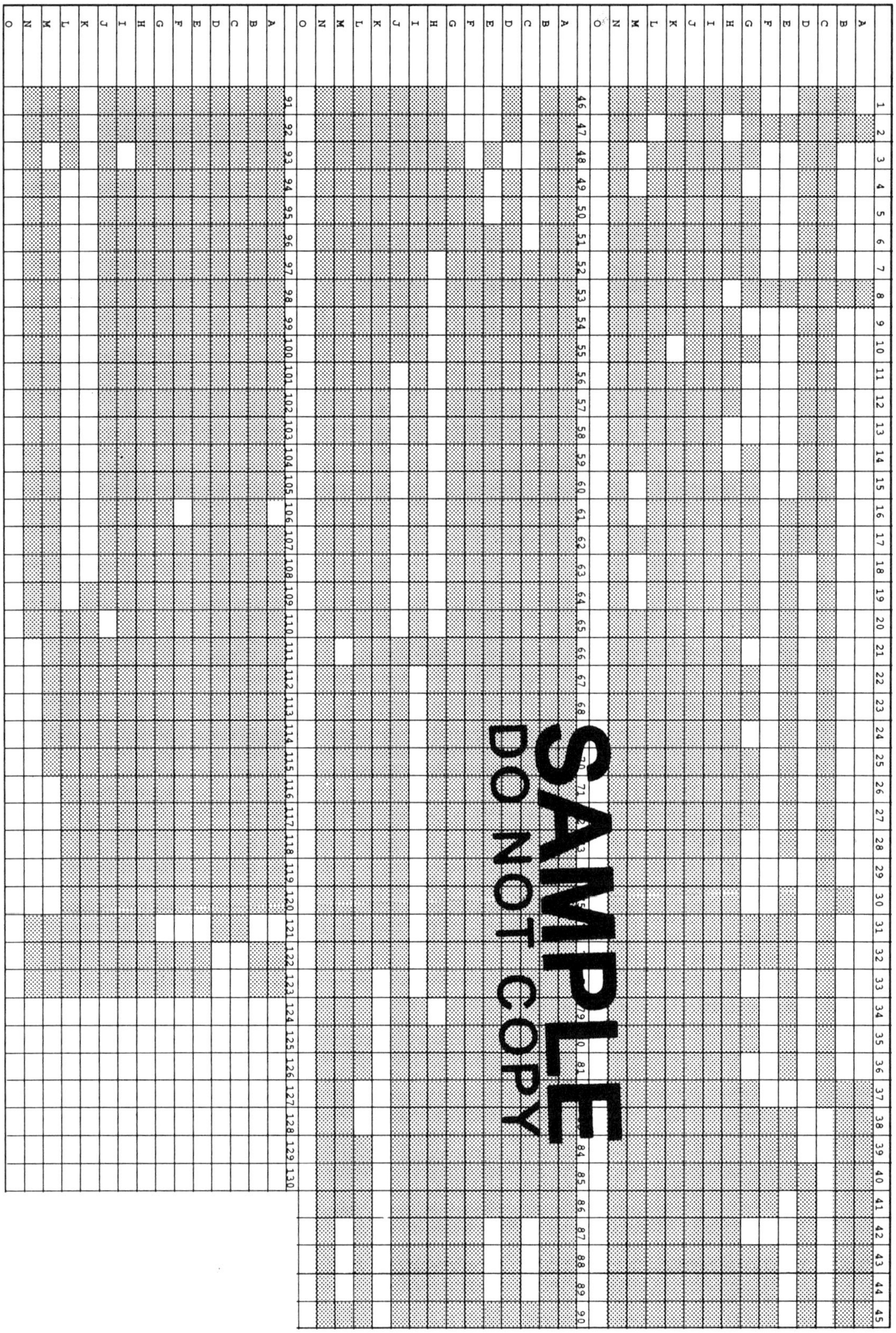

Client's Name	Physician	Admit #	Room/Bed

LEISURE MOTIVATION SCALE

Name: Leisure Motivation Scale

Also Known As: LMS

Authors: Jacob G. Beard and Mounir G. Ragheb developed the Leisure Motivation Scale. The Leisure Motivation Scale Manual and the Summary Page of the LMS were written by joan burlingame with the permission of Beard and Ragheb.

Time Needed to Administer: Idyll Arbor, Inc. staff did two separate time trials to determine the length of time that was required to administer the LMS.

The first set of trials timed a group of seven women (ages between 28 years and 42 years). All seven women had been evaluated to be 'gifted' and had worked in a professional capacity for part of their adult lives. None of them were under any kind of medical or psychological care. The time to administer the assessment tool (they read the front side themselves) was between 4 minutes and 17 minutes.

The second set of trials timed a group of adults whose primary diagnosis was mental retardation (moderate to mild). The time to administer the assessment tool (the therapist read the front side to the client) was between 8 minutes and 27 minutes.

Time Needed to Score: Scoring the LMS (both sides of the form) took under 10 minutes for each person tested.

Recommended Disability Group: Because of the extent of validity testing conducted on the LMS, it would be a good assessment to use on clients who have the cognitive ability to understand the questions.

Purpose of the Assessment: The purpose of the LMS is to measure a client's motivation(s) for engaging in leisure activities.

What Does theAssessment Measure?: The LMS measures the client's motivation for leisure activities. Based on extensive literature searches the authors found four primary factors which motivated individuals to recreate: 1) Intellectual, 2) Social, 3) Competence - Mastery, and 4) Stimulus - Avoidance.

Supplies Needed: LMS Manual and Score Sheet

Reliability/Validity: Validity and reliability information available.

Degree of Skill Required to Administer and Score: The LMS was developed to be used with 'normal' populations to self-administer and score. The back side requires the skills of a Certified Therapeutic Recreation Specialist to measure client behavior and to summarize the information to make recommendations for treatment.

Comments: The LMS has been available to professionals in the leisure counseling field since the early 1980's. In all of the facilities that Idyll Arbor, Inc. field tested the 'therapy version', the LMS received strong support from the recreational therapists involved. (Idyll Arbor, Inc. field tested the LMS in three different types of settings: 1) rehab., 2) psych., and 3) MR/DD.)

The LMS is part of the Idyll Arbor Leisure Battery which also includes the Leisure Satisfaction Measure, the Leisure Interest Measure, and the Leisure Attitude Measure.

Suggested Levels: Ranchos Los Amigos Level: 7 or above. Developmental Level: 12 or above. Reality Orientation Level: Mild to No Impairment.

Distributor: Idyll Arbor, Inc., 25119 SE 262 Street, PO Box 720, Ravensdale, WA 98051-0720 (206) 432-3231 (area code 425 after April 1997).

LEISURE MOTIVATION SCALE MANUAL

The Leisure Motivation Scale (LMS) was developed by Jacob G. Beard and Mounir G. Ragheb and published in the *Journal of Leisure Research,* 1983 Volume 15, Number 3, pp. 219-228. This version was developed by Idyll Arbor, Inc. with the permission of Beard and Ragheb. The original 48 statements have remained unchanged. Idyll Arbor, Inc. modified the assessment form and wrote a manual for the benefit of the recreational therapists who choose to administer the LMS. The back summary page of the LMS was developed by Idyll Arbor, Inc. and was not part of the original instrument.

PURPOSE: The purpose of the LMS is to measure a patient's motivation(s) for engaging in leisure activities.

AREAS MEASURED: This assessment measures a patient's motivation for leisure activities. Based on extensive literature searches the authors found four primary factors which motivated individuals to recreate. This instrument was built to reflect these four areas:

(The following four descriptions are taken from the *Journal of Leisure Research,* 1983, Vol. 15, Number 3, pp. 225.)

The **Intellectual** component of leisure motivation assesses the extent to which individuals are motivated to engage in leisure activities which involve substantial mental activities such as learning, exploring, discovering, creating, or imagining.

The **Social** component assesses the extent to which individuals engage in leisure activities for social reasons. This component includes two basic needs. The first is the need for friendship and interpersonal relationships, while the second is the need for the esteem of others.

The **Competence-Mastery** component assesses the extent to which individuals engage in leisure activities in order to achieve, master, challenge, and compete. The activities are usually physical in nature.

The **Stimulus-Avoidance** component of leisure motivation assesses the drive to escape and get away from over-stimulating life situations. It is the need for some individuals to avoid social contacts, to seek solitude and calm conditions; for others it is to seek rest and to unwind themselves.

SUPPLIES NEEDED: Idyll Arbor, Inc. score sheet #149, pen, LMS Manual. (No additional copies of the score sheet may be made. The therapist may order more score sheets from Idyll Arbor, Inc. 25119 SE 262 Street, PO Box 720, Ravensdale, WA 98051-0720. (206) 432-3231.)

POPULATIONS: Idyll Arbor, Inc. staff recommend the following guidelines to help determine if a patient is cognitively able to comprehend the statements.

*Adapted IQ of 80 or above
*Mental Age of 12 years or above
*Ranchos Los Amigos Level of 7 or above
*Reality Orientation Level of 'Mild to No Orientation Disability'

TIME NEEDED: The recreational therapist should allow between 5 and 25 minutes for the patient to answer all 48 statements. Scoring (both sides of the score sheet) should take the therapist under 10 minutes. In most cases the recreational therapist should be able to administer the assessment, score it and write a brief summary/recommendation statement in 30 minutes or less.

RELIABILITY AND VALIDITY: The LMS has two forms; the Full Scale which contains 48 statements (and is the one included in this assessment package), and the Short Scale which contains 32 statements. While both scales proved to have strong content validity and strong internal consistency, the Full Scale proved slightly more reliable. Please refer to Beard's article in the *Journal of Leisure Research,* 1983 for more detail.

WHEN TO ADMINISTER: The LMS ideally should be administered between the 4th and 7th day after admission. If the assessment is administered prior to the 4th day, the results may be undesirably impacted by transitional depression (the normal physiological reaction of people to an unfamiliar environment). If the therapist waits until sometime after the 7th day of admission, s/he may run into two problems: the first being the need to start treatment prior to knowing what is a motivator for the patient, and the second being that the patient may be adapting too well to being in an institution (developing an institutionalization mentality) and the score achieved may reflect that.

IN CONJUNCTION WITH PSYCHOTROPIC MEDICATIONS: Psychotropic medications may change a patient's leisure motivations. (Whether the change is a positive or negative one may require further assessment and discussion by the treatment team and the patient.) On units that frequently use psychotropic medications as one method of treatment, the recreational therapist should routinely administer the LMS prior to the medication being introduced or changed, and again after the medication has stabilized in the patient's system.

INSTRUCTIONS FOR ADMINISTERING THE LEISURE MOTIVATION SCALE

VERBAL INSTRUCTIONS: It is important that the recreational therapist gives each patient the same instructions for completing the assessment. The instructions should be the same whether the patient is self-administering the assessment or if the therapist is reading the assessment to the patient.

The therapist should first explain to the patient the purpose of the assessment and how the results could benefit the patient. This explanation should not take more than four or five brief sentences. The therapist should also inform the patient that there are no 'right' or 'wrong' answers.

Next, the therapist should read the directions right from the score sheet and then ask the patient if they understand the instructions. If the therapist is going to be reading the statements for the patient, the therapist should place an example of the 1 - 5 bar graph with the corresponding words (i.e.; 'Never True') in front of the patient to help cue him/her.

ENVIRONMENT: The therapist should obtain better results if the assessment is administered in a stimulus-reduced environment. A comfortable room with adequate light, limited visual and auditory distractions should be the therapist's goal.

PATIENT SELF-ADMINISTERED VS THERAPIST READ: Up to 20% of the population of the United States of America are non-functional readers (World Book Encyclopedia, 1989). In addition, numerous patients have visual disabilities making it difficult for them to self-administer this assessment. The therapist should always err on the conservative side. If s/he feels that the patient's reading level or visual acuity may affect the patient's score, the statements should be read out loud.

INSTRUCTIONS FOR FILLING OUT THE FIRST PAGE OF THE LMS FORM

The purpose of the first page of the LMS is to present the 48 statements to the patient. The therapist will need to ensure:

1. that the patient understands the statements
2. that the basic patient information is placed across the bottom of the form.

DIRECTIONS: The LMS (Full Scale) contains 48 statements. Each one begins with the phrase: 'One of my reasons for engaging in leisure activities is...'. To the right of each statements is a line to indicate how true that statement is. A '1' means that the statement is never true, a '2' means that the statement is seldom true, a '3' means that the statement is somewhat true, a '4' means that the statement is often true, and a '5' means the statement is always true. Write down the number that best fits your (the patient's) situation.

Instruct the patient to select one whole number between 1 and 5 (i.e, '2' not '2.5') for each statement.

The therapist may want to measure the length of time it takes for the patient to answer the statements. By collecting this data and comparing it with the times of other patients with similar disabilities and illnesses the therapist will have a more realistic understanding of the actual time required to administer (and score) the LMS within the facility. If this is being done, the therapist needs to let the patient know that s/he is being timed. The patient should be less threatened if s/he understands that the information is taken to establish the time needed to be allocated for patients in the future.

INSTRUCTIONS FOR FILLING OUT THE SECOND PAGE OF THE LMS

The purpose of the second page of the LMS is to:

1. provide a summary of the patient's scores related to motivation for leisure, and
2. provide a summary of the patient's affect and mannerisms during the assessment process.

The recreational therapist should complete the entire summary page within 24 hours of the patient's completing the LMS questionnaire. The best guideline would be to finish the summary sheet within an hour after the patient finished.

CHECK ONE: This part of the summary gives the therapist two choices: 'Patient self-administered assessment' and 'Therapist administered assessment'. *Only one* of the two squares may be checked.

'Self Administered' means that the patient read the entire LMS questionnaire himself/herself *and wrote* in his/her own scores.

'Therapist Administered' means that the patient required minimal to maximal assistance in reading the statements *and/or* in writing down his/her scores.

MEDICATIONS THAT COULD IMPACT RESULTS: This space is for the therapist to write in any medications that the patient is currently taking (on standard orders *or* PRN which may change the patient's scores.) Medications included in this category would be medications that ***may*** cause a personality change, cause dizziness or lethargy, modify attention span, or change coordination.

If possible, the therapist should note the name of the medication and dosage. This is especially important as a historical record. If this assessment is re-administered at a later date, it could be very important to factor in the possible effect medications may have had in any measured change in the patient's scores.

If the patient has received a PRN medication within the last eight hours, and if this medication could impact the assessment results, this medication should be highlighted. If might also be a good idea to indicate the length of time between the administration of the medication and the administration of the LMS questionnaire. Please note if the PRN medication was administered P.O., I.V., or I.M.

If the patient is receiving medications for pain, the recreational therapist should indicate if the patient perceives the pain medications as adequate to control the pain. A patient who perceives a lack of control over his/her pain could have significantly different perception of motivators than if s/he perceived his/her pain was under control.

DATE ASSESSMENT GIVEN: Place the month, day, and year that the patient completed the LMS questionnaire in this space (i.e., 9/20/90).

NOTE: The therapist will find the terms 'situational and cultural standards' frequently in the descriptors below. The therapist should take into account whether the patient is unable to meet the descriptor because of a physical disability (i.e., being on bedrest) or because of a cultural standard (i.e., women from the middle east will frequently refuse to establish and maintain eye contact with men).

When the therapist modifies his/her selection of a descriptor category because of a situational or cultural standard, the modification must be noted right on the score sheet.

APPEARANCE:
Appropriate, good hygiene: The patient is dressed according to situational and cultural standards. Skin and hair are relatively soil and oil free; good dental hygiene evident. Patient's body is free of noticeable odor (free from body odor as well as free from excess cologne or perfume). If make-up is used, it is within situational and cultural norms.
Clothing and/or hygiene slightly dirty or smelly: Upon close observation, clothing and/or hygiene falls short of situational and cultural standards. Patient's body may be emitting odor noticeable upon close proximity. If make-up is used, its use is slightly outside of situational and cultural norms.
Clothing noticeably spotted an/or lack of good hygiene draws attention: Patient's clothing and hygiene obviously falls short of situational and cultural expectations. If make-up is used, use is noticeably outside of situational and cultural norms.
Very wrinkled and soiled clothing, poor hygiene: Clothing and hygiene noticeably poor, even from a distance of 20 feet or more. Dress and hygiene significantly substandard to situational and cultural expectations. Hygiene inadequate enough to be a potential health risk for patient and/or others near him/her. If make-up is used, it is totally inappropriate to situational and cultural norms; may be applyed in a clumsy and excessive manner.

ATTENTION SPAN:
Attend to staff during assessment: No difficulty with attention span; is able to attend to activity with little or no inattention demonstrated for up to 20 minutes.
Occasionally needed to be cued to pay attention: Demonstrates inability to attend to assessment for 20 minutes (or for the length of time it takes to complete the questionnaire if it takes less than 20 minutes). Requires up to one cue every five minutes. When the patient is distracted, s/he is inattentive for up to 5 seconds, frequently requiring a cue to re-focus. Even with distractibility, patient is able to demonstrate enough short term memory to return to correct section of questionnaire.
Frequently needed to be cued to pay attention: Requires more than one cue every 5 minutes to attend, concentration is broken for periods greater than 5 seconds. Even with cueing is not always able to concentrate on issue at hand.
Could not focus attention and keep attention to task: Patient startles when spoken to or when s/he is distracted by peripheral movement and sounds and/or patient's attention is taken up by internal stimuli, self-stimulation, and other non-interactive activities.
Patient Self-Administered Assessment: Patient completed assessment away from the visual or hearing range of the therapist.

ATTITUDE DURING ASSESSMENT:
Enthusiastic and Interested: Patient attends to assessments process. Actively participates, responsive, eye contact, alert, enthusiastic, willingly participates, engrossed in activity.
Indifferent: Patient demonstrates basic cooperation through the assessment process. Facial gestures change multiple times during assessment process from smiles, to neutral, to frowns. Tonation of voice is not flat, but is not exuberant either.
Hostile but cooperative: Patient has not refused to participate in the assessment process but demonstrates impatience, rudeness, or anger toward the assessment process and/or the therapist.
Hostile, uncooperative: Patient has not refused to participate in the assessment process but demonstrates enough disruptive behavior to make the administration difficult to impossible.

NOTE: The choice of **refusing to cooperate with assessment process** is not included in this section because the patient has the right to refuse to take this assessment or to participate in any specific treatment unless ordered to by the courts. The recreational therapist may encourage the patient to take the assessment but may not force the patient to participate.

BODY POSTURE:
Erect: Patient demonstrates appropriate body posture based on situational and cultural standards.
Rounded Shoulders: Patient demonstrates a body posture and countenance which is slightly rounded, and somewhat 'closed' in nature.
Slouched, Head Down: Patient demonstrates a slumped posture which is obviously beyond situational and cultural standards.
Limp, unable/unwilling to participate: Patient maintains a body posture which effectively makes the assessment impossible to administer.

EYE CONTACT:
Good, appropriate: Patient demonstrates culturally and situationally appropriate eye contact.
Looked away occasionally: Patient broke eye contact with therapist in a situationally and culturally inappropriate manner one to two times during a five minute period.
Looked away frequently: Patient broke eye contact with therapist in a situationally and culturally inappropriate manner 3 or more times during a five minute period.
Little to no eye contact: Patient did not demonstrate the ability and/or desire to establish eye contact with therapist given situational and/or cultural standards.

FRUSTRATION/AGITATION LEVEL:
Participated without frustration/agitation: Patient participates without appearing frustrated/agitated; at times may appear discouraged or puzzled but completes assessment.
Occasionally frustrated/agitated: Patient will generally stick to the assessment process for up to 20 minutes before giving up. Patient does not demonstrate significant frustration/agitation behaviors which disrupt those around him/her.
Often frustrated/agitated: Patient becomes easily frustrated/agitated and as a result, is functionally unable to participate in the assessment process for up to 5 minutes at a time.
Frustrated/agitated; is unable to participate: Patient is functionally unable to participate in the assessment process for five minutes or more during the administration of the assessment.

APPARENT COMPREHENSION:

NOTE: This section is labeled **apparent comprehension** because the therapist could potentially change the outcome of the assessment by asking the patient if they understood this word or that word. The therapist should observe the patient closely during the assessment process and use his/her professional judgment as to how well the patient understands the statements. For patients who have Spanish as their primary language, the therapist should use the LMS questionnaire form in their native language. The LMS questionnaire is also available in Spanish.

Good Comprehension: The patient is able to answer the statements using a steady pace; s/he does not appear to struggle over the meaning of the statements.
Basic Comprehension: The patient appears to slow down when reading sentences which contain one or more words with three syllables. A steady pace is generally maintained with little to no noticeable problems with word/concept comprehension.
Poor Comprehension: The patient appears to be having difficulty reading and comprehending the material; may even ask for word or concept clarification two or more times during the assessment process.

RESPONSE TIME:
Answered most statements immediately: Patient appeared to give thought to his/her answers, but generally took less than 5 seconds to answer each statement.
Needed some thought to come up with answers: Patient appeared to give thought to his/her answers and generally took less than 10 seconds to answer between 1 and 5 of the statements.
Needed a lot of time to respond: Patient appeared to give thought to his/her answers, and generally took more than 10 seconds to answer between 6 and 10 of the statements.
Extreme difficulty to inability to respond: Patient appeared to give excessive thought to answers and took over 10 seconds on 11 or more of the statements *or* patient demonstrated an inability to respond to statements in a timely manner. (A timely manner means that the patient took 30 seconds or less to answer each statement.)

NOTE: The descriptors in this section place a heavy emphasis on response time. Response time means the time it took the client to determine the answers s/he wanted to give *and does not* mean the amount of time it took the patient to communicate his/her choice to the therapist. If the patient is having enough difficulty in responding that the therapist is actually timing the response, timing should stop as soon as the patient initiates the process to communicate his/her selection to the therapist.

SCORING INSTRUCTIONS: The therapist will need to determine four separate subscores. The subscore with the highest total score will indicate the primary motivating force in the patient's leisure activities. The lowest score(s) will indicate the least motivating force(s). A very low score may indicate that those kinds of motivators actually cause a person to avoid the leisure activity.

Subscore A: Intellectual: To determine the patient's score in this area use the following equation:

Add the numerical value of the answers given to the first 12 statements to achieve a total.

Scores from: (1+2+3+4+5+6+7+8+9+10+11+12)

Subscore B: Social: To determine the patient's score in this area use the following equation:

Add the numerical value of statements 13-24 to achieve a total.

Scores from: (13+14+15+16+17+18+19+20+21+22+23+24)

Subscore C: Competence-Mastery: To determine the patient's score in this area use the following equation:

Add the numerical value of statements 25-36 to achieve a total.

Scores from: (25+26+27+28+29+30+31+32+33+34+35+36)

Subscore D: Stimulus Avoidance: To determine the patient's score in this area use the following equation:

Add the numerical value of statements 37-48 to achieve a total.

Scores from: (37+38+39+40+41+42+43+44+45+46+47+48)

NOTE: A TOTAL SCORE FOR ALL 48 STATEMENTS HAS NOT BEEN SHOWN TO HAVE ANY CLEAR MEANING. DO NOT ADD THE SUBSCORES TOGETHER FOR A TOTAL.

COMPARISONS OF TWO CASE STUDIES

The LMS questionnaire was administered to two clients, both females, who have extensive testing in leisure attitudes, abilities, etc., as well as extensive testing in other fields.

'Tammy' is a 30 year old female with a primary diagnosis of Prader-Willi Syndrome and a secondary diagnosis of diabetes and mild mental retardation. She is currently living in a group home outside of Seattle, Washington. Tammy scored at ten years or above in all areas of the General Recreation Screening Tool (GRST) and preferred activities in the group/social activities area of the Leisurescope. On the WRAT Scoring/Grade Equivalent: READING = 8th grade, end of; SPELLING = 9th grade, beginning of; MATH = 9th grade, beginning of. On the Peabody she achieved a receptive score of 18 years. Her I.Q. was measured at 100 with noted difficulty in reality orientation and judgment.

Tammy took less than 8 minutes to complete all of the statements on the LMS. (The therapist read each item to her and she then indicated her response.) Her scores indicated a close parallel to both her scores on the Leisurescope and with her actual participation patterns. (The Recreation Participation Data Sheet, RPD, has been used to measure her leisure participation patterns for the past 33 months.) An element of her leisure which did not come out on the Leisurescope but which has been noted as a trend on the RPD was Tammy's desire to engage in competitive situations. Competitiveness as a motivator for her received a high score.

Tammy had difficulty understanding the following words: 'stimulation, original, competent, engaging, and unstructured'.

'Megan' is a 35 year old female with a primary diagnosis of Prader-Willi Syndrome. She is currently living in a group home outside of Seattle, Washington. In all areas of the General Recreation Screening Tool (GRST) she scored at the 10+ years age level. Using the Leisurescope she showed a strong preference for activities that emphasized mental stimulation and a strong preference to avoid social situations. Her scores on the Vineland Adaptive Behavior Scale were as follows: Socialization = 13.9 years, Coping Skills = 15.3 years, Interpersonal = 16.0 years, and Play and Leisure = 9.8 years. Her Quick Test IQ = 77.

It became very obvious to the therapist that Megan was not able to understand how feelings could correlate to numbers. Even before reading the statements the therapist modified the responses to include only the numbers '1' and '3' and '5'. This simplification seemed to help Megan understand the type of response desired. After some trials to determine if Megan did understand the numbering system, the therapist felt confident that the results obtained would not be grossly invalid with this modification.

Megan took just over 20 minutes to complete all of the LMS. (The therapist read the statements to her and Megan then responded with her answer.) Megan's scores indicated that intellectual stimulation was a great motivator for her and that social situations were a low motivator for her. These findings correlated well with both the Leisurescope findings and her leisure participation patterns as measured over the last 36 months (using the RPD).

Megan had difficulty understanding the following words: 'expand, stimulation, satisfy, original, interact, reveal, competent, achievement, mastery, unstructured, and responsibilities'.

WHAT IF'S:

1. What if the patient does not understand the definition of 'Leisure'?

An extensive discussion on the topic of leisure prior to the administration could influence the patient's score, possibly producing less valid results. The therapist may offer the patient the definition on the score sheet. If the patient asks for a more detailed definition, gently state that it is important for him/her to answer the statements using the definition on the score sheet.

2. What if the patient does not understand some of the words used in the statements?

It is very likely that patients with any measurable degree of cognitive disability, with limited education, or who have English as a second language will have difficulty with understanding some of the words used. The therapist should try to help the patient with necessary definitions. Use as little detail as possible and then redirect the patient back to the statements. For those with Spanish as a primary language, the recreational therapist should use the LMS questionnaire in that language. The instruction manual is available in only English for both versions.

The recreational therapist should strive to speak only the words written on the score sheet. Any additional conversation during the assessment process may affect the assessment results.

LEISURE MOTIVATION SCALE (LMS)

PURPOSE: The purpose of this scale is to help the patient and the therapist work together to find out, in part, why the patient chooses to engage in leisure activities.

DIRECTIONS: Listed below are 48 statements. Each one begins with the phrase: 'One of my reasons for engaging in leisure activities is...'. To the left of each statements is a line to indicate how true that statement is. A '1' means that the statement is **never** true, '2' means that it is **seldom** true, '3' means that it is **sometimes** true, '4' means that it is **often** true, and '5' means that it is **always** true. Write down the number that best fits your situation.

DEFINITION: 'Leisure Activities' are those things that you do that are not part of your work and are not part of your basic grooming needs.

1	2	3	4	5
NEVER TRUE	SELDOM TRUE	SOMEWHAT TRUE	OFTEN TRUE	ALWAYS TRUE

One of my reasons for engaging in leisure activities is ...

_____ 1. to expand my interests
_____ 2. to seek stimulation
_____ 3. to make things more meaningful for me
_____ 4. to learn about things around me
_____ 5. to satisfy my curiosity
_____ 6. to explore my knowledge

_____ 7. to learn about myself
_____ 8. to expand my knowledge
_____ 9. to discover new things
_____ 10. to be creative
_____ 11. to be original
_____ 12. to use my imagination

_____ 13. to be with others
_____ 14. to build friendships with others
_____ 15. to interact with others
_____ 16. to develop close friendships
_____ 17. to meet new and different people
_____ 18. to help others

_____ 19. so others will think well of me for doing it
_____ 20. to reveal my thoughts, feeling, or physical skills to others
_____ 21. to influence others
_____ 22. to be socially competent and skillful
_____ 23. to gain a feeling of belonging
_____ 24. to gain other's respect

_____ 25. to get a feeling of achievement
_____ 26. to see what my abilities are
_____ 27. to challenge my abilities
_____ 28. because I enjoy mastering things
_____ 29. to be good in doing them
_____ 30. to improve skill and ability in doing them

_____ 31. to compete against others
_____ 32. to be active
_____ 33. to develop physical skills and abilities
_____ 34. to keep in shape physically
_____ 35. to use my physical abilities
_____ 36. to develop my physical fitness

_____ 37. to be in a calm atmosphere
_____ 38. to avoid crowded areas
_____ 39. to slow down
_____ 40. because I sometimes like to be alone
_____ 41. to relax physically
_____ 42. to relax mentally

_____ 43. to avoid the hustle and bustle of daily activities
_____ 44. to rest
_____ 45. to relieve stress and tension
_____ 46. to do something simple and easy
_____ 47. to unstructure my time
_____ 48. to get away from the responsibilities of my everyday life

Patient's Name	Physician	Admit#	Room/Bed

LEISURE MOTIVATION SCALE
SUMMARY PAGE

CLIENT BEHAVIOR

A. APPEARANCE
- ☐ appropriate, good hygiene
- ☐ clothing and/or hygiene slightly dirty or smelly
- ☐ clothing noticeably spotted and/or lack of good hygiene draws attention
- ☐ very wrinkled and soiled clothing, poor hygiene

B. ATTENTION SPAN
- ☐ attended to staff during entire assessment
- ☐ occasionally needed to be cued to pay attention
- ☐ frequently needed to be cued to pay attention
- ☐ could not get attention and keep attention
- ☐ patient self-administered assessment

C. ATTITUDE DURING ASSESSMENT
- ☐ enthusiastic and interested
- ☐ indifferent
- ☐ hostile but cooperative
- ☐ hostile, uncooperative

D. BODY POSTURE
- ☐ erect
- ☐ rounded shoulders
- ☐ slouched, head down
- ☐ limp, unable/unwilling to participate

E. EYE CONTACT
- ☐ good, appropriate
- ☐ looked away occasionally
- ☐ looked away frequently
- ☐ little to no eye contact

F. FRUSTRATION/AGITATION LEVEL
- ☐ participated without frustration/agitation
- ☐ occasionally frustrated/agitated
- ☐ often frustrated/agitated
- ☐ frustrated/agitated; unable to participate

G. APPARENT COMPREHENSION
- ☐ good comprehension
- ☐ basic comprehension
- ☐ poor comprehension

H. RESPONSE TIME
- ☐ answered most questions immediately
- ☐ needed some thought to come up with answers
- ☐ needed a lot of time to respond
- ☐ did not respond

SCORING

Check One:
- ☐ Patient Self-Administered Assessment
- ☐ Therapist Administered Assessment

Date Assessment Given:

Medications That Could Impact Results:

Length of Time to Administer: **Length of Time to Score:**

NOTE: The higher the score in any subsection, the more motivating that type of activity should be for the patient.

Subsection A: Intellectual ____________ **Subsection C: Competence-Mastery** ____________

Subsection B: Social ____________ **Subsection D: Stimulus-Avoidance** ____________

SUMMARY/RECOMMENDATIONS:

Therapist: **Date:**

Patient's Name	Physician	Admit #	Room/Bed

LEISURE DIAGNOSTIC BATTERY

Name: Leisure Diagnostic Battery

Also Known As: LDB

Authors: Peter Witt and Gary Ellis

Time Needed to Administer: The LDB has numerous forms and scales. Idyll Arbor, Inc. staff usually allow between 20 minutes and 40 minutes to administer the LDB.

Time Needed to Score: The LDB is a difficult assessment to score (due to the format). Idyll Arbor, Inc. staff usually allow at least 20 minutes to score the LDB. The computerized version can greatly reduce the time it takes to score.

Purpose of the Assessment: The purpose of the LDB is:
1) To enable the therapist to assess their client's leisure functioning,
2) To enable the therapist to determine the areas in which improvement of current leisure functioning is needed,
3) To enable the therapist to determine the impact of offered services on the client's leisure functioning, and
4) To facilitate research on the structure of leisure to enable a better understanding of the value, purpose, and outcomes of leisure experiences.

What Does the Assessment Measure?: The various sections of the LDB measure the following areas: 1) perceived leisure competence, 2) perceived leisure control, 3) leisure needs, 4) depth of involvement in leisure, and 5) playfulness scale.

NOTE: The LDB used to have a section called 'The Knowledge of Leisure Opportunities Test'. This section of the LDB did not have the same degree of reliability and validity as the other instruments and thus has been removed from the overall battery.

Supplies Needed: The LDB Manual and the appropriate score sheets.

Reliability/Validity: Extensive documentation and information on validity and reliability available.

Degree of Skill Required to Administer and Score: The LDB requires the skills of Certified Therapeutic Recreation Specialist to administer, score, and interpret the results.

Comments: The LDB is one of the better known assessments in the field of recreational therapy. Its greatest drawback is the length of time required to score the paper version.

Suggested Levels: Ranchos Los Amigos Level: 7 or above (Idyll Arbor, Inc. staff have achieved some success in using it with clients as low Level 6.) Developmental Level: 9 years and above. Reality Orientation: Mild to No Impairment.

Distributor: Venture Publishing, 1999 Cato Ave., State College, PA 16801 (814) 234-4561.

Leisure Diagnostic Battery (LDB)

I. Introduction

The Leisure Diagnostic Battery (LDB) is a copyrighted collection of instruments designed to enable the assessment of the leisure functioning for a wide range of disabled and non-disabled individuals. The LDB is available in paper and pencil format or in computer format for IBM compatible computers. The computer version was designed as a user-friendly, menu driven means of administering and scoring the various LDB scales.

Both long and short forms of most of a family of instruments forming the battery have been developed. In addition, long and short form versions designed specifically for adolescents and adults have also been developed. The LDB has been used for both assessment and research purposes in both institutional and community settings.

The original version of the LDB is composed of seven components grouped into two sections.

Section One

Scale A: Perceived Leisure Competence Scale
Scale B: Perceived Leisure Control Scale
Scale C: Leisure Needs Scale
Scale D: Depth of Involvement in Leisure Scale
Scale E: Playfulness Scale
Note: Combining the scores from Scales A to E enables the calculation of a 'Perceived Freedom in Leisure' score.

Section Two

Scale F: Barriers to Leisure Involvement Scale
Scale G: Leisure Preferences Inventory
Note: The Knowledge of Leisure Opportunities Test is no longer part of the LDB. The test did not have the same degree of reliability and validity as the other instruments and thus has been removed from the overall battery.

Several variations of this original set of scales have been developed. At present the following groups of instruments are available.

Long Forms

Version A: This version was originally designed for 9 to 14 year old orthopedically impaired individuals, and/or higher functioning level educable mentally retarded individuals. However, the instruments have also been successfully used with individuals ages 9 through 18, either disabled or non-disabled. Version A consists of all LDB components.

Version C: An adult version of the long form has been created by adapting the wording of Version A items to be more suitable for adults. Version C consists of all LDB components except the Knowledge of Leisure Opportunities Test (Scale H).

Note: As part of the original LDB Project, Version B of the LDB Long Form was developed for use with individuals who are lower functioning and educable mentally retarded. However, the authors were not satisfied with the psychometric properties of this version and thus, it is not currently available for distribution.

Short Forms

Version A: This version consists of 25 items taken from the first five scales (A-E) of the LDB Long Form, Version A. Together these scales are thought to measure 'perceived freedom in leisure'. Short Form A was originally designed for use with 9 to 14 year old nondisabled or orthopedically impaired individuals and/or higher functioning level educable mentally retarded individuals. This instrument, however, has also been successfully used with individuals age 9 to 18, either disabled or non-disabled.

Version B: An adult version of the short form has been created by adapting the wording of Short Form Version A items to be more suitable for adults.

The following sections of this document describe the conceptual basis of the LDB, the various components that make up the LDB, the development of the LDB, available reliability and validity data, and procedures for scoring and interpreting LDB results.

II. Conceptual Basis of the LDB

The most unique feature of the LDB is its overall conceptualization. Recognizing the inherent shortcomings and limitations of the time and activity participation approaches to the assessment of leisure functioning, the development of the LDB was based on a more holistic view of leisure, with emphasis on leisure as a state of mind as the basis for understanding leisure functioning.

Under the time and activity approaches, leisure has been viewed objectively as a particular block of time or one of a particular set of activities. Under the subjective or state of mind view, almost any human endeavor has the potential to be experienced as leisure. Leisure is thus seen as an experience that can occur at any time, during any activity. Under the objective view, defining leisure is a matter of agreeing on time periods or activities that will be categorized as leisure or not leisure. Under the subjective view, it is necessary to agree on the feelings or perceptions that an individual will experience in order for a given endeavor to be referred to as leisure.

While many practitioners and some theorists have argued that making distinctions between objective and subjective definitions of leisure is the 'play' of academics, the distinctions have important implications for both theory and practice. For example, viewing leisure as time or activity suggests different approaches to leadership and programming than the state of mind view. Under the former paradigm, we worry about scheduling, whether people will show up, and we use measures of attendance as a basis for judging success of our programming efforts. Under the state of mind view, we would be more concerned with creating environments and utilizing leadership strategies that will maximize feelings and perceptions that have been denoted as typifying leisure.

In the area of assessment, the activity and time approaches to defining leisure have focused on the assessment of psychomotor or social skills, as well as activity participation and interests. Under these approaches, the presumption has been that the main problems that individuals face in maximizing leisure are such things as the lack of skills to successfully participate or the lack of available opportunities for participation.

However, by viewing leisure from a state of mind perspective, an individual could have the requisite skills to participate but still view him/herself as unable to fully enjoy and derive optimal benefits from participation. While skills are important to participating in an activity, self-definitions of success, competence, and ability, as opposed to objectively rated skills based on externally judged standards, seem to be an unexplored avenue for developing assessment approaches and associated remediation strategies.

Thus, the LDB was developed utilizing a state of mind approach to understanding leisure functioning. The term 'leisure functioning' describes how an individual feels about his/her leisure experiences and what kinds of outcomes result from these experiences. One assumption which underlies the LDB is that involvements become leisure experiences when certain conditions are met. These conditions involve an individual perceiving him/herself as competent, being able to control the initiation and outcomes of experiences, and participating in activities more out of intrinsic desire than extrinsic reward expectations. Individuals who meet these conditions are thought to be in a better position to derive maximum benefits from their recreation activity involvements.

Collectively, perceived leisure competence and perceived leisure control describe characteristics of an individual who perceives freedom in leisure. *The LDB, therefore, involves the assessment of a client's perceived freedom in leisure and factors which are potential barriers to this freedom.* In the absence of such barriers, it can be expected that the individual will have a higher probability of experiencing a sense of freedom in leisure and therefore will derive maximum benefits from activity participation.

Due to the impact of leisure on the life of an individual, assessment of leisure functioning becomes an important need. Through assessment, it becomes possible to identify deficiencies in leisure functioning and to take remedial action in identified deficit areas. In this manner, individuals may obtain optimal benefits from their leisure experiences. The results of the LDB can provide the user with a necessary resource for planning strategies to optimize leisure functioning. In this process, input from the client is critical. All too often input from the individual is neglected or made secondary to 'professional judgments' of functioning level. Thus, the LDB provides a source of information which will help to fulfill the mandate for assessment/diagnosis/prescription information required in many educational settings due to the mandate of P.L. 94-142. That law requires that an assessment of leisure functioning be a part of an overall Individualized Education Plan (IEP). In addition, the LDB should be useful in other settings such as community agencies and institutions.

The purposes of the LDB are thus fourfold.

1) To enable users to assess their clients' leisure functioning.
2) To enable users to determine areas in which improvement of current leisure functioning is needed.
3) To enable users to determine the impact of offered services on leisure functioning.
4) To facilitate research on the structure of leisure to enable a better understanding of the value, purpose, and outcomes of leisure experiences.

The two major sections of the LDB each relate to a different part of the assessment process. Section 1 contains the scales which assess the client's attainment of the conditions which are considered essential to successful leisure functioning. Section 2 scales are intended to be administered if results from Section 1 indicate deficit leisure functioning scores for a given individual. Information from Section 2 scales can be used to generate additional information to help initiate a remediation process.

Conceptualization

For a detailed discussion of the conceptualization of the LDB, the reader is referred to the LDB Manual. This material is essential for individuals planning to administer and interpret the results of the LDB.

Components of the Leisure Diagnostic Battery

The LDB is designed to enable the user to identify an individual's perception of freedom in leisure, and for those individuals identified as exhibiting deficiencies (i.e. feelings of helplessness), to further identify the causative factors limiting perceived freedom. Each section of the LDB serves a distinct function in this process.

Scales included in Section 1 are designed to provide the user with an indication of the individual's perception of freedom in leisure. These scales include the Perceived Leisure Competence Scale, the Perceived Leisure Control Scale, the Leisure Needs Scale, the Depth of Involvement in Leisure Scale, and the Playfulness Scale. The sum of scores across these scales provides an indication of an individual's degree of perceived freedom in leisure.

Perceived Leisure Competence Scale: The Perceived Leisure Competence Scale is designed to measure the extent to which an individual believes s/he is competent in leisure. Four domains of competence are included: cognitive competence, physical competence, social competence, and general competence (Harter, 1979). Perceived competence is a part of perceived freedom because it describes an individual's beliefs about his/her ability to control outcomes and to avoid failure. Perceived competence, therefore, is a probabilistic perception the individual holds about his/her ability to determine what happens in the course of an activity. The individual who perceives that success or a positive outcome is likely be cause of his/her own personal skills and abilities will feel freer to be involved in leisure pursuits.

Perceived Leisure Control Scale: The Perceived Leisure Control Scale measures an aspect of freedom closely related to that assessed by the Perceived Leisure Competence Scale. Like the Perceived Leisure Competence Scale, results of the Perceived Leisure Control Scale suggest the degree to which an individual feels that s/he can determine what happens in the course of his/her leisure activities. Thus, the Perceived Leisure Control Scale provides an indication of the individual's perceived freedom to control the process and outcome of leisure endeavors. The difference in the two scales is that in the Perceived Leisure Competence Scale, control of outcomes is determined by a sense of being 'good at' specific tasks and behaviors. In the case of the Perceived Leisure Control Scale, initiation and outcomes are determined by a sense of 'I control'. In this latter case, the control may be a result of being competent in the task or behavior or it may be the result of being persuasive, crafty, or of functioning in an environment in which the individual is frequently encouraged or allowed to make choices.

Leisure Needs Scale: The Leisure Needs Scale and the Depth of Involvement in Leisure Scale each measure a different aspect of freedom. Activities in which people participate out of intrinsic desire tend to result in positive feelings of freedom. These two scales are designed to provide insights into that process. The Leisure Needs Scale generates information about the extent to which involvement in recreation activities satisfies intrinsic needs and wants. The specific needs included in the scale were derived from classical, recent, and modern theories of play (M. J. Ellis, 1970; Havinghurst, 1957; Donald & Havinghurst, 1959; Tinsley, Barrett, & Kass, 1977; London, Crandall, & Fitzgibbons, 1977). Included are questions concerning the use of recreation activities to satisfy such needs as catharsis, relaxation, compensation, gregariousness, novelty, arousal, and a need for creative expression. The individual who is able to use recreation to satisfy such intrinsic needs feels a sense of freedom in leisure and is thought to derive optimal benefits from leisure.

Depth of Involvement in Leisure Scale: While the Leisure Needs Scale involves assessment of activity outcomes relative to a broad array of needs, the Depth of Involvement in Leisure Scale is focused more on one specific need and on the process of activities. The scale is based on Csikszentmihalyi's (1975) description of 'flow' and 'microflow' and on M. J. Ellis' (1970) description of play as a mechanism to meet a human need for optimal arousal. Items for this scale ask subjects to indicate the extent to which a merging of action and awareness, a centering of attention, an altered perception of time, and feelings of power and control occur when they are involved in recreation activities. Generated information provides an indication of what feelings an individual has during his/her preferred activities. The individual who feels a degree of excitement, enthusiasm, control, and depth of involvement in his/her activities can be thought of as feeling free during involvement in the activities. In the process, intrinsic needs are satisfied and the individual's overall leisure functioning is optimized.

Playfulness Scale: The final component of perceived freedom in leisure is measured by the Playfulness Scale. Playfulness is seen as a behavioral component of perceived freedom. By definition, the playful individual is free to do the unexpected, i.e. behavior is not limited to the normative or situational expectations of others. A perception of competence, control, and a desire for novelty and dissonance may provide a framework within which playful behavior may occur.

Lieberman's (1977) analysis of playfulness in high school and kindergarten students served as the basis for development of the Playfulness Scale. Playfulness, Lieberman found, is composed of cognitive spontaneity, physical spontaneity, social spontaneity, manifest joy, and a sense of humor. Although manifest joy and a sense of humor may reflect freedom via social competence, the spontaneity elements are perhaps the most intimately associated with freedom. In order to be spontaneous, one must feel a degree of freedom. Following the behaviorist line of thinking, if spontaneous behavior is punished or is not rewarded, the behavior will cease. An individual whose spontaneous behaviors consistently lead to negative consequences such as failure, peer disapproval, or adult rebuttal will perceive a more limited realm of acceptable behaviors; freedom will thus be limited.

Perceived Freedom in Leisure - Total Score: Collectively, the sum of scores on the Perceived Leisure Competence Scale, the Perceived Leisure Control Scale, the Leisure Needs Scale, the Depth of Involvement in Leisure Scale, and the Playfulness Scale reflect the degree to which an individual perceives freedom in leisure. The scales can be summed to yield a total measure of Perceived Freedom in Leisure or used separately to indicate deficit areas more precisely. An individual may, for example, have feelings of helplessness stemming from a low perception of competence. An individual may also feel limited freedom because s/he is given no choices or control in his/her life. Or, perhaps one's playful, spontaneous behaviors have been squelched by overbearing parents, peers, or significant others.

In addition to deficits in areas measured by the Section 1 or perceived freedom in leisure scales, numerous other factors are thought to limit an individual's perceived freedom in leisure. These factors may include lack of knowledge of opportunities for participation, poor social skills, inadequate motor skills, negative attitudes toward leisure, inaccessible facilities, poor health, financial constraints, lack of transportation, and lack of encouragement. While the LDB does not address all of these areas, Section 2 components yield information about several of the factors which may inhibit an individual's leisure functioning. Section 2 components include the Barriers to Leisure Involvement Scale, and Leisure Preferences Inventory.

Barriers to Leisure Involvement Scale: Perceived competence, control, intrinsic motivation, and playfulness provide an individual with feelings of 'freedom to' pursue recreation and leisure experiences. In addition to this sense of 'freedom to', previous authors have suggested that freedom has a second dimension, which can be thought of as 'freedom from' (Fromm, 1941; Bregha, 1985). Whereas 'freedom to' is determined by factors which are internal to the individual, the extent to which an individual has feelings of 'freedom from' depends upon external, environmental contingencies. These external factors may be thought of as 'barriers to leisure opportunities'. Barriers are of central importance to a comprehensive leisure assessment because they can inhibit perceived freedom and preclude participation in recreation activities.

The Barriers to Leisure Involvement Scale, therefore, can be used to generate information concerning the extent to which an individual perceives that barriers to participation exist in his/her environment. The inventory asks questions about the following types of barriers: communication and social skills, decision-making and lack of desire, time and monetary constraints, and accessibility. The total score across all of these areas is suggestive of the presence of a general perception of personal or environmental barriers to participation in preferred recreation activities. In order to make this information useful, the user must identify the source of this perception. Some barriers may be thought of as 'real' and may be directly associated with a causative factor in the environment. Other barriers are only perceived by the individual even though an objective analysis of the environment does not reveal the existence of the barrier.

Leisure Preferences Inventory: The final component of Section 2 is the Leisure Preferences Inventory. The existence of a preference for an activity suggests the presence of some degree of competence and control in that activity. Because the overall goal of remediation is to maximize perceived freedom, it is logical to begin remediation with preferred activities in which perceived freedom exists to some degree. The Leisure Preferences Inventory is designed to identify preferences among five activity domains as well as among three styles of participation. Activity domains assessed include sports, arts and crafts, music and drama, nature and outdoor recreation, and mental and linguistic activities. Style domains assessed include preferences for active vs. passive, individual vs. group, and risk vs. non-risk involvements.

Scales of Measurement and Number of Items Per Component

To complete each component of the LDB, subjects read (or can be read) a series of statements and indicate their responses using one of several different response formats. The number of items and response formats for each version of the LDB are summarized in Figure 1.

The five components comprising Section 1 have from 17 to 20 items each. A total of 95 items comprise Section 1. For these scales, Long Form Version A uses a three point response format of 'doesn't sound like me', 'sounds a little like me', 'sounds a lot like me'. Items are worded so that more positive responses, i.e. 'sounds a lot like me', are indicative of more perceived leisure

Figure 1. Response Formats for the Long and Short Versions of the Leisure Diagnostic Battery

		Long Form		Short Form	
	# of Items	Version A	Version C	Version A	Version B
Section 1					
Leisure Competence	20	M	P		
Leisure Control	17	M	P		
Leisure Needs	20	M	P		
Depth of Involvement	18	M	P		
Playfulness	20	M	P		
Section 2					
Barriers to Leisure	24	M	P		
Preferences	60	O	O		
Short Forms				M	P

Format M - Doesn't sound like me, Sounds a little like me, Sounds like me (3 point scale)
Format O - Forced choice
Format P - Strongly disagree to Strongly agree (5 point scale)

competence, perceived leisure control, etc. Long Form Version C uses a five point response format from 'strongly agree' to 'strongly disagree'. Again, items are worded so that more positive responses, i.e. 'strongly agree', are indicative of more perceived leisure control, etc.

For Section 2 components, two different response formats are utilized. The 24 item Barriers Scale uses the same response format as the Section 1 components for both Versions A and C respectively. However, 'sounds a lot like me' responses are indicative of a perception of greater barriers. The Leisure Preferences Inventory has 60 items and uses a forced choice format in which subjects must indicate their preference for one of two types of activities or one of two styles of activity participation.

The two short form versions each have 25 items. Version A uses the same response format as Section 1 components of the Long Form Version A, while Short Form Version B uses the same response format as Section 1 components of Long Form Version C. It should be noted that several LDB users have successfully employed the 5 point 'strongly agree' to 'strongly disagree' response format for the Section 1 scales of Long Form Version A and Short Form Version A. The decision on which response format to employ depends on the comprehension level of the subjects to whom the LDB is to be administered.

LIFE SATISFACTION SCALE

Name: Life Satisfaction Scale

Also Known As: LSS

Authors: Variations of a Life Satisfaction Scale have been around for many years in many different forms. Some of the questions are similar to the Philadelphia Geriatric Center Morale Scale, the Life Satisfaction Index, and possibly the Oberleder Attitude Scale. Nancy Lohmann did research measuring the various questions against each other, and this Life Satisfaction Scale is a result of that research.

Time Needed to Administer: The LSS (either read by the client or to the client) should take no more than 20 minutes to administer.

Time Needed to Score: The LSS can be scored and summarized in approximately 10 minutes.

Purpose of the Assessment: The purpose of the LSS is to measure the client's perceived satisfaction with his/her life.

What Does the Assessment Measure?: The LSS measures 5 dimensions of satisfaction: 1) pleasure versus apathy, 2) determination, 3) difference between desired and achieved goals, 4) mood at time of assessment, and 5) self-concept. The scoring appears to be based on cultural stereotypes and expectations.

Supplies Needed: Life Satisfaction Score Sheet and LSS Answer Sheet.

Reliability/Validity: Reliability and validity studies have been conducted on this assessment.

Degree of Skill Required to Administer and Score: As with all assessment used in treatment, it is best to have professionally trained staff administer and score this assessment.

Comments: The LSS is an assessment to use to help measure the client's degree of satisfaction. This type of assessment (and the accompanying care plan to improve low satisfaction) demonstrates that a facility is working to assure client rights.

Suggested Levels: Rancho Los Amigos Level: 7 or above. Developmental Level: Due to the types of questions asked, this assessment is best used with client's who are chronologically 35 or over and cognitively 10 or above. Reality Orientation: Moderate to No Impairment.

Distributor: Dr. Nancy Lohmann, Office of the Provost, West Virginia University, 206 Stewart Hall, PO Box 6203, Morgantown, WV 26506-6203. The assessment may be used free of charge as long as the copyright notice appears on all materials.

LIFE SATISFACTION SCALE
(LSS)

NAME: ______________________________ DATE: ________________

INSTRUCTIONS: Read each statement. If you agree with the statement, place an 'X' in the 'AGREE' column. If you disagree with the statement, place an 'X' in the 'DISAGREE' column.

QUESTIONS	AGREE	DISAGREE
1. I feel just miserable most of the time.	☐	☐
2. I never dreamed that I could be as lonely as I am now.	☐	☐
3. I never felt better in my life.	☐	☐
4. I have no one to talk to about personal things.	☐	☐
5. I have so few friends that I'm lonely much of the time.	☐	☐
6. I can no longer do any kind of useful work.	☐	☐
7. This is the most useful period of my life.	☐	☐
8. I have more free time than I know how to use.	☐	☐
9. I do better work than ever before.	☐	☐
10. I haven't a cent in the world.	☐	☐
11. I have no use for religion.	☐	☐
12. My life is meaningless now.	☐	☐
13. I am just as happy as when I was younger.	☐	☐
14. Sometimes I feel there is no point in living.	☐	☐
15. I can't help feeling now that my life isn't very useful.	☐	☐
16. My life is full of worry.	☐	☐
17. This is the dreariest time of my life.	☐	☐
18. My life is still busy and useful.	☐	☐
19. I like being the age I am.	☐	☐
20. I seem to have less and less reason to live.	☐	☐
21. Most of the things I do are boring or monotonous.	☐	☐
22. I often feel lonely.	☐	☐
23. Compared to other people, I get down in the dumps too often.	☐	☐
24. Things keep getting worse as I get older.	☐	☐
25. These are the best years of my life.	☐	☐
26. I have a lot to be sad about.	☐	☐
27. I sometimes worry so much that I can't sleep.	☐	☐
28. I am as happy now as I ever was.	☐	☐
29. I feel old and somewhat tired.	☐	☐
30. The older I get, the worse everything is.	☐	☐
31. My life could be happier than it is now.	☐	☐
32. Life is hard for me most of the time.	☐	☐

LIFE SATISFACTION SCALE
(LSS)
Lohmann 1976

The Life Satisfaction Scale is an assessment that measures perceived satisfaction with life. It is an easy and quick assessment to give.

WHEN TO ADMINISTER THE LSS:

1. When the resident has a relatively intact thought process, memory, and is oriented to reality.
2. When the recreational therapist (or other health care provider) wants to establish a baseline of satisfaction with life or wants compare a change in satisfaction over a period of time.

HOW TO ADMINISTER THE LSS:

1. If the resident is able to read and write independently the recreational therapist may have the resident fill out the answers himself/herself.
2. If the resident has some difficulty reading or writing independently the recreational therapist may orally give the assessment to the resident.

SUPPLIES NEEDED TO ADMINISTER THE LSS:

1. LSS Score Sheet
2. Pencil or Pen

SCORING:

Compare the resident's answers to the answers given below. Each time the resident's answers match the ones listed below, s/he receives one point. A total of 32 points are possible. The higher the score, the greater the resident's perceived satisfaction with life. This assessment is best used to compare a resident's perceived satisfaction with life from one year to another.

ANSWERS THAT INDICATE SATISFACTION:

1. D	8. D	15. D	22. D	29. D
2. D	9. A	16. D	23. D	30. D
3. A	10. D	17. D	24. D	31. D
4. D	11. D	18. A	25. A	32. D
5. D	12. D	19. A	26. D	
6. D	13. A	20. D	27. D	
7. A	14. D	21. D	28. A	

WHAT AM I DOING?

Name: What Am I Doing?

Also Known As: WAID

Author: John Neulinger

Time Needed to Administer: The WAID is used as a log to increase the client's awareness of how and why s/he spends his/her time the way that s/he does. The client will need over 20 minutes a day for a period of five to seven days.

Time Needed to Score: Schedule an hour or more. The WAID is intended to be scored by the client. In health care situations, the therapist will want to review the client's results with him/her. As the WAID is a tool to promote self-awareness, the therapist's primary responsibility is to guide the process, not to lead it.

Recommended Disability Group: Adult clients with little to no cognitive impairment.

Purpose of the Assessment: To help the client discover more about his/her leisure/perceived freedom.

What Does the Assessment Measure?: The WAID measures the subjective state of choice, reason, and feeling.

Supplies Needed: The WAID Manual, the WAID score sheets. Also recommended is the book **The Road to Eden, After All: A Human Metamorphosis** (1990) by John Neulinger.

Reliability/Validity: Validity and reliability reported; normative scores available.

Degree of Skill Required to Administer and Score: High. For a 'prescriptive' use of this form, and the integration of the normative data, the recreational therapist should have an extensive understanding of perceived freedom and how disability impacts perceived freedom.

Comments: The WAID is a good tool to use with clients who have the cognitive capability to fill out the form and who have the desire to learn more about themselves. John Neulinger's book, **Eden, After All,** is recommended reading for all recreational therapists. While the book is short (only 154 pages) it provides the reader with a history of the development of leisure philosophy as well as some concrete examples of how leisure goes beyond 'play'. Most therapists will find justifications for their treatment in the book.

Suggested Levels: Ranchos Los Amigos Level: 8 (Level 7 may be tried). Developmental: Age 12 cognitively. Reality Orientation: Mild to No Impairment.

Distributor: This testing tool is no longer available and has not been released into the public domain.

WHAT AM I DOING?
THE WAID

NOTE: The documentation included in this book contains approximately one third of the WAID Assessment Manual. The therapist will need to obtain the complete manual to be able to adequately interpret a client's scores.

INTRODUCTION

Have you ever tried the impossible? Were you ever told that what you were up to, cannot possibly succeed? I certainly have, and what I am about to undertake is one of those instances. I am introducing a technique that is designed to enable you to measure the quality of your life, your unique sense of well-being or lack thereof. I shall introduce the technique, but for the success in measuring the quality of your life, your cooperation is the essential ingredient. We shall have to look closely at what you do and how you spend your time. More importantly, we shall concern ourselves with how and what you feel. We shall examine your everyday experiences and translate these into an index of well-being.

Many people, including some social scientists, still feel that this cannot be done. They are under the impression that private experiences are to subjective, so unique, that scientists cannot touch them. They insist that it is impossible to measure or quantify them or that to do so, is somehow objectionable.

MEASURING VERSUS KNOWING

Much of this negative attitude stems from confusing 'measuring' with 'knowing'. When I measure a person's fever (that is, temperature), I do not become aware of his/her experience of the fever; I do not know how or what the person feels. I merely get an indication (an index) of his/her state of being. The measured temperature tells me something quite objective about the person's subjective well-being, without however denying this person's uniqueness or private experience.

It is amazing how many people confuse the act of measuring characteristics of an individual with 'knowing' the individual. If I measure a person's shoe, hat and glove size, would I assume that I now really know that person? Hardly. But when it comes to measuring subjective states or personality dimensions, people seem to adopt a different mindset. They assume that by having measured one or two or even a dozen such characteristics, they have grasped the essence of the person. Nonsense!

This kind of thinking distorts the intent of measurement and quantification. Yes, in quantification we may indeed count 'beings'. We distinguish one person from another; we count: one person, two persons, ten people, a hundred, a thousand, a million. We do this in terms of certain characteristics that distinguish one person from the next. But in doing so we are not claiming to have comprehended each person's unique being. We merely distinguish one from the other on the basis of certain characteristics they may share.

We are taking the time to discuss this confusion so you understand what we are trying to do and also, what we are not trying to do. A reluctance to engage in subjective self-examination often has its root in this kind of misunderstanding. We want you to recognize that we are not trying to do the impossible. We shall merely help you learn about the factors that influence your temperature one way or another.

MEASURING SUBJECTIVE STATES

Most people are unaware of the fact that psychologists had accomplished the task of measuring subjective states way back during the latter half of the nineteenth century. Such subjective phenomena as brightness, loudness, and other sensed qualities were then measured with considerable accuracy. These techniques were later translated into methods of measuring values, attitudes, and other psychological states. Present-day computer-facilitated methodologies have attained most respectable standards for measuring almost any subjective state, given appropriate research conditions.

Scientists, however, tend to be most reluctant to 'popularize' these techniques, that is, to have people use them who may not have an understanding of the limitations of these methods. Findings obtained from group studies are not necessarily applicable to any one individual within the group. Such findings, furthermore, are limited to the population used in the particular study. Use of findings often required expert interpretation for the meaning of the measures used. And there are more such reasons for being hesitant about letting a lay-person use professional tools.

However, there are times when these considerations are carried too far, particularly when they do not seriously apply. I get very annoyed when a nurse refuses to let me see my temperature, as if that knowledge would hurt me or as if I could not handle that information properly.

With appropriate care, meaningful information about subjective states can be gathered by individuals for themselves. In such instances, we are not generalizing to others; we are not facing the issue of using the information inappropriately to affect someone else's life. The information is gathered not only with the person's consent, but in line with the person's wish to do so. Moreover, the person has the information anyhow; we are merely helping to put it into focus. We are providing glasses so people can see what previously had escaped their attention or had only been perceived dimly.

THE TASK AT HAND

It is our intention to help you obtain a clearer and more informative picture of your life than you now have. Let me assure you that you will find some of this work quite pleasant, satisfying and perhaps even fascinating. But the task will not be a quick and easy one. It involves a great deal more than filling out a short questionnaire. I like to compare the process of becoming acquainted with this technique to learning a new language. Fortunately, this language has a very brief vocabulary. However, the specific terms used have very distinct meanings that you need to understand well. These terms are the key to your perceiving yourself and the quality of your life in a way that you can translate into an index of well-being.

Our technique provides you with a perspective on life that is bound to make you reflect on what you are doing. You many want to leave it at that. Or, having acquired the skill of quantifying your well-being, you may wish to chart fluctuations in this state. You might merely want to observe ups and downs or you may wish to do something about them. That, of course, will be up to you. But by then, we shall have alerted you to factors that are critical in bringing about these fluctuations.

Let us recapitulate. In line with your desire to get a clearer picture of the quality of your life, we are introducing a technique that will help you to do so. This process requires looking at yourself in a particular way. You need to learn the meaning of certain concepts and, in this context, become familiar with the instrument 'WHAT AM I DOING?' or, as we shall refer to it, the WAID. This instrument gives you not only a measure of the quality of your life, but also of certain dimensions that are critical to that quality. It lets you express what you probably know already, but may not be able to put into words or even less so, on a scale.

OTHER-COMPARISONS VERSUS SELF-COMPARISONS

Before introducing the WAID, let us consider an important distinction between two kinds of comparisons. One, we compare our experience to those of others. Two, we compare our own experiences.

'Eat your spinach! Clean up your plate! Think of all the starving children in China' (or more recently, 'in Bangladesh')! You may still hear your mother's voice. Very stern, very factual, slightly guilt arousing, but overall quite ineffective. We rarely pay much attention to that sort of comparison. It does not hit home; it is not easy to relate to.

'I tell you, this year's vacation was much better than last year's.' 'I have eaten better food than this.' 'What a day this was!' These are also comparisons, but they are quite different. They refer to our own experiences and we judge one experience against another. Our own experiences become the baseline and therefore these comparisons are meaningful; we can relate to them. We know what we are talking about.

These, then, are two quite distinct ways of making comparisons. Yet, they are closely intertwined. What we expect of life, what we judge as adequate and satisfying, depends largely on our reference groups, those we compare ourselves to. 'Other-comparisons' are intimately linked to the norms we have incorporated into our life-styles. Within this context, we see things as getting better or worse most immediately in terms of what we experienced previously in our lives. 'Self-comparisons' relate most directly to our everyday feeling of well-being.

Our efforts will be directed primarily at these 'self-comparisons' and this is the great advantage of our technique. 'Other-comparisons' (comparing oneself to others) necessitate sophisticated research efforts involving large samples. 'Self-comparisons', however, can be carried out quite validly by an individual on his/her own and without requiring complicated statistical analyses. This is the road you will take in examining the quality of your life.

THE WAID: AN OVERVIEW

The WAID instrument (What Am I Doing? Exploring the Quality of Your Life) consists of three parts: An INTRODUCTION, a brief reminder of its propose and goal; INSTRUCTIONS on how to complete the instrument; and the 24 hours WAID LOG, the form on which you will record a day's experiences.

TIME-BUDGETS

The WAID is a time budget instrument. A time-budget is similar to a money-budget. Everyone knows what a money-budget is. It accounts for a given amount of money. It tells how much was spent (or is planned to be spent) on what.

A time-budget accounts for a given amount of time. It tells how much time was spent (or is planned to be spent) in what activity.

Time-budgets have one great advantage over money-budgets; they start at the same baseline. Let me explain. People vary greatly in the amount of money available to them; there are the rich and the super-rich, the poor and the even poorer and those in the middle; somewhere along there are you and me. Each person's money assets also vary over time. This same person may be poor one day and rich the next, or it may go the other way around. People's money-budgets, accordingly, may start off at very different baselines from each other, and even from themselves, at different times. One person's budget, say for a month, may be $1,000, another's $2,000, and a third one's $5,000. Or the same person's budget may fluctuate; one month it may be $2,500 and the next it could be $3,000.

Time-budgets, on the other hand, have the same baseline for everyone. If, for example, we pick one day as our unit of analysis (and that is the most frequently picked unit), then we all start with 24 hours or 1440 minutes. This amount is the same for all people, whoever they are and throughout their whole life. It is one way in which everyone is equal. We all have the same amount of time per day. What we do with that time and how we experience it, however, varies tremendously. And that is precisely what we plan to explore.

OBJECTIVE DIMENSIONS

A time-budget instrument, then, makes you record how you spend your time, in chronological order, one activity after another. You also record WHERE the activity takes place and WITH WHOM or WITH HOW MANY people you engage in the activity. WHEN the activity takes place is given by the order of the events.

You can easily see why this additional information is important. For example, reading a newspaper while commuting on the train is different from reading a newspaper while on the job (WHERE). Sleeping with one's spouse is different from sleeping with one's neighbor's spouse (WITH WHOM). Or having a cocktail at eight a.m. is different from having one at eight p.m. (WHEN).

The dimensions dealt with so far are generally considered to be objective, that is, the information gathered could be obtained by 'objective' observers, who would more or less agree on what they record. A record of the person's behavior and the context within which it takes place, could be obtained without inquiry into the person's state of mind. Such information can be readily verified and does not depend on the individual's subjective report of thoughts, feelings and desires, or intended actions. However, such information consequently tells us very little, if anything, about these mental states. If we want to find out what people experience, that is, what they think, feel, what their motivations are, and so on, we have to go one step further. We have to enter a different level of investigation.

SUBJECTIVE DIMENSIONS

We have done this. We have added subjective dimensions to time-budgets and that is the essential aspect of the WAID. We are exploring states of mind or experiences and motivations. The quality of life, not the quantity, is our main interest. Thus, in addition to objective dimensions, we inquire into subjective dimensions as they occur with each activity. When you actually get into doing that, you will recognize what a completely different task that is from merely recording activities and their content.

A TWO STEP PROCEDURE

To facilitate the completion of the WAID, we are proceeding in two steps. In Step I, we ascertain objective dimensions; the activity itself, the WHEN, WHERE, and WITH HOW MANY. In Step II, we concern ourselves with certain subjective dimensions that are associated with these activities and that are relevant to our purpose, the description of the quality of your life.

We shall discuss different ways of using the information you gather about yourself after you have become familiar with the WAID instrument and procedure, and after you have collected some actual data. The discussion will then be much more meaningful than it would be now.

THE WAID: STEP I

Following are instructions for Step I of the WAID log procedure. We recommend that you try your hand at completing a log as you read these instructions, but that you keep an open mind about revising your entries as you get to understand the procedure and relevant terms better. We are telling you here what to do and how to do it, without going into reasons why. At this point, we are mainly concerned that you understand the procedure and that, in the next chapter, you become thoroughly familiar with the meaning of the terms used in Step II.

Start when you have an hour that you can set aside for this task. You may not need the full hour, but you want to make sure not to feel rushed.

First, take a look at the WAID log, Step I. Notice that the log covers a 24 hour period, starting at midnight and running through noon of the target day to once again midnight. The log is divided into 24 rows, each representing one hour. There is room at the bottom for summary data that you will compute after the log is completed.

The log is also divided into columns. Furthest left is the TIME column, indicating for which hour of the day you are recording. Step I covers three columns: ACTIVITY, WHERE, and WITH HOW MANY. Step II also covers three columns and we shall deal with those a little later on.

ACTIVITY: For each 1 hour interval, record your *primary* activity, that is, the most important thing you did during that interval. If that activity lasted more than one hour, simply draw an arrow to when the activity ended.

You will develop a feeling for what you choose as primary activities, as you go along. You will also learn how to group specific activities into more comprehensive ones. For example, 'getting up' may consist of getting out of bed, going to the bathroom, cleaning your teeth, taking a shower, and getting dressed. 'Getting dressed' may itself consist of selecting your clothing, putting on socks, underwear, suit or dress, shoes, and so on. You are the best judge on whether a broader category may, in fact, cover any number of more specific activities.

There may be instances, probably rare, when you feel that you would want to record more than one *important* activity per hour. We shall handle such instances later, when dealing with coding issues. For the moment, try to restrict yourself to one primary, that is, the most important activity per hour.

WHERE: Where did the activity take place. to simplify matters, we suggest that you use the following code:

0 - in your home: your residence, apartment, house, or wherever you live.
1 - commuting: as between your home and place of employment or education, or other travel.
2 - at place of employment or self-employment.
3 - at school: formal or informal educational institutions.
4 - other: any place other than above.

If you discover that your 'other' category contains repeatedly the same place, you may want to form additional categories, that is, 5, 6, and so on. The main purpose of using a code rather than words is simplicity, both in terms of recording and later on, interpreting your data.

WITH HOW MANY: Were you alone or were you with somebody, and with how many people, as you engaged in the activity? Once again, a code will simplify matters.

0 - alone
1 - with one other
2 - with two others
3 - with three others
4 - with four others
5 - with five or more others

We are restricting ourselves at the present to the simplest way of recording WITH WHOM, namely to only the number of people. At some point, when you are more familiar with the procedure, you may wish to provide information about WHO these others are, particularly if they represent important people in your life. You will then have to adjust your coding system accordingly.

Complete Step I of the log by consecutively recording each activity and WHERE and WITH HOW MANY it took place. Only after you have done this for the full 24 hour period, go on to Step II.

Now begin Step I. Record in the space provided the DATE OF THE TARGET DAY (that is, the day logged) and what DAY OF THE WEEK it was (Monday, Tuesday, etc.). ***Your recording should always take place on the day immediately following the target day.***

Then, describe the target day, covering 24 hours. Thus, if you happen to be doing this on a Thursday, describe the previous Wednesday (the target day). *Start from the time you woke up* and code the next 24 hours, hour by hour. For example, if you awoke between 6 and 7 a.m., on Wednesday, you record your activities through Thursday, 5 - 6 a.m.. Or if you are a late sleeper and you woke up Wednesday morning between 9 and 10, you would record through Thursday morning, 8 - 9 a.m.

Record activities that took place after midnight (running into the next day, but needed to complete 24 hours!) at the beginning of the target day, into the spaces you left blank when you started recording. Just keep in mind that this time period is, in fact, the beginning of the day after the target day. You will get the idea quickly, once you do it a couple of times.

Start recording now into the appropriate hour slot of the time you awoke in the target day. Enter the primary activity that you were engaged in during that hour, where it took place and how many people were with you. Continue doing this for each of the 24 hours.

Having done so will give you a record of one 24 hour segment of your life. This, of course, was the easy part. The real work, but also the part that you may find most meaningful and revealing, is yet to come. Next we shall discuss Step II, adding subjective dimensions to the information you have provided.

THE WAID: STEP II
THREE CRITICAL DIMENSIONS

Before you start working on Step II, we need to discuss the basic vocabulary of the WAID. Three subjective dimensions are critical for the evaluation of the quality of life. We consider next to health, '*perceived freedom*' (CHOICE) and '*intrinsic motivation*' (REASON) to be the most essential conditions for the good life. This is not the place to offer our rationale for this viewpoint; you may find a full discussion elsewhere (Neulinger, 1981; 1984). At this point, we want you to get as complete an understanding of these dimensions as is possible. You are to develop a 'feeling' for them, so that you will be aware of how they apply to your life and to your personal activities and experiences. Only then will you be able to complete Step II of the WAID in a really meaningful manner.

The third dimension, which we call '*feeling tone*' (FEELING), reflects your affect, the way you feel. It is a direct measure, a subjective indicator of whether you feel good or bad, at any given point in time.

The first two dimensions are important because they influence how you feel. They tend to be causally related to the third dimension. This is the reason why we want you to become thoroughly aware of what role they play in your daily life. They are the conditions you might eventually want to do something about, if you find the quality of your life less than satisfactory.

For the sake of clarity, let us restate the above once more. The first two dimensions (CHOICE and REASON) are conditions that affect the quality of your life; the third dimension (FEELING) is, in fact, a measure of the quality of your life.

All three dimensions are subjective, that is, you and only you can experience them or have a direct knowledge of them. Others can neither see them, nor hear them, nor touch them. They can only *infer* them by observing your behavior or studying your physiology. You, the one who actually experiences these dimensions, are the only one who can describe them and give direct estimates of their quality and intensity. You do have access to your state of mind.

Becoming aware of the quality of these dimensions and estimating their intensity is not the sort of thing we generally do. We get used to doing things without questioning our motives. We could not function efficiently, were we to engage in this kind of mind searching all the time. So we establish habits, customs, ways of life. And then, most of us just drift along.

This, however, is the time to do some mind searching and to examine these dimensions very closely. This task will not be an easy one. You need to approach the process with an open mind. Look at yourself as you've never done before. Be honest; doubt your first impression; ponder each question you confront. *Do not make value judgements* as to whether it is good or bad, how you answer or whether somebody might approve or disapprove of how you respond. Be as descriptive, as true to your knowledge of yourself, as possible.

Here are the dimensions you are to describe.

PERCEIVED FREEDOM: CHOICE

To become aware of the degree of perceived freedom you experienced in a given activity, ask yourself the following questions:

> Who made me do it? Was I the origin of my actions, or did I merely do it because I had to?
>
> Did I have any choice in what I was doing? Some choice? Or no choice at all?
>
> Am I sure that I really wanted to do it? Or did I only partly want to do it or perhaps not at all, if I had had a chance?

Use the numbers from ZERO to 100 to reflect the degree of perceived freedom you experienced.

Use 100 to indicate that the activity was 'totally your choice', that you experienced no pressure whatsoever to engage in the activity.

Use ZERO to indicate that you felt 'no choice at all', 'absolutely no sense of perceived freedom'.

Use any of the numbers between ZERO and 100 to indicate that your feelings of perceived freedom was somewhere in between these two extremes.

INTRINSIC MOTIVATION: REASON

To become aware of your reasons for having engaged in a given activity, ask yourself the following questions:

> What did I do the activity for? What did I want to get out of it?
>
> Did I engage in the activity for its own sake, just for the satisfaction I got out of doing it? Or did I do it for a pay-off, or perhaps to avoid a negative consequence? Did I do it because someone else expected or demanded that I do it?
>
> To what degree was it a matter of one or/and the other?

Use the numbers from ZERO to 100 to reflect your judgment as to the reason why you engaged in the activity.

Use 100 to indicate that the reason was purely intrinsic, that you did it only because of the satisfaction derived from the activity. You engaged in the activity purely for its own sake.

Use ZERO to indicate that the reason was not at all intrinsic, that is, you did it *not at all* for the satisfaction or pleasure of the activity itself, but totally for a pay-off, a consequence, thus in order to satisfy someone else.

To the degree that your reasons may have been partly intrinsic and partly extrinsic, use the numbers in between ZERO and 100. The number you choose will be the proportion of intrinsic motivation; the proportion of extrinsic motivation will be 100 minus the number chosen. For example, if you indicate 80, that means the reason was 80% intrinsic and 20% (that is, 100 - 80 = 20) extrinsic. If you choose 50, the intrinsic reason was 50% intrinsic and 50 % (100-50 = 50) extrinsic. And if you choose 10, the reason was 10% intrinsic and 90% (100 - 19 = 90) extrinsic. Thus, ZERO (100 - 0 = 100) implies a 100% extrinsic reason.

FEELING TONE: FEELING

To become aware of how you felt when you engaged in the activity you are describing, as yourself the following questions:

> Did I feel good, positive, happy, while I engaged in the activity?
>
> Did I feel neutral, so-so; was there hardly any feeling at all? Did I feel some good and some bad, so it sort of cancelled out?
>
> Did I feel bad, negative, unhappy, while I engaged in the activity?

Use the numbers from ZERO to 100 to reflect your feeling.

Use 100 to reflect the most positive or best feeling you can imagine.

Use ZERO for the most negative or worst possible feeling.

Use 50 for the midpoint between good and bad, or when you feel neutral or are not aware of any feeling at all. Use any of the other numbers between ZERO and 100 to indicate the degree of good or bad between the extremes and the midpoint.

These, then, are the three dimensions in terms of which you are going to explore the quality of your life. We are sure that you will have any questions as you start compiling WAID logs. Not all will be clear; you may find the task easy or totally impossible. In any case, do it! As you proceed and practice, you will find that you acquire a feeling for the dimensions that you are trying to describe and that these dimensions are very real and important factors in your everyday life.

At this point the main concern is that you complete the log as it is meant to be. Let us therefore spend some time discussing issues that tend to come up, when people complete the form.

For the professional use of the WAID, the therapist will need to become intimately familiar with (1) the concept of *leisure*, understood as a state of mind (e.g., as described in Neulinger's 1990 **The Road to Eden, After All: A Human Metamorphosis**) and (2) with all of the WAID manual. The manual's other chapters include: A Sample Log, Subtleties of Subjective Dimension, Misuses of the WAID, and Uses of the WAID (including: The Impressionistic Approach, the Experience of Completing the WAID logs, The Statistical Approach, Establishing Baselines, Reading Meaning into the Baseline, Identifying your 'Comfort Zones', and a WHERE and WITH HOW MANY analysis.

The therapist will also want to obtain a copy of **Annual in Therapeutic Recreation,** Volume One, 1990. This joint effort of the American Therapeutic Recreation Association and the American Association for Leisure and Recreation contains two excellent articles which will provide the therapist with numerous baseline tables to be used when interpreting the results.

WHAT AM I DOING ?
THE WAID
EXPLORING THE QUALITY OF YOUR LIFE*

The purpose of this form is to help you look at yourself and get to know yourself better. It is not likely that you have ever taken account of yourself in this particular way: exploring dimensions that are critically related to the quality of and meaning in your life.

What you are about to do will take time and effort. To be worthwhile, it needs to be done right. The task requires thoughtful consideration and you should not attempt it unless you have at least an hour's time. Remember that you are doing this for a reason: to help you improve the quality of your life.

This method of looking at yourself is based on certain assumptions about what is important in life. These assumptions are outlined in full elsewhere (Neulinger, 1984). The procedure to follow is given in this form and is elaborated on in the WAID guide (Neulinger, 1986). **This guide needs to be read prior to completing this form,** unless you are completing the WAID under the supervision of a counselor.

What can you expect from completing these forms? Minimally, some enlightening hours exploring yourself and your particular life style. But it may well be more than that. You may not only attain a new sense of self, but also a direction as to where you want to go and some help in getting you there.

Your pay-off will be in direct relation to the amount of effort you are willing to put into this task and of course, to the degree to which the quality of your life needs improvement.

INSTRUCTIONS

1. Read these instructions carefully. This technique requires that you become familiar with certain concepts, as if learning a new language with which you can talk to yourself.

2. Record the date of the target day (the day you are describing) and what day of the week it was.

STEP I: Enter information for ACTIVITY, WHERE and WITH HOW MANY. Start in the hour period during which you woke up. Enter information past midnight at the beginning of the log.

3. ACTIVITY: For each hourly period, record your **primary** activity, that is, the most important thing you did during that interval. If the activity lasted more than an hour, simply draw an arrow to when the activity ended.

4. WHERE: Use the following code...

0- in your home
1- commuting or travelling
2- place of employment or self-employment
3- at school (formal or informal educational institution)
4- other

(Instructions continued on back page)

* A TECHNIQUE DESIGNED TO HELP YOU MEASURE AND IMPROVE THE QUALITY OF YOUR LIFE

WAID LOG
(What Am I Doing?)

	STEP I			STEP II		
TIME	ACTIVITY	WHERE	WITH HOW MANY	CHOICE YOU - 100 OTHER - 0	REASON OWN SAKE 100 OTHER - 0	FEELING + 100 = 50 - 0
Mid-night						
1 a.m.						
2 a.m.						
3 a.m.						
4 a.m.						
5 a.m.						
6 a.m.						
7 a.m.						
8 a.m.						
9 a.m.						
10 a.m.						
11 a.m.						

(Please continue on next page)

Day logged: ☐Mon; ☐Tue; ☐Wed; ☐Thu; ☐Fri; ☐Sat; ☐Sun.

Date of day logged (TARGET DAY): _____/_____/_____/.
(Month) (Day) (Year)

WAID continued.

	STEP I			STEP II		
TIME	ACTIVITY	WHERE	WITH HOW MANY	CHOICE YOU - 100 OTHER - 0	REASON OWN SAKE 100 OTHER - 0	FEELING + 100 = 50 - 0
noon						
1 p.m.						
2 p.m.						
3 p.m.						
4 p.m.						
5 p.m.						
6 p.m.						
7 p.m.						
8 p.m.						
9 p.m.						
10 p.m.						
11 p.m.						

(Continue at beginning of page 1, unless you started at midnight)

SUMMARY DATA:	0 ____ 1 ____ 2 ____ 3 ____ 4 ____	0 ____ 1 ____ 2 ____ 3 ____ 4 ____ 5 ____	MEAN CHOICE	MEAN REASON	MEAN FEELING
	24	24			

(Instructions continued)

5. WITH HOW MANY: Use the following code...

0- alone
1- with one other
2- with two others
3- with three others
4- with four others
5- with five or more others

STEP II: Enter information for CHOICE, REASON and FEELING.

6. CHOICE: Who made you do it? Did you have a choice in what you were doing? Were you the origin of your actions or did you do it because you had to? To what degree was it a matter of one or the other?

Use the numbers from ZERO to 100 to reflect your choice:

0 100

0	100
Not my choice at all; had to do it	Totally my choice; I decided

7. REASON: What did you do it for ? Did you do it for its own sake, because you like doing it? Just for the satisfaction you get out of doing it? Or did you do it for a pay-off or to avoid a negative consequence? To what degree was it a matter of one or the other?

Use the numbers from ZERO to 100 to reflect your reason:

0 100

0	100
For pay-off only; No satisfaction from activity itself	For its own sake; Satisfaction from activity only

(If your reasons were mixed, pick an appropriate middle point)

8. FEELING: Did you feel good, positive, happy while engaged in the activity? Did you feel neutral, so-so; no feeling at all? Did you feel bad, negative, unhappy?

Use the numbers from ZERO to 100 to reflect your feeling:

0 .... 50 100

0		50		100
Extremely bad or negative	(bad)	neutral no feeling;	(good)	exrtemely good or positive

Information for research studies only:

#: NAME: SEX: male( ) female ( )

AGE: A: B: C: D:

THE LEISURE INSTITUTE

FORM# 486-A

LEISURESCOPE PLUS

Name: Leisurescope Plus, versions for adults and teens

Also Known As: Earlier versions were known as Leisurescope and Teenscope.

Time Needed to Administer: Depending on the format and clients, between 20 minutes and 40 minutes.

Time Needed to Score: Scoring takes place as the assessment tool is used. Only additional time is in reporting the summary. It rarely took Idyll Arbor, Inc. staff over 10 minutes to develop the summary statement after administering the assessment.

Recommended Disability Group: Adolescent and adult clients with little to no cognitive impairment. Test manuals state that clients with IQs below 60 should not be given this assessment.

Purpose of Assessment: The purpose of the Leisurescope is threefold:
1) to have a means to determine a client's leisure preferences without limiting him/her to a predetermined check list,
2) to have a means to determine how a client feels about the activities that s/he likes best and how extensive his/her vocabulary is as it relates to feelings and leisure, and
3) to measure the client's perceived need for risk taking experiences.

What Does the Assessment Measure?: The Leisurescope Plus measures the client's preferences for activity types (e.g., sports versus crafts), emotional motivation for participation, and need for high arousal experiences.

Supplies Needed: The Leisurescope Plus pictures (which come in two formats: laminated cards or slides), manual, and a score sheet.

Reliability/Validity: Reliability and Validity reported.

Degree of Skill Required to Administer and Score: To ensure that the assessment tool is measuring what it says it is measuring, we recommend that a recreational therapist certified at the CTRS level administer and interpret the results. Idyll Arbor, Inc. staff have found that some clients interpret the pictures differently than intended. Some clients were found to select the last three cards because they thought that the pictures meant 'dating' or they liked the way the people looked.

Comments: This assessment is very easy to use and is well-received by clients.

Suggested Levels: Rancho Los Amigos Level: 7 or above. Developmental Level: 7 or above. (We had difficulty feeling comfortable with results obtained with clients whose IQs were below 60.) Reality Orientation Score: Moderate to No Impairment.

Distributor: Leisure Dynamics, 5199 Icicle Hill, Tallahassee, FL 32303 (904) 562-9750.

LEISURESCOPE PLUS

(Note: To practice administering this assessment you will need to borrow the Leisurescope Plus supplies from a therapist who has them.)

The Leisurescope Plus is an assessment tool which helps the therapist assess the client's leisure preferences. These preferences are divided into ten categories related to leisure: 1) games, 2) sports, 3) nature, 4) collection, 5) crafts, 6) art and music, 7) entertainment, 8) helping others/volunteerism, 9) social affiliation, and 10) adventure. Unlike most leisure interest assessments, this one is a nice change from the typical check list. The client is shown ten different collages, each with a set of eight photographs of activities. There is one collage for each category of leisure. The eight photographs in each collage depict a different aspect of that category. The crafts collage, for example, has color photographs of a potter's wheel, tie dye, cooking, model building, engine repair, cross stitch, woodworking, and leather work.

The purpose of the assessment tool is threefold:

1) to determine a client's leisure preferences without limiting him/her to a predetermined check list,

2) to determine how a client feels about the activities that s/he likes best *and* how extensive his/her vocabulary is as it relates to feelings and leisure, and

3) to measure the client's perceived need for high arousal experiences (risk taking).

The way in which the therapist administers the assessment helps achieve all three purposes. The therapist places collage #1 and collage #2 in front of the client and asks him/her which one s/he likes best, or finds most pleasing. The therapist also asks how much more does the client like the selected collage over the other collage and asks the client to select a word which describes how s/he feels about the activities in the collage. The therapist compares each collage against all the others until all 45 comparisons are made. By using a simple coding system and marking directly on the score sheet, the results are easy to obtain and interpret.

There are two versions of the Leisurescope Plus available. One is specifically developed for adults, the other for adolescents.

The therapist also has a selection of formats. The assessment tool can be purchased as a set of ten 5" x 7" laminated cards of good quality, or as a set of ten slides which are also of good quality. Since most of the assessments that Idyll Arbor, Inc. does are done one on one, we choose to use the cards. The slide format would be ideal for administering the assessment to a group of clients who have the skills to mark their own score sheets or who are visually impaired. These formats require approximately 15 - 20 minutes for administration. Idyll Arbor, Inc. staff have found that this tool works best with clients with an adapted IQ greater than 60 and a Rancho Los Amigos level of 7 or greater.

Leisurescope Plus was developed out of Connie Nall Schenk's own frustration. She found that clients became bored and disinterested with the traditional methods used for determining leisure interests. Knowing that the majority of people are 'visual', it seemed logical to her to design an instrument which would satisfy the need for acquiring leisure interest information through a method that would also be enjoyable for participants. After making this basic assumption, she began her research and design of the photographic tool now known as Leisurescope Plus.

Activity categories are based on the *Avocational Activities Inventory* (AAI) (Dr. Robert Overs, 1977). The AAI listed over 800 leisure activities and was developed to help classify avocational activities. One of the ways that the AAI was used was to stimulate conversation about the breadth of activities available to the client. However, the AAI proved to be a cumbersome instrument to use. The Leisurescope Plus draws upon the strengths of the AAI without having many of the drawbacks.

The adventure/high arousal seeking element of this tool was correlated with the *Sensation Seeking Tool* by Zukerman. Zukerman's scale found four dimensions to adventure seeking: experience seeking, dishibition, boredom susceptibility, and adventure seeking.

Experience seeking is defined as activities which stimulate many senses and also tend to be spontaneous in nature. Dishibition is defined as a nonconformity usually related to noncompliance with 'prudent' use of alcohol, partying, sex, and gambling. Boredom susceptibility is defined as having a low tolerance for the expected. Thrill and adventure seeking is defined as risk taking, usually of a physical nature, which is usually within the bounds of socially acceptable activities.

One of the most important aspects of any assessment tool is that it should clearly indicate the types of intervention indicated. The Leisurescope Plus does this in two ways.

For many therapists it becomes very obvious after just a few times administering the Leisurescope Plus that few people have an extensive vocabulary covering feelings related to leisure. This seems even more true of clients who have had a long term disability or illness. For many clients this is an obvious need after completing the Leisurescope Plus. The recreational therapist should work very closely with the speech therapist to help expand the client's selection of words (and to understand their meaning) as they relate to leisure.

The second type of intervention that is apparent after administering the Leisurescope Plus is the areas of leisure that the client enjoys and should take part. This is especially true when trying to help a client find new activities in an area of interest. A spinal cord injury may limit a client's ability to participate in his/her old favorite pastime, but the Leisurescope Plus makes it easier to determine appropriate new activities to pursue.

The Leisurescope Plus has an extensive activity resource filing system for practitioners to use with their clients. The client and/or therapist takes the scored preferences from the assessment tool and goes to the LEISURE ACTIVITIES FILING SYSTEM (LAFS) to pull the file folder which contains information about the area of preference.

Each folder contains information about local leisure opportunities. The therapist and/or the clients locate the information and continually update the information in the files. While this type of intervention is often not considered 'therapy', it does assist the client in locating activities to help maintain a healthy, satisfying leisure lifestyle.

We have a story to explain why we think so highly of the Leisurescope Plus. Idyll Arbor, Inc. staff have over 30 formal assessment tools available for use when a client is assessed. In 1987 joan walked into a group home to conduct an assessment. Before she could start the assessment, she found herself face to face with the one state surveyor who seemed void of any humor and warmth. He immediately barked that he wanted to discuss the validity of the assessments the Idyll Arbor, Inc. staff used. He was wondering why Idyll Arbor, Inc. staff had assessments that no other recreational therapist had. Going on gut feelings, joan chose the older version of the Leisurescope to demonstrate how the assessments worked. She helped him fill out his own score sheet and, when joan interpreted the results for him, he sat back and smiled. Then he said after a pause, 'Your assessments must be good because no one has ever been able to 'peg' me so well!'

The assessment (and LAFS) are available through Leisure Dynamics, 5199 Icicle Hill, Tallahassee, FL 30302 (904) 562-9750.

LEISURESCOPE *PLUS*

a leisure interest assessment

step 1

Leisure Categories Chart

• You will be shown 10 groups of pictures (collages) which illustrate leisure activities. You will be shown two "collages" at a time, and will be comparing all pairs. • Begin by comparing collage #1 with collage #2. Decide quickly which collage you like better (your first impression is best) • Decide <u>how much</u> better you like your choice. • Then on the row number of your choice, shade in 1, 2, or 3 squares. Example: if you like collage #2 "a lot better" than collage #1, shade three squares on row #2. <u>Note:</u> as you work through the pairs, you will continue adding shaded squares to the rows.

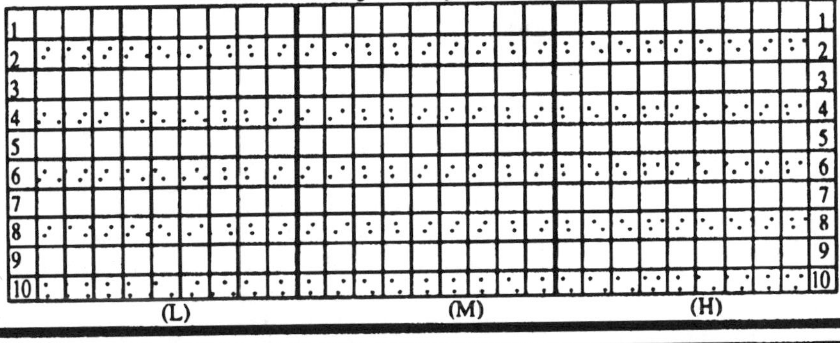

EXAMPLE

Slightly More Interest	Shade 1 Square
Moderately More Interest	Shade 2 Squares
Extremely More Interest	Shade 3 Squares

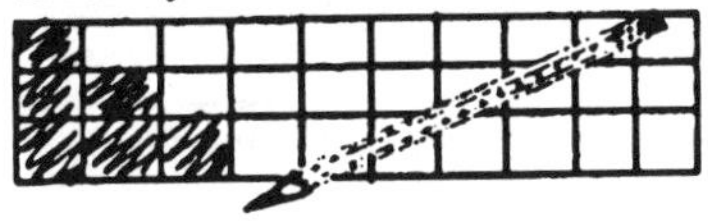

step 2

Feelings Chart

• Read the list of words that describe <u>feelings</u> • Choose one word that describes how you <u>feel</u> when you look at the collage you just selected. If none match your feelings, write a word that does, in one of the blank spaces provided. • Make a tally (/) in the correct box to record your feelings. Example: if you chose Collage #2 in step 1, and you decide it is "fun" for you, put your tally in the box where the column "Collage #2" and "Fun" meet. Note: you will choose only one word for each comparison. If you select the same collage more than once, you do <u>not</u> have to use the same word each time. • When all comparisons have been made, use the Total column to add your tally marks across each row.

Your Feelings	Collage 1	Collage 2	Collage 3	Collage 4	Collage 5	Collage 6	Collage 7	Collage 8	Collage 9	Collage 10	TOTAL
Relaxed											
Accomplishment/ Satisfaction											
Fun											
Healthy											
Escape											
Contentment/ Pleasure											
Rejuvenation											
Tension Reduction											
Companionship											
Excitement											

step 3

Collage Comparisons

Use the following chart to keep track of each comparison you make. Example: place a checkmark next to the comparison you just completed (1 vs 2). • Repeat steps 1, 2 and 3, using the next pair (1 vs 3). Continue until all pairs have been completed.

1 vs 2 ______	1 vs 9 ______	2 vs 8 ______	3 vs 8 ______	4 vs 9 ______	6 vs 7 ______	8 vs 9 ______
1 vs 3 ______	1 vs 10 ______	2 vs 9 ______	3 vs 9 ______	4 vs 10 ______	6 vs 8 ______	8 vs 10 ______
1 vs 4 ______	2 vs 3 ______	2 vs 10 ______	3 vs 10 ______	5 vs 6 ______	6 vs 9 ______	9 vs 10 ______
1 vs 5 ______	2 vs 4 ______	3 vs 4 ______	4 vs 5 ______	5 vs 7 ______	6 vs 10 ______	
1 vs 6 ______	2 vs 5 ______	3 vs 5 ______	4 vs 6 ______	5 vs 8 ______	7 vs 8 ______	
1 vs 7 ______	2 vs 6 ______	3 vs 6 ______	4 vs 7 ______	5 vs 9 ______	7 vs 9 ______	
1 vs 8 ______	2 vs 7 ______	3 vs 7 ______	4 vs 8 ______	5 vs 10 ______	7 vs 10 ______	

When you have completed all comparisons, turn scoresheet over for your interpretations.

LEISURESCOPE *PLUS* INTERPRETATION

step 1

• For each of the 10 Leisure Categories, (step 1, other side) note where your line of shaded squares ends. Below the chart are (L) for low, (M) for medium and (H) for high. • Now circle your score here for each category.

Leisure Categories	Circle Your Score
1 Games	L M H
2 Sports	L M H
3 Nature	L M H
4 Collection	L M H
5 Crafts	L M H
6 Art & Music	L M H
7 Entertainment	L M H
8 Helping Others/ Volunteerism	L M H
9 Social Affiliation	L M H
10 Adventure	L M H

step 2

• Now list the categories in order, by looking at your longest line of shaded squares (step 1, other side). Write that category name here as your 1st choice and highest interest. • Look at the next longest line, and write that category name as your 2nd choice. • Continue until all 10 categories have been listed. Naturally, the line with the fewest (or no) shaded squares will be your 10th and lowest interest.

1st ____________________

2nd ____________________

3rd ____________________

4th ____________________

5th ____________________

6th ____________________

7th ____________________

8th ____________________

9th ____________________

10th ____________________

step 3

• Look at the Total column (step 2, other side) and find your three highest tally totals. • Now list the three feelings tied to these three totals. Your highest total shows what feeling is most important to you.

1st ____________________

2nd ____________________

3rd ____________________

step 4

• What leisure categories give you this feeling? (Step 2, other side - use either category names or numbers for each feeling)

____

____

Produced by
Leisure Dynamics
5199 Icicle Hill
Tallahassee, Florida 32303
(904) 562-9750

RECREATION PARTICIPATION DATA SHEET

Name: Recreation Participation Data Sheet

Also Known As: RPD

Authors: joan burlingame and Johna Peterson

Time Needed to Administer: The RPD is a data collection system. Experience has shown that it has taken aides (nursing aides and/or direct care staff) less than two minutes per client to fill this form out daily.

Time Needed to Score: The Idyll Arbor, Inc. staff found that they were spending 30 - 45 minutes per client per quarter analyzing the data and comparing the changes from the previous quarter.

Recommended Disability Groups: All

Purpose of Assessment: The purpose of the RPD is to monitor a client's leisure activities to promote a balanced leisure lifestyle.

What Does the Assessment Measure?: The RPD helps the recreational therapist keep track of the client's demonstrated functional ability in the following areas: 1) participation, 2) initiation, 3) independence, 4) physical output, 5) satisfaction, 6) average size of leisure groups, and 7) average time spent engaging in activities.

Supplies Needed: RPD sheets (the therapist may also use the supplemental physical activity sheet) and a calculator.

Reliability/Validity: No formal reliability or validity testing has been done at this point. A clear correlation has been found between the RPD findings and either the Leisurescope or the LET'S* activity assessment with 12 clients whose primary diagnosis is Prader-Willi Syndrome.

Degree of Skill Required to Administer and Score: The RPD was designed to be filled out by direct care staff and analyzed by a recreational therapist certified at the CTRS level. Because of the degree of professional judgment required in determining the appropriate balance of activities, a CTRS familiar with the disabling conditions of the clients is necessary.

---

*LET'S is a set of assessment tools and training programs developed by Lori Lund. The LET'S is currently out of print.

Comments: The RPD has worked well in the 6 group homes it was developed for in 1985. For an example of how this information is used in an assessment report, the therapist should turn to Chapter 8 and read the **Recreation Participation** section of Jenny Doe's report.

Suggested Levels: Rancho Los Amigos Level: 3 and up. Developmental Level: birth and up. Reality Orientation Level: Severe and up.

Distributor: Idyll Arbor, Inc. 25119 S.E. 262 Street, PO Box 720, Ravensdale, WA 98051-0720 (206) 432-3231. (Area code 425 after April 1997.)

RECREATION PARTICIPATION DATA SHEET
RPD

PURPOSE: The purpose of the Recreation Participation Data Sheet (RPD) is to monitor a client's leisure activities. In many ways the RPD is an attendance sheet that also provides the recreational therapist with a means to record functional skills.

When used over a period of time, the RPD helps measure a client's leisure participation patterns.

WHAT DOES THE RPD MEASURE?: The RPD helps the recreational therapist keep track of the client's demonstrated functional ability in the following areas: 1) participation, 2) initiation, 3) independence, 4) physical output, 5) satisfaction, 6) average size of leisure groups, and 7) average time spent engaging in activities.

SUPPLIES NEEDED: The recreational therapist will need to have one RPD score sheet for each client. The other supplies needed depend on the activity.

WHEN SHOULD THE RPD BE FILLED OUT?: The RPD is usually filled out at the end of each day. The staff should decide which leisure activities should be recorded. For most clients in institutional settings and group homes, their daily schedule is so full of training programs and activities of daily living that they have little free time. A typical series of entries might look like: Monday: watched one hour of TV, Tuesday: van ride to grocery store for fruit, Wednesday: coffee and chit-chat with favorite staff person, Thursday: social group at local parks department, Friday: movie with 3 peers from group home, etc.

DEVELOPMENT: The RPD was first developed to help the therapist monitor whether the direct care staff in group homes were offering the clients a balance of activities. A 'balance of activities' was defined as a variety of activities in all domains (cognitive, social, physical) with no one domain accounting for more than 50% of all activities in a one month period.

The information recorded on the RPD was usually recorded by the direct care staff after an inservice by the recreational therapist. One of the criteria for the development of the form was to be able to glean as much useful information as possible and to be able to get this information with less than 30 seconds recording time for each client (including locating the sheet itself).

ISSUES SURROUNDING POOR DOCUMENTATION TECHNIQUES BY DIRECT CARE STAFF: Therapists who have used the RPD for any length of time realize how vulnerable the tool is to substandard documentation by the direct care staff and to the selection of activities that the direct care staff choose to write down. The use of the RPD is a good way to measure the direct care staff's understanding of what makes a balanced leisure lifestyle and helps pinpoint the need for staff inservices.

Whenever a problem is noted related to a client's leisure activity patterns, the therapist should first rule out the possibility that the documentation represents a problem with staff performance. It is a good idea for the therapist to carry staff inservice forms to help document all training of direct care staff. This also allows the direct care staff to document his/her on-going involvement in professional development.

SOME SUGGESTED USES:

Over time the RPD was modified and after five years of use it has reached its current form. Some of the modifications, and the reasons for them, are listed below:

A. RPD Supplemental Physical Activity Sheet: In certain situations the treatment team felt that a client's cardiovascular endurance was low enough to potentially place that client at risk. The two most common reasons were obesity (the need to increase activity while decreasing caloric intake) and medications (the need to increase blood flow through the kidneys to decrease the potential kidney damage caused by medications).

A set of general treatment protocols was set up to indicate when the treatment team needed to implement increased physical activity. This increase needed to be monitored. The RPD supplemental Physical Activity Sheet was placed behind the client's regular RPD each month (or as needed).

Two of the group homes that the RPD was developed for had individuals with Prader-Willi Syndrome. Prader-Willi Syndrome is caused by a genetic defect. The presenting disability associated with Prader-Willi Syndrome is the uncontrollable urge to eat food. By age three or four most of these individuals require a living situation with all food cabinets and refrigerator doors locked shut. The most devastating side effect of this syndrome is that, the more they eat and gain weight, the lower their IQ drops. If they then loose the weight they do not gain back the IQ. For this group of individuals the team eventually found that an average of nine hours of physical exercise a month at levels one or two was indicated. For some of these individuals it took two years for the client (with the help of the recreational therapist) to develop a group of physical activities that s/he enjoyed enough to average nine hours. For clients on medications such as Depo Provera, an additional one hour per month was encouraged. (Depo Provera has a potential side effect of causing damage to the kidneys.)

B. Group Size: Normally leisure activities take place in groups of less than four people. Not only is it not usual to have more than 50% of your activities in large groups (i.e., over four people), but large groups also creates significantly different social dynamics requiring different skills than one-on-one interactions. Idyll Arbor, Inc. staff try to encourage the direct care staff to have

80% or more of the activities take place with fewer than four people.

C. Comment Section — Eating: Frequently clients in institutions are overweight. In two group homes for which this seemed to be a general problem, Idyll Arbor, Inc. had standing orders that all leisure activities that involved food (besides regular meal time) be recorded. For some clients over 65% of their leisure activities involved such things as trips to McDonalds! The recreational therapist, by working with the direct care staff, taught both the clients and staff appropriate, enjoyable activities and social skills that did not require the use of food. To help avoid a significant shock and possible rebellion (by either the clients or the staff) the percentage of activities involving food was not immediately cut, but was dropped 5%-10% a month until it reached about 10%.

D. Comment Section — Money: Often clients are on the three to five year plan for discharge to an independent living situation. In those cases the therapist would have staff record the actual cost of the outing for the client (i.e., movie $6.00, popcorn $2.00, soda pop $1.50 = $9.50). The recreational therapist would (with the help of the case manager) anticipate the amount of discretionary money the client would have for leisure per month. After that amount is determined, the recreational therapist would work with both the client and the direct care staff to develop a repertoire of satisfying leisure activities that were within the client's monthly budget.

E. Initiation Level and Potential for Isolation from Activity: The degree to which a client initiated activities was closely watched. For a client within a few years of discharge it was imperative that s/he develop the desire and ability to independently initiate the activities. The ability to demonstrate the skill to initiate is one of the most primary skills required for a healthy leisure lifestyle. Whether the inability to initiate is due to an organic dysfunction or to an institutional environment (and is probably a combination of the two), an intervention strategy should be developed. The therapist must first ensure that the client has learned at least five appropriate activities and then, as a team, develop behavioral rewards to encourage the client's participation in those activities.

SCORING:

The way that the RPD is scored is by comparing the client's demonstrated leisure patterns from one month to the next (or from any given time period, i.e., a quarter, to the next).

Idyll Arbor, Inc. staff would calculate the average number of hours of physical exercise (level 1 or 2) that a client participated in per month. This would be graphed to show a trend over time.

Degree of satisfaction was also tracked. The recreational therapist would help the client problem solve so that the majority of the client's leisure activities were satisfying to him/her (level 1 or 2).

One other area that was closely watched was initiation. For any client with an average level of 2.5 - 3.0, specific training to develop the ability to initiate activities was considered.

For an example of how the information gleaned from the RPD can be used, the reader should turn to Chapter 8 of this book to review a sample assessment report.

RPD
RECREATION PARTICIPATION DATA SHEET
Coding Guide

Date: Enter the date that the activity took place.

Activity: The purpose of this entry is to allow the recreational therapist to have enough description of the activity so they can develop a mental picture of what transpired, e.g.; walk to store, bike, T-Ball, water play, table game (name game), arts and crafts (name), etc.

Treatment Code: If the activity that the staff is recording is part of a client's formal treatment, enter the number of the treatment code.

Participation Level:

1. Active: actively participates, responsive, eye contact, alert, enthusiastic, willingly participates, engrossed in the activity.

2. Semi - Active: participates with encouragement, wants staff assistance but does not necessarily require it, needs cues to willingly participate, needs staff encouragement.

3. Passive: fringe participant, prefers to observe only, requires frequent staff encouragement.

4. Declines: does not participate, resistive, non-cooperative, refuses to stay in area, demonstrates inappropriate behaviors, interferes with the activity, disruptive.

5. Medically unable to participate.

Initiation Level:

1. Independent: independently initiates activity without cuing from staff.

2. Semi - Independent: initiates activity after being cued by, 'What would you like to do now?' or 'What recreational activity would you like to do now?'

3. Dependent: requires staff assistance to participate in activity, does not indicate desire to participate and/or initiate activity.

Independence Level:

1. Independent: independently participate, does not require physical support from staff or peers to participate in the activity; no special adaptations required of equipment or activity.

2. Semi - Independent: semi-independently participates, requires little modification to activity or equipment to be able to physically take part in the activity successfully.

3. Semi - Dependent: semi-dependently participates, requires special adaptations of activity or equipment, or needs specially ordered equipment to physically take part in the activity successfully. Requires occasional physical assistance from staff or peers.

4. Dependent: requires special adaptation of activity and/or specially ordered equipment *and* requires physical assistance from staff or peers even with the equipment to take part in the activity.

Physical Level:

1. High: high physical output including: increased heart beat sustained over 10 minutes time, sweat, potentially winded.

2. Medium: medium physical output including: increased heart beat sustained for less than 10 minutes but more than 3 minutes.

3. Low: low physical output including: little to no change in heart beat, normal breathing, no sweat related to activity.

Satisfaction Level:

1. High: enjoyed activity, smiled, other physical and/or verbal cues indicating satisfaction with activity.

2. Moderate: general satisfaction and pleasure with activity.

3. Low: disliked activity, unenthusiastic, angry, sad.

Size of Group:

1. Solitary: activity done alone.

2. Dyad: one-on-one activity with staff, family, or peer.

3. Small Group: group containing four or less people.

4. Large Group: group containing five or more people.

Total Time Activity Run:

Enter the total number of minutes the client was involved in the activity.

Comments:

Enter any additional information that might assist the recreational therapist in his/her assessment of the client's participation in this activity, e.g.; 'Said he loved the outing', 'Smiled a lot today', 'Refused to get involved', 'Cooperated well'.

RPD

Recreation Participation Data Sheet

Year:______________

Date:	Activity:	Treatment Code	Participation (1-4)	Initiation (1-3)	Independence (1-4)	Physical (1-3)	Satisfaction (1-3)	Group (1-4)	Time	Comments:

Name:
House:
Birthdate:
Admission Date:

RPD
SUPPLEMENTAL PHYSICAL ACTIVITY SHEET
ACTIVITY GUIDELINES

The following activities *would* be considered physical activities at Level 1, provided that they are done for at least 10 - 15 minutes, without stopping:

1. Swimming (Not standing around in the pool)
2. Water Aerobics
3. Low Impact Aerobics
4. Hiking
5. Bike Riding (Stationary or Freestanding)
6. Walking Fast
7. Walking Up Stairs
8. Walking Up Hills or Steep Inclines
9. Trampoline
10. Outdoor Games/New Games, (tag, relays, etc.)
11. Snow Skiing
12. Running/Jogging
13. Ball Games (not necessarily baseball)
14. Volleyball and Basket Drills
15. Dancing

And lots more activities too - be creative!

The following activities *would not* be considered physical activities at Level 1, unless you can prove that the heart rate stays up for a consistent 10 minutes.

1. Bowling
2. Push Ups
3. Van Rides
4. Playing the Organ
5. Visiting with Others
6. Eating at Burger King
7. Standing around in the swimming pool

Heart Rates:

1. The average adult's heart beats between 70 and 80 times per minute (about once per second).

2. To exercise the heart muscle the heart needs to beat faster. This exercise increases the heart muscle's ability to do work. Exercise increases the heart's ability to get the blood pumped through the body more efficiently.

5. To take the heart rate, check a persons wrist, count the heart beats for 6 seconds. Multiply the number of heart beats counted in 6 seconds by ten to get the beats per minute.

6. Prior to any client engaging in high physical activity, the client must first be cleared by his/her physician to do so. This approval should be renewed on a quarterly basis, or more often, depending on the client's health.

RPD

SUPPLEMENTAL PHYSICAL ACTIVITY SHEET

Purpose: The purpose of the Supplemental Physical Activity Sheet of the RPD is to consolidate all the information on a client's physical activity onto one sheet for easier review.

Recreational Therapy Objective: The client will be involved in activities that will increase his/her heart rate to a physical level of 1 or 2*, at least three times per week, for a minimum of 15 minutes each time.

Date	Activity	Level	Time	Comments

Key to be used for Physical Levels:

1 = High: high physical output including: increased heart beat sustained over 10 minutes time, sweat, potentially winded

2 = Medium: medium physical output including: increased heart beat sustained for less than 10 minutes but more than 3 minutes

3 = Low: low physical output including: little to no change in heart beat, normal breathing, no sweat related to activity

*Note: Physical Levels as described in the RPD by Idyll Arbor, Inc.

Target Heart Rate:

Client's Name	Physician	Admit #	Room/Bed

Chapter 5

MEASURING FUNCTIONAL SKILLS

One of the treatment areas that we have in common with the other therapies is functional skills. A functional skill is an action or thought which can be measured. The unique aspect of recreational therapy is that we address the development *and* integration of these skills using leisure activities.

Functional skills lend themselves to be measured using criterion-referenced assessment tools. A criterion-referenced assessment measures a client's skill level based on a continuum from 'no or low skill' to 'high skill'.

The purpose of this chapter is to provide the recreational therapist with some samples of assessments which address the client's demonstrated functional skill.

Table 5 - 1 Suggested Levels

The Idyll Arbor, Inc. staff reviewed the assessments contained in this book to *estimate* which groups the assessments may be given to. The determinations were based on their experience administering the assessments with the clients that they have worked with. (Idyll Arbor, Inc. has a general practice, admitting clients with all diagnoses except clients with a primary diagnosis of addiction). There has been no formal testing to establish these recommended guidelines. Each therapist will need to evaluate whether any specific assessment will work with the clients that s/he serves.

The shaded areas on the charts below indicate that the assessment is recommended for use with clients functioning at that level. To determine if an assessment is appropriate to use, determine the functional level of the client and then read the chart to determine if the assessment is appropriate for that client.

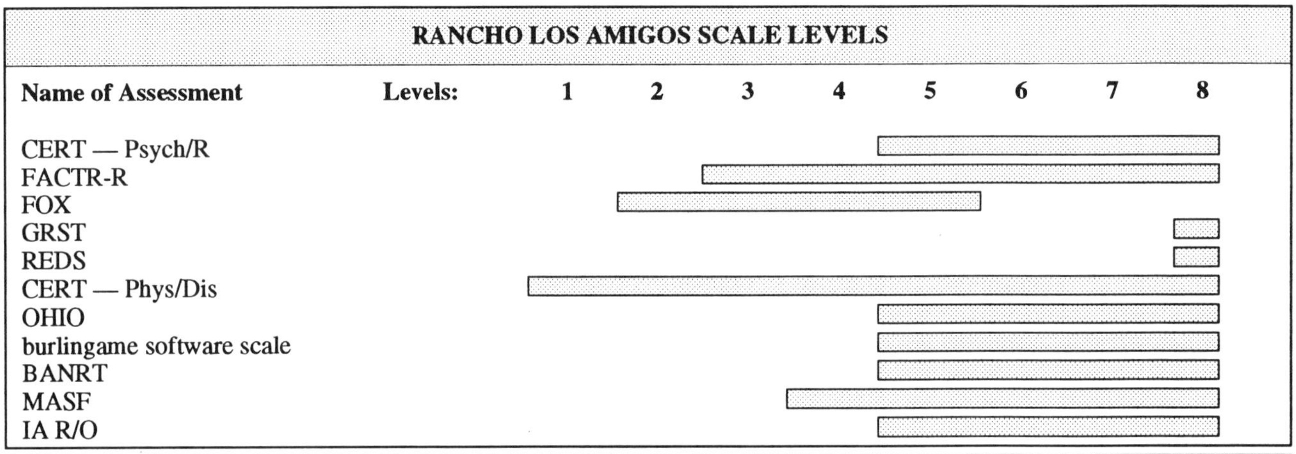

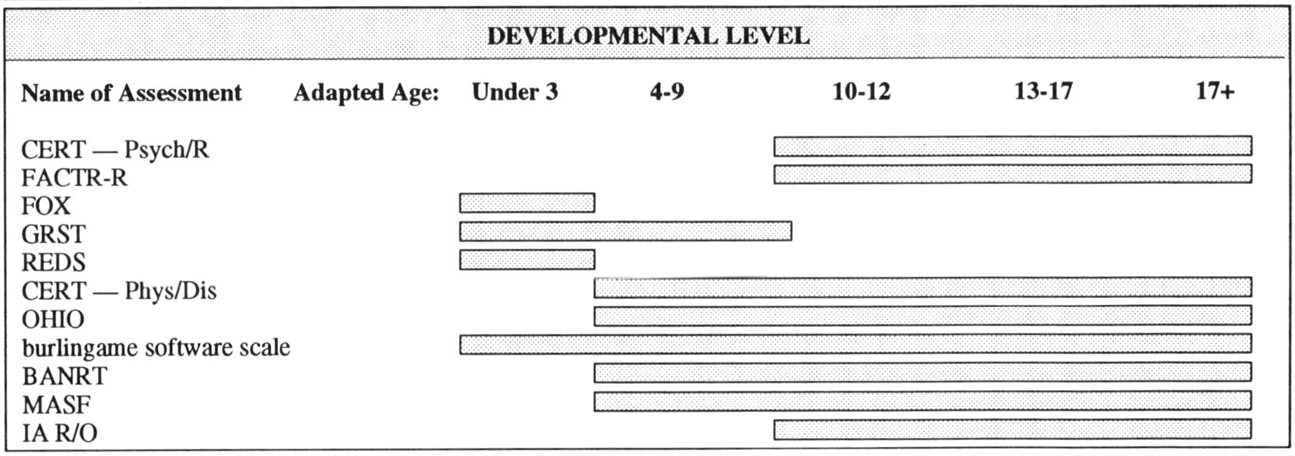

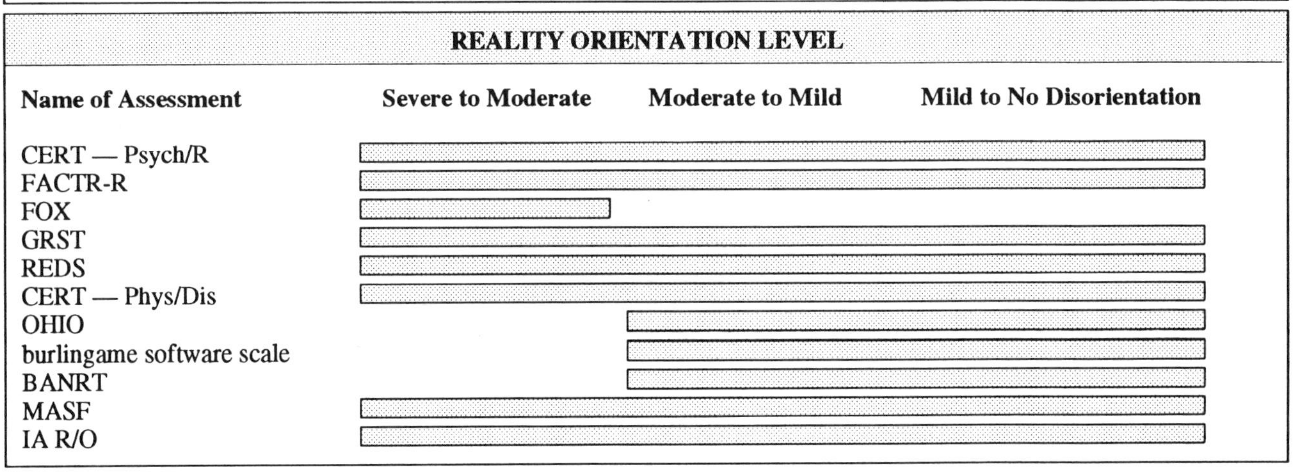

COMPREHENSIVE EVALUATION IN RECREATIONAL THERAPY — PSYCH/BEHAVIORAL, REVISED

Name: Comprehensive Evaluation in Recreational Therapy — Psych/Behavioral, Revised

Also Known As: CERT — Psych/R

Authors: Robert A. Parker, Curtis H. Ellison, Thomas F. Kirby, and M. J. Short, MD

Time Needed to Administer: The CERT — Psych/R is scored after observing the client in a group activity. There is no administration time separate from the activity.

Time Needed to Score: The CERT — Psych/R takes approximately 5 minutes per client to score after the therapist observes the client in a group activity.

Recommended Disability Group: Youth and adult clients with a developmental age of at least 10 years. This assessment works very well with both psychiatric and rehabilitation populations. The School Social Behavior Scale (Merrell, 1993, Clinical Psychology Publishing Company, Inc. Brandon, VT) is more developmentally appropriate for youth from six to fifteen.

Purpose of the Assessment: The purpose of the CERT — Psych/R is to identify, define, and evaluate behaviors relevant to a person's ability to successfully integrate into society using his/her social interaction skills.

What Does the Assessment Measure?: The CERT — Psych/R measures three performance areas: General, Individual Performance, and Group Performance.

Supplies Needed: The therapist will need to provide the supplies that s/he would normally supply for the activity. In addition, the therapist will need one CERT — Psych/R form #116 for each client being evaluated. The Idyll Arbor, Inc. version of this assessment has been designed to be used up to ten times for each client.

Reliability/Validity: Initial validity and reliability studies reported for the original version. The changes in the revised version should not change the original findings significantly.

Degree of Skill Required to Administer and Score: A therapist certified at the CTRS level by the National Council for Therapeutic Recreation Certification is qualified to administer, score, and interpret the results obtained on the CERT — Psych/R.

Comments: The CERT — Psych/R is one of the more usable assessment tools for many populations. It is a good tool to: 1) document client interactions after each treatment session, 2) measure changes possibly due to medications, and 3) to identify change over a period of time. At the time of the 1996 printing of this book, the CERT — Psych was being used with over 8,000 clients a year.

Suggested Levels: Rancho Los Amigos Level 5 or above. Developmental Level: 10 or above. Reality Orientation Level: Severe and above.

Distributor: Idyll Arbor, Inc., 25119 S.E. 262 Street, PO Box 720, Ravensdale, WA 98051 (206) 432-3231. (Area code 425 after April 1997.)

Comprehensive Evaluation in Recreational Therapy — Psych/Behavioral, Revised
CERT — Psych/R

PURPOSE: The purpose of the CERT — Psych/R is to identify, define, and evaluate behaviors relevant to a person's ability to successfully integrate into society using his/her social interaction skills.

The assessment has changed slightly from the original form published in the *Therapeutic Recreation Journal* in 1975. The question related to sexual roles was changed and reformatting was done to help speed up the scoring process.

SUPPLIES NEEDED

The CERT — Psych/R is meant to be used after observing the client in a variety of leisure activities (primarily in group activities). The therapist will need to provide the supplies that would normally be used for the activity. In addition, the therapist will need one CERT — Psych/R form #116 for each client being evaluated. The Idyll Arbor, Inc. version of this assessment has been designed to be used up to ten times for each client.

TIME NEEDED

The assessment score sheet that accompanies this manual was formatted to be used to measure a client's skill development or deterioration during his/her involvement in a therapy program. Two therapists would take less than 20 minutes to assess 15-20 clients who were in an activity together.

USES OF THE CERT — PSYCH/R

The CERT — Psych/R is one of the oldest functionally-based assessments in the field of recreational therapy. It is used in acute care settings as an intake assessment to determine appropriate therapy goals. The CERT — Psych/R is also used extensively to document changes in a client's social interaction skills resulting from longer-term therapy programs, especially in large state facilities. Clients are evaluated at regular intervals to document the amount of change.

In addition, the health care environment has become increasingly sensitive to the prescription and use of medications that control a client's behavior. This assessment has been used more and more as a means to document even subtle changes in a client's demonstrated functional skills induced by medication changes. The usual protocol for using the CERT — Psych/R in this case is to administer the assessment five times prior to the medication change using a variety of activities. After the medicine has stabilized in the client's system the assessment is readministered five times using similar situations to determine the amount of change.

BACKGROUND

The information provided below is an update of the information that was provided by Robert A. Parker in the original journal article. The original authors of the assessment and documentation are Robert A. Parker, Curtis H. Ellison, Thomas F. Kirby, and M. J. Short, MD. Idyll Arbor, Inc. appreciates Robert Parker's willingness to share his work with the other therapists in the field.

With the current trend toward greater accountability in health care, professionals treating clients with mental illness and other disorders must take steps to define the behaviors they are treating in order to clarify the treatment process taking place. To help clarify the process for recreational therapists, a rating scale, the Comprehensive Evaluation in Recreational Therapy Scale — Psych/Behavioral (CERT Psych) was developed. It identifies and defines behaviors relevant to recreational therapy and provides a more objective means for rating clients on these behaviors.

The development and use of a rating scale is not a new idea as most recreational therapists have used a variety of scales and have, in turn, developed their own to meet particular needs. However, this in itself is a problem. There are many departmentally developed rating scales used at individual facilities, but there is no one scale uniformly used that provides a common point of reference for recreational therapy.

The CERT — Psych was initially designed for use in a short term, acute care, psychiatric setting. In Marshall I. Pickens Hospital, a 50 bed hospital where the scale was developed, adults and adolescents have an average length of stay of 11 days and attend recreational therapy programs an average of eight times. Recreational therapy groups range in size from 8 to 12 and are staffed by one registered recreational therapist and one recreational therapy assistant.

DEVELOPMENT OF THE SCALE

In developing the scale, the Recreational Therapy Department of Marshal I. Pickens Hospital began work with two objectives in mind. The first was to identify behaviors that were relevant to the recreational therapy process. The second was to develop behavioral definitions so the behaviors could be reliably evaluated by two or more people. The purpose of the scale was to provide a means of evaluating a client and of reflecting progress or lack of progress by the client while in recreational therapy. The scale is a part of the client's chart and provides essential information for the treatment team in developing and modifying the individual treatment plan.

After reviewing numerous scales used throughout the United States, the Recreational Therapy Department selected three areas of an individual's behavior to be evaluated: General, Individual, and Group Performance. A total of 25 behaviors were identified: five were in the General category and ten each in Individual Performance and Group Performance. The ratings are from 0 to 4 with 0 being 'normal' and 4 indicating a severe problem. Thus, the higher the score, the greater is the severity of the problems, with a score of 100 being the highest possible. The format of the scale is such that it provides a graph effect when several ratings have been completed.

After reviewing changes in the laws regarding discrimination based on sexual orientation, item E in the Group Preformance section regarding sexual roles in the group was changed in 1996 to reflect problems arising from sexual actions rather than descriptions of gender roles. (There was a version of the CERT — Psych used between 1992 and 1996 which omitted the question entirely.) Unless there is a specific concern with interpersonal expressions of sexuality, the scoring of all three versions is compatible.

DESCRIPTION OF THE SCALE

Because there are many scales used in Recreational Therapy and many different behaviors on these scales, the rational and clinical implications for each of the 25 behaviors selected is given.

GENERAL CATEGORY

The behaviors for the General category are not all specifically relevant to recreational therapy. They are behaviors that provide the therapist with an indication of the client's general lifestyle.

ATTENDANCE: Attendance reflects the client's attitude toward norms and/or how well s/he is able to follow these norms. It also gives some indications as to how a client handles responsibility.

APPEARANCE: Appearance tells how the client is caring for himself/herself. If s/he is very meticulous, his/her lifestyle may also be this way and may be creating problems for him/her. A very sloppy appearance may indicate a 'don't care' attitude, giving up, depression or rebellion. For ratings 2 and 3, the pertinent behavior must be underlined.

ATTITUDE TOWARD RECREATIONAL THERAPY: Attitude toward recreational therapy gives an indication as to the client's adaptability and to whether certain situations may be difficult for his/her coping skills. It might be that the client dislikes recreational therapy because it threatens him/her or s/he may like it because it is the only place s/he can excel.

POSTURE: Posture reflects body tone and is a type of body language that can give clues about the client's feelings.

INDIVIDUAL AND GROUP PERFORMANCE

Individual and Group Performance have been separated because of the different behaviors that take place in each of the two situations and because some clients can accept a one-to-one situation better, or vice versa. Thus, a comparison of the ratings can indicate the best initial mode of treatment as well as future treatment needs.

INDIVIDUAL PERFORMANCE

RESPONSE TO THERAPIST'S STRUCTURE: One-to-one is a behavior that reflects how a client responds, how receptive the client is to seeking help in a one-to-one relationship and how the client handles authority. It can give clues as to whether a group or an individual approach would be best in therapy.

DECISION MAKING ABILITY: Decision making ability is an important behavior because of the many choices a person encounters. The therapist has to ascertain whether or not the client is capable of making decisions and, if s/he is not, then pursuing the reason for his/her problem. This question looks at the process of deciding. Judgment looks at the quality of the decisions.

JUDGMENT ABILITY: The client's judgment ability is related to decision making. Some patients make decisions well but their judgment is poor, while others have trouble deciding but their judgment is good. This question looks at the quality of the decisions, not the quality of the process. How the client progresses in his/her ability to function in the community is often reflected by his/her judgment ability.

ABILITY TO FORM INDIVIDUAL RELATIONSHIPS: The ability to form individual relationships speaks to our social way of life. The way in which a client is capable of relating and interacting effectively with his/her peers is a major key in therapy. In order to fully evaluate this behavior, the therapist may need to observe the client over a three-day period. The client will usually need some time in the group to adjust to a new situation.

EXPRESSION OF HOSTILITY: Expression of hostility reflects how the client handles anger, and this may be inward of outward, thus indicating the need for an 'a' or 'b' category. The client may withdraw or s/he may direct his/her anger outward and tend to over-express himself/herself. Regardless of his/her pathological style of expression, it will almost directly relate to the client's problem and give definite clues as to style and approach to therapy.

PERFORMANCE IN ORGANIZED ACTIVITIES: Performance in organized activities can indicate whether the client is capable of participating in a carefully organized and structured activity, which gives the therapist a clue to the client's emotional organization. If the client is able to function in only an organized activity but not an unorganized activity, this may reflect on his/her needs and lifestyle in society with regard to his/her dependence or independence. This behavior also reflects his/her ability to function in individual and group relationships that are structured which may, in turn, reflect some problems with authority.

PERFORMANCE IN FREE ACTIVITIES: Performance in free activities is an indicator of the client's ability to be independent and to rely on his/her own resources. Free activities provide him/her the opportunity to structure his/her own time, and they provide a contrasting situation with organized activities. The therapist can explore any differences. The behavior may have to be observed during evening and weekend free choice activities for a complete evaluation. Most formal recreational therapy groups are not free time nor choice activities.

ATTENTION SPAN: Attention span is an indicator of the client's ability to apply himself/herself to a task as well as an indication of his/her awareness of surroundings and his/her ability to maintain interaction with them. Difficulties in this area may indicate conflict, simple boredom, preoccupation, or confusion.

FRUSTRATION TOLERANCE LEVEL: Frustration tolerance level often reflects how well a client is able to tolerate an average situation and what sort of impulse control s/he has. If his/her frustration tolerance is low, the therapist can explore how this affects his/her everyday life.

STRENGTH/ENDURANCE: Strength/Endurance is a behavior that reflects the client's ability to carry through with activities of daily living. The client who is depressed often shows very little strength or endurance. Lack of endurance should be pursued in therapy.

GROUP PERFORMANCE

The Recreational Therapy Department of Marshal I. Pickens Hospital is group-oriented and therapy is viewed as a process which uses activity as a treatment medium. The treatment process is viewed as an action (as contrasted to strictly verbal) group therapy model. Sometimes, the activity is pre-selected for its ability to elicit or approximate certain behaviors. At other times, the therapist selects an activity specifically to deal with behaviors already demonstrated by the group.

MEMORY FOR GROUP ACTIVITIES: Memory for group activities is used to tell how well the client can remember from one day to the next, which may relate to how s/he functions on his/her job or at home. It is an indicator of confusion and tells the therapist how well the individual can remember what has taken place in the group.

RESPONSE TO GROUP STRUCTURE: Response to group structure reflects whether a client can relate to the group and follow group instructions and can be compared to how the client responds in a one-to-one situation. Response to group structure also reflects how the client handles authority.

LEADERSHIP ABILITY IN GROUPS: Leadership ability in groups or lack of it tells the therapist about the client's lifestyle and may indicate a cause for some of his/her problems. If s/he is a leader, what support does s/he need; if s/he is not a leader, does this create problems or conflicts for him/her?

GROUP CONVERSATION: Group conversation behavior identifies self-expression problems and also indicates whether feelings are expressed inwardly or outwardly. This behavior may also show how the client would function with a group of peers and how s/he would be perceived by the group. If problems do arise, the therapist may get some indication of the client's problems in peer groups outside the hospital. The client should be given time to adjust to the group before this behavior can be adequately evaluated.

SEXUAL ROLE IN THE GROUP: Sexual role in the group indicates how well a client fits into society's sexual norms. Appropriate sexual behavior is a major determinant of success in group situations. Problems can arise when the client acts in a sexually ianappropriate way or when the client perceives appropriate behavior as sexually threatening. Indicate if the problem is in the client's actions or perceptions. (When this assessment was originally developed, this question dealt with whether a man was effeminate or a woman was masculine. Since then, many government agencies have made it illegal to discriminate in any way against a person who is bisexual or a person who is homosexual. The question now looks at how the client expresses his/her sexuality as it relates to how well s/he will fit into the rest of society. Sexual orientation is not the issue. Proper expression of sexuality is the key.)

STYLE OF GROUP INTERACTION: Style of group interaction may also be measured on an inward or outward scale and tells how the client interacts in a group which, in turn, tells about his/her lifestyle in group situations. The therapist observes each client's style and attempts to determine if a client's ability or lack of same is causing him/her problems.

HANDLES CONFLICT IN GROUP WHEN INDIRECTLY INVOLVED: How well the client handles conflict s/he is not directly involved in shows the client's understanding of his/her personal boundaries, ability to distinguish between self and others, and assurance in dealing with uncomfortable situations.

HANDLES CONFLICTS IN GROUP WHEN DIRECTLY INVOLVED: How the client handles conflicts in a group in which s/he is directly involved indicates how the client behaves in a situation where s/he must choose some course of action. This behavior can take the form of inward or outward expression and calls for a double scale. The manner in which an individual behaves can give clues to the therapist about the client's insight, ego strength, coping behaviors, and general stability. Also important for the therapist to observe is the degree of the client's reaction and the appropriateness of the reaction to the conflict that was involved. Only rate this in sessions where it occurs.

COMPETITION IN GROUP: Competition in a group is part of our culture and is a behavior that may be directed inward or outward. It also reflects to what degree a person will go to get something s/he wants. The therapist observes how appropriate the client's competitive behavior is for the situation that exists.

ATTITUDE TOWARD GROUP DECISIONS: A client's attitude toward group decisions reflects whether or not s/he is able to follow a decision made by the group as a whole and may relate to how the client functions with his/her family, work group, and community.

RELIABILITY

To determine the reliability between different therapists using the scale, percent agreement between the ratings of two therapists was computed in the following manner. After a one-hour session in recreational therapy, two therapist independently rated the same patient on the 25 behaviors of this scale. A criterion of ratings within one of each other (0-1, 1-2, 3-4) for each behavior was considered acceptable. Percent agreements were calculated by dividing the number of agreements by the number of agreements plus disagreements. Percent agreements between therapist for 38 clients ranged from 67% to 100% and averaged 91%. Percent agreements were also calculated for exact agreement of the ratings between therapists on the same clients and they ranged from 25% to 100% and averaged 51%. A total of five therapists, resulting in 7 different pairings, were involved.

VALIDITY

In the first edition of this book we reported that formal evaluation of the validity of the scale was in progress. The primary focus was to study predictive validity to show that a decrease in total score indicated improvement in the client's condition and readiness for discharge. No results have been reported since the first release of this book in 1990. Given that this is, by far, the most frequently used assessment tool in recreational therapy, the lack of research is surprising.

DISCUSSION

The authors feel that the CERT — Psych/R has much to offer the profession of recreational therapy. It provides clearly defined behaviors that practicing recreational therapists have identified as being particularly relevant to recreational therapy in short-term, acute care psychiatric and rehabilitation settings and in longer term therapy situations. The reliability with which these behaviors can be observed and rated speaks to their clear definitions.

The way the scale is set up also allows it to be used as both an initial assessment and as progress notes. As an initial assessment, the scale provides the therapy team with information on 25 different behaviors. After the treatment program has been written, the scale then indicates the client's progress or lack of it. This allows program evaluation as well as client assessment and the information provided can be reviewed in a very short time. In addition, use of the scale as progress notes saves the therapist a great deal of writing time and allows him/her more time to make notes on the more significant behaviors that occur. Using the scale this way also gives the therapist more time for active treatment. It should be noted that the scale in no way takes the place of treatment notes.

Another use of the scale is related to the organization of the treatment program in many facilities. When all of the departments — nursing, recreational therapy, social work, psychology, and occupational therapy — contribute equally in team meetings where the client's treatment milieu is planned and assessed, the CERT — Psych/R allows recreational therapists to clearly communicate with the other departments and to relate client's progress.

Another use for the scale is related to a problem faced by recreational therapy. Third party payers do not routinely cover recreational therapy as a treatment process, even when it is directly ordered by the physician. However, the services of RT are often covered as part of the 'milieu therapy' provided in a psychiatric setting. In the past Blue Cross - Blue Shield has denied several claims because milieu therapy was included in the treatment regime and milieu therapy was specifically not covered by the particular Blue Cross policy (McDonald, 1975). In the debate over coverage of milieu therapy, Dr. Robert Laur, vice-president of the Blue Cross Association and the National Association of Blue Shield Plans, testified before the House Subcommittee on Retirement, Insurance, and Health Benefits that one of the requirements mental health coverages should meet is that, 'The service to be covered must be capable of definition, so that subscribers, providers, and carriers will have a reasonable understanding of what will be paid for.' (1974). Thus, in order to be covered directly by third party payment or as a part of milieu therapy, the recreational therapist must be able to define recreational therapy and show what is done, how it is done, and why it is done — to anyone concerned. The CERT — Psych is a means for helping recreational therapists achieve these goals.

SUMMARY

The CERT — Psych/R has been developed for use in a short-term, acute care psychiatric setting and consists of 25 behaviors that are particularly relevant to recreational therapy. The scale can be used both as an initial evaluation and as progress notes. The behaviors have been carefully defined and the agreement between therapist's ratings has been high. The CERT — Psych/R is a valuable instrument to be used by recreational therapy as the profession faces the current demands for accountability and definition of services.

CERT — Psych/R

Comprehensive Evaluation in Recreational Therapy — Psych/Behavioral, Revised

Name: ______________________ Unit: ____________

Date of Birth: ______________________ Admit: ____________

I. General

Date: / / / / / / / / / /

A. Attendance
- (0) Attends
- (1) Attended, but late or left early
- (2) Absent occasionally without cause
- (3) Rarely attends
- (4) Refuses or never attends

(0) ☐ ☐ ☐ ☐ ☐ ☐ ☐ ☐ ☐ ☐
(1) ☐ ☐ ☐ ☐ ☐ ☐ ☐ ☐ ☐ ☐
(2) ☐ ☐ ☐ ☐ ☐ ☐ ☐ ☐ ☐ ☐
(3) ☐ ☐ ☐ ☐ ☐ ☐ ☐ ☐ ☐ ☐
(4) ☐ ☐ ☐ ☐ ☐ ☐ ☐ ☐ ☐ ☐

B. Appearance (for ratings of 2 or 3 underline the behavior being rated)
- (0) Appropriate
- (1) Disarranged clothing
- (2) Suggestive dress *or* any wrinkled and soiled clothing
- (3) Very meticulous *or* very wrinkled and soiled clothing
- (4) Very wrinkled & soiled clothing & poor hygiene

(0) ☐ ☐ ☐ ☐ ☐ ☐ ☐ ☐ ☐ ☐
(1) ☐ ☐ ☐ ☐ ☐ ☐ ☐ ☐ ☐ ☐
(2) ☐ ☐ ☐ ☐ ☐ ☐ ☐ ☐ ☐ ☐
(3) ☐ ☐ ☐ ☐ ☐ ☐ ☐ ☐ ☐ ☐
(4) ☐ ☐ ☐ ☐ ☐ ☐ ☐ ☐ ☐ ☐

C. Attitude Toward Recreational Therapy
- (0) Enthusiastic
- (1) Interested
- (2) Indifferent
- (3) Intense dislike
- (4) Hostile

(0) ☐ ☐ ☐ ☐ ☐ ☐ ☐ ☐ ☐ ☐
(1) ☐ ☐ ☐ ☐ ☐ ☐ ☐ ☐ ☐ ☐
(2) ☐ ☐ ☐ ☐ ☐ ☐ ☐ ☐ ☐ ☐
(3) ☐ ☐ ☐ ☐ ☐ ☐ ☐ ☐ ☐ ☐
(4) ☐ ☐ ☐ ☐ ☐ ☐ ☐ ☐ ☐ ☐

D. Coordination
- (0) Well coordinated gait
- (1) Shuffling gait
- (2) Stiff, awkward gait
- (3) Spastic, draws attention
- (4) Unable to walk

(0) ☐ ☐ ☐ ☐ ☐ ☐ ☐ ☐ ☐ ☐
(1) ☐ ☐ ☐ ☐ ☐ ☐ ☐ ☐ ☐ ☐
(2) ☐ ☐ ☐ ☐ ☐ ☐ ☐ ☐ ☐ ☐
(3) ☐ ☐ ☐ ☐ ☐ ☐ ☐ ☐ ☐ ☐
(4) ☐ ☐ ☐ ☐ ☐ ☐ ☐ ☐ ☐ ☐

E. Posture
- (0) Erect
- (1) Round Shouldered
- (2) Slouched
- (3) Sagging
- (4) Limp, unable to participate

(0) ☐ ☐ ☐ ☐ ☐ ☐ ☐ ☐ ☐ ☐
(1) ☐ ☐ ☐ ☐ ☐ ☐ ☐ ☐ ☐ ☐
(2) ☐ ☐ ☐ ☐ ☐ ☐ ☐ ☐ ☐ ☐
(3) ☐ ☐ ☐ ☐ ☐ ☐ ☐ ☐ ☐ ☐
(4) ☐ ☐ ☐ ☐ ☐ ☐ ☐ ☐ ☐ ☐

Sub Total __ __ __ __ __ __ __ __ __ __

II. Individual Performance

Date: / / / / / / / / / /

A. Response to Therapist's Structure: One-to-One
- (0) Accepts well
- (1) Accepts with question
- (2) Occasionally accepts
- (3) Rarely accepts
- (4) Rejects

(0) ☐ ☐ ☐ ☐ ☐ ☐ ☐ ☐ ☐ ☐
(1) ☐ ☐ ☐ ☐ ☐ ☐ ☐ ☐ ☐ ☐
(2) ☐ ☐ ☐ ☐ ☐ ☐ ☐ ☐ ☐ ☐
(3) ☐ ☐ ☐ ☐ ☐ ☐ ☐ ☐ ☐ ☐
(4) ☐ ☐ ☐ ☐ ☐ ☐ ☐ ☐ ☐ ☐

B. Decision Making Ability
- (0) Independent
- (1) Needs support
- (2) Indifferent
- (3) Indecisive
- (4) Totally dependent

(0) ☐ ☐ ☐ ☐ ☐ ☐ ☐ ☐ ☐ ☐
(1) ☐ ☐ ☐ ☐ ☐ ☐ ☐ ☐ ☐ ☐
(2) ☐ ☐ ☐ ☐ ☐ ☐ ☐ ☐ ☐ ☐
(3) ☐ ☐ ☐ ☐ ☐ ☐ ☐ ☐ ☐ ☐
(4) ☐ ☐ ☐ ☐ ☐ ☐ ☐ ☐ ☐ ☐

CERT — Psych/R

Name ______________________

II. Individual Performance (continued)

Date: / / / / / / / / / /

C. Judgment Ability

- (0) Good Ability
- (1) Needs occasional advice
- (2) Needs constant advice
- (3) Irresponsible
- (4) No ability

D. Ability to Form Individual Relationships (Evaluate after three days)

- (0) Relates readily
- (1) Hesitant
- (2) Superficial
- (3) Distant
- (4) Rejecting

E. Expression of Hostility (a or b)

a.
- (0) Appropriate
- (1) Verbally aggressive (curses, slanders, etc.)
- (2) Belligerent (sulks, refuses)
- (3) Physically destructive
- (4) Physically combative

b.
- (0) Appropriate
- (1) Withdraws
- (2) Verbally negates self
- (3) Verbally abuses self
- (4) Suicidal

F. Performance in Organized Activities

- (0) Grasps situation
- (1) Needs minimal instructions
- (2) Needs frequent instructions
- (3) Needs constant instructions to participate
- (4) Unable to participate

G. Performance in Free Activities (Evaluate from evening and weekend activities)

- (0) Acts on own initiative
- (1) Participates after activity starts
- (2) Participates after encouragement
- (3) Starts & Stops: frequent encouragement required
- (4) No interest and/or refuses

H. Attention Span

- (0) Attends to activity
- (1) Occasionally does not attend (preoccupied)
- (2) Frequently does not attend (distracted)
- (3) Rarely attends to activity
- (4) Does not attend (detached)

I. Frustration Tolerance Level

- (0) Participates without appearing frustrated
- (1) Occasionally becomes frustrated
- (2) Often becomes frustrated
- (3) Appears frustrated most of the time
- (4) So frustrated unable to participate

J. Strength/Endurance

- (0) Good tone
- (1) Able to participate in 3/4 of any activity
- (2) Tires if activity requires being on feet
- (3) Tires even in seated activities
- (4) Unable to participate

Sub Total ___ ___ ___ ___ ___ ___ ___ ___ ___ ___

CERT — Psych/R

Name ____________

III. Group Performance

Date: / / / / / / / / / /

A. Memory for Group Activities
- (0) Good recall
- (1) Remembers most activities
- (2) Remembers few activities (selective)
- (3) Confused, seldom remembers activities
- (4) No recall

B. Response to Group Structure
- (0) Accepts well
- (1) Accepts with questions
- (2) Rarely accepts
- (3) Rejects structure
- (4) Rejects structure & becomes hostile

C. Leadership Ability in Groups
- (0) Can be a leader
- (1) A leader if encouraged
- (2) Co-leader ability
- (3) Some leadership with constant support
- (4) No ability

D. Group Conversation (a or b) (Evaluate only when situation occurs)

a.
- (0) Converses well with groups
- (1) Converses well but sometimes is too loud
- (2) Overly talkative at times
- (3) Overly talkative during most of activity
- (4) Incessant talking

b.
- (0) Converses well with groups
- (1) Converses only occasionally
- (2) Converses but is guarded
- (3) Attempts to converse but appears to block
- (4) Unable to converse with groups

E. Sexual Role in Group (Indicate if the problem is in actions or perceptions.)
- (0) Meets society's norms
- (1) Inappropriate dress, speech or body language
- (2) Poor understanding of personal space
- (3) Inappropriate physical contact or fear of appropriate contact
- (4) Unable to control sexual impulses or fears

F. Style of Group Interaction (a or b)

a.
- (0) Assertive
- (1) Tries to control
- (2) Argumentive
- (3) Dominant interrupter
- (4) Hostile

b.
- (0) Assertive
- (1) Assertive with support
- (2) Only sits quietly
- (3) Detaches from group, participates
- (4) Withdraws from group and participation

G. Handles Conflict in Group When Indirectly Involved
- (0) Handles well
- (1) Sometimes will not get involved
- (2) Personalizes the conflict
- (3) Rarely gets involved
- (4) Ignores or runs away

CERT — Psych/R

Name ____________________

III. Group Performance (continued)

Date: / / / / / / / / / /

H. Handles Conflict in Group When Directly Involved (a or b)

a. (0) Handles well (0) ☐ ☐ ☐ ☐ ☐ ☐ ☐ ☐ ☐ ☐
(1) Verbally defensive (1) ☐ ☐ ☐ ☐ ☐ ☐ ☐ ☐ ☐ ☐
(2) Verbally aggressive (2) ☐ ☐ ☐ ☐ ☐ ☐ ☐ ☐ ☐ ☐
(3) Becomes physically agitated (3) ☐ ☐ ☐ ☐ ☐ ☐ ☐ ☐ ☐ ☐
(4) Becomes physically abusive (4) ☐ ☐ ☐ ☐ ☐ ☐ ☐ ☐ ☐ ☐

b. (0) Handles well (0) ☐ ☐ ☐ ☐ ☐ ☐ ☐ ☐ ☐ ☐
(1) Apologetic (1) ☐ ☐ ☐ ☐ ☐ ☐ ☐ ☐ ☐ ☐
(2) Self-depreciating (2) ☐ ☐ ☐ ☐ ☐ ☐ ☐ ☐ ☐ ☐
(3) Withdraws, but continues in activity (3) ☐ ☐ ☐ ☐ ☐ ☐ ☐ ☐ ☐ ☐
(4) Withdraws from activity (4) ☐ ☐ ☐ ☐ ☐ ☐ ☐ ☐ ☐ ☐

I. Competition in Group (a or b)

a. (0) Sufficient (0) ☐ ☐ ☐ ☐ ☐ ☐ ☐ ☐ ☐ ☐
(1) Occasionally is aggressive (1) ☐ ☐ ☐ ☐ ☐ ☐ ☐ ☐ ☐ ☐
(2) Often over-competitive (2) ☐ ☐ ☐ ☐ ☐ ☐ ☐ ☐ ☐ ☐
(3) Must always win (3) ☐ ☐ ☐ ☐ ☐ ☐ ☐ ☐ ☐ ☐
(4) Lies or breaks rules to win (4) ☐ ☐ ☐ ☐ ☐ ☐ ☐ ☐ ☐ ☐

b. (0) Sufficient (0) ☐ ☐ ☐ ☐ ☐ ☐ ☐ ☐ ☐ ☐
(1) Tries, but occasionally gives up (1) ☐ ☐ ☐ ☐ ☐ ☐ ☐ ☐ ☐ ☐
(2) Tries, but often gives up (2) ☐ ☐ ☐ ☐ ☐ ☐ ☐ ☐ ☐ ☐
(3) Doesn't try to win (3) ☐ ☐ ☐ ☐ ☐ ☐ ☐ ☐ ☐ ☐
(4) Doesn't care/refuses to participate (4) ☐ ☐ ☐ ☐ ☐ ☐ ☐ ☐ ☐ ☐

J. Attitude Toward Group Decisions

(0) Follows group decisions (0) ☐ ☐ ☐ ☐ ☐ ☐ ☐ ☐ ☐ ☐
(1) Accepts most of time (1) ☐ ☐ ☐ ☐ ☐ ☐ ☐ ☐ ☐ ☐
(2) Hesitant (2) ☐ ☐ ☐ ☐ ☐ ☐ ☐ ☐ ☐ ☐
(3) Resists (3) ☐ ☐ ☐ ☐ ☐ ☐ ☐ ☐ ☐ ☐
(4) Rejects (4) ☐ ☐ ☐ ☐ ☐ ☐ ☐ ☐ ☐ ☐

Sub Total __ __ __ __ __ __ __ __ __ __

Scoring

Suggested Scoring Range

	Outstanding	Good	Functional	Problematic
General	0-1	2-3	4-5	6-20
Individual	0-1	2-5	6-10	11-40
Group	0-1	2-5	6-10	11-40

Date	/	/	/	/	/	/	/	/	/	/
General										
Individual										
Group										
Overall										
Staff										

Summary/Recommendations

Date ____________________ Signature ____________________

FUNCTIONAL ASSESSMENT OF CHARACTERISTICS FOR THERAPEUTIC RECREATION, REVISED

Name: Functional Assessment of Characteristics for Therapeutic Recreation, Revised.

Also Known As: FACTR-R. The previous version was known as the FACTR.

Authors: The authors for the assessment are Peterson, Dunn, and Carruthers (1983). The primary author for the assessment manual is joan burlingame.

Time Needed to Administer: It should take the therapist less than 20 minutes to administer and score after observing the client in multiple group activities and reviewing the client's chart.

Time Needed to Score: Administration and scoring are done at the same time.

Recommended Disability Groups: All groups with developmental levels over 10 years.

Purpose of the Assessment: The purpose of the FACTR-R is to determine client's needs related to his/her basic functional skills and behaviors.

What Does the Assessment Measure?: The FACTR-R measures eleven areas in each of three domains: Physical, Cognitive, and Social/Emotional.

Supplies Needed: The FACTR Manual and score sheet #113.

Reliability/Validity: Some reliability studies reported, no validity reported.

Degree of Skill Required to Administer: A recreational therapist certified at the CTRS level by the National Council for Therapeutic Recreation Certification has the skills to administer, score, and interpret the FACTR-R.

Comments: The FACTR-R is used to help identify: 1) if a client qualifies for recreational therapy services and 2) the domain most likely to improve with recreational therapy services.

Question 2.11 'Purposeful Interaction with the Environment' and Question 3.11 'Decision Making Ability' were switched in the revised version of the FACTR-R to place the items in the domains they are more generally considered to be a part of.

Suggested Levels: Rancho Los Amigos Level: 3 and above. Developmental Level: 10 years and above. Reality Orientation: Severe and above.

Distributor: Idyll Arbor, Inc., 25119 S.E. 262 Street, PO Box 720, Ravensdale, WA 90851 (206) 432-3231. (Area code 425 after April 1997.)

FACTR-R

Functional Assessment of Characteristics for Therapeutic Recreation, Revised

Purpose: The purpose of the Functional Assessment of Characteristics for Therapeutic Recreation, Revised (FACTR-R) is to determine client needs relative to his/her basic functional skills and behaviors. The FACTR-R may be used as an initial screening tool for most populations. Further testing is usually indicated for all clients except those on a short term stay.

Time Needed to Administer the FACTR-R: The FACTR-R is a screening tool administered after observing the client in multiple group activities and reviewing the client's chart. Under these conditions, it should take less than 20 minutes to administer and score.

Background Information: Functional behaviors and abilities selected for inclusion in the screening are those behaviors that are determined to be prerequisite or generally required within leisure participation. Low scores on the three categories of functional skills indicate that clinical program intervention is needed or desirable.

Three areas of functional ability have been selected for the initial screening. These areas are *physical, cognitive, and social/ emotional*. These will be described and elaborated on below. These three categories represent basic and commonly identified domains of ability, skills, and behavior which cut across all illnesses and disabilities. The intent is to identify functional limitations that may interfere with, or make difficult, the self-directed leisure involvement of clients. Thus, these three behavioral categories become target areas for treatment and clinical services since leisure participation is dependent on certain identifiable functional behaviors.

1. Physical: Eleven areas of physical functioning are used in the screening process. With the exception of the first four (vision, hearing, ambulation, and bowel and bladder), all other items indicate areas of physical functioning that can be improved (treated) through clinical leisure services. *In the initial screening process, judgments will need to be made regarding whether a given physical behavioral area can be improved and if it is problematic enough to warrant program intervention.*

2. Cognitive: Eleven areas of cognitive functioning are used in the screening. All eleven areas are areas that can be impacted by clinical leisure programming. All eleven are viewed as functional areas with relevance for leisure involvement, thus, they are critical areas for possible program intervention. Again, judgments will need to be made regarding the significance of behavioral ability for the individual client in question.

3. Social/Emotional: Eleven items comprise this section. These eleven areas address functional abilities in social interaction and emotional expression. They are dealt with in one major combined category since so much of emotional behavior is addressed in a general way as opposed to a pathological or diagnostic manner. All eleven areas can be impacted by clinical leisure services. Judgment regarding the importance of the given item must be made for each individual client.

The FACTR was developed in 1983 by Peterson, Dunn, and Carruthers. Idyll Arbor, Inc. reformatted the assessment and made it available to therapists in 1988. This current version of the documentation for the FACTR was developed by the Idyll Arbor, Inc. staff in 1990. In 1996 two questions were exchanged to place them in domains more generally recognized as appropriate. Question 2.11 'Purposeful Interaction with the Environment' was moved into the Social/Emotional domain. Question 3.11 'Decision Making Ability' was moved into the cognitive domain. (The numbers were changed, too.) The original version of the FACTR and the revised version, FACTR-R, cannot be compared if the need for therapeutic recreation services was noted in either of these areas.

Administration and Scoring:

The screening for areas of need is conducted through *observation* of the client and *review of the medical record*. If the therapist administering the screening is familiar with the client, the evaluation should be relatively easy to make and take very little time.

Scoring, analysis, and interpretation are an important part of the FACTR-R. ***There are no absolutes relative to leisure functioning*** and thus no definite way to determine if a given functional behavior will create problems in future independent leisure involvement. The items of the instrument do, however, identify significant functional behaviors that are related to leisure participation. Thus, a low score in any of the three categories or in all three components, can be interpreted as a logical indication of need for clinical program intervention. Equally important to the category score is the analysis of individual items in each category. Program referral should be made based on prioritized functional need assessment of specific items. The category score will only identify if one or more categories are extremely low or high. The specific items, however, will indicate what behaviors or skills need improvement.

Scoring Procedure: Each item has a list of descriptive statements. The therapist who is conducting the screening should mark an 'X' on the line in front of the one descriptive statement that best describes the client's functional behavior related to that item.

The therapist administering the assessment should refer to the detailed definition of each description (see below) to help him/ her make the *best* choice based on a common definition. By using the definitions supplied with this assessment, the inter-rater reliability of this assessment should be very high. In trials run by Idyll Arbor, Inc. staff in 1988 and 1989 the inter-rater reliability without using the definitions was poor.

The next step is for the therapist to determine if this is a behavior that can be improved through recreational therapy services and if that behavior is problematic enough to warrant program intervention. If the answer to both of these questions is 'yes', then an 'X' is placed in the corresponding square to the right of the item.

There are three categories of the FACTR-R: Physical, cognitive, and social/emotional. After the evaluations are made in all three components, scores are tabulated. For each component, total the number of 'no' responses from the columns with the square. The three different components are clearly marked. Place the totals at the top of page 1 in the upper right hand corner. The 'no' response indicates functional ability. High scores indicate functional ability and adequacy. Low scores indicate greater problems in functional areas. Thus, the lower the score, the greater the need for clinical program intervention.

Indications for Further Testing:

After administering and scoring the FACTR-R, the therapist may determine that further testing is needed to better define the specific functional skills in need of intervention in the domain of greatest need.

Additional assessment to determine the client's leisure preferences and patterns of participation should also be completed.

FILLING OUT THE CLIENT INFORMATION SECTION

Name: Include the client's full name and any appropriate 'nicknames'.

Staff: Print the name of the staff person administering the assessment. The staff person should also include the appropriate credential abbreviation after his/her name (e.g., CTRS). After the appropriate credential abbreviation, the staff person should place his/her initials to indicate that they were truly the one to administer the assessment.

Unit: Indicate the unit and the current room number (e.g., Rehab 103W or Chartely House, #05).

Birthday: Indicate the client's date of birth.

Date: Indicate the date that the assessment is given. On clients whose ability fluctuates noticeably throughout the day, also include the starting time of the assessment using military time (a 24 hour clock).

Admit: Write in the current admission date. If the client was first admitted to ICU (intensive care unit) then transferred to rehab. three weeks later, indicate both dates (e.g., ICU 9/12/89: Rehab. 10/3/89).

Physical/Cognitive/Social Emotional: These three sections are to be completed only after the assessment has been fully administered. This is the section in which the therapist indicates the client's scores.

FILLING OUT 1.0 THE PHYSICAL DOMAIN SECTION

Note: Questions #1.1 - 1.4 may not be amenable to improvement through recreational therapy. However, knowledge of them is necessary for programming.

1.1 Sight/Vision: Check the appropriate statement. 'Correctable' means that the client has good enough vision to function on a day-to-day basis with the aid of glasses. Just because a client has glasses does not mean that s/he uses them. If the client's vision is correctable and s/he usually chooses not to wear his/her glasses, note that in the space just to the right of the question.

1.2 Hearing: Check the appropriate statement. 'Correctable' means that the client has good enough hearing to function on a day-to-day basis with the help of a hearing aid. Just because a client has a hearing aid does not mean that s/he usually wears his/her hearing aid. If the client's hearing is correctable and s/he usually chooses not to wear his/her hearing aid, note that in the space just to the right of the question.

1.3 Ambulation:
a. Normal: No difficulty in higher order ambulatory skills (e.g., negotiates stairs, runs and/or jumps, hops in place on each foot). Has adequate endurance to walk for 10 minutes around facility without the need for a rest.
b. Ambulates with Difficulty (no aids): demonstrates an inability to meet all of the criteria listed under normal *and* does not use any aids.
c. Ambulates with Aids: (circle one or more of: crutches, cane, walker. If aid is not listed (e.g., leg braces) write that information in to the right of the question.) If this choice is selected, note to the right of the question the degree of impairment in ambulation when the client is using the aid (e.g., 'the client climbed a 14,000 foot mountain with her leg braces, no noticeable limitation').
d. Wheelchair (difficulty in use) client uses a w/c for locomotion. If the client does not have significant difficulty using his/her w/c, note that to the right of the question (e.g., 'w/c athlete: very skilled in use of w/c').
e. Wheelchair (unable to use independently) Client is placed in w/c to aid in locomotion. Client is 100% dependent on others to move self through space.
f. No ambulation (bedridden) There is an extremely large variation of movement in clients who are 'bedridden'. To the right of the question indicate the amount of independent movement the client is able to demonstrate (e.g., traction due to spinal fx and Rt femur fx — little to no movement of trunk and legs possible).
Note: If client uses a gurney or a banana cart as a means to move around, check the appropriate selection under w/c — then indicate the vehicle of locomotion to the right of the question.

1.4 Bowel and Bladder:

a. Normal Bowel and Bladder: Client demonstrates the ability to be continent day and night; able to anticipate needs to toilet and does not exhibit a great sudden urgency to void to avoid incontinence.

b. Occasional Incontinence Problems: Client is incontinent less than 1x week; staff and client cannot anticipate timing or activity associated with incontinence (e.g., coughing which leads to incontinence).

c. Incontinent: Client has a high probability of being incontinent during at least one leisure activity over a 7 day period of time. Indicate frequency of incontinence and whether the incontinence is just nocturnal in nature to the right of the question.

d. Uses Adaptive Devices: If the client uses appliances check here **and** indicate both the type(s) of appliance and the client's independence in changing the appliances to the right of the question. *Also* check one of the other 3 choices under Bowel and Bladder to indicate how successful the appliance is in aiding the client to be fully continent.

Note: If the client is at risk for autonomic dysreflexia, note that to the right of the question and circle it in red to flag the concern.

1.5 Upper Extremity Manipulation:

a. Normal: Client is able to manipulate 1/8" objects with ease with both hands; uses a pincer grasp appropriately, has no difficulty in movement and demonstrates full (or almost full) range in upper extremities.

b. Stiffness: Client is not able to fully range joints; tone of muscles in upper extremity less than normal range.

c. Weakness: Client requires at least one rest period for even light upper extremity activity lasting less than 10 minutes. Upper extremity does not have the muscle strength to complete normal activity (e.g., twisting top off of a jar or pushing w/c along hallway).

d. Uses Adaptive Devices: If the client uses adaptive devices check here **and** indicate both the type(s) of devices and the client's degree of skill for upper extremity manipulation while using the devices.

1.6 General Coordination:

a. Normal: The client demonstrates full functional use and control of neck, trunk, and extremities. No difficulty with balance and agility; no difficulty integrating actions of both arms and of both legs. Independently sequences most movements/ actions logically and with relative grace.

b. Minor Coordination Problems: The client demonstrates some limitation in use and control of neck, trunk, and extremities. Demonstrates ability to maintain balance while standing or sitting but has difficulty integrating balance while sequencing complex tasks (e.g.; walking over uneven terrain). Has difficulty sequencing motor tasks logically and gracefully.

c. Major Coordination Problems: Demonstrates limitations in the use and control of neck, trunk, and extremities which cause a significant inability to carry out normal leisure tasks. Ambulation is significantly limited or impossible due to the inability to coordinate movement.

1.7 Hand-Eye Coordination:

a. Normal: The client can select one of many small objects (1/8") in a group and pick up desired object. Is able to connect numbered dots on a piece of paper in an error free manner. Demonstrates no problems when reaching for objects in a difficult figure-ground situation. Does not over or under reach. Demonstrates appropriate pressure of grasp on objects held (e.g., not too tight, not too loose).

b. Minor Hand-Eye Coordination: Client has enough impairment in this area to be considered below 'normal' but is not impaired enough to exclude him/her from most normal leisure activities.

c. Major Hand-Eye Coordination: Client has enough impairment in this area to be significantly limited in his/her participation in normal leisure activities.

1.8 Strength:

a. Normal: Endurance and strength adequate to complete tasks attempted. Requires little to no rest period after a heavy muscular activity.

b. Minor Weakness: Requires rest periods during activities that require moderate strength and endurance. Strength is almost adequate to allow normal participation in leisure activities.

c. Major Weakness: Client tires almost immediately upon attempting to utilize muscles groups. Requires frequent rest periods. Normal leisure participation is not attainable due to lack of strength.

1.9 Cardiovascular Functioning:

a. Excellent: Client's heart beat and respiratory rate do not show significant increase after 10 minutes of moderate physical activity. Recovery takes place in less than 5 minutes.

b. Normal: Client's heart beat and respiratory rate show large increase during a 10 minute period of moderate physical activity. Recovery takes place in less than 10 minutes but more than 5 minutes.

c. Poor: Client's heart beat and respiratory rate are limited to the point of the client not being able to participate in moderate physical exercise for 10 minutes; recovery takes greater than 10 minutes.

1.10 Weight:

Note: Some facilities use 'Ideal Body Weight' (IBW) and some use 'Normal Body Weight' (NBW). Check the appropriate selection as indicated by the dietitian *and* to the right of the question indicate whether the IBW or the NBW was used.

1.11 Balance:

a. Normal: No difficulty with static and dynamic balance and agility; no devices used.

b. Minor Balance Difficulties: Static and dynamic balance and agility functional under normal, non-stress situations; some difficulty with uneven terrains, sudden movements, and in over-stimulating environments.

c. Major Balance Difficulties: Static and dynamic balance impaired enough to significantly limit client's participation in normal leisure activities.

FILLING OUT 2.0 THE COGNITIVE DOMAIN

2.1 Orientation:
a. Normal: Client is oriented to person, place, and time. If a reality orientation assessment is given, client falls within the category of 'mild to no impairment'.
b. Confused and Disoriented Occasionally: Client demonstrates disorientation once or twice a day for short periods of time (e.g.; right after waking up; or when placed in an unfamiliar situation). Client is still able to function in society with a relative degree of personal safety even when disoriented.
c. Confused and Disoriented Most of the Time: Client lacks the ability to demonstrate orientation to person, place, and time 2 out of 3 trials which are given over an 8 hour period of time. The therapist has significant doubt about the client's ability to function in society with a relative degree of personal safety.
d. Confused and Disoriented All of the Time: Client is consistently disoriented to 2 out of 3 (person, place, time) more than 90% of the time.
Note: Obviously if a client has been scored as being confused and disoriented most or all of the time, s/he will score poorly on the rest of this section. A formal, standardized reality orientation assessment should be given to any client who has scored poorly in this area in addition to scoring questions 2.2 - 2.11 on the FACTR-R. Often the medications a client is being given decrease his/her scores in this area. The therapist's close measurement in this area can help the physician and the rest of the team to determine if a change in medications is indicated.

2.2 Oral Expressive Language:
a. Very Articulate: No expressive verbal language deficits. Converses well with groups on a variety of topics.
b. Average Articulation: A few expressive verbal language deficits; has some difficulty conversing well with groups.
c. Poor Articulation: Noted difficulty with pronunciation, obvious problems with word finding skills, tends to use jargon, perseveration possible, possible motor planning problems or general slowness.
d. No Oral Expressive Language: Does not demonstrate the ability to produce intelligible language.

Manual Communication:
Suggested modification of this section of the assessment: Do not limit the response to manual communication (e.g.; sign language) if the client utilizes some other means of augmented communication. Use the criteria listed below to determine the degree of skill demonstrated by the client. To the right of the descriptors indicate the type of augmented communication used by the client.
a. Excellent: No noted slowness, few if any errors in processing and output of augmented communication. Communication output flows naturally.
b. Average: General slowness related to motor planning problems, or cognitive processing difficulties.
c. Poor: Severely limited ability to utilize system, major motor planning problems or delayed responses.

2.3 Receptive Language:
a. Can Process and Act on Directions Immediately: Demonstrates working understanding of language. Demonstrates the ability to discern key points; does not get lost in details. Demonstrates the ability to filter out noises and stimuli to concentrate on speaker.
b. Needs Time to Process and Act on Directions: Demonstrates ability to understand language, however a noted delay is evident in the client's ability to hear and then respond. At times has difficulty with language comprehension leading to inaccurate responses or to getting lost in detail.
c. Needs Cues, Prompts, or Second Set of Directions: The client has difficulty in organizing and integrating words and concepts when presented, makes weak or bizarre associations.
d. Does Not Process Directions: The client does not demonstrate an awareness of what words mean. Any reaction to spoken word is reaction to tonation of voice, not to the actual words.

2.4 Attending and Concentrating:
a. Concentrates and Focuses Well: No difficulty with attention span; is able to attend to activity with little or no inattention demonstrated for up to 20 minutes. Can stick to a subject that s/he enjoys for over 20 minutes.
b. Concentration and Focus Drifts or is Easily Distracted: Demonstrates inability to attend to a topic (even one that s/he is interested in) for 20 minutes. Requires up to one cue every five minutes. When client is distracted s/he is inattentive for up to 5 seconds, frequently requiring a cue to re-focus. Even with distractibility, client is able to retain knowledge of subject.
c. Major Difficulties Attending and Concentrating: Requires more than one cue every 5 minutes to attend, concentration is broken for periods greater than 5 seconds. Even with cueing is not always able to concentrate on issue at hand.
d. Seems Functionally Unaware of People and Objects in the Environment: Client startles when spoken to or when s/he sees a person *or* client demonstrates little to no recognition of others. Client's attention is taken up by internal stimuli, self-stimulation, and other non-interactive activities.

2.5 Long Term Memory
a. Clear Recall of Past Events: Client is able to recall 80% of events from the past 7 days; is also able to demonstrate a knowledge of his/her personal history (date of birth, length of time in school, mother's maiden name, etc.)
b. Vague or Occasional Recall of Past Events: Client has difficulty remembering personal history; is able to remember person, place and time between 40% - 80% of the time.
c. Unrealistic or Distorted Recall: Client reports incorrect answers over 40% of the time; demonstrates some belief that s/he is giving the correct answer. Recall of time is distorted.
d. No Recall of Past Events: Client is unable to provide information due to cognitive impairment.

2.6 Short Term Memory:
a. Clear Recall of Recent Events: Client demonstrates the ability to retain 70% or more of pertinent information for up to 1 hour. Recall has little to no errors.
b. Vague or Occasional Recall of Recent Events: Client is able to recall between 25% - 70% of pertinent information for up to 1 hour. Noted difficulty in reporting information correctly due to cognitive confusion. Even if information recalled from short term memory is distorted, it is at least related to actual event.
c. No Recall of Recent Events: Client is unable to report back up to 25% of pertinent information and/or information reported has little to nothing to do with actual event.

2.7 Thought Process (logic, problem solving, creativity, abstraction):
a. Excellent: Client is able to process information quickly with little to no distortion. Actions taken demonstrate that multi-step reasoning has taken place, including the anticipation of possible consequences for one's actions. Awareness of more than one solution to most problems. Client demonstrates the ability to predict other's reactions to his/her decisions at least 60% of the time.
b. Average: Client is able to process most information if given adequate time. Because of an incomplete comprehension of the material presented, client may demonstrate a slightly distorted understanding. Many, but not all, actions are thought through for potential consequences. Especially under pressure the client has difficulty developing more than one solution to the problem. Client is, at times, surprised at the reaction of others.
c. Poor: Client has difficulty processing information. Actions taken demonstrate little to no understanding of cause and effect; of multiple step planning; or awareness of the consequences for ones actions. Client reacts to problems instead of taking time to cognitively process solutions.

2.8 Learning:
a. Learns New Material Quickly and Easily: Client grasps ideas with little instruction needed. New information is quickly integrated with already acquired knowledge; the client's knowledge base expands synergistically. Client finds the assimilation of new ideas easy and usually enjoyable.
b. Average Learning Ability: Client is able to understand most concepts with adequate instruction and experience. New information is retained but not automatically integrated with already acquired knowledge; the client's knowledge base continues to expand with each new bit of information but not synergistically. Client demonstrates some inattention and frustration when learning information that challenges his/her capabilities.
c. Slow Learning Ability: Client has difficulty understanding and retaining new concepts, even with skilled instruction using multi-learning methods (e.g., seeing a demonstration and reading or hearing about it).

2.9 Literacy:
a. Good Reading Ability: Client is able to read any book or magazine; able to learn new skills just by reading instructions.
b. Basic Reading Ability: Client is able to read most books and magazines; is able to learn some new skills just by reading instructions.
c. No Functional Reading Ability: Client is either a non-reader or has limited reading ability.
Note: The basic ability to read important signs, activity calendars, and books (letters, etc.) is often taken for granted. Even prior to being admitted into a health care system between 11% to 20% of the people in the United States are non-functional readers. (Based on the studies listed in the World Book Encyclopedia, 1989). In this assessment reading means not only being able to read the words out loud. It also means the ability to remember the basic point of what was read five minutes later. This criterion would mean that many individuals who are moderately to severely impaired on a reality orientation assessment would be rated as 'non-readers'.

2.10 Math Concepts
a. Above Average Mathematical Computation Ability (add, subtract, divide, and multiply): Client is able to add, subtract, multiply, and divide two digit numbers in his/her head quickly with less than a 5% error rate.
b. Average Mathematical Computation Ability: Client can balance a check book, can determine how much an individual item is if its price is 3 for $1.20 without using paper, has only limited difficulty determining 15% of a food bill to leave a tip.
c. Basic Computation (add, subtract): Client is able to add or subtract numbers with two or three digits. Client demonstrates an error rate of 30% or more if computation is executed in his/her head. Client does not demonstrate the ability to determine 15% of a food bill to leave a tip.
d. No Functional Mathematical Computation Ability: Client is not able to manage a check book, even with the use of a calculator. Requires assistance from others to select the correct coin combinations to pay for simple purchases. Client has extreme difficulty to no ability to count up to $20.00 of change using nickles, dimes, quarters, and one dollar bills.

2.11 Decision Making Ability
a. Survey Alternatives and Selects Positive Approach: Client is able to anticipate outcomes to actions prior to taking the action and makes a reasonable choice given that knowledge.
b. Somewhat Ambivalent and Uncertain in Decision Making: Client has noted difficulty in making a choice, seems unsure about course of action to take, not convinced of choice after decision was made.
c. Extremely Ambivalent and Uncertain in Decision Making: Client is significantly impaired in his/her ability to make decisions. Functional ability in the community is at risk due to this limitation.

FILLING OUT 3.0 THE SOCIAL/EMOTIONAL DOMAIN

3.1 Dyad (2 person):
a. Initiates and Maintains Dyad Situations/Conversations: Client interacts freely with another individual of his/her choice. Few if any uncomfortable, awkward moments. Initiates conversations at a socially appropriate rate; maintains conversations to their logical end.
b. Responds to and Maintains Dyad Situation when Initiated by Others: Client interacts freely with another person of his/her choice but actual initiation of conversation is not frequently demonstrated by client. Client will maintain a conversation begun by another to its logical end.
c. Responds Minimally to Dyad Situations: Client demonstrates limited initiation of conversation in dyad situations and does not usually carry out conversations to their logical end.
d. Does Not Respond to Dyad Situations: Client does not initiate, respond to, or maintain conversations with another person.

3.2 Small Group (3 - 8 persons)
a. Initiates and Maintains Small Group Interactions: Client interacts freely with two or more individuals of his/her choice. Few, if any uncomfortable, awkward moments. Initiates and maintains conversations at socially appropriate rate; maintains conversations to their logical end.
b. Responds To and Maintains Small Group Situations When Initiated by Others: Client interacts freely with two or more people of his/her choice but actual initiation of conversation is not frequently demonstrated by client. Client will maintain a conversation begun by another to its logical end.
c. Responds Minimally in Small Group Interactions: Client demonstrates very limited initiation of conversation in small group situations and does not usually carry out conversations to their logical end. Does not contribute new content or questions to conversation.
d. Does Not Respond in Small Group Situations: Client does not initiate, respond to, or maintain conversations with individuals while in a group situation.

3.3 Social Interest
a. Seeks Social Contacts/Situations: The client demonstrates an interest in others, demonstrates enjoyment in the close proximity of other people.
b. Doesn't Initiate, But Doesn't Avoid Social Contacts/Situations: Client initiates less than 20% of his/her social contacts; few, if any, avoidance techniques are exhibited by client to avoid others.
c. Avoids Social Contacts/Situations: The client demonstrates a variety of maneuvers to avoid having to interact with other people. Demonstrates the desire to end conversations before their logical end.
d. Excessive Need for Social Contact: Client over-initiates interactions with others. Demonstrates a lack of understanding of body language which indicates another person's desire to be left alone. Tries to carry conversations beyond their logical end.

3.4 General Participation:
a. Self-Initiation: Client independently initiates activity without cueing from staff. Actively participates, responsive, eye contact, alert, enthusiastic, willingly participates, engrossed in activity.
b. Voluntarily Complies with Activities Initiated by Others: Initiates activity after being cued by staff. Participates with encouragement, wants staff assistance but does not necessarily require it, needs cues to willingly participate, needs staff encouragement.
c. Responds to Direct Commands or Instructions: Requires staff cueing and assistance to participate in activity, does not indicate desire to participate and/or initiate activity.
d. Does Not Engage in Cooperative Behavior: Client declines, does not participate, resistive, non-cooperative, refuses to stay in area, demonstrates inappropriate behaviors, interferes with the activity, disruptive.

3.5 Cooperation (compliments, shares voluntarily, comments of emotional support, etc.)
a. Understands and Engages in Cooperative Behavior: Client demonstrates the ability to get along with others; to be flexible; to share and go along with another person's wish.
b. Cooperation with Prompting and Reinforcement: Client demonstrates the ability to be cooperative, but seldom initiates that behavior.
c. Does Not Engage in Cooperative Behavior: Client is unable to, or unwilling to, cooperate with others.

3.6 Competition:
a. Understands and Engages in Competitive Behavior Appropriately: Client demonstrates enough competitive behavior to fit into the social group. Is competitive for the fun of it, not to 'get others'.
b. Overly Aggressive in Competitive Behavior: Tries to win to the point of physically or emotionally hurting others in the group. Client appears to be almost 'driven' to win.
c. Overly Passive in Competitive Behavior: Client is unable to, or chooses not to, engage in competitive behavior with others in the group. Client is frequently at a disadvantage because of the lack of competitive behavior.

3.7 Conflict/Argument:
a. Appropriate Communication and Behavior in an Argument/Conflict Situation: Client maintains emotional and physical control and verbally responds appropriately.
b. Loses Emotional and/or Physical Control in Argument/Conflict Situations: Client has noted difficulty in maintaining emotional and/or physical control during heated arguments. Client talks in a raised or threatening voice.
c. Passively Submits in Argument/Conflict Situations: Client does not take actions to defend self when threatening situations arise.

3.8 Emotional Expression
a. Appropriate Emotional Response to Situations: Client demonstrates logical emotional responses to situations, degree of control exhibited is culturally appropriate.
b. Excessive Emotional Response: Client demonstrates an over-reaction to a situation; the reaction is beyond logical and cultural norms.
c. Withholds Emotional Response: Client demonstrates less emotional response than the situation normally would dictate; response is understated given cultural background.
d. Inappropriate Emotional Expression: Unlike a client who demonstrates either an excessive or an understated response, the client demonstrates an illogical response (e.g., laughs at his/her own pain).

3.9 Authority/Leadership
a. Responds Appropriately to Authority: Client responds in a culturally appropriate manner when presented with a request from someone with authority.
b. Defies or Actively Resists Authority: Client demonstrates behavior contrary to what is expected of him/her. This defiance is an active, knowledgeable choice on the part of the client.
c. Overly Passive With Authority: Client does not stand up for his/her rights; goes along with leader or group suggestions even if s/he does not feel good about doing so. This is an active, knowledgeable choice on the part of the client.
Note: If the client is not cognitively able to respond to authority in a purposeful manner, write N/A to the left of the choices and then make a note to the right of the question.

3.10 Frustration
a. High Tolerance for Frustration: Client participates without appearing frustrated; at times may appear discourage but completes activity.
b. Average Frustration Tolerance: Client will generally stick to an activity for up to 20 minutes before giving up. Client does not demonstrate significant frustration behaviors which disrupt those around him/her.
c. Frequent Frustration Behavior: Client becomes easily frustrated and as a result, is functionally unable to complete an activity. At times the client will be too frustrated to respond or to participate.

3.11 Purposeful Interaction with Environment:
a. Interacts Purposefully with Other Persons and Objects: Client initiates and maintains social interactions; demonstrates a cooperative nature with others in the environment a majority of the time. Demonstrates an interest and awareness of objects in the environment.
b. Intermittent Purposeful Interaction with Environment: A consistent pattern of meaningful and purposeful interaction with others and objects is not maintained. At times the client is internally distracted, causing inattentiveness to the environment. Does not always respond to cueing.
c. Minimal Purposeful Interaction with Environment: Client interacts with the environment only to meet personal needs; frequently cannot or will not interact with others.

FACTR—R

Functional Assessment of Characteristics for Therapeutic Recreation, Revised

Name ______________________ Birthdate ____________ Physical ________ /11
Staff ______________________ Date ____________ Cognitive ________ /11
Unit ______________________ Admit ____________ Social/Emotional ________ /11

Functional Skills Related to Leisure	Will Influence Program Participation: yes	Will Influence Program Participation: no	Can Be Improved thru RT and Needs Improvement: yes	Can Be Improved thru RT and Needs Improvement: no
1.0 Physical				
1.1 Sight/Vision: *	❑	❑	❑	❑
___ Normal ___ Partial or impaired (corrected with lenses) ___ Partial or impaired (not correctable with lenses) ___ Legally blind - no vision				
1.2 Hearing: *	❑	❑	❑	❑
___ Normal ___ Hearing impaired (corrected) ___ Hearing impaired (not correctable) ___ Deaf				
1.3 Ambulation: *	❑	❑	❑	❑
___ Normal ___ Ambulates with difficulty (no aids) ___ Ambulates with aids (crutches, cane, walker) ___ Wheelchair (difficulty in use) ___ Wheelchair (unable to use independently) ___ No ambulation (bedridden)				
1.4 Bowel and Bladder*	❑	❑	❑	❑
___ Normal bowel and bladder for age population ___ Occasional incontinence problems ___ Incontinent ___ Uses bowel and bladder appliances				
1.5 Upper Extremity Manipulation (arms, hands, grasp)			❑	❑
___ Normal ___ Stiffness ___ Weakness ___ Uses adaptive devices				
1.6 General Coordination (major body parts)			❑	❑
___ Normal ___ Minor coordination problems ___ Major coordination problems				
1.7 Hand Eye Coordination			❑	❑
___ Normal ___ Minor hand eye coordination difficulties ___ Major hand eye coordination difficulties				
1.8 Strength			❑	❑
___ Normal ___ Minor weakness ___ Major weakness				

Functional Skills Related to Leisure	Can Be Improved thru RT and Needs Improvement: yes	Can Be Improved thru RT and Needs Improvement: no
1.0 Physical (continued)		
1.9 Cardio-vascular Functioning (endurance)	❑	❑
___ Excellent ___ Normal ___ Poor		
1.10 Weight	❑	❑
___ Normal ___ Overweight ___ Underweight		
1.11 Balance	❑	❑
___ Normal ___ Minor balance difficulties ___ Major balance difficulties		

* These 4 areas are not amenable to improvement, although knowledge of them is necessary for programming.

end of physical

Functional Skills Related to Leisure	Can Be Improved thru RT and Needs Improvement: yes	Can Be Improved thru RT and Needs Improvement: no
2.0 Cognitive		
2.1 Orientation	❑	❑
___ Normal ___ Confused & disoriented occasionally ___ Confused & disoriented most of the time** ___ Confused & disoriented all of the time **		

** Note: If either of these are checked, it may be impossible to accurately assess other cognitive or social/ emotional items.

Functional Skills Related to Leisure	Can Be Improved thru RT and Needs Improvement: yes	Can Be Improved thru RT and Needs Improvement: no
2.2 Oral Expressive Language	❑	❑
___ Very articulate ___ Average articulation ___ Poor articulation ___ No oral expressive laguage		

Note: If manual communication (signing) is the primary communication method, indicate the level of manual communication skill.

___ Excellent
___ Average
___ Poor

Functional Skills Related to Leisure	Can Be Improved thru RT and Needs Improvement: yes	Can Be Improved thru RT and Needs Improvement: no
2.3 Receptive Language	❑	❑
___ Can process and act on directions immediately ___ Needs time to process and act on directions ___ Needs cues, prompts or second set of directions ___ Does not process directions		

Functional Skills Related to Leisure	Can Be Improved thru RT and Needs Improvement	
	yes	no

2.0 Cognitive (continued)

2.4 Attending and Concentrating ☐ ☐
- ___ Concentrates and focuses well
- ___ Concentration and focus drifts or is easily distracted
- ___ Major difficulties attending and concentrating
- ___ Seems functionally unaware of people and objects in environment

2.5 Long Term Memory ☐ ☐
- ___ Clear recall of past events
- ___ Vague or occasional recall of past events
- ___ Unrealistic or distorted recall
- ___ No recall of past events

2.6 Short Term Memory ☐ ☐
- ___ Clear recall of recent events
- ___ Vague or occasional recall of recent events
- ___ No recall of recent events

2.7 Thought Process ☐ ☐
(logic, problem solving, creativity, abstraction)
- ___ Excellent
- ___ Average
- ___ Poor

2.8 Learning ☐ ☐
- ___ Learns new material quickly and easily
- ___ Average learning ability
- ___ Slow learning ability

2.9 Literacy ☐ ☐
- ___ Good reading ability
- ___ Basic reading ability
- ___ No functional reading ability

2.10 Math Concepts ☐ ☐
- ___ Above average mathematical computation ability (add, subtract, divide, multiply)
- ___ Average mathematical computation ability
- ___ Basic computations (add & subtract)
- ___ No functional mathematical computation ability

2.11 Decision making ability ☐ ☐
- ___ Survey alternatives and selects positive approach
- ___ Somewhat ambivalent and uncertain in decision making
- ___ Extremely ambivalent and uncertain in decision making

end of cognitive

\- - - - - - - - - - - -

3.0 Social/Emotional

3.1 Dyad (2 persons) ☐ ☐
- ___ Initiates and maintains dyad situations/conversations
- ___ Responds to and maintains dyad situation when initiated by others
- ___ Responds minimally in dyad situations (does not contribute new content or questions)
- ___ Does not respond in dyad situations

3.2 Small Group (3-8 persons) ☐ ☐
- ___ Initiates and maintains small group interactions
- ___ Responds to and maintains small group situations when initiated by others
- ___ Responds minimally in small group interactions (does not contribute new content or questions)
- ___ Does not respond in small group situations

Functional Skills Related to Leisure	Can Be Improved thru RT and Needs Improvement	
	yes	no

3.3 Social Interest ☐ ☐
- ___ Seeks social contacts/situations
- ___ Doesn't initiate, but doesn't avoid social contacts/situations
- ___ Avoids social contacts/situations
- ___ Excessive need for social contact

3.4 General Participation ☐ ☐
- ___ Self-Initiating
- ___ Voluntarily complies with activities initiated by others
- ___ Responds to direct commands or instructions
- ___ Non-participative

3.5 Cooperation (compliments, shares voluntarily, comments of emotional support, etc.) ☐ ☐
- ___ Understands & engages in cooperative behavior
- ___ Cooperation with prompting and reinforcement
- ___ Does not engage in cooperative behavior

3.6 Competition ☐ ☐
- ___ Understands and engages in competitive behavior appropriately
- ___ Overly aggressive in competitive behavior
- ___ Overly passive in competitive behavior

3.7 Conflict/Argument ☐ ☐
- ___ Appropriate communication and behavior in an argument/conflict situation (maintains emotional and physical control and verbally responds appropriately.)
- ___ Loses emotional and/or physical control in argument/conflict situations
- ___ Passively submits in argument/conflict situations

3.8 Emotional Expression ☐ ☐
- ___ Appropriate emotional response to situations
- ___ Excessive emotional response
- ___ Withholds emotional response
- ___ Inappropriate emotional expression

3.9 Authority/Leadership ☐ ☐
- ___ Responds appropriately to authority
- ___ Defies or actively resists authority
- ___ Overly passive with authority

3.10 Frustration ☐ ☐
- ___ High tolerance for frustration
- ___ Average frustration tolerance
- ___ Frequent frustration behavior

3.11 Purposive interaction with environment ☐ ☐
- ___ Interacts purposively with other persons and objects
- ___ Intermittent purposive interaction with environment
- ___ Minimal purposive interaction with environment

end of social/emotional

\- - - - - - - - - - - - - - -

Total the number of "no" responses for each category and record on page 1

Idyll Arbor, Inc.
P.O. Box 720
Ravensdale, WA 98051-0720
(206) 432-3231

FOX

Name: FOX

Also Known As: This version of the assessment is known as 'The FOX'. An earlier version is called 'The Fox Activity Therapy Social Skills Baseline'.

Authors: Rodney Patterson is credited with the development of the Fox Activity Therapy Social Skills Assessment. The questions from the Fox Activity Therapy Social Skills Assessment were re-ordered by the Idyll Arbor, Inc. staff after initial testing pointed out reliability problems. The FOX is the assessment contained in this book.

Time Needed to Administer: The FOX usually takes 20 minutes or less per client.

Time Needed to Score: Scoring and interpretation of the results will usually take the therapist under 15 minutes per client.

Recommended Disability Groups: Individuals with a primary or secondary diagnosis of dementia, mental retardation, or developmental disability.

Purpose of the Assessment: The purpose of the FOX is to evaluate the client's relative level of skills in the social/affective domain. Most of the skills included in this assessment are important building blocks to the development of a mature leisure lifestyle.

What Does the Assessment Measure?: The FOX measures six areas in the social domain:

1) client's reaction to others
2) client's reaction to objects
3) client's seeking attention from others to manipulate the environment
4) client's interaction with objects
5) client's concept of self
6) client's interaction with others

Supplies Needed: The therapist will need to determine which levels of the FOX s/he may administer to ensure that all of the required objects are nearby. In addition, the therapist will need the FOX manual and score sheet #106.

Reliability/Validity: Validity and reliability studies in progress.

Degree of Skill Required to Administer and Score: Due to the lack of established validity and reliability this assessment is best scored and interpreted by a recreational therapist who is certified at the CTRS level by the National Council for Therapeutic Recreation Certification.

Comments: The FOX provides the therapist working in an Intermediate Care Facility for the Mentally Retarded (ICF-MR), on an Alzheimer's unit, or in a school setting with a good set of progressive training goals once the client's social baseline is established.

Suggested Level: Rancho Los Amigos Level: 2 - 5. Developmental Level: Birth to 5 years. Reality Orientation Level: Severe to Moderate

Distributor: Idyll Arbor, Inc., 25119 SE 262 Street, PO Box 720, Ravensdale, WA 98051-0720 (206) 432-3231. (Area code 425 after April 1997.)

FOX
Activity Therapy Skills Baseline

PURPOSE: The purpose of the FOX is to evaluate the client's relative level of skills in the social/affective domain. Most of the skills included in this assessment are important building blocks to the development of a mature leisure lifestyle.

TIME NEEDED TO ADMINISTER THE FOX: The FOX is a relatively quick assessment to administer, usually taking 20 minutes or less per client.

The recreational therapist should be familiar enough with the assessment and the client to be able to guess which questions to begin with. *This assessment is not intended to be administered by starting with the first question in the test manual and going all the way through the assessment.* The therapist may find that s/he needs to start at level three for a client who is severely retarded or who is significantly impaired with dementia of the Alzheimer's type. The therapist should only continue the assessment until the client is not able to score any points in any given level of the section being tested.

An example of how to decrease the time required to administer the assessment can be found by examining Section VI: INTERACTIONS WITH OTHERS. The therapist will note that levels IX - XII all have a category called GREETS ANOTHER PERSON. Only one trial is needed to evaluate all 4 levels. By having a stranger walk into the room while the therapist is observing, the therapist can easily mark the most appropriate level.

BACKGROUND INFORMATION: The FOX is a revision of a training sequence of Basic Social Skills Development as outlined in a paper presented at the 1977 Annual Statewide Institute for Educators of the Severely and Profoundly Handicapped. The FOX was designed to: 1) evaluate the client's present level of social skill development, 2) assist in determining the client's training priorities, 3) serve as a basis for establishing new therapy programs when necessary, and 4) evaluate the effectiveness of program delivery in the area of social skill development.

The primary population that this assessment has been used with has been youth and adults with developmental disabilities. The FOX has also been used with three other populations: adults with dementia, youth and adults with brain injuries, and adolescents and adults with severe psychological disorders.

The therapist will find the FOX a good assessment to use with clients who are functioning socially at or below the level of a pre-schooler. Caution should be used when interpreting the results of this assessment. While the Idyll Arbor, Inc. staff found that each section followed a general developmental sequence, there was not a good correlation between the levels and a specific developmental age. In other words, Level IX did not represent the same developmental level across all sections.

The FOX assessment is divided into twelve levels of ability, the lowest level being Social Level I. The skill areas tested include:

1. The client's reaction to others
2. The client's reaction to objects
3. The client's seeking attention from others to manipulate the environment
4. The client's interaction with objects
5. The client's concept of self
6. The client's interaction with others

A point value is assigned to each skill tested according to the complexity of the response. For example:

Social Level III, Section IV, 'B' has three response levels:

Grasps and hold objects for specified duration: When staff holds a squeaky toy against the palm of the client's hand and says, 'hold toy', the client will palm-grasp the object and hold it for

(05 points) 4 seconds
(10 points) 6 seconds
(15 points) 10 seconds

If the client being tested is physically disabled so that the test needs to be modified to be administered, the modifications used must be described in the comment section.

A client is considered to have adequate skills to have 'passed' any given level if s/he meets or exceeds the number of points indicated in the upper right corner of the square. (Check the score sheet for the number of points required for each specific skill area.) When the client has gone one or two levels without obtaining enough points to 'pass' in any given skill area, the therapist should end testing in that skill area and go on to the next skill area. The test is complete when the client has reached his/her maximum level in all six skill areas.

When testing has been completed, the therapist should take a colored pen and draw a line on the right side of the box which showed the highest level that the client reached in each skill area. This allows the therapist to quickly determine which skill areas need the greatest amount of development.

I. REACTION TO OTHERS

SOCIAL LEVEL I

A. Reacts to being touched by others
(05) When a staff hugs, touches, or pats the client, the client will not push the staff away, tense muscles, or pull body away.

B. Turns toward a staff who calls his/her name
When a staff stands beside the client and says the client's name, the client will, within 5 seconds:

(05) Turn 45 degrees in the direction of the noise
(10) Turn toward and look at the staff
(15) Turn toward and establish eye contact with the staff

SOCIAL LEVEL II

A. Reacts to being touched by others
When a staff tickles, touches, or pats the client, the client will:

(05) Turn face toward staff
(10) Turn face toward and look at staff
(15) Turn face toward and establish eye contact with the staff for at least 2 seconds

B. Turns toward a staff who calls his/her name
When a staff stands 5 feet from the client and calls the client's name, the client will, within 10 seconds:

(05) Turn toward the staff
(10) Turn toward and look at the staff
(15) Turn toward and establish eye contact with the staff for at least 2 seconds

C. Turns toward a peer who calls his/her name
When a peer is positioned beside the client and calls his/her name or makes some kind of a sound, the client will:

(05) Turn toward the peer
(10) Turn toward and look at the peer
(15) Turn toward and establish 2 second eye contact with peer

SOCIAL LEVEL III

A. Turns toward a staff who calls his/her name
When a staff stands across the room from the client and says the client's name, the client will, within 10 seconds:

(05) Turn toward the staff
(10) Turn toward and look at the staff
(15) Turn toward and establish 2 second eye contact

B. Turns toward a peer who calls his/her name
When a peer is positioned 5 feet from the client and calls the client's name or makes a noise, the client will:

(05) Turn toward the peer
(10) Turn toward and look at the peer
(15) Turn toward and establish eye contact with peer

C. Turns toward a person who enters the room
When the client is located within 3 feet of the entrance to a room and a person enters the room, the client will:

(05) Turn toward the person
(10) Turn toward and look at the person

D. Watches the movements of others
When a staff bounces a ball within 3 feet of the client, the client will watch the staff's movements for a minimum of:

(05) 2 seconds
(10) 4 seconds
(15) 6 seconds

SOCIAL LEVEL IV

A. Turns toward a person who enters the room
When the client is located within 10 feet of the entrance of the room and a person enters the room, the client will:

(05) Turn toward the person
(10) Turn toward and look at the person
(15) Turn toward and establish eye contact

B. Watches the movement of others
When a staff claps his/her hands within 3 feet of the client, the client will watch the staff's movements for a minimum of:

(05) 2 seconds
(10) 4 seconds
(15) 6 seconds

C. Establishes and maintains eye contact
When a staff is sitting opposite the client and calls the client's name, the client will establish and maintain eye contact for:

(05) 2 seconds
(10) 4 seconds
(15) 6 seconds

SOCIAL LEVEL V

A. Turns toward a person who enters the room
When the client is located across the room from the entrance to the room and a person enters the room, the client will:

(05) turn toward the person
(10) turn toward and look at the person

B. Watches the movements of others
When a staff pours juice within 3 feet of the client, the client will watch the movements of the staff for a minimum of:

(05) 2 seconds
(10) 4 seconds
(15) 6 seconds

C. Establishes and maintains eye contact
(05) When a peer is sitting near the client and touches the client's arm/shoulder and/or calls the client's name, the client will establish and maintain eye contact with the peer for at least 1 second.

D. Turns toward, looks at, and maintains gaze in the direction of a speaker who addresses the whole group.
(05) When a staff, standing in front of the whole group, gives a verbal attention signal ('Look at me') the client will turn and look at the staff for at least 2 seconds.

SOCIAL LEVEL VI

A. Watches the movement of others
When a staff walks across the room, the client will watch the staff's movements for a minimum of:

(05) 2 seconds
(10) 6 seconds
(15) 8 seconds

B. Establishes and maintains eye contact
When a peer is sitting near the client and touches the client's arm/shoulder and/or calls the client's name, the client will respond by establishing and maintaining eye contact with the peer for:

(05) 2 seconds
(10) 4 seconds
(15) 8 seconds

C. Turns toward, looks at, and maintains gaze in the direction of a speaker who addresses the whole group
When a staff gives a verbal attention signal ('Look at me') to the entire group, and continues to address the group, the client will turn toward and look at the staff for:

(05) 8 seconds
(10) 10 seconds
(15) 12 seconds

D. Follows simple commands
When a staff gives a simple command such as 'Clap your hands', the client will follow the command:

(05) with a gestural prompt
(10) with a verbal prompt

SOCIAL LEVEL VII

A. Establishes and maintains eye contact
When a unfamiliar staff is sitting near the client and calls the client's name, the client will establish and maintain eye contact for:

(05) 2 seconds
(10) 4 seconds
(15) 6 seconds

B. Turns toward, looks at, and maintains gaze in the direction of a speaker who addresses the whole group
When an unfamiliar staff gives a verbal attention signal to the group and continues to address the group, the client will turn toward and look at the staff for:

(05) 8 seconds
(10) 10 seconds
(15) 12 seconds

C. Follows simple commands
(05) When a staff gives a simple command such as 'Clap your hands', the client will follow the command without a gestural cue.

SOCIAL LEVEL VIII

A. Follows simple commands
(05) When, during the course of an activity session, the staff gives three separate simple commands, the client will follow each command with a verbal cue.

B. Imitates actions of others
(05) In a group setting, the client will imitate a gross motor behavior when given the command 'Do this'.

SOCIAL LEVEL IX

A. Follows simple commands
(05) When a staff gives a simple command requiring gross motor body movement ('raise your hand'), the client will respond correctly.

B. Imitates actions of others
(05) When a staff says 'Do this', and models waving 'Hi' for 3 seconds, the client will wave 'Hi'.

END OF REACTION TO OTHERS SECTION

II. REACTION TO OBJECTS

SOCIAL LEVEL I

A. Turns in direction of a noise
When a staff stands behind the client and makes a loud noise with a bell, a drum, or a shaker, within 3 inches of the client's ear, the client will:

(05) turn 45 degrees in the direction of the noise
(10) turn 90 degrees in the direction of the noise
(15) turn and glance at the noise producing object

B. Looks at moving objects
(05) When a staff says 'Look' and moves, from the client's left to right, a large reinforcing object (that requires two hands to hold) within 18 inches of the client, the client will look at the object for 1 second.

SOCIAL LEVEL II

A. Turns in the direction of a noise
When a staff stands behind the client and makes a quiet noise (music box) within 3 inches of the client's ear, the client will:

(05) turn 45 degrees in the direction of the noise
(10) turn 90 degrees in the direction of the noise
(15) turn and glance at the object

B. Looks at moving object
(05) When a staff says 'Look', and moves, from the client's left to right, a small reinforcing object within 18 inches of the client, the client will look at the object for 1 second.

SOCIAL LEVEL III

A. Turns in the direction of a noise
When a staff stands behind the client and makes a quiet noise within 3 feet of the client's ear, the client will:

(05) turn 45 degrees in the direction of the noise
(10) turn 90 degrees in the direction of the noise
(15) turn and glance at the object

B. Looks at moving objects
(05) When a staff moves from the client's left to right, a small reinforcing object within 3 feet of the client, the client will look at the object for 1 second.

C. Maintains visual contact on a stationary object
When a staff says 'Look at this', and holds a small reinforcing object 18 inches from the client, at eye level, the client will maintain visual contact for:

(05) 3 seconds
(10) 4 seconds
(15) 5 seconds

SOCIAL LEVEL IV

A. Maintains visual contact on a stationary object
When a staff says 'Look at this', and holds a small reinforcing object 18 inches from the client, at eye level, the client will maintain visual contact for:

(05) 3 seconds
(10) 4 seconds
(15) 5 seconds

SOCIAL LEVEL V

A. Looks at and tracks moving objects
When a staff stands within 18 inches of the client and says 'Look at this', and moves a small reinforcing object from the client's left to right, the client will look at the object and track the object for a distance of:

(05) 1 foot
(10) 2 feet
(15) 3 feet

SOCIAL LEVEL VI

A. Looks at and tracks moving objects
(05) When a staff stands approximately 3 feet from the client and says 'Look at this', and moves a small reinforcing object from the client's left to right, the client will look at the object and track the object.

END OF REACTION TO OBJECTS

III. SEEKS ATTENTION

(This section begins at Social Level Five)

SOCIAL LEVEL V

A. Seeks attention for personal assistance in manipulating the environment
When the client sees food out of his/her reach, the client will direct others' attention to the food by:

(05) gesture
(10) noise (other than crying)
(15) symbolic sound, words, or alternative communication

SOCIAL LEVEL VI

A. Seeks attention for personal assistance in manipulating the environment
When the client drops an object out of reach, the client will direct others' attention to the object by:

(05) gesture
(10) noise (other than crying)
(15) symbolic sound, words, or alternative communication

B. Approaches another person and seeks attention
Before the client demands attention from a person located across the room, the client:

(05) will approach the other person by crawling, creeping, or scooting.
(10) Will approach the person by walking, walking with prosthetic, or by moving a wheelchair.
(15) (If nonambulatory) will attract the person's attention with gesture, noise (other than crying) or symbolic sound, words or alternate communication.

SOCIAL LEVEL VII

A. Seeks attention for personal assistance in manipulating the environment
When the client is in an unnatural position (body part stuck, fallen on floor) and unable to re-position, the client will direct others' attention to the situation by:

(05) gesture
(10) noise (other than crying)
(15) symbolic sound, words, or alternative communication

SOCIAL LEVEL VIII

A. Seeks attention for personal assistance in manipulating the environment
When the client is unable to move from one location to another, the client will direct others' attention to the situation by:

(05) gesture
(10) noise (other than crying)
(15) symbolic sound, words, or alternative communication

B. Seeks attention for assistance to bodily needs
(05) When the client needs to use the toilet (if toilet trained), the client will seek others' attention to obtain permission to go, seeking assistance in going to the bathroom.

SOCIAL LEVEL IX

A. Waits to demand attention until the person is free to respond
(05) When the client approaches a person who is interacting with another person, the client will wait until the interaction is terminated.

END OF SEEKS ATTENTION

IV. INTERACTION WITH OBJECTS

SOCIAL LEVEL I

A. Grasps objects when it is presented near hand
(05) When staff holds the handle of a bell against the client's palm and says, 'Hold bell', the resident will palm-grasp the object.

SOCIAL LEVEL II

A. Grasps objects when it is presented near hand
(05) When a staff holds a small squeaky toy against the palm of the client's hand and says 'Hold toy', the client will palm-grasp the object.

B. Grasps and holds objects for a specified duration
When a staff holds the handle of a bell against the client's palm and says 'Hold bell', the client will grasp the handle and hold the object for:

(05) 4 seconds
(10) 6 seconds
(15) 10 seconds

SOCIAL LEVEL III

A. Grasps object when it is presented near hand
(05) When a staff holds the handle of a spoon against the palm of the client's hand and says 'Hold spoon', the client will palm-grasp the spoon.

B. Grasps and holds objects for specified duration
When a staff holds a squeaky toy against the palm of the client's hand and says 'Hold toy', the client will palm-grasp the object and hold it for:

(05) 4 seconds
(10) 6 seconds
(15) 10 seconds

C. Reaches toward, grasps, and holds object
(05) When staff holds the handle of a bell within 3 inches of the client's hand and says 'Get bell', the client will reach for, grasp, and hold the bell for at least 2 seconds.

SOCIAL LEVEL IV

A. Grasps and holds an object for a specified duration of time
When a staff holds the handle of a spoon against the palm of the client's hand and says 'Hold spoon', the client will palm-grasp the spoon for:

(05) 4 seconds
(10) 6 seconds
(15) 10 seconds

B. Reaches toward, grasps, and holds an object
(05) When a staff holds the handle of the spoon within 6 inches of the client's hand and says, 'Get spoon', the client will reach for, grasp, and hold the spoon for at least 2 seconds.

C. Picks up and holds objects with two hands
When the client is seated at a table with his/her hands on the table and the staffs places a large reinforcing object on the table between the client's hands and says, 'Pick up _____', the client will grasp the object with one hand on each side, lift it up, and hold the object for:

(05) 4 seconds
(10) 6 seconds
(15) 10 seconds

SOCIAL LEVEL V

A. Reaches towards, grasps, and holds an object
(05) When a staff holds a small squeaky toy within 12 inches of the client's hand and says, 'Get toy', the client will reach for, grasp, and hold the toy for at least 2 seconds.

B. Uses objects appropriately
When a client is seated at a table and a staff places an object with movable parts on the table in front of the client and says, 'Play with ____', the client will manipulate the movable parts to make an observable change in the object with:

(05) 3 responses within 30 seconds
(10) 5 responses within 30 seconds
(15) 7 responses within 30 seconds

SOCIAL LEVEL VI

A. Reaches towards, grasps, and holds an object
(05) When the client is seated at a table with his/her hands on the table and the staff places a spoon on the table 3 inches from the client's hand and says, 'Get spoon', the client will reach, grasp, and hold the spoon.

B. Uses objects appropriately
(05) When a staff presents an object that can be appropriately manipulated by pulling and says 'Pull', the client will pull the object a minimum of 3 times.

C. Takes objects in and out of containers
(05) When a staff provides an empty box or container for collection of play objects or parts of objects and says 'Put them away', the client will pick up the objects and place them in the container.

SOCIAL LEVEL VII

A. Reaches toward, grasps and holds an object

(05) When client is seated at a table with his/her hands on the table and the staff places an object on the table 8 inches from the client's hands and says, 'Get ________,' the client will reach, grasp and hold the object.

B. Uses objects appropriately

(05) When staff presents an object that can be appropriately manipulated by pushing and says, 'Push,' the client will respond by pushing the object.

C. Initiated play with objects

When staff places a play object or container within reach of the client's hand, the client will reach for the object and play with it using previously trained manipulations for:

(05) 2 minutes
(10) 4 minutes
(15) 10 minutes

SOCIAL LEVEL VIII

A. Uses object appropriately

(05) When staff presents an object that can be appropriately manipulated by shaking and says, 'Shake', the client will shake the object 3 times.

SOCIAL LEVEL IX

A. Uses play objects appropriately

(05) When a staff presents an object that can be appropriately used by hitting (drums, xylophone, pegs and hammer) and says 'Hit ____', the client will hit the object 3 three times.

B. Initiates play with objects

When the client has a period of unstructured time, s/he will go to the location where play materials are kept, select a container/play object, take to the play area and play using previously trained manipulations for:

(05) 2 minutes
(10) 4 minutes
(15) 10 minutes

SOCIAL LEVEL X

A. Uses objects appropriately

When a staff presents a play object and says 'Play with ____', the client will make previously trained manipulations appropriate to that object for:

(05) 2 minutes
(10) 4 minutes
(15) 10 minutes

END OF INTERACTION WITH OBJECTS

V. SELF-CONCEPT

(Self-Concept begins at Social Level III)

SOCIAL LEVEL III

A. Responds to own name when spoken
(05) When a staff says, 'Where is (client's name)', the client will respond by raising his/her hand.

B. Labels own body parts
When a staff says 'Touch your (large body part, i.e., head), the client will touch the body part named:

(05) with gestural cue
(10) with only verbal cue

SOCIAL LEVEL IV

A. Touches small body part
(05) When a staff says 'Touch your (small body part, i.e., nose)', the client will touch the body part named.

SOCIAL LEVEL V

A. Labels own body parts
When a staff touches one of the client's body parts and says 'Is this your ____?', the client will respond correctly with:

(05) Gesture
(10) Symbolic sound, words, or alternative communication

OR

When a staff touches one of the client's body parts and says 'What is this?', the client will respond with:

(15) symbolic sound, words, or alternate communication

B. Discriminates own body parts from others
(05) When a staff says 'Touch my (body part)', the client will respond by touching the staff's named body part.

SOCIAL LEVEL VI

A. Discriminates own body parts from others'
When a staff touches one of the client's body parts and says, 'Whose ____ is this?', the client will respond by:

(05) Pointing to self
(10) Saying/signing his/her name
(15) Saying/signing possessive pronoun (my, mine)

B. Identifies own image in mirror
(05) When the client is standing alone in the mirror and the staffs says, 'Show me (client's name)', the client will touch his/her image in the mirror.

SOCIAL LEVEL VII

A) Discriminates own body parts from others
When a staff touches one of his/her own body parts and says, 'Whose ____ is this?', the client will respond by:

(05) Pointing to the staff
(10) Saying/signing the staff's name
(15) Saying/signing possessive pronoun (you/yours)

B. Identifies own image in mirror
(05) When the client and a staff are standing in front of a mirror and the staff says, 'Show me (client's name)', the client will touch his/her own image in the mirror.

SOCIAL LEVEL VIII

A. Identifies own image in mirror
(05) When the client and a peer are standing in front of a mirror and the staffs says, 'Show me (client's name)', the client will touch his/her image in the mirror.

B. Identifies self in photograph
(05) When the staff presents a photograph of the client pictured alone and says, 'Show me (client's name)', the client will touch his/her image in the photograph.

C. Identifies family or familiar adults
(05) When the staff provides a photograph of a family member (or familiar adult) and says, 'Show me (the person in the photograph)', the client will touch the image of the person named.

D. Identifies self by name
(05) When the staff says 'Who are you?', the client will say/sign his/her first name.

SOCIAL LEVEL IX

A. Identifies self in photograph
(05) When the staff presents the client with a photograph of the client pictured with the staff (or another person) and says 'Show me (client's name)', the client will touch his image in the photograph.

B. Identifies family members or familiar adults
(05) When the staff presents a photograph of the client's family (or a group of familiar adults) and says 'Show me (name of person in group photograph)', the client will respond by touching the image of the person named.

C. Identifies self by name
(05) When a unfamiliar staff or adult says, 'Who are you?', the client will respond by saying/signing his/her name or pointing to his/her name on a language board.

D. Identifies self as male/female
When the staff asks, 'Are you a (male/boy/female/girl)?', the client will respond by:

(05) Nodding/shaking head
(10) Saying/signing yes or no
(15) Pointing to yes or no on language board

SOCIAL LEVEL X

A. Identifies self in photograph
(05) When staff presents a photograph of the client pictured with a peer and says, 'Show me (client's name)', the client will touch his/her image in the photograph.

B. Identifies family member or familiar adults in photograph
(05) When the staff provides a photograph of the client's family or a group of familiar adults and says, 'Show me (name of one group member)', the client will touch the image of the person named.

C. Identifies self as male/female
When staff says 'Are you a (male/boy or a female/girl?' the client will respond with:

(05) One word (male/boy/female/girl)
(10) Two words (a male/boy/female/girl)
(15) Three or more words (I a boy/I a girl)

D. Identifies others as male or female
When staff points to another client and says 'Is (name) a (male/boy/female/girl)?' the client will respond by:

(05) One word (male/boy/female/girl)
(10) Two words (a male/boy/female/girl)
(15) Three or more words ((name) a male/boy/female/girl)

E. Identifies others as male or female
When adult points to another client and says. 'Is (name) a (male/boy/female/girl)?' the client will respond by:

(05) Nodding/shaking his/her head
(10) Pointing to yes or no on a language board
(15) Saying/signing yes or no

SOCIAL LEVEL XI

A. Identifies family members or familiar adults in photograph
When staff presents a photograph of the client's family or a group of familiar adults and peers, points to one of the persons in the photograph and says, 'Who is this?', the client will respond by:

(05) Saying/signing the name
(10) Pointing to name on language board

B. Identifies others as male or female
When staff points to another client and says, 'Is (name) a male/boy/female/girl?', the client will respond by saying/signing (or using language board) a response of:

(05) One word (male/boy/female/girl)
(10) Two words (a male/boy/female/girl)
(15) Three or more words

SOCIAL LEVEL XII - NA

END OF SELF-CONCEPT

VI. INTERACTION WITH OTHERS

This section begins with Social Level III

SOCIAL LEVEL III

A. Receives Interaction

(05) When a staff or other adult who is familiar to the client hugs the client, the client will position his/her arms around the adult's torso and apply pressure and then release.

SOCIAL LEVEL IV

A. Returns a smile

(05) When staff positions his/her face within 1 foot and level with the client's face and smiles, the client will respond by smiling.

B. Receives interaction from peers

(05) When a peer hugs or pats the client, the client will return the interaction.

SOCIAL LEVEL V

A. Receives interaction

(05) When the staff points to an object near the client and requests the object by saying, 'Will you give me ____?', the client will respond by handing the object to the staff.

B. Returns a hug from an unfamiliar adult

(05) When an unfamiliar adult hugs the client, the client will return the hug.

C. Returns a smile

(05) When a familiar staff stands 3 feet in front of the client, establishes eye contact with the client, and smiles, the client will respond by smiling.

SOCIAL SKILL LEVEL VI

A. Returns smile from peers

(05) When a peer stands approximately 3 feet from the client, establishes eye contact, and smiles, the client will respond by smiling.

B. Shares objects with peers

(05) When a peer requests an object that is near the client by pointing to the object and (if verbal) asks, 'Will you give me the ____?', the client will hand the object to peer.

C. Returns a greeting from adults

When an adult says 'Hi (client's name)', and waves to the client, the client will return the greeting by:

(05) Waving
(10) Saying/signing 'Hi'
(15) Saying/signing 'Hi (adult's name)'

SOCIAL LEVEL VII

A. Returns greeting from staff

When adult says, 'Hi (client's name)', without waving, the client will return the greeting by:

(05) Waving
(10) Saying/signing 'Hi'
(15) Saying/signing 'Hi (adult's name)'

B. Interaction with peers

(05) When a peer stands approximately 3 feet from the client, establishes eye contact, and smiles, the client will respond by smiling.

C. Plays with play objects in group setting

(05) When a staff presents a play object to the client and says, 'Let's play', the client will accept the object and remain in proximity of the staff for a minimum of 10 seconds.

SOCIAL LEVEL VIII

A. Returns greeting to peer

When a peer says 'Hi' and/or waves to the client, the client will return the greeting by;

(05) Waving
(10) Saying/signing 'Hi'
(15) Saying/signing 'He (peer's name)'

B. Appropriately plays with play object in group setting

(05) When staff presents a play object to the client and says, 'Let's play', the client will accept the object, remain in proximity of the staff while beginning to use the object with previously trained manipulations.

C. Responds to questions with 'yes' or 'no'

When staff asks a question requiring a 'yes' or 'no' answer, the client will respond by:

(05) Gesture
(10) Saying/signing 'yes' or 'no'
(15) Using language board

D. Initiates interaction
When staff approaches the client and stands approximately 3 feet from the client, the client will greet the staff within 30 seconds by:

(05) Smiling
(10) Smiling and waving
(15) Saying/signing a greeting

SOCIAL LEVEL IX

A. Returns greeting
When an unfamiliar adult says, 'Hi' to the client, the client will return the greeting by:

(05) Waving
(10) Saying/signing 'Hi'

B. Receives cooperative play
(05) When an unfamiliar adult presents a play object to the client and says, 'Let's play', the client will accept the object and remain in proximity of the adult while beginning to use the object with previously trained manipulations.

C. Answers questions
When an unfamiliar adult asks a question requiring a yes/no answer, the client will respond by:

(05) Nodding/shaking head
(10) Saying/signing yes or no
(15) Pointing to yes or no on a language board

D. Recognizes peers, family members, teachers by name
When client is seated between two other people and the staff says, 'Where is (name of another person in the group)?' the client will respond by:

(05) Looking toward the person named
(10) Pointing towards/touching the person named
(15) Saying/signing 'There'

E. Greets another person
When an unfamiliar adult stands approximately 3 feet from the client, the client will greet the adult within 30 seconds by:

(05) Smiling
(10) Smiling and waving
(15) Saying/signing a greeting

F. Requests objects from another person
When staff holds a reinforcing object in front of the client, the client will request the object by:

(05) Pointing
(10) Saying/signing the request

SOCIAL LEVEL X

A. Receives object cooperatively
(05) When a peer presents a common play object to the client, the client will accept the object, remain in proximity of the peer while beginning to use the object with previously learned manipulations.

B. Answers questions
When a peer asks a question requiring a yes or no answer, the client will respond by:

(05) Nodding/shaking head
(10) Using language board to point to yes or no
(15) Saying/signing yes or no

C. Recognizes peers, family members, teachers by name
When the client is in a group of 3 or more and the staff in charge says, 'Where is ____?', the client will respond by:

(05) Looking toward the person named
(10) Pointing towards/touching the person named
(15) Saying/signing 'There'

D. Shows approval of others' work, skill, or possessions
When a peer achieves a goal (earns treat, does good work, completes a task, hits the target), and the staff prompts the client to show approval, ('____ did a good job, let's clap hands'), the client will demonstrate approval by:

(05) Smiling at peer
(10) Hugging/patting peer; clapping for peer
(15) Saying/signing praise

E. Greets another person
When peer approaches the client and stands approximately 3 feet from the client, the client will greet the peer within 30 seconds by:
(05) Smiling
(10) Smiling and waving
(15) Smiling/signing a greeting

F. Requests object from others
When staff is seated near a reinforcing object, the client will request the object by:
(05) Pointing
(10) Saying/signing the request
(15) Using language board

SOCIAL LEVEL XI

A. Receives cooperative play

(05) When staff presents 3 common play objects which the client has previously labeled receptively, and says, 'Let's play with the ____', the client will get the object named and begin to use the object with previously trained manipulations.

B. Answers questions

When a staff asks a question that requires a response other than yes or no, the client will respond (saying/signing or using a language board) a response of:

(05) One word
(10) Two words
(15) Three words

C. Recognizes peers, family members, teachers by name

(05) When a staff points to another person whom the client has previously labeled receptively, the client will respond by saying/signing the person's name or pointing to the name on a language board.

D. Shows approval of others' work, skill, or possession

When a peer achieves a goal and shows it to the client, and the staff says a reminder ('____ did a good job. How do we show him/her?'), the client will demonstrate approval by:

(05) Smiling at peer
(10) Hugging/patting peer; clapping for peer
(15) Saying/signing praise

E. Discriminates appropriate time, place, and situation for receiving interaction

When the staff initiates an activity that is appropriate to the time and situation and says, 'Should we play here?' the client will respond by:

(05) Nodding/shaking his/her head
(10) Using language board
(15) Saying/signing yes/no

F. Greets another person

When a peer, familiar or unfamiliar adult enters the room and makes eye contact with the client, the client will greet the person within 30 seconds by:

(05) Smiling
(10) Smiling and waving
(15) Saying/signing a greeting

G. Requests objects from another person

When a peer is playing with an object near the client, the client will request the object by:

(05) Pointing
(10) Saying/signing the request
(15) Using language board

H. Initiates cooperative play

(05) When the client has an unstructured period of time, the client will approach a staff and initiate play by signing/saying or using language board.

I. Seeks approval from others for work, skill, or possession

When the client achieves a goal (earns a treat, does good work, makes all his/her points, hits the target, etc.) or acquires a new possession, the client will show the product to the staff by:

(05) Holding up product
(10) Pointing to object and saying/signing 'Look'
(15) Describing achievement

J. Seeks affiliation (physical contact or proximity with familiar person) while performing actions

(05) When a staff says, 'Walk with a friend', the client will select a peer and walk with him/her or push his/her wheelchair until they reach their destination.

K. Helps one who has difficulty manipulating the environment

(05) When the client sees a peer attempting to grasp an object out of reach, the client will assist the peer by handing him/her the object or by directing an adult's attention to the situation.

L. Discriminates appropriate time, place situation for initiation of interaction

When the client initiates an interaction that is appropriate to place and the staff says, 'Is this the time for ____?', and 'Should you be ____?', the client will respond by:

(05) Nodding/shaking head
(10) Using language board
(15) Saying/signing yes or no

The client will continue or terminate the interaction accordingly.

M. Sustains ongoing cooperative play activity after activity has been initiated and received

(05) When the client is participating in a play interaction, the client will remain in a situation appropriately in proximity to the other player(s) until the interaction is terminated (by end of game or end of session).

N. Terminates cooperative play activity
When, in a structured session the adult gives a verbal cue to terminate the activity, the client will finish his/her turn (if applicable) and terminate the activity by:

(05) Gathering materials and/or placing them in their containers
(10) Returning collected materials to the appropriate storage place
(15) Returning materials to storage and cleaning the area

SOCIAL LEVEL XII

A. Receives cooperative play
When peer asks, 'Do you want to play ____?', the client will respond by:

(05) Nodding/shaking his/her head
(10) Using language board
(15) Saying/signing yes or no

B. Answering questions
When a peer asks a question that requires a response other then yes/no, the client will sign/say or use language board for a response of:

(05) One word
(10) Two words

C. Discriminates appropriate time, place, and situation for receiving interaction
(05) When a peer initiates an interaction, the client will discriminate if the interaction is appropriate to the time, place and situation and participate or terminate the interaction accordingly.

D. Greets another person
(05) Once the client's greeting to another person has been reciprocated, the client will not repeat greetings to that person.

E. Requests objects from others
When an object is not available, the client will request the object from an adult by saying/signing or using language board:

(05) (Object)
(10) Want (object)
(15) I want (object)

F. Initiates cooperative play
(05) When the client has an unstructured period of time, the client will approach a peer and initiate play by signing/saying or using language board.

G. Seeks approval from other for work, skill or possession
(05) When the client achieves a goal or acquires a new possession, the client will show the product to a peer.

H. Seeks affiliation with familiar person while performing actions
(05) When adult says, 'Sit with a friend', the client will select a peer and sit down with him/her.

I. Helps one who has difficulty manipulating the environment
(05) When the client sees a person who is calling attention to his/her inability to move from one location to another, the client will assist that person by helping him/her to move or directing an adult's attention to the situation.

J. Sustains ongoing cooperative play activity after the activity has been initiated and received
(05) When the client is participating in a play interaction, the client will share the materials with the other players, remain in proximity to them, attend to the other players as they take their turns, take his/her turn, using materials correctly and at an appropriate rate until the game is terminated.

END OF INTERACTION WITH OTHERS

FOX

Information on obtaining additional copies of this or other forms may be obtained from Idyll Arbor, Inc., 25119 SE 262nd Street, Ravensdale, WA 98051-9763 (206) 432-3231.

Social Level	I	II	III	IV	V	VI	VII	VIII	IX	X	XI	XII
I Reaction to Others	A– /10 B–	A– /15 B– C–	A– /20 B– C– D–	A– /15 B– C–	A– /20 B– C– D–	A– /20 B– C– D–	A– /15 B– C–	A– /10 B–	A– /10 B–	N/A	N/A	N/A
II Reaction to Objects	A– /10 B–	A– /10 B–	A– [illegible] B– C–	A– [illegible]	A– [illegible]	A– /5	N/A	N/A	N/A	N/A	N/A	N/A
III Attention Seeking	N/A	N/A	N/A	N/A	A– /5	A– /10 B–	A– /5	A– /10 B–	A– /5	N/A	N/A	N/A
IV Interaction with Objects	A– /5	A– /10 B–	A– /15 B– C–	A– /15 B– C–	A– /10 B–	A– /15 B– C–	A– /15 B– C–	A– /5	A– /10 B–	A– /5	A– /5	N/A
V Concept of Self	N/A	N/A	A– /10 B–	A– /5	A– /10 B–	A– /10 B–	A– /10 B–	A– /20 B– C– D–	A– /20 B– C– D–	A– /25 B– C– D– E–	A– /10 B–	N/A
VI Interaction with Others	N/A	N/A	A– /5	A– /10 B–	A– /15 B– C–	A– /15 B– C–	A– /15 B– C–	A– /20 B– C– D–	A– /30 B– C– D– E– F–	A– /30 B– C– D– E– F–	A– /70 B– C– D– E– F– G– H– I – J – K– L– M– N–	A– /50 B– C– D– E– F– G– H– I – J –

Comments:

Name ______________________ Admit ______________________

D.O.B. ______________________ Therapist ______________________

Living Unit ______________________

GENERAL RECREATION SCREENING TOOL

Name: General Recreation Screening Tool

Also Known As: GRST (pronounced 'grist', rhymes with 'list')

Author: joan burlingame

Time Needed to Administer: The GRST is usually scored after the therapist has observed the client in five or more activities. In this situation, very few specific skills will need to be tested. Idyll Arbor, Inc. staff usually scheduled 15 minutes or less to spot test the skills that the staff were not sure about.

Time Needed to Score: The GRST usually takes 10 minutes to score.

Recommended Disability Groups: The GRST is recommended for MR/DD populations. It has been used on pediatric populations in children's hospitals with moderate success.

Purpose of the Assessment: The purpose of the GRST is to help determine the client's functional level in eighteen skill areas related to leisure.

What Does the Assessment Measure?: The GRST measures the general developmental level of the client in the following areas: 1) gross motor, 2) fine motor, 3) eye-hand coordination, 4) play behavior, 5) play structure, 6) language use, 7) language comprehension, 8) understanding of numbers, 9) object use, 10) following directions, 11) problem solving, 12) attending behavior, 13) possessions, 14) emotional control, 15) imitation play, 16) people skills, 17) music, and 18) stories/drama.

Supplies Needed: The type of supplies needed depends on the specific developmental areas that the therapist needs to evaluate. The therapist should read the assessment tool prior to administering. The assessment manual and score sheet #111 are also needed.

Reliability/Validity: The GRST was developed after an extensive literature search on developmental milestones. Over 30 different developmental charts and studies were compared and no single item was selected for inclusion in the GRST unless it had at least three sources in agreement. No reliability testing is reported.

Degree of Skill Required to Administer and Score: A recreational therapist who is certified at the CTRS level by the National Council for Therapeutic Recreation Certification should be able to administer, score, and interpret the results.

Comments: The GRST is a useful general screening tool to be used with clients in Intermediate Care Facilities for the Mentally Retarded (ICF-MRs). It is a widely used assessment tool and one of the few functional assessment tools available for recreational therapists working with clients with mental retardation or other severe learning disabilities.

Suggested Levels: Rancho Los Amigos Level: 8 (not appropriate if there is any head injury). Developmental Level: birth to 10 years. Reality Orientation Level: any level, reality orientation is not generally used for ages under 10.

Distributor: Idyll Arbor, Inc., 25119 SE 262 Street, PO Box 720, Ravensdale, WA 98051-0720 (206) 432-3231. (Area code 425 after April 1997.)

GENERAL RECREATION SCREENING TOOL (GRST)

The purpose of this screening tool is to help determine the client's functional level in eighteen skill areas related to leisure. The original version of the GRST was developed at Rainier School in Buckley, Washington. In this version the assessment has remained basically the same, with the primary changes being an updating of the terms used to reflect the 1988 ICF-MR (Intermediate Care Facility for the Mentally Retarded) regulations. The original score sheet, Idyll Arbor, Inc. #111 is used with this version of the assessment.

This assessment helps determine the strengths and weaknesses of the client. The results also provide a developmental level for each assessed functional skill as it relates to the client's leisure capabilities. The material within the developmental levels was complied from more than 12 different development charts, each one selected because it had been tested for the accuracy of the stated developmental ages.

SCORING THE GRST

The GRST provides the recreational therapist with two or more skills associated with each developmental level. Read the developmental skills listed in each age group for each of the functional leisure skill categories. If the client has demonstrated 50% to 75% of the skills listed within the age group, draw a dashed line through that age group. If the client has demonstrated 75% or more of the skills listed within the age group, draw a solid line through that age group. (Please refer to the score sheet for an example.) The skills listed within each category may not be in exact developmental order, so it is important to read the entire paragraph prior to scoring.

Idyll Arbor, Inc. staff have found that the accuracy of the results increases significantly if the recreational therapist has observed the client in various activities in a variety of settings prior to filling out the assessment.

PHYSICAL DOMAIN

GROSS MOTOR

0-6 months — The client needs some assistance to support head/trunk when in sitting position. When an object, like a maracas, is placed in his/her hand, client is not able to (or has difficulty) shaking object. Client is able to turn head from side to side when lying on back. Can momentarily lift head from bed.

6-12 months — Client can sit without support, pulls self to standing. Client is able to crawl, is able to support head in upright position when sitting. Client can roll from back to abdomen.

1-3 years — Client can lift chest and abdomen off ground when on belly. Client is able to sit in supportive chair (up to 10 minutes). Client is able to change from lying-down position to sitting position. Walks with some supportive help.

3-6 years — Client can walk/run without help. Kneeling, standing, throwing ball, and going up stairs (2 feet on each step) possible without falling. Client is developing skills to pick up ball or to kick ball while maintaining balance. When jumping, jumps with both feet. Enjoys jumping off low step. Client is able to stand on one foot for a very short time and can tip-toe a short distance.

7-10 years — Client goes up stairs using alternate feet. Client is learning to skip and hop, maybe even skate. Can walk backwards with heel to toes. Can catch and throw ball reliably. Can throw ball overhand.

FINE MOTOR

0-6 months	Client's hand will usually clench toys placed in hand, but will not reach for them. Client will clutch own hand, pull at blankets and clothes. Client will try to reach toys with hand but will frequently overshoot them. Client will attempt to place toys in his/her mouth. Client cannot pick toy up after s/he drops it.
6-12 months	Client will pick up a dropped toy. When client has one toy in his/her hand and is offered another one, will drop first. May be able to transfer from one hand to the other. Client enjoys banging toys on table. When grasping for a toy, may begin to use pincer grasp using index, 4th, and 5th fingers against lower part of thumb. Client may attempt to hold crayon. Reaches persistently for toys out of reach.
1-3 years	Client turns pages of books, one page at a time. When playing with blocks, can build tower to eight blocks high. Client is developing the skills to move fingers independently.
3-6 years	Client can construct bridges with 3 cubes. Client accurately places small objects in narrow-necked bottle (or other small opening). When drawing, client can imitate a cross, copy diamonds, copy circles, and can name what s/he has drawn. Toward end of this developmental grouping, the client can draw stick man, numbers, letters, or words. Client uses scissors, simple tools, or pencil well.

EYE-HAND COORDINATION

0-6 months	Client is able to follow moving objects with eyes for short periods of time (under 10 seconds). Client will visually track object by turning head up to 180 degrees.
6-12 months	Client is able to maintain visual contact with small objects that s/he is interested in (not just blank staring).
1-3 years	Client demonstrates intense interest in picture books, will turn pages of book while 'reading'. Client will build tower of cubes or will align two or more objects like a train. In drawing, the client imitates vertical and circular strokes.
3-6 years	Client is able to copy simple geometric figures, places geometric forms into the correct opening of form board.
7-10 years	Client is aware of the fact that his/her hand can be used as a tool to get things done. Client likes to draw, print, and color.

COGNITIVE DOMAIN

PLAY BEHAVIOR

0-6 months	Client does not seem to be playing but watches movement/turns head toward sounds in room for short periods of time. Client plays with his/her body; follows others without purpose; does gross motor activity without purpose. Client just sits looking around.
6-9 months	Client watches others play, might even communicate with them, but does not actively participate.
9 months to 3 years	Client engages in playful activity alone and independently. Others may be playing nearby, but their play does not influence client's own play activity.
3-4 years	Client plays with toys; engages in activities similar to the other clients/staff nearby, but plays next to, instead of with, others.
4-5 years	Client plays with others. There is no organization of play activities, no division of labor, and no product. Each client acts independently; the client's interest and actions are directed toward being with the other clients instead of directed toward the play activity.
5-10 years	The client plays with other clients in an organized manner for a purpose (eg; making something, formal games). The client feels like s/he belongs to the group. The client plays a role (leader/ follower) and the others support that role to some degree.

STRUCTURE OF PLAY

0-12 months	Client explores world visually by random movement. As ability to grasp and ability to put things in his/her mouth develops, explores the world this way also.
1-5 years	Client engages in make-believe and dramatic play.
5-10 years	Client engages in playful activities that tend to produce an end product or be part of a formal game.
10+ years	Client's playful activities become more complex with planning for future goals and activities included. Daydreaming and introspection evident.

LANGUAGE USE

0-6 months	Client will use simple body language to communicate (eg; holding hands out to be hugged). Client can make consonant sounds 'n','k','g','p','b', and vowel like cooing sounds interspersed with consonantal sounds (eg; ah-goo).
6-12 months	Client begins to laugh out loud. Client takes pleasure in hearing his/her own sounds. Client is able to produce vowel sounds and chain syllables (baba, dada). Client 'talks' (produces sounds) to imitate talking when others are talking. Client may say one word ('he', 'bye', 'what', 'no'). Client can make consonant sounds 't', 'd', and 'w'.
1-3 years	Client can say two or more words ('up', 'down', 'come', and 'go') with meaning. Client is beginning to understand the concept of time; waits in response to 'just a minute'. Client refers to self by name.
3-6 years	Client now has a vocabulary greater than 900 words and can give his/her first and last name. Client uses three to four words in his/her sentences. Client tends to tell exaggerated stories.
7-10 years	Client is fascinated by rhymes, alliteration, anagrams, codes and ciphers, foreign words and phrases, puns and onomatopoeia. S/he likes to play with the ambiguities of language, as in 'You want me to take my vitamins? Okay, I'll take them to my room.'.

LANGUAGE COMPREHENSION

0-6 months	Client will squeal aloud to show pleasure, coos, babbles, and chuckles. Client just beginning to imitate (cough, protraction of tongue).
6-12 months	Client comprehends 'no-no' and can inhibit behaviors to verbal command of 'no-no'. Client can respond to simple verbal commands. Client reacts to staff anger; cries or pouts when scolded. Client responds to his/her own name. Client takes pleasure in hearing his/her own voice.
1-3 years	Client can comprehend meaning of several words (comprehension always precedes verbalization). Client understands simple verbal commands (eg; 'Give it to me.', 'Show me your eyes.').
3-6 years	Client obeys four prepositional phrases (under, on top of, in back of, or in front of). Client is beginning to be able to follow up to three commands in succession.
7-10 years	Client can define common objects, such as fork and chair, in terms of their use. Client can describe the objects in a picture instead of just naming what they are. The client does not doubt the accuracy of the written word, just because it's in print.

NUMBERS

3-6 years	Client can repeat four digits. Client is beginning to be able to name coins (nickle, dime, etc.). Client may begin to show some understanding of numbers through counting objects. Client may pretend to tell time.
7-10 years	Client reads ordinary clock or watch correctly to nearest quarter hour. Client can make change for a quarter. Client can count pennies.

OBJECT USE AND UNDERSTANDING

0-6 months	Client begins to recognize familiar faces and objects. Client anticipates feeding when s/he sees familiar luncheon ware. Client is discovering parts of his/her body, but does not really know what they 'do'.
6-12 months	Client begins to be aware of depth and space in play. Client can hold a crayon to make a mark on paper. Client explores objects more thoroughly (eg; clapper inside of bell used during music time).
1-3 years	Client knows to turn pages of book, but turns many pages at a time. Client begins to recognize objects by name. Client experiences joy and satisfaction when a task is mastered.
3-6 years	Client is able to copy geometric figure with crayon or pencil. Client develops a curiosity about the world around him/her and is constantly asking questions. Client knows simple songs. Client is beginning to use time-oriented words (eg; soon, later) with increased understanding.
7-10 years	Client can make use of common tools such as a hammer, saw, or screwdriver. Client uses clocks and watches for practical purposes. Client can learn to count backwards from 20 to 1. Client can describe common objects in detail, not merely their use. Client is becoming more proficient at common kitchen and sewing utensils. Client usually understands, and likes, being part of a reward system.

FOLLOWS DIRECTIONS

6-12 months — Client comprehends 'no-no'.

1-3 years — Client understands simple commands (eg; 'Give it to me.' 'Show me your eyes.'). May say 'no' even while agreeing to the request.

3-6 years — Client begins to learn simple games and meanings of rules, but follows them according to self-interpretation.

7-10 years — Client can share and cooperate but occasionally needs cueing from staff.

PROBLEM SOLVING

0-6 months — Client is beginning to localize sounds made below ear level. Client demands attention by being fussy, becomes bored if left alone.

6-12 months — Client will search for an object if s/he sees it hidden. Client will tug at the clothing of another person to attract their attention. Client reacts to restrictions with frustration. Client localizes sound by turning head diagonally and directly toward sound. Client can localize sounds made above ear.

1-3 years — Client may have a 'security blanket' or favorite toy. Thinking is characterized by lumping many things together (global organization of thought) and s/he may explain many everyday occurrences as being the result of magic (magical thinking). Client realizes that just because something is out of sight, it's not necessarily out of reach, so will look for 'hidden object' (object permanence).

3-6 years — Client may feel the 'need to win' so will cheat to win. Client has improved concept of time and may talk about the past and the future, as much as about the present.

7-10 years — Client is beginning to be able to put himself/herself in another's place to understand other side of the problem. Client begins to use elementary logic. Client notices that certain parts are missing from pictures. Client has very few socially acceptable tension outlets.

ATTENDING BEHAVIOR

0-6 months — Client, visually, usually prefers people to objects. Client shows much interest in surroundings. Prefers more complex visual stimuli.

6-12 months — Client listens selectively to familiar words. Client looks at and follows pictures in a book for up to five minutes. Client can stare at a very small object for a period of time. Client can visually follow a rapidly moving objects.

1-3 years — Client's attention span increasing to 20 minutes or more. Displays an intense and prolonged interest in pictures.

3-6 years — Client tries to attend, but is easily distracted. Develops a simple organizational framework for play and other tasks. Client can usually wait his/her turn. The client often finishes what s/he starts.

7-10 years — Client notices that certain parts are missing from pictures. Client is aware of time of day. Client is observant enough to say which is pretty and which is ugly in a series of drawings of faces.

AFFECTIVE DOMAIN

POSSESSIONS

0-6 months	Client is not aware of the concept of ownership.
6-12 months	Client begins to develop awareness of ownership; will complain about objects being taken away that s/he had/wants.
1-3 years	Client will claim and defend possessions.
3-6 years	Client is generally able to share toys and other possessions, although expresses ideas of 'mine' frequently. Client sometimes will steal money and other attractive items.
7-10 years	Client can share and cooperate. Stealing may still be a problem.

EMOTIONAL CONTROL

0-6 month	Client has frequent mood swings — from crying and laughing, with little or no provocation. Reacts to restrictions with frustration.
6-12 months	Client shows emotions, has temper tantrums. Client has few, if any, other positive ways of dealing with frustration.
1-3 years	Temper tantrums increase in intensity as way to deal with stress. Client does not have the reasoning ability to solve many problems, seeks staff help. Client may use magical thinking to 'solve' problems (eg; a monster will come and eat you up).
3-6 years	Client demonstrates more aggressive behavior including motor activity and shocking language. Client requires increased attention from staff for emotional support dues to his/her emotional insecurity and fear of loss of love.
7-10 years	Client has very few tension outlets; s/he is decreasing old tension-reducing habits; attempts to control those that remain. Client bites nails, picks at fingers, scowls, stomps feet, taps pencil, draws in lips.

IMITATION PLAY

0-6 months	Client begins imitation play (protrusion of tongue).
6-12 months	Client will imitate facial expressions. Client imitates simple acts and noises.
1-3 years	Client begins to imitate care-givers in such activities as cleaning residence. Client becomes a 'great' imitator, taking delight in copying other peoples' actions.
3-6 years	Client often does what s/he sees staff and peers doing, even copying undesirable behavior and language. (Mild swear words may begin surfacing.)
7-10 years	Client likes to put on dramatic shows that combine imitations of events, people, actions previously observed.

PEOPLE SKILLS

0-6 months	Client will cease crying/fussing when favorite staff comes into room. Client enjoys social interaction with people.
6-12 months	Client demonstrates such emotions as jealousy, affection, anger, fear. Client will stop many activities when told 'no-no'. Client may hand a toy to another person, but does not let go to share. Client will repeat actions that attract attention and that are laughed at. Client may be fearful of strangers.
1-3 years	Client is less fearful of strangers. Client may infer a cause by associating two or more experiences (such as candy missing, roommate smiling).
3-6 years	Client begins to interact in play and take turns. Client selects his/her own friends.
7-10 years	Client enjoys being part of a 'family' unit. Client enjoys competitive games but requires supervision as unsupervised play frequently ends in brawl.

REACTION TO MUSIC

0-6 months	Client enjoys background music. Soothing music seems to have a calming effect on client.
6-12 months	Client moves to music, not necessarily in time.
1-3 years	Client knows phrases of songs. Client will dramatize songs.

STORIES AND DRAMATIC PLAY

0-6 months	Client may attend to staff's voice while being read a story, but does not follow story line. Client does not participate in dramatic play.
6-12 months	Client plays peek-a-boo type games. Client plays interactive games such as pat-a-cake.
1-3 years	Client listens to short, simple stories, makes relevant comments about stories. 'Reads' from pictures.
3-6 years	Client begins to work out social interactions through play. Client may replay (dramatize) stressful or pleasant events until s/he resolves conflict or moves on to next experience.
7-10 years	Client dramatizes many conversations and situations.

GRST: General Recreation Screening Tool (Score Sheet)

Name ______________________________ Date of Birth ____________ Staff ________________

Unit ________________________ Date of Assessment ________________

The purpose of this screening tool is to provide the therapist with a general assessment which helps determine the strengths and weaknesses of the client. The results also provide a developmental level for each assessed functional skill that relates to the client's leisure capabilities. Please note that the skills listed within each category may not be in exact developmental order. — **Scoring:** Read the developmental skills listed in each age group for each functional leisure skill category. If the client is able to demonstrate between 50% to 75% of the skills listed within the age group, draw a dashed line through that age group. If the client is able to demonstrate 75% or more of the skills listed within the age group, draw a solid line through that age group.

Example:

	0-6 mos.	6-12 mos.	1-3 yrs.	3-6 yrs.	7-10 yrs.
Fine Motor	━━━━	━━━━	■ ■ ■ ■ ■		

DEVELOPMENTAL GROUPS

	Functional Leisure Skills	0-6 mos.	6-12 mos.	1-3 yrs.	3-6 yrs.	7-10 yrs.	10+
Physical	Gross Motor						
	Fine Motor						
	Eye-Hand						
Cognitive	Play Behavior		6mos.-9mos.	9mos.-3yrs.	3-4yrs. 4-5yrs.	5-10yrs.	
	Play Structure			1-5 yrs.		5-10yrs.	10+
	Language Use						
	Language Compr.						
	Numbers						
	Object Use						
	Follow-Directions						
	Problem Solving						
	Attending Behavior						
Affective	Possessions						
	Emotional Control						
	Imitation Play						
	People Skills						
	Music						
	Stories/Drama						

Summary / Recommendations:

RECREATION EARLY DEVELOPMENT SCREENING TOOL

Name: Recreation Early Development Screening Tool

Also Known As: REDS

Author: joan burlingame

Time Needed to Administer: 20 minutes

Time Needed to Score: 10 minutes

Recommended Disability Group: Individuals with severe or profound MR/DD who are adaptively under 1 year of age.

Purpose of the Assessment: The purpose of the REDS is to assess the developmental level of clients who are functioning at or below one year of age.

What Does the Assessment Measure?: The REDS assess five areas as they relate to leisure: 1) play, 2) fine motor, 3) gross motor, 4) sensory, and 5) social/cognition.

Supplies Needed: Common household and play items are required for the assessment. In addition, the therapist will need the REDS manual and the score sheet #112.

Reliability/Validity: The REDS was developed after an extensive literature search and the review of over 30 developmental charts and studies. Initial field testing showed that the REDs places more emphasis on visual and hearing skills than is appropriate. It is for this reason that caution should be used when deciding if to use this assessment with clients with visual or auditory deficits. No reliability studies are reported.

Degree of Skill Required to Administer and Score: Due to the limited amount of validity data (as well as the known weakness of over emphasizing visual and auditory skills) the skills of a recreational therapist certified at the CTRS level by the National Council for Therapeutic Recreation Certification may be required.

Comments: The REDS is one of the only assessments in the field of recreational therapy which measures clients who are extremely disabled.

Suggested Levels: Rancho Los Amigos Level: inappropriate. Developmental Level: Adapted level of Birth to 1 year. Reality Orientation: inappropriate.

Distributor: Idyll Arbor, Inc. 25119 S.E. 262 Street, PO Box 720, Ravensdale, WA 98051 (206) 432-3231. (Area code 425 after April 1997.)

RECREATION EARLY DEVELOPMENT SCREENING TOOL (REDS)

The purpose of the REDS is to assess the developmental level of clients who are functioning at or below one year of age. The REDS assesses five areas as they relate to leisure: 1) Play, 2) Fine Motor, 3) Gross Motor, 4) Sensory, and 5) Social/Cognition. The therapist will be able to pinpoint the developmental age in each category (e.g., Play = 4 - 8 months, Fine Motor = 3 months, Gross Motor = 5 months, Sensory = 3 months, and Social/Cognition = 3 months).

It is through play that all humans learn the basic skills that they will need later to participate in meaningful relationships and to successfully hold down a job. Normally in the first year of life a child makes some of his/her most important discoveries about the world around him/her. The child begins to learn how s/he can manipulate the world (an important skill for survival). The first stepping stones toward an understanding about space, structure, trust, and cause and effect are learned during this year.

For the individual who has either a disability or handicap which interrupts the achievement of these first year developmental skills, the recreational therapist's job is to nurture the individual along toward achieving them. This is done both through direct intervention (therapy) and through structuring the environment to promote the skill development and skill maintenance desired.

The words 'DISABILITY' and 'HANDICAP' do not have the same definition: do not use them interchangeably. Disability refers to a functional physical, sensory, or cognitive limitation which interferes with a person's ability. Handicap refers to: a society-imposed condition or barrier; a self-imposed condition or barrier; or a natural condition or barrier in the environment which impedes the individual's ability to function.

PLAY refers to the individual's integration of multiple sensory/learning actions which s/he is internalizing. The individual may be letting go of a block (fine motor) and watching it drop to the floor (visual tracking), waiting with great anticipation to see if someone then picks it back up (cause and effect). In normal development, the individual will repeat playful actions that bring pleasure.

FINE MOTOR refers to the use of one's hands (and when needed, one's toes) to manipulate the environment.

GROSS MOTOR refers to the use of one's trunk and extremities for movement through space, balance, and relative strength to complete the task.

SENSORY refers to the stimulation of the body's sensory organs and the reaction/response that results. This element of play is the nonsocial stimulating experience which primarily arises from outside of the individual.

SOCIAL/COGNITION refers to the element of play which involves pleasure derived from relationships with people, animals, and other objects in the environment. In normal development the individual learns very quickly to elicit desired responses through such behaviors as imitation and making sounds.

The developmental material used in this screening tool was taken from a series of developmental charts, primarily from Whaley and Wong, 1985. Each skill listed in the REDS was confirmed by at least one other source. Initial testing with 75 clients showed that it did not work well with clients who were legally blind or deaf. The REDS may still be used with those two populations but with less confidence in the validity of the results.

This manual is an updated version of the original REDS which was developed for Rainier School in Buckley, Washington. In this version the assessment has remained basically the same, with most changes reflecting vocabulary changes in the 1988 ICF-MR (Intermediate Care Facility for the Mentally Retarded) regulations. The original score sheet, Idyll Arbor #112, may still be used.

The REDS was developed specifically for use with adolescents and adults who are mentally retarded or developmentally delayed. It has been used in a variety of pediatric hospitals around the United States. Mixed reviews have been given about its use with pediatric populations. Therapists have limited choices for pediatric populations, with this being the only recreational therapy tool for children under one year.

Please note that it is normal for the individual to have 'spotty' scores. When an individual starts demonstrating functional skills around the 4 month level, s/he will need to stop demonstrating some of the earlier skills. An example would be the sequence of hand grasps. The individual should advance from the palmer grasp to the pincer grasp. A therapist will know which skills to work on by examining the skills listed in the assessment to determine the appropriate next step (or skill) to improve the quality of playfulness.

SUPPLIES NEEDED:

CAUTION: DO NOT LEAVE THE CLIENT UNATTENDED WITH THE TESTING SUPPLIES. MANY OF THEM ARE SMALL ENOUGH FOR HIM/HER TO CHOKE ON!

1. Matchbox car or Fisher Price car
2. Board to set up incline to roll car down
3. Maracas light enough for client to pick up
4. Cloth napkin
5. Six wooden blocks, approx. 1.25 to 1.5 inches square
6. See-through plastic bottle with opening approximately 2 inches in diameter
7. TV or radio with volume knobs which turn clockwise/counter clockwise
8. Set of stacking cups, smallest being 1 inch in diameter
9. Large crayons (approx. 9/16 x 5 inches long)
10. Drawing paper, (white) 8.5 x 11 inches
11. Hand bell, approx. 5 inches tall (including handle)
12. Ten colorful wooden beads, 1 inch in diameter
13. Picture book, no larger than 9 inches by 10 inches
14. Watch that can measure seconds as well as minutes
15. Object that has been in the freezer and is cold
16. One square block or bead that is 1/2 inch across
17. Pen flash light
18. Colorful picture of people's faces and/or flowers
19. Three pictures of simple geometric forms in primary colors: one picture of a red circle 4 inches across on a white background, one picture of a green square 4 inches across on a white background, and one yellow triangle with 4 inches sides on a white background.
20. Toy that client likes
21. Non-breakable mirror, approx. 10 inches x 10 inches
22. String measuring 8 inches in length

TIME NEEDED:

The REDS is an assessment that is easily done during different play periods. The therapist will find that in most cases, s/he will need less than 20 minutes to administer the assessment.

PLAY ACTIVITIES

0 - 1 MONTH

1. The client moves in response to things in the environment (reflexes, other movements).
2. Little noticeable learning taking place. The client does not seem to be imitating staff, or to be learning from the environment.
3. Activities do not really count as play; no noted purposeful activity for enjoyment sake.

2 - 4 MONTHS

4. The client demonstrates interest in engaging in self-exploratory and/or self-stimulating activities.
5. Practice games (repeating activities) make up the major part of the client's play (opening mouth, sticking out tongue in imitation of staff, playing peek-a-boo).
6. The client seems to enjoy watching his/her hands, engages in simple repetition of body movements (e.g., kicking legs, moving arms in simple patterns) to experience the sensation of his/her body moving.
7. Client repeats his/her vocal sounds for pleasure.

4 - 8 MONTHS

8. The client will repeat actions to prolong activity/result that s/he finds interesting (purposeful manipulation of his/her body to produce desired results).

9. The client will occasionally vary his/her play action a slight bit to see if the result is different (e.g., turning head to side AND kicking to see if that allows him/her to roll over and is SURPRISED if s/he does roll over).

8-12 MONTHS

10. The client has clearly begun to purposely repeat playful movements of his/her body to produce desired, enjoyable results.
11. The client uses fine and gross motor skills to start purposely manipulating his/her environment. A classic example of this would be a client dropping a toy as soon as the staff pick it up and give it back to him/her. This important game helps teach object permanence (a concept not fully developed yet). This game also helps teach the client that s/he is capable of manipulating things in the environment other than his/her body.
12. The actual process of doing the activity is more important than the end result.
13. The client enjoys putting things inside of containers and setting one object upon another.
14. The client knows by trial and error that s/he cannot rest a plaything on a vertical or steeply sloping surface, but this learning does not teach him/her that s/he can roll a car down an incline.
15. The client is aware that some things have a 'correct' up-down spatial orientation and goes around almost compulsively righting overturned objects.

FINE MOTOR ACTIVITY

0 - 1 MONTH

16. The client's hands are usually in a closed position.
17. If a toy is placed in the client's hands, the client will usually grasp it (because of a natural reflex, not due to a conscious desire to hold anything).

2 MONTHS

18. The client's hands relax and are open at least as often as they are in the closed position.
19. The client will not always grasp a toy placed in his/her hand as the 'grasp reflex' is now fading.

3 MONTHS

20. The client's hands are predominantly open; grasp reflex is now absent.
21. The client will actively hold a rattle, maracas, handbell, or other similarly shaped toy, but if s/he drops it, s/he will not reach for it.
22. Client finds enjoyment in pulling at his/her clothes and blankets and in clutching his/her own hands.

4 MONTHS

23. The client plays by actively exploring his/her own hands.
24. The client will grasp clothing or blanket or pull it over his/her face.
25. The client will try to reach for objects that s/he sees and wants to play with, but often over-reaches.
26. The client may grasp a toy with both hands when one is placed in his/her hand.
27. The client will play with a rattle, maracas, handbell, or similar object.
28. The client begins to place objects in his/her mouth.

5 MONTHS

29. The client is able to grasp objects voluntarily.
30. The client uses the 'palmer grasp' (using the whole hand) instead of the 'pincer grasp' (using the thumb and index finger).
31. If given the opportunity, the client will play with his/her toes, other body parts.
32. The client will hold one cube while looking at another, but will not be able to reach for and hold two cubes.

6 MONTHS

33. The client can pick up a toy that s/he has dropped.
34. The client will drop the cube s/he is holding when another cube is given to him/her.
35. The client may try to grab his/her feet and pull them to his/ her mouth.

7 MONTHS

36. The client is able to transfer a toy from one hand to the other.
37. One of the ways that a client may 'play' with a toy is by banging it on the table.
38. The client uses a 'raking' motion with his/her hands to obtain toys near him/her.

8 MONTHS

39. The client alternates between using the palmer grasp and using a modified 'pincer grasp' using the index, fourth, and fifth fingers against the lower part of the thumb.
40. The client is able to release held toys at will.
41. The client will draw a toy closer to him/her by pulling on the string attached to the toy.
42. The client frequently reaches for toys out of his/her reach (not able to judge distance vs. arm length).

9 MONTHS

43. The client uses only his/her thumb and index finger in a crude manner as s/he picks up toys.
44. The client displays a preference for either his/her right or left hand in play.

10 MONTHS

45. The client will clap his/her hands together at midline, but not necessarily hard enough to make a clapping sound.
46. The client will throw his/her toy but with very poor (if any) aim.
47. The client is able to retrieve a bead or cube out of a see-through plastic bottle.
48. The client can switch on a TV set or radio and twist the knobs to increase/decrease the volume.
49. The client may turn the knobs clockwise with the right hand and counter-clockwise with the left hand.
50. The client can take apart semi-complex toys (puzzles, stacked cups, etc.) but does not demonstrate a consistent skill to put them back together.

11 MONTHS

51. The client can hold a crayon and make a mark on paper.
52. The client begins to re-explore things s/he explored before, only this time in more detail. The clapper on bells and the spinning wheels on toy cars seem to draw his/her attention for minutes at a time.

12 MONTHS

53. The client is able to pick up toys using a neat pincer grasp.
54. The client enjoys fine motor play that involves sequential play (e.g., placing a bead in a cup, bead after bead).
55. The client attempts to build a two-block tower, but fails.
56. The client tries to insert a small object into a narrow-necked bottle but fails.
57. The client 'reads' books and magazines by turning many pages at a time.

GROSS MOTOR ACTIVITY

0 - 1 MONTHS

58. The client can turn his/her head from side-to-side when prone (lying face down); can lift head momentarily from his/her bed.
59. The client's head has a marked head lag when s/he is being pulled from the lying to sitting position.
60. The client tends to assume a flexed position with pelvis high, but knees not under abdomen when prone.
61. The client cannot maintain his/her head in an upright position when sitting.

2 MONTHS

62. The client assumes a less flexed position when prone — hips flat, legs extended, arms flexed, and head to side.
63. The client demonstrates only moderate head lag when pulled to sitting position.
64. The client can lift his/her head almost 45 degrees off the floor when in prone position.
65. The client can usually maintain his/her head in an upright position when sitting, but his/her head still bobs forward some.

3 MONTHS

66. The client is able to raise head and shoulders from prone position to a 45 to 90 degree angle when on floor.
67. The client can bear weight on his/her forearms when prone on floor.

4 MONTHS

68. The client demonstrates good head balance when sitting.
69. The client is able to raise his/her head and chest off a soft surface (e.g., couch) to an angle of 90 degrees.
70. The client can roll from his/her back to his/her side.
71. The client is able to sit erect if propped up.

5 MONTHS

72. The client demonstrates no head lag when pulled into the sitting position.
73. The client is able to hold his/her head steady and erect while sitting.
74. The client is able to sit for periods of time as long as his/her back is well-supported.
75. The client can turn over from his/her abdomen to his/her back.

6 MONTHS

76. The client can lift his/her chest and upper abdomen off the floor, bearing the weight on his/her hands.
77. The client can sit with his/her back straight while in a chair with a back.
78. The client can roll from his/her back to his/her abdomen.

7 MONTHS

79. The client can sit independently on the floor, but leans forward on both hands to balance.
80. The client can actively bounce when supported in the standing position.

8 MONTHS

81. The client can sit steadily, unsupported.

9 - 10 MONTHS

82. The client is able to crawl, may crawl backwards at first.
83. The client can sit steadily on the floor for over 10 minutes.
84. The client can recover his/her balance when s/he leans forward but cannot do so when leaning sideways.
85. The client can pull himself/herself into a standing position.
86. The client can go from a prone position to a sitting position.

11-12 MONTHS

87. The client can sit down from a standing position.
88. The client can walk while holding a staff's hand for support.

SENSORY

0 - 1 MONTHS

89. The client is able to visually fixate on a slowly moving object.
90. The client will visually follow a light to midline.
91. The client will quiet when s/he hears a voice.

2 MONTHS

92. The client will visually follow a dangling toy from side to a point beyond midline.
93. The client will visually search to locate a sound.
94. The client will turn his/her head to the side when the sound is made at the level of his/her ear.

3 MONTHS

95. The client will follow a toy to periphery (180 degrees).
96. The client will locate a sound by turning his/her head to the side and looking in the same direction.
97. The client inconsistently demonstrates the ability to coordinate stimuli from various sense organs (e.g., looks toward cold object that his/her hand touches).

4 MONTHS

98. The client can focus on a 1/2 inch block.
99. The client is beginning to demonstrate some eye-hand coordination (e.g., by reaching for objects, but not necessarily touching them).

5 MONTHS

100. The client visually pursues a dropped object.
101. The client is able to sustain visual inspection of an object.
102. The client is able to locate sounds made below his/her ear.

6 MONTHS

103. The client will adjust his/her posture to see an object.
104. The client prefers more complex visual stimuli (e.g., a picture of flowers or people's faces to simple geometric shapes).
105. The client can localize sounds made above his/her ears.
106. The client will turn his/her head to the side, then look up or down.

7 MONTHS

107. The client will turn his/her head to the sound of his/her name.
108. The client localizes sound by turning his/her head in a curving arch.
109. The client has 'taste' preferences for food and games.

8 - 10 MONTHS

110. The client locates sounds by turning his/her head diagonally and directly toward the sound.
111. The client inconsistently demonstrates an awareness of depth and space in his/her play.

11 - 12 MONTHS

112. The client can discriminate (and point to) simple forms (e.g., circle).
113. The client can follow a rapidly moving object with his/her eyes.
114. The client can control and adjust his/her responses to sound (not startling all the time to sharp sounds).
115. The client will listen for a sound to recur.

SOCIALIZATION/COGNITION

0 - 1 MONTHS

116. The client will watch the staff's face intently as s/he talks to him/her.
117. The client is totally self-centered, that is, the client is not aware that s/he is a separate being from the world around him/her. The client has little understanding of how to purposely control either himself/herself or the world around him/her.

2 MONTHS

118. The client will smile in response to a variety of things s/he finds pleasure in.
119. The client visually prefers people to objects.
120. The client demonstrates an excitement in anticipation of seeing toys that s/he likes.

3 MONTHS

121. The client demonstrates a great interest in his/her surroundings by watching the activity and objects around him/her.
122. The client can recognize familiar faces and objects (e.g., staff, favorite toys).

4 MONTHS

123. The client demands attention by fussing, becomes bored if left alone.
124. The client enjoys social interaction with others.
125. The client shows excitement with his/her whole body, squeals, breathes heavily.
126. The client demonstrates memory; is aware of strange surroundings.

5 MONTHS

127. The client will smile at an image of himself/herself in a mirror.
128. The client is able to discriminate strangers from regular staff and housemates.
129. The client will vocalize displeasure when an object is taken away.

6 MONTHS

130. The client begins to fear strangers.
131. The client inconsistently demonstrates the ability to imitate staff in play.
132. The client will briefly search for a dropped object.

7 MONTHS

133. The client is able to demonstrate the imitation of very simple acts and noises 50% or more of the time.
134. The client will actively play peek-a-boo with staff.

8 - 9 MONTHS

135. The client will respond to the command 'NO'.
136. The client is demonstrating the desire to please staff.
137. The client is demonstrating a developing fear of the dark and/or of being left alone.
138. The client will search for a toy if s/he sees it hidden.

10 - 11 MONTHS

139. The client will inhibit behavior to the verbal command of 'No-No', or by the use of his/her own name.
140. The client imitates facial expressions.
141. The client is able to wave good-bye upon command or cue.
142. The client will extend a toy to another person but will not release it.
143. The client repeats actions that attract attention and are laughed at.
144. The client will cry when scolded by staff, or react in a manner that demonstrates his/her distress at the staff being angry.
145. The client will look at and follow pictures in a book.

11 - 12 MONTHS

146. The client demonstrates joy and satisfaction when a task is mastered.
147. The client shows emotions such as jealousy, affection, anger, and fear.
148. The client enjoys familiar surroundings but will explore away from his/her residence.
149. The client may develop a 'security blanket' or favorite toy.
150. The client will search for an object even if s/he hasn't seen it hidden, but only where it was last seen.

REDS

Recreation Early Development Screening Tool

Score Sheet

Name: ____________________ Date of Assessment: ____________________

Living Unit: ____________________ Staff: ____________________

Birthdate: ____________________

Admission Date: ____________________

Use this form to record the scores from the Recreation Early Development Screening Tool. Place an 'X' next to the number corresponding to a positive answer. This assessment is not meant to be given to residents who are either blind or deaf.

Play	Fine Motor Activity			Gross Motor			Sensory		Social/Cognition		
1☐	16☐	29☐	43☐	58☐	72☐	82☐	89☐	103☐	116☐	130☐	146☐
2☐	17☐	30☐	44☐	59☐	73☐	83☐	90☐	104☐	117☐	131☐	147☐
3☐		31☐		60☐	74☐	84☐	91☐	105☐		132☐	148☐
	18☐	32☐	45☐	61☐	75☐	85☐		106☐	118☐		149☐
4☐	19☐		46☐			86☐	92☐		119☐	133☐	150☐
5☐		33☐	47☐	62☐	76☐		93☐	107☐	120☐	134☐	
6☐	20☐	34☐	48☐	63☐	77☐	87☐	94☐	108☐			
7☐	21☐	35☐	49☐	64☐	78☐	88☐		109☐	121☐	135☐	
	22☐		50☐	65☐			95☐		122☐	136☐	
8☐		36☐			79☐		96☐	110☐		137☐	
9☐	23☐	37☐	51☐	66☐	80☐		97☐	111☐	123☐	138☐	
	24☐	38☐	52☐	67☐					124☐		
10☐	25☐				81☐		98☐	112☐	125☐	139☐	
11☐	26☐	39☐	53☐	68☐			99☐	113☐	126☐	140☐	
12☐	27☐	40☐	54☐	69☐				114☐		141☐	
13☐	28☐	41☐	55☐	70☐			100☐	115☐	127☐	142☐	
14☐		42☐	56☐	71☐			101☐		128☐	143☐	
15☐			57☐				102☐		129☐	144☐	
										145☐	

Scoring

Using a magic marker, draw a line through each number group below in which the resident received at least one positive answer.

Example: Resident's 'X' had a positive answer to question #'s 2,3,5 & 7. Resident 'X' is functioning at approximately 4 months of age in skills related to play.

	1	2	3	4	5	6
Play	1-3	4-7	4-7	4-7	8-9	8-9

Developmental Graph (Months)

	1	2	3	4	5	6	7	8	9	10	11	12
Play	1-3	4-7	4-7	4-7	8-9	8-9	8-9	8-9	10-15	10-15	10-15	10-15
Fine Motor	16-17	18-19	20-22	23-28	29-32	33-35	36-38	39-42	43-44	45-50	51-52	53-57
Gross Motor	58-61	62-65	66-67	68-71	72-75	76-78	79-80	81	82-86	82-86	87-88	87-88
Sensory	89-91	92-94	95-97	98-99	100-102	103-106	107-1[illegible]	110[illegible]	1[illegible]	[illegible]0-111	[illegible]-115	112-115
Social Cognition	116-117	118-120	121-122	123-126	127-129	130-132	133-134	135-138	135-138	139-145	146-150	146-150

Summary:

Recommendations:

COMPREHENSIVE EVALUATION IN RECREATIONAL THERAPY — PHYSICAL DISABILITIES

Name: Comprehensive Evaluation in Recreational Therapy — Physical Disabilities.

Also Known As: CERT — Phys/Dis., CERT — Rehab.

Author: Robert Parker

Time Needed to Administer: One hour

Time Needed to Score: Most of the scoring takes place during the administration of the assessment. An additional 15 minutes should be scheduled to score and interpret the results.

Recommended Disability Group: Physical Disabilities

Purpose of the Assessment: The CERT — Physical Disabilities establishes a baseline of a patient's functional skills related to leisure activities. Re-assessment of the same patient helps to establish skill recovery or loss.

What Does the Assessment Measure?: The CERT — Physical Disabilities measures functional ability in eight areas: 1) gross motor function, 2) fine movement, 3) locomotion, 4) motor skills, 5) sensory, 6) cognition, 7) communication, and 8) behavior.

Supplies Needed: Matt table (helpful, not required), small objects (diameters = 1/8", 1", 2", 3", 6"), checker set (or other activity to measure manual endurance), a variety of surfaces to try w/c or ambulation skills, hallway with distance marked off every 10 feet, stairs, 4 musical instruments, watch or clock, a set of Figure versus Ground pictures, pencil and paper, and score sheet (#121).

Reliability/Validity: Validity and reliability studies reported.

Degree of Skill Required to Administer and Score: A recreational therapist certified at the CTRS level by the National Council for Therapeutic Recreation Certification should be able to administer, score, and interpret this assessment.

Comments: The CERT — Physical Disability Assessment provides a comprehensive functional assessment, especially if the recreational therapist is the only therapist in the facility (e.g., no O.T. or P.T.). This testing tool is rarely used any more in the United States, probably because of the length of time required to obtain the information.

Suggested Levels: Rancho Los Amigos Level: 1 - 8. Developmental Level: Most items will allow a developmental level of 5 years or above. Reality Orientation Level: Severe and above.

Distributor: Idyll Arbor, Inc., 25119 SE 262 Street, PO Box 720, Ravensdale, WA 98051-0720 (206) 432-3231. (Area code 425 after April 1997.)

COMPREHENSIVE EVALUATION IN RECREATIONAL THERAPY CERT — PHYSICAL DISABILITIES

PURPOSE: The CERT — Physical Disabilities establishes a baseline of a patient's functional skills related to leisure activities. Re-assessment of the same patient helps to establish skill recovery or loss.

SUPPLIES NEEDED

Mat table (helpful, not required)
Small objects (diameters = 1/8", 1", 2", 3", 6")
Checker set (or other activity to measure manual endurance)
A variety of surfaces to try w/c or ambulation skills
Hallway with distance marked off every 10 feet
Stairs
4 Musical instruments (a set of bells with different tones is good)
Watch or clock
A set of Figure vs. Ground pictures (a felt board is ok)
Pencil and paper
Score sheet

TIME NEEDED

One hour plus observation of patient in a variety of leisure activities.

This assessment is a fairly lengthy one, made easier if the therapist observes the patient in a few small group activities prior to the full assessment. Do not let the length of the assessment discourage you from using it if you have the time necessary. The use of this assessment will help you comply with the standards and regulations outlined by many accrediting agencies.

Below is the documentation that came with the original assessment. The documentation is an unpublished paper written by Robert A. Parker, Kathie Keller, Marguette Davis, and Robert Downie at the Greenville Hospital System, Greenville, South Carolina.

In addition to the applications described in the paper, this assessment can help Recreational Therapists and Activity Directors working in Long Term Care facilities assess the functional needs of clients. A leisure history/leisure preference assessment should also be given in this case. In Long Term Care facilities this assessment should be given upon admission, after major illnesses, and at each yearly anniversary of admission.

(Idyll Arbor, Inc. re-formatted the assessment itself to provide a more professional looking tool to be placed in patient charts.)

ABSTRACT

The Comprehensive Evaluation in Recreational Therapy Scale — Physical Disability (CERT — Phys/Dis) has been developed to help Recreational Therapists assess, measure, and record patient's progress. The CERT — Phys/Dis consists of fifty items which are arranged into eight sections: Gross Motor Function, Fine Movement, Locomotion, Motor Skills, Sensory, Cognition, Communication, and Behavior. Each section measures various functional abilities. The therapists can establish a numerical functional assessment score after completing an evaluation. An evaluation is done on admission, at selected intervals during hospitalization, at discharge, and during appropriate follow-up. Appropriate management planning can be made, using the data collected.

OVERVIEW

In 1975 a rating scale was introduced to Recreational Therapy called the Comprehensive Evaluation in Recreational Therapy Scale. (Form #116 available from Idyll Arbor, Inc.) The instrument was developed by the Recreational Therapy Department at Marshall I. Pickens Hospital which is a 68 bed inpatient psychiatric facility of the Greenville Hospital System in Greenville, South Carolina. The CERT — Psych./Behavioral, as it is commonly referred to today, was designed to help Recreational Therapists objectively assess, measure, and record patient progress in psychiatric settings (Parker, Ellison, Kirby, and Short, 1975). The CERT — Psych/Behavioral is presently being utilized extensively throughout the United States.

The development of another Comprehensive Evaluation in Recreational Therapy Scale for Rehabilitation (CERT Scale — Rehab.) has now been completed by the same Recreation Therapy Department in the Roger C. Peace Rehabilitation Hospital, an acute 36 bed inpatient medical rehabilitation facility. The average length of stay varies with the disability, and encompasses a large variety of diagnostic categories including strokes, spinal cord injuries, brain injuries, multiple sclerosis, Guillian Barre', etc. The facility accepts adults and older adolescents. The Recreational Therapy Department is staffed with three registered Recreational Therapists and two Recreational Therapy Assistants who treat patients daily on a one-to-one basis. The department is staffed seven days a week, including evenings. The evening and weekend programming is conducted primarily by the Recreational Therapy Assistants and consists of group type recreational activities.

DEVELOPMENT OF THE SCALE

Development of the Scale began in 1977, with a number of objectives in mind. One was to design an objective rating scale or instrument that would show progress or lack of progress by patients being treated in Recreational Therapy. After much consideration it seemed obvious that another 'Recreation Lifestyle' or 'Recreation Interest Survey' tool for the client with a disability was not needed because there seemed to be a sufficient number available (Howe, 1984). There also seemed to be adequate 'Activities of Daily Living' instruments as well, such as the Barthel Index (Mahoney and Barthel, 1965) and others. It was felt that the need was for an instrument that would evaluate the overall functional ability of an individual. Simply stated, Recreational Therapists need to be able to assess and measure, 'what works and what does not', with regard to a patient's ability to use his/her body to his/her best benefit.

Another objective was to develop the scale in such a manner that rater reliability between therapists would not present a problem. Discussion of this process is outlined later.

The third objective was to simplify the scale so a patient could be evaluated using easily acquired activities and functions found in almost any recreational therapy department in a rehabilitation hospital.

After reviewing some instruments used in rehabilitation programs, we felt that the same basic format of the CERT Scale developed for psychiatry could be used. Many more areas were needed, however, and more functions had to be identified. After several years of trial and error, the CERT Scale for Rehabilitation emerged as a 50 item scale arranged in eight sections: Gross Muscular Function, Fine Movement, Locomotion, Motor Skills, Sensory, Cognition, Communication, and Behavior. Each section contained variable numbers of items for assessment, each with five numerical ratings. Though the basic formats of both the CERT and the CERT Rehab are similar, there is a specific difference in scoring and interpreting the scores. With the Scale in Psychiatry the objective is to look for the absence of behavioral pathology, thereby, making the scores approaching zero more desirable. With the Scale in Rehabilitation, the objective is to look for the presence of functional ability, thereby, making higher scores more desirable. After completion of an evaluation, a numerical functional assessment score can be established. During periodic re-evaluations the patient's progress and overall functional ability can be rated and recorded.

DESCRIPTION OF THE SCALE

As indicated earlier, there are eight sections on the scale in which a Recreational Therapist can evaluate basic functional ability; these include 50 different items to assess. Because of the vast number of activities that a therapist utilizes while working with a patient, it is relatively easy to evaluate all of the functional areas using very simple and familiar tasks. Some of the areas cross over in such a manner that multiple areas are evaluated at the same time. Most of the 50 items are self explanatory, but basic descriptions of the eight categories and some individual items are provided below.

GROSS MUSCULAR FUNCTION is defined as 'bodily and extremity movements or stabilizations confined to one's personal space'. This section looks at gross muscular movements in the neck, trunk, and extremities including both endurance and movement ability. In 'B' on the scale, the statement on 'short sitting position' refers to a patient sitting on the front portion of a chair without arm or back support and with knees flexed.

FINE MOVEMENT is limited to and defined as that 'movement confined to the hands'. Here again, movement ability as well as endurance must be addressed.

LOCOMOTION refers to 'skills limited to the movement of the body from one place to another'. The area addresses whether one needs to use a wheelchair and also deals with transfers. The objective is to measure the level at which a patient can relocate himself independently from one place to another in whatever way that may be. In 'B' in this section it should be noted that after the main heading the evaluator must 'circle' whether or not assistive devices are needed.

Basically, MOTOR SKILLS is the 'actions or sequences of actions resulting from the processing of information'. This, of course, has a cognitive, neurological, and physiological aspect to it just as most of the other areas do. We have found air hockey, a large ball suspended on a long string, balloon badminton, and ping pong useful activities to measure Reaction Time. Movement Planning Ability can be assessed with something as simple as checkers or as complex as mazes or video games. This area can be evaluated also through demonstration of mental processes as well as through physical movements.

In the SENSORY section the evaluator is looking for the patient's 'demonstrated awareness due to stimulation of a sense organ' and 'the use of hearing aids/glasses when needed'. The area basically has to do with sight, hearing, and tactile sensation of the extremities. Under the areas of Visual Acuity any objects of the size indicated may be used; care should be taken to make sure they are familiar to the patient. With regard to Ocular Pursuit, air hockey, again, is an excellent activity. Activities such as pool and billiards are also very useful. When checking for Extremity Tactile Sensation always remember to cover the patient's eyes to make sure s/he is not using visual clues. Under Auditory Discrimination use of musical instruments is advised but is not mandatory. The primary objective is the determination of the patient's ability to discriminate sounds and determine the general location or direction of the sound.

COGNITION basically relates to 'the higher mental processes involving awareness of objects, of thought, or of perception'. Most of the items are relatively clear, but some suggestions are provided. For Problems Solving, mazes, math, and money problems are often used. Many other activities, however, may provide problem solving types of tasks. Laterality relates to the difficulty some patients have with neglect of one side or the other. Directionality relates to the basic spatial concepts of over and under, in front of, behind, beside, beneath, and other similar instruction. With Form Perception/Constancy a commercially available game, Perfection, serves as a good activity to deal with geometric shapes. Another object is the Tupperware ball that utilizes geometric shapes and can be easily acquired. In Figure Ground Discrimination a felt board is used. Increasingly more complex arrangements are presented, and the patient locates or identifies what is requested. Another activity that works well is the hidden picture within a picture drawings commonly found in children's puzzle books

COMMUNICATION relates to the 'skills involved in receiving and relaying messages'. Verbal as well as written expressive and receptive skills are measured. Alternate methods of communication of ideas or concepts are also addressed.

BEHAVIOR deals with 'actions considered to be a reflection of one's feelings'. The items are simple and straightforward and do not require any additional explanation.

SCORING

During the evaluation all 50 items are assessed and the number of the statement most appropriately describing the patient's functional ability is placed in the square to the left of each item. Each of the eight sections is then totaled and that figure transposed to the scoring grid on the last page of the scale. The scores for the eight sections are totaled and then divided by two, giving the overall functional assessment score ranging from 0 to 100. The scale is designed to be used for four different ratings. The first rating is used as the initial evaluation and the last is done just before discharge. Other ratings might be done at whatever intervals are felt appropriate by the therapist. Should more than four ratings be needed or desired, additional scales can be included and dated, consecutively.

Immediately following the scoring grid on the scale is an area for the therapist to state the goals for treatment in very specific terms, based on the results from the CERT Scale — Physical Disabilities. Also avocational interests should be assessed and documented for each patient. The comments section can be used to record a variety of items. We use it to record information not addressed by the Scale and to collect data for the discharge summary. Therapists should keep in mind that this instrument does not take the place of weekly progress notes. Therapists will still need to continue their periodic notes to record progress toward treatment goals and any modifications of those goals.

RELIABILITY

In order to establish reliability in the scale, extreme care went into developing functional descriptors in very 'concrete' terms. Therapists continually worked together (for 3 to 4 years) comparing evaluation results on all 50 items until consistent agreement was reached on all descriptors. The scale was then tested for a year and minor adjustments were made to the descriptors and became part of the final scale. Inter-rater reliability remained consistently high.

After the design was finished, one additional reliability evaluation was done by having two individuals evaluate the same patient at the same time on all 50 items on the scale without comparing results until the total evaluation was completed. A criterion of rating within one of each other (0-1,1-2,2-3,3-4) for each item was considered acceptable. Percent agreement was calculated by dividing the number of agreements by the number of agreements plus disagreements. Percent agreements between therapists for 10 patients ranged from 84 percent to 100 percent and averaged 95 percent. Percent agreement was also calculated for exact agreement of ratings between therapists on the same patients and they ranged from 32 to 94 percent and averaged 68 percent. A total of five therapists resulting in 6 different pair combinations were involved.

DISCUSSION

The CERT Scale — Physical Disability has much to offer the professional in recreational therapy in a rehabilitation or long term care setting. It covers most functional abilities and allows the results to be expressed by an objective numerical rating. It is easy to administer and does not require a great deal of sophisticated equipment or procedures. Rater reliability is good because most of the descritors are very concrete. Therapists should be able to complete the test in two treatment hours.

The CERT Scale — Physical Disability does not address recreation or leisure in the specific sense of the words. This will, no doubt, distress some recreational therapists. However, it should be kept in mind that rehabilitation patients are in the hospital for functional evaluation and disability management, and the recreational therapist has a primary responsibility in these efforts. The therapist uses activities as tools to evaluate the 50 items on the scale. The scale provides the mechanism and structure needed to evaluate and re-evaluate a patient in an objective manner, over a period of time and thus contributes significant information to the team process. Parker and Downie (1981) proposed a 'Model for Recreational Therapy' in a rehabilitation setting that more explicitly details the philosophical approach referred to here.

The scale took approximately six years to develop and has been used as the department's evaluation instrument since February 1983. Since that time all admission and discharge scores have been recorded by diagnostic categories. During the time this department was using the Scale, New England Sinai Hospital in Massachusetts evaluated some of their patients using this instrument. While the number of patients evaluated was relatively small, the scores were in the same range of those at Roger C. Peace Hospital.

SUMMARY

The CERT Scale — Physical Disability is an evaluation tool that can be used by recreational therapists in a rehabilitation or long term care setting. It consists of eight sections containing a total of 50 items to be scored. The scale is used for initial evaluations and can measure changes of patient's functional ability during treatment in their rehabilitation program. The CERT Scale — Physical Disability just as the CERT Scale for Psychiatry (Idyll Arbor, Inc. form #116) appears to be a valuable instrument for recreational therapist as the profession faces the increasing demands for accountability and definition of services.

REFERENCES

Howe, C.Z. (1984). Leisure Assessment and Instrumentation in Therapeutic Recreation. *Therapeutic Recreation Journal* 18 (2), 14-24.

Mahoney, F.I., and Barthel, D.W., (1985). Functional Evaluation: The Barthel Index. *Maryland State Medical Journal* 14, 61-65.

Parker, R.A. and Downie, G.R. (1981) Recreational Therapy: A Model for Consideration. *Therapeutic Recreation Journal* 15 (3), 22-26.

Parker, R.A., Ellison, C.H., Kirby, T.F., and Short, M.J. (1975) The Comprehensive Evaluation in Recreational Therapy Scale; A Tool For Patient Evaluation. *Therapeutic Recreation Journal* 9 (4), 143-152.

Comprehensive Evaluation in Recreational Therapy

CERT

Physical Disabilities

Name ____________ Unit ____________

Date of Birth ____________ Admit ____________

Date of 1st Asssesment ________ Date of 2nd Asssesment ________ Date of 3rd Assesment ________ Date of 4th Assesment ________

I. Gross Muscular Function

(bodily and extremity movements or stabilizations confined to one's personal space)

☐☐☐☐ A. **Neck Control**
- 0 - no stability or movement in neck.
- 1 - moves neck but cannot reposition upright.
- 2 - moves neck and can reposition upright only.
- 3 - can control neck but still has some limitations.
- 4 - full functional neck use and control.

☐☐☐☐ B. **Trunk Control** (short-sitting position)
- 0 - with support cannot maintain an erect sitting position.
- 1 - only with support maintains an erect sitting position.
- 2 - without support maintains an erect sitting position.
- 3 - controls trunk though still has some instability.
- 4 - full functional trunk use and control.

☐☐☐☐ C. **Right Upper Extremity Movement Ability**
- 0 - cannot move voluntarily.
- 1 - moves slightly but is nonfunctional.
- 2 - moves in synergistic patterns only.
- 3 - produces most isolated movements but is still limited.
- 4 - no difficulty in strength and range.

☐☐☐☐ D. **Left Upper Extremity Movement Ability**
- 0 - cannot move voluntarily.
- 1 - moves slightly but is essentially nonfunctional.
- 2 - moves in synergistic patterns only.
- 3 - produces most isolated movements but is still limited.
- 4 - no difficulty in strength and range.

☐☐☐☐ E. **Right Upper Extremity Endurance**
- 0 - no movement.
- 1 - tires almost immediately upon attempting to utilize.
- 2 - requires rest periods for even light muscular activity.
- 3 - requires rest periods for only heavy muscular activity.
- 4 - endurance adequate to complete tasks attempted.

☐☐☐☐ F. **Left Upper Extremity Endurance**
- 0 - no movement.
- 1 - tires almost immediately upon attempting to utilize.
- 2 - requires rest periods for even light muscular activity.
- 3 - requires rest periods for only heavy muscular activity.
- 4 - endurance adequate to complete tasks attempted.

☐☐☐☐ G. **Weight-Bearing Ability**
- 0 - no functional weight-bearing ability on either leg.
- 1 - with much support/device(s) bears weight on one or both legs.
- 2 - with some support/device(s) bears weight on one or both legs.
- 3 - with slight support/device(s) bears weight on one or both legs.
- 4 - full weight-bearing on both legs without support/device(s).

☐☐☐☐ H. **Right Lower Extremity Movement Ability**
- 0 - cannot move voluntarily.
- 1 - moves slightly but is nonfunctional.
- 2 - moves in synergistic patterns only.
- 3 - produces most isolated movements but still limited.
- 4 - has no difficulty in strength and range.

☐☐☐☐ I. **Left Lower Extremity Movement Ability**
- 0 - cannot move voluntarily.
- 1 - moves slightly but is nonfunctional.
- 2 - moves in synergistic patterns only.
- 3 - produces most isolated movements but still limited.
- 4 - has no difficulty in strength and range.

Sub Total I ☐☐☐☐

II. Fine Movement

☐☐☐☐ A. **Right Manual Movement Ability**
- 0 - cannot move voluntarily.
- 1 - moves slightly but is nonfunctional.
- 2 - mass grasps objects at least two inches in diameter.
- 3 - utilizes pinch to handle objects less than two inches in diameter.
- 4 - no difficulty in the areas of strength and range.

☐☐☐☐ B. **Left Manual Movement Ability**
- 0 - cannot move voluntarily.
- 1 - moves slightly but is nonfunctional.
- 2 - mass grasps objects at least two inches in diameter.
- 3 - utilizes pinch to handle objects less than two inches in diameter.
- 4 - no difficulty in the areas of strength and range.

☐☐☐☐ C. **Right Manual Movement Endurance**
- 0 - no movement.
- 1 - tires almost immediately upon attempting to utilize.
- 2 - requires more than two rest periods to complete task.
- 3 - requires two or less rest periods to complete task.
- 4 - endurance adequate to complete tasks.

☐☐☐☐ D. **Left Manual Movement Endurance**
- 0 - no movement.
- 1 - tires almost immediately upon attempting to utilize.
- 2 - requires more than two rest periods to complete task.
- 3 - requires two or less rest periods to complete task.
- 4 - endurance adequate to complete tasks attempted.

Sub Total II ☐☐☐☐

III. Locomotion

(skills limited to movement of the body from one place to another)

☐☐☐☐ A. **Wheelchair Maneuverability**
- 0 - no ability to propel wheelchair.
- 1 - attempts wheelchair propulsion but ability nonfunctional.
- 2 - propels wheelchair independently on level surfaces.
- 3 - manages rough surfaces and moderate inclines.
- 4 - independent in all basic wheelchair skills or N/A.

☐☐☐☐ B. **Transfer Ability**
(circle : assistive device — no assistive device)
- 0 - no ability to assist self in a transfer.
- 1 - transfers self but requires much assistance.
- 2 - transfers self but requires some assistance.
- 3 - transfers self with supervision.
- 4 - transfers self independently.

☐☐☐☐ C. **Ambulatory Ability**
- 0 - no ability to ambulate.
- 1 - ambulates up to 20 feet on level surface with much assistance.
- 2 - ambulates up to 150 feet on level surface with some assistance.
- 3 - ambulates independently with devices on most surfaces.
- 4 - ambulates independently without devices on any surface.

☐☐☐☐ D. **Higher-Ordered Ambulatory Skills**
(without human assistance)
- 0 - no ability to perform higher ordered ambulatory skills.
- 1 - negotiates stairs.
- 2 - runs and/or jumps.
- 3 - hops in place on each foot.
- 4 - no difficulty in higher-ordered ambulatory skills.

Sub Total III ☐☐☐☐

CERT (Physical Disabilities)

IV. Motor Skills

(actions or sequences of actions resulting from the processing of information)

☐☐☐☐ A. **Static and Dynamic Balance** (standing/ambulatory)
- 0 - cannot stand.
- 1 - maintains a stationary standing position with support.
- 2 - maintains an independent, stationary standing position.
- 3 - maintains balance while ambulating, with device.
- 4 - no difficulty with balance and agility, no devices.

☐☐☐☐ B. **Fine Motor Coordination** (hands)
- 0 - cannot make any purposeful movement with either hand.
- 1 - one or both hands mass grasps handsized objects.
- 2 - one or both hands picks up/places 1" objects.
- 3 - at least one hand manipulates 1/8" objects with ease.
- 4 - both hands manipulate 1/8" objects with ease.

☐☐☐☐ C. **Gross Motor Coordination** (arms)
- 0 - cannot make any purposeful movement with either arm.
- 1 - only one arm moves in limited actions.
- 2 - both arms move in limited actions.
- 3 - at least one arm has no difficulty integrating most actions.
- 4 - no difficulty integrating actions of both arms.

☐☐☐☐ D. **Reaction Time**
- 0 - unable to time movements to react.
- 1 - needs preparation for even slow speed reactions.
- 2 - requires more than two rest periods to complete task.
- 3 - reaction time only occasionally impaired.
- 4 - no difficulty integrating actions of both arms.

☐☐☐☐ E. **Movement Planning Ability**
- 0 - unable to sequence steps even with assistance.
- 1 - sequences only two to three step tasks with much assistance.
- 2 - needs assistance for sequencing only complex tasks.
- 3 - sequences complex tasks with only occasional assistance.
- 4 - independently sequences steps logically.

Sub Total IV ☐☐☐☐

V. Sensory

(demonstrated awareness due to stimulation of a sense organ - assumes use of hearing aid/glasses when needed)

☐☐☐☐ A. **Visual Acuity** (at distances of approximately 2 feet)
- 0 - unable to distinguish any size object.
- 1 - distinguishes objects larger than 6 inches in diameter.
- 2 - distinguishes objects as small as 3 inches in diameter.
- 3 - distinguishes objects as small as 1 inch in diameter.
- 4 - distinguishes any size object.

☐☐☐☐ B. **Ocular Pursuit**
- 0 - unable to track any moving object.
- 1 - when cued tracks moving objects in only 1/2 of visual field.
- 2 - spontaneously tracks moving objects in 1/2 of visual field.
- 3 - needs occasional cueing to track in total visual field.
- 4 - spontaneously tracks moving objects in total visual field.

☐☐☐☐ C. **Depth Perception** (using two identical objects with plane and depth held constant; which object is closer to self)
- 0 - unable to judge any depth between objects.
- 1 - judges depth between objects no greater than 2 feet from self.
- 2 - judges depth between objects no greater than 10 feet from self.
- 3 - judges depth between objects no greater than 30 feet from self.
- 4 - no difficulty with depth perception.

☐☐☐☐ D. **Extremity Tactile Sensation** (rate each extremity then average score)
- 0 - unable to perceive any amount of touch applied.
- 1 - detects touch applied with extreme pressure to a small area only.
- 2 - detects touch applied with some pressure to most of area.
- 3 - detects light touch applied to most of area.
- 4 - detects any touch applied.

☐☐☐☐ E. **Auditory Acuity**
- 0 - does not acknowledge any sound.
- 1 - acknowledges only loud startling sounds.
- 2 - acknowledges only loud conversational sounds.
- 3 - usually acknowledges most conversational tones.
- 4 - no difficulty with auditory acuity.

☐☐☐☐ F. **Auditory Discrimination** (use musical instruments)
- 0 - unable to differentiate sounds.
- 1 - differentiates between two grossly dissimilar sounds only.
- 2 - differentiates between similar sounds.
- 3 - diff[illegible]iate[illegible]tw[illegible]r s[illegible]nds and [illegible]y locate sou[illegible]
- 4 - [illegible]o d[illegible]ud[illegible]scrim[illegible]ation.

Sub Total V ☐☐☐☐

VI. Cognition

(the higher mental processes involving the awareness of objects of thought or perception)

☐☐☐☐ A. **Judgment/Decision Making Ability** (common sense)
- 0 - appears unable to make any appropriate choice.
- 1 - even with constant guidance, inconsistently makes appropriate choices.
- 2 - with constant guidance, usually makes appropriate choices.
- 3 - with occasional guidance makes appropriate choices.
- 4 - independently makes appropriate choices.

☐☐☐☐ B. **Attention Span**
- 0 - does not attend to activity.
- 1 - with many cues and no distracting stimuli is attentive up to 5 minutes.
- 2 - with some cueing and no distracting stimuli is attentive up to 10 minutes.
- 3 - with distracting stimuli is attentive up to 15 minutes.
- 4 - no difficulty with attention span.

☐☐☐☐ C. **Memory**
- 0 - demonstrates no ability to recall.
- 1 - only recalls a one step activity.
- 2 - recalls simple activities after five minutes.
- 3 - recalls most activities after 30 minutes.
- 4 - from one day to the next, recalls most activities.

☐☐☐☐ D. **Orientation**
- 0 - appears disoriented to time, place and person.
- 1 - knows name, but usually disoriented to time, place, and other person.
- 2 - usually disoriented to time and/or place only.
- 3 - sometimes disoriented to time and/or place only.
- 4 - no difficulty with orientation.

CERT (Physical Disabilities)

Name:

☐☐☐☐ E. **Feedback Utilization**
- 0 - appears unable to utilize any type of feedback.
- 1 - occasionally processes simple information for improving performance.
- 2 - consistently processes simple information for improving performance.
- 3 - occasionally processes complex information for improving performance.
- 4 - appears to utilize all feedback appropriately.

☐☐☐☐ F. **Problem Solving** (tasks)
- 0 - appears unable to solve any problem.
- 1 - occasionally solves one step problems.
- 2 - consistently solves one step problems.
- 3 - occasionally solves problems of two or more steps.
- 4 - solves problems adequately.

☐☐☐☐ G. **Laterality**
- 0 - denies and disregards one side of his body.
- 1 - constantly disregards one side of his body.
- 2 - disregards one side of body but occasionally self corrects.
- 3 - disregards one side of body but consistantly self corrects.
- 4 - no problem with laterality.

☐☐☐☐ H. **Directionality**
- 0 - no concept of spatial relationships.
- 1 - occasionally relates to single, directional command and to objects.
- 2 - consistently relates to single, directional command and to objects.
- 3 - occasionally relates to multiple directional commands and to objects.
- 4 - no problem with directionality.

☐☐☐☐ I. **Right-Left Discrimination**
- 0 - unable to discriminate right from left.
- 1 - inconsistently identifies right and left on self.
- 2 - consistently identifies right and left on self.
- 3 - inconsistently identifies right and left of person facing self.
- 4 - no problem in right-left discrimination.

☐☐☐☐ J. **Form Perception/Constancy** (geometric shapes)
- 0 - appears unable to differentiate/categorize shapes.
- 1 - differentiates/categorizes only some common, distinct shapes.
- 2 - differentiates/categorizes most common, distinct shapes.
- 3 - differentiates/categorizes some complicated, similar shapes.
- 4 - no problem in form perception/constancy.

☐☐☐☐ K. **Figure-Ground Discrimination**
- 0 - appears unable to extract any object from a background.
- 1 - occasionally extracts common shapes from a bland background.
- 2 - consistently extracts common shapes from a bland background.
- 3 - occasionally extracts shapes from a complicated background.
- 4 - no problem in figure-ground discriminations.

Sub Total VI ☐☐☐☐

VII. Communication

(skills involved in receiving and relaying messages)

☐☐☐☐ A. **Verbal Expressive Skills**
- 0 - aphonic.
- 1 - uses jargon.
- 2 - uses single words inappropriately.
- 3 - uses words or phrases appropriately.
- 4 - no expressive verbal language deficits.

☐☐☐☐ B. **Verbal Receptive Skills**
- 0 - appears unable to listen and comprehend verbalization.
- 1 - responds appropriately to a single verbal command.
- 2 - responds appropriately to a simple verbal phrase.
- 3 - responds appropriately to a verbal sentence.
- 4 - responds appropriately to all verbal expressions.

☐☐☐☐ C. **Written Expressive Skills** (cursive or printed)
- 0 - appears unable to write anything legibly.
- 1 - forms some letters but script is illegible.
- 2 - writes but script is only occasionally legible.
- 3 - conveys messages but script appears scrawled.
- 4 - writes precisely and conveys messages.

☐☐☐☐ D. **Written Receptive Skills** (cursive or printed)
- 0 - appears unable to read and comprehend writing.
- 1 - responds appropriately to single word, written commands.
- 2 - responds appropriately to a simple, written phrase.
- 3 - responds appropriately to a written sentence.
- 4 - responds appropriately to all written expressions.

☐☐☐☐ E. **Al[illegible]nate [illegible]ns [illegible]ati[illegible]** (e.g. ge[illegible] [illegible]ictures, [illegible].)
- [illegible] a[illegible]ear[illegible] ty[illegible] of adap[illegible]
- [illegible]mu[illegible]c[illegible] "[illegible]s" [illegible]no" conc[illegible]t.
- [illegible] - co[illegible]ca[illegible] a [illegible]w [illegible]ngle con[illegible]
- 3 - c[illegible]u[illegible]ca[illegible]s a [illegible]w co[illegible]p[illegible] [illegible]
- 4 - c[illegible]u[illegible]icat[illegible]s e[illegible]fective[illegible]

Sub Total VII ☐☐☐☐

VIII. Behavior

(actions considered to be a reflection of one's feelings)

☐☐☐☐ A. **Adjustment to Disability**
- 0 - denies or appears unable to comprehend disability.
- 1 - denies extent of disability and has unrealistic goals.
- 2 - questions extent of disability and searches for answers.
- 3 - accepts disability but has no well defined personal goals.
- 4 - accepts disability and is goal directed.

☐☐☐☐ B. **Social Interaction Skills** (ability to relate to others)
- 0 - cannot or will not interact with others.
- 1 - interacts only to meet personal needs.
- 2 - appears uncomfortable when others interact with him/her.
- 3 - initiates social interaction with some individuals only.
- 4 - readily initiates social interaction.

☐☐☐☐ C. **Frustration Tolerance Level**
- 0 - appears unresponsive or is too frustrated to participate.
- 1 - terminates activity after three minutes.
- 2 - terminates activity after 5 to 10 minutes due to frustration.
- 3 - appears discouraged but completes any activity.
- 4 - participates without appearing frustrated.

☐☐☐☐ D. **Initiative/Motivation**
- 0 - shows no initiative/motivation.
- 1 - only with much encouragement will apply self.
- 2 - applies self but does not offer opinions.
- 3 - applies self and occasionally offers opinions.
- 4 - readily applies self and freely offers opinions.

☐☐☐☐ E. **Display of Emotions** (lability)
- 0 - appears unresponsive or is uncontrollably emotional.
- 1 - usually ceases activity due to inappropriate emotions.
- 2 - occasionally ceases activity due to inappropriate emotions.
- 3 - difficulty controlling emotions, but completes any activity.
- 4 - displays emotions appropriately.

☐☐☐☐ F. **Attitude Toward Recreational Therapy**
- 0 - appears unresponsive or is hostile.
- 1 - participates but is resistive.
- 2 - participates but is indifferent.
- 3 - participates and usually shows interest.
- 4 - participates enthusiastically.

Sub Total VIII ☐☐☐☐

CERT (Physical Disabilities)

Scoring

Date/Initials	Section	I + II + III + IV + V + VI + VII + VIII	Total
	Sub Totals 1st rating	____ + ____ + ____ + ____ + ____ + ____ + ____ + ____ = ____ / 2 =	
	Sub Totals 2nd rating	____ + ____ + ____ + ____ + ____ + ____ + ____ + ____ = ____ / 2 =	
	Sub Totals 3rd rating	____ + ____ + ____ + ____ + ____ + ____ + ____ + ____ = ____ / 2 =	
	Sub Totals 4th rating	____ + ____ + ____ + ____ + ____ + ____ + ____ + ____ = ____ / 2 =	

Comments: ______________________________

Summary/Recommendations: ______________________________

Additional Forms may be ordered from:

Idyll Arbor, Inc.
PO Box 720
Ravensdale, WA 98051-0720

OHIO FUNCTIONAL ASSESSMENT BATTERY

Name: Ohio Functional Assessment Battery

Also Known As: 'OHIO', previously known as the Ohio Leisure Skills Scales on Normal Functioning ('OLSSON')

Author: Roy Olsson

Time Needed to Administer: Approximately 45 minutes to one hour, depending on the portion of the battery used.

Time Needed to Score: Scoring takes approximately 20 minutes.

Recommended Disability Group: The OHIO was originally developed to be used with individuals with a primary diagnosis of MR/DD. Over time, the assessment has been marketed more agressively for adults with brain injuries or adults in nursing homes.

Purpose of the Assessment: The purpose of the OHIO is to obtain the functioning level of a patient in order to develop measurable treatment goals and objectives.

What Does the Assessment Measure?: The OHIO is heavily weighted toward the measurement of cognitive skills and memory. It also provides some measurement of communication skills, money management skills, leisure interest, and gross/fine motor skills.

Supplies Needed: The supplies needed to administer the OHIO come with the assessment kit.

Reliability/Validity: Validity and reliability studies reported.

Degree of Skill Required to Administer and Score: A recreational therapist certified at the CTRS level by the National Council for Therapeutic Recreation Certification should have the background to administer and score this assessment.

Comments: As with its precursor, the scoring and other directions for this assessment are clearly stated. Interviews with recreational therapists in the field who used the OHIO drew mixed reviews. Comments ranged from 'well-defined steps' to 'results hard to translate into community treatment goals' and 'too cumbersome'. The greatest satisfaction came from individuals who served adults with a primary diagnosis of MR/DD. Some long term care facilities have stopped using it because the clients themselves felt that it was age-inappropriate.

Suggested Levels: Rancho Los Amigos: 5 or above. Development Level: The various sections of the assessment cover a wide range of developmental levels. Age 5 and above should cover most of the sections. Reality Orientation: Moderate and above.

Distributor: Psychological Corporation, 555 Academic Court, San Antonio, TX 78204-2498, (800) 228-0752.

OHIO FUNCTIONAL ASSESSMENT BATTERY

NOTE: To be able to practice administering this assessment, the therapist will need to purchase the Ohio Functional Assessment Battery. The assessment has a set of supplies in addition to the score sheet. These supplies are needed to administer this assessment.

The Ohio Functional Assessment Battery (OHIO) is an assessment tool designed to obtain the functional level of a patient. The assessment contains a very detailed set of directions for administering the assessment, score sheets, and a set of supplies. The supplies used are familiar objects (e.g., domino's, wooden beads, pencils, etc.). A set of photographs is also included. Assembly of the testing kit is required.

The OHIO has three different testing options within the Battery: the Functional Living Skills Assessment (FLSA), the Quick Functional Screening Test (QFST) and the Recreation and Leisure Profile (RLP).

The Functional Living Skills Assessment (FLSA) form has five sections. *Section 1: Information* contains the standard intake information including the patient's name, date of admission, etc. *Section 2: Observations of Cognitive/Communication Skills* contains areas for the therapist to summarize the patient's demonstrated functional ability in six different activities. These activities include the Recreation and Leisure Profile (RLP), domino patterns, draw a box, beads, sporting goods shopping trip and rainy day test sequences. *Section 3: Observation of Behavioral Skills* contains six areas for the therapist to measure the patient's attitudes and social behaviors including self-esteem, frustration tolerance, attention-seeking behavior, motivation, nonproductive behavior and cooperation. *Section 4: Clinical Impressions* contains the section of the test where the summarizes the patient's scores. *Section 5: Treatment Plan* contains space for the therapist to outline the patient's treatment plan. The FLSA part of the battery is best given to patient's with cognitive impairment. The Recreation and Leisure Profile section of this battery may not be able to be given to patients with moderate to severe cognitive impairments. The therapist will want to schedule approximately 45 minutes to administer the FLSA.

The Quick Functional Screening Test (QFST) has functional sections similar to the full battery (the Functional Living Skills Assessment) but has the patient complete only one of the six activities (the Recreation and Leisure Profile). From the administration of this one activity the therapist is to summarize the patient's skills in multiple areas of cognition, communication, attitude, and motor performance. The Quick Functional Screening Test is counter-indicated for patients with significant cognitive impairment. The therapist will want to schedule approximately 15 to 20 minutes to administer the QFST.

The Recreation and Leisure Profile (RLP) uses a series of photographs of recreational activities which the patient is asked to rank in order of preference, name at least one specific location to enjoy his/her five top choices, list the reasons (motivation) for liking the activities and list any possible barriers to engaging in the activities.

While the OHIO is a nicely packaged testing tool and is relatively easy to administer after the therapist becomes familiar with it, the authors have serious concerns about this testing tool. While the inter-rater reliability and reported validity appear to be supportive of a solid testing tool, the authors have difficulty with the overall construct validity. One example of our concern is that the OHIO scores attention span at the same degree of difficulty as managing a budget and maintaining a check book. While having a good attention span is an important aspect of enjoying one's free time, it is not on the same developmental level, or as complex, as the multiple skills required to manage money. Another example is the division of leisure activities into categories. The Leisure Diagnostic Battery, the Leisure Interest Measure (Ragheb and Beard, 1991) and the Leisurescope Plus divide leisure activities into categories based on research and theory. The division of interest areas in the OHIO reflects little knowledge of the generally accepted divisions within the field of leisure studies.

The assessment package comes complete with verbatim instructions, all materials needed to administer the test activities (except pencils, paper, etc.), a reference manual and scoring sheets.

VALIDITY

The author of the OHIO reports that the content validity was established by: 1) a search of the literature to determine functional parameters used with the following disability groups: mentally retarded, physically disabled, mentally ill, and impaired elderly; 2) face validity (validation by experts in the field of recreational therapy to determine appropriateness of the functional parameters as well as the ability of the activities selected to test the functional parameters); and 3) by determining a validity coefficient with the Comprehensive Evaluation in Recreational Therapy Scale (CERT — Phys./Dis.). Note that the OHIO was measured against the CERT — Phys./Dis. which does not have any actual measured validity beyond a limited peer review. Criterion-related validity was also measured against the Comprehensive Occupational Therapy Evaluation Scale (COTES).

RELIABILITY

The reliability of the OHIO was established by determining if two individuals who observed the same event would record the results in the same way. The observers were recreational therapy students trained by the author to administer and score the OHIO.

Functional Living Skills Assessment

Example 2

The Functional Living Skills Assessment is a therapy tool designed to obtain the functional level of a client in order to develop measurable treatment objectives.

Section 1: Information

Name: Jane Groves Sex: Female Age: 15

Date of: Admission n/a Referral 8/14 Assessment 8/16

Race: Caucasian Client No.: 515-64-5671 Religion: n/a

Admission diagnosis: Educable mentally retarded

Medication(s) and implications: ______

Other pertinent information: ______

REALITY ORIENTATION
The following factors are involved: orientation to (1) person, (2) place, (3) time, (4) situation (why the client is here).
(0) No problem with any factor.
1 Problem with 1 factor. (list # ______)
2 Problem with 2 factors. (list #s ______)
3 Problem with 3 factors. (list #s ______)
4 Problem with more than 3 factors. (list #s ______)
5 Not assessed at this time.

Section 2: Observations of Cognitive/Communication Skills

Recreation and Leisure Profile (RLP)

MOTOR PERFORMANCE
The following factors are involved: (1) hand-eye coordination (places chips within activity areas), (2) left/right discrimination, (3) opposite-hand fine motor skills (manipulation of chips), (4) primary-hand fine motor skills (manipulation of writing materials), (5) hemispatial neglect.
0 No problem with any factor.
(1) Problem with 1 factor. (list # 3)
2 Problem with 2 factors. (list #s ______)
3 Problem with 3 factors. (list #s ______)
4 Problem with more than 3 factors. (list #s ______)
5 Not assessed at this time.

VERBAL COMMUNICATION
The following factors are involved: (1) answers questions directed toward him or her, (2) answers questions completely, (3) exhibits logical conversation, (4) speaks clearly.
0 No problem with any factor.
(1) Problem with 1 factor. (list # 2)
2 Problem with 2 factors. (list #s ______)
3 Problem with 3 factors. (list #s ______)
4 Problem with more than 3 factors. (list #s ______)
5 Not assessed at this time.

NONVERBAL COMMUNICATION
The following factors are involved: (1) maintains eye contact, (2) nonverbal communication congruent with verbal communication, (3) shows emotion, (4) uses gestures.
0 No problem with any factor.
(1) Problem with 1 factor. (list # 1)
2 Problem with 2 factors. (list #s ______)
3 Problem with 3 factors. (list #s ______)
4 Problem with more than 3 factors. (list #s ______)
5 Not assessed at this time.

RETENTION SPAN/NEW LEARNING

1st	2nd	
0	0	Restates instructions including all 4 details.
1	1	Restates instructions including 3 of 4 details.
(2)	(2)	Restates instructions including 2 of 4 details.
3	3	Restates instructions including 1 of 4 details.
4	4	Cannot restate 1 detail from the instructions.
5	5	Not assessed at this time.

ATTENTION SPAN
The degree to which the client is distracted from the task (off task).
0 No difficulty attending to task.
(1) Off task less than 25% of time.
2 Off task 25% to 49% of time.
3 Off task 50% to 75% of the time.
4 Off task more than 75% of time.
5 Not assessed at this time.

MONEY MANAGEMENT SKILLS
The following factors are involved: (1) adds numbers correctly, (2) subtracts numbers correctly, (3) writes numbers from chips in correct spaces, (4) writes total area numbers in correct space.
0 No problem with any factor.
(1) Problem with 1 factor. (list # 2)
2 Problem with 2 factors. (list #s ______)
3 Problem with 3 factors. (list #s ______)
4 Problem with more than 3 factors. (list #s ______)
5 Not assessed at this time.

Section 2: Observations of Cognitive/Communication Skills (continued)

Domino Patterns

NEW LEARNING

- 0 Completes all domino patterns without visual cues.
- 1 Completes all domino patterns, but needs visual cue for design pattern of 4.
- 2 Needs visual cue for design pattern of 3 but can complete design pattern of 2 without visual cue.
- (3) Needs visual cue for design pattern of 2 but can complete design pattern of 1 without visual cue.
- 4 Cannot complete design pattern of 1 without visual cue.
- 5 Not assessed at this time.

ATTENTION SPAN

The degree to which the client is distracted from the task (off task).

- 0 No difficulty attending to task.
- (1) Off task less than 25% of time.
- 2 Off task 25% to 49% of time.
- 3 Off task 50% to 75% of time.
- 4 Off task more than 75% of time.
- 5 Not assessed at this time.

RETENTION SPAN/NEW LEARNING

- 0 Restates instructions including all 4 details.
- 1 Restates instructions including 3 of 4 details.
- (2) Restates instructions including 2 of 4 details.
- 3 Restates instructions including 1 of 4 details.
- 4 Cannot restate 1 detail from the instructions.
- 5 Not assessed at this time.

Draw a Box

ATTENTION SPAN

The degree to which the client is distracted from the task (off task).

- (0) No difficulty attending to task.
- 1 Off task less than 25% of time.
- 2 Off task 25% to 49% of time.
- 3 Off task 50% to 75% of time.
- 4 Off task more than 75% of time.
- 5 Not assessed at this time.

RETENTION SPAN/NEW LEARNING

- 0 Restates instructions including all 4 details.
- 1 Restates instructions including 3 of 4 details.
- (2) Restates instructions including 2 of 4 details.
- 3 Restates instructions including 1 of 4 details.
- 4 Cannot restate 1 detail from the instructions.
- 5 Not assessed at this time.

FOLLOWS DIRECTIONS/NEW LEARNING

- 0 Carries out all details of the task as instructed.
- 1 Needs verbal step-by-step directions for 1 or 2 details.
- (2) Needs verbal step-by-step directions for 3 or 4 details.
- 3 Needs verbal step-by-step directions and visual cues for 1 or 2 details.
- 4 Needs verbal step-by-step directions and visual cues for 3 or 4 details.
- 5 Not assessed at this time.

MOTOR PERFORMANCE

The following factors are involved: (1) hand-eye coordination (drawing lines and coloring within lines), (2) color discrimination, (3) left/right discrimination, (4) fine motor skills (manipulation of materials), (5) hemispatial neglect, (6) perseveration.

- (0) No problem with any factor.
- 1 Problem with 1 factor. (list # ________)
- 2 Problem with 2 factors. (list #s ________)
- 3 Problem with 3 factors. (list #s ________)
- 4 Problem with more than 3 factors. (list #s ________)
- 5 Not assessed at this time.

Beads

MOTOR PERFORMANCE

The following factors are involved: (1) hand-eye coordination (threading beads), (2) color discrimination, (3) size discrimination, (4) shape discrimination, (5) fine motor skills (manipulation of materials), (6) hemispatial neglect.

- (0) No problem with any factor.
- 1 Problem with 1 factor. (list # ________)
- 2 Problem with 2 factors. (list #s ________)
- 3 Problem with 3 factors. (list #s ________)
- 4 Problem with more than 3 factors. (list #s ________)
- 5 Not assessed at this time.

ATTENTION SPAN

The degree to which the client is distracted from the task (off task).

- (0) No difficulty attending to task.
- 1 Off task less than 25% of time.
- 2 Off task 25% to 49% of time.
- 3 Off task 50% to 75% of the time.
- 4 Off task more than 75% of time.
- 5 Not assessed at this time.

RETENTION SPAN/NEW LEARNING

- 0 Restates instructions including all 4 details.
- 1 Restates instructions including 3 of 4 details.
- (2) Restates instructions including 2 of 4 details.
- 3 Restates instructions including 1 of 4 details.
- 4 Cannot restate 1 detail from the instructions.
- 5 Not assessed at this time.

ORGANIZATION OF TIME AND MATERIAL

The following factors are involved: (1) uses all beads, (2) uses all strings, (3) logical progression (e.g., puts all beads on one string before starting another string), (4) completes task within time limits, (5) attempts task.

- 0 No problem with any factor.
- 1 Problem with 1 factor. (list # ________)
- (2) Problem with 2 factors. (list #s 3, 4)
- 3 Problem with 3 factors. (list #s ________)
- 4 Problem with more than 3 factors. (list #s ________)
- 5 Not assessed at this time.

Sporting Goods Shopping Trip

MONEY MANAGEMENT SKILLS

The following factors are involved: (1) identifies money, (2) adds money correctly, (3) subtracts money correctly, (4) writes check correctly.

- 0 No problem with any factor.
- (1) Problem with 1 factor. (list # 4)
- 2 Problem with 2 factors. (list #s ________)
- 3 Problem with 3 factors. (list #s ________)
- 4 Problem with more than 3 factors. (list #s ________)
- 5 Not assessed at this time.

ATTENTION SPAN

The degree to which the client is distracted from the task (off task).

- (0) No difficulty attending to task.
- 1 Off task less than 25% of time.
- 2 Off task 25% to 49% of time.
- 3 Off task 50% to 75% of time.
- 4 Off task more than 75% of time.
- 5 Not assessed at this time.

Section 2: Observations of Cognitive/Communication Skills (continued)

Rainy Day

PROBLEM SOLVING

Note: *assistance* = (a) identify viable activities, (b) identify an advantage or disadvantage of viable activities.

0 Recognizes and solves problem without therapist's assistance.
1 Recognizes and solves problem but needs assistance once from therapist.
2 Recognizes and solves problem but needs assistance twice from therapist.
3 Recognizes but cannot solve problem without assistance from therapist more than twice.
4 Cannot recognize problem without therapist's help.
5 Not assessed at this time.

OLD LEARNING

0 Can identify 80% or more of the pictures (≥13).
1 Can identify 65% to 75% of the pictures (11-12).
2 Can identify 55% to 62% of the pictures (9-10).
3 Can identify 50% of the pictures (8).
4 Cannot identify 50% of the pictures.
5 Not assessed at this time.

DECISION MAKING

0 Makes own decisions (chooses activities).
1 Makes own decisions but seeks therapist's approval/intervention once.
2 Makes own decisions but seeks therapist's approval/intervention more than once.
3 Makes decisions when given only 2 choices (chooses between activity pictures).
4 Cannot make or refuses to make any decision (does not choose between activity pictures).
5 Not assessed at this time.

ATTENTION SPAN

The degree to which the client is distracted from the task (off task).

0 No difficulty attending to task.
1 Off task less than 25% of time.
2 Off task 25% to 49% of time.
3 Off task 50% to 75% of time.
4 Off task more than 75% of time.
5 Not assessed at this time.

Section 3: Observations of Behavioral Skills

SELF-ESTEEM

The following factors are involved: (1) neat/clean appearance, (2) makes three positive statements about self, (3) smiles, (4) perceives people like him/her, (5) assertive, (6) positive self-image (makes no self-deprecating remarks).

0 No problem with any factor.
1 Problem with 1 factor. (list # ________)
2 Problem with 2 factors. (list #s __4, 5__)
3 Problem with 3 factors. (list #s ________)
4 Problem with more than 3 factors. (list #s ________)
5 Not assessed at this time.

FRUSTRATION TOLERANCE

0 Handled all tasks without becoming overly frustrated.
1 Became frustrated once, but frustration did not interfere with completion of any activity.
2 Became frustrated twice, but frustration did not interfere with completion of any activity.
3 Became frustrated more than twice or frustration inhibited completion of any one activity.
4 Became so frustrated that the client was unable to complete two or more activities.
5 Not assessed at this time.

ATTENTION-SEEKING BEHAVIOR

0 No attention-seeking behavior.
1 Attention-seeking behavior less than 25% of time.
2 Attention-seeking behavior 25% to 49% of time.
3 Attention-seeking behavior 50% to 75% of time.
4 Attention-seeking behavior more than 75% of time.
5 Not assessed at this time.

MOTIVATION

The following factors are involved: (1) engagement, (2) neatness, (3) interest in activities, (4) interest in accomplishment, (5) finishes activities that he or she is able to do.

0 No problem with any factor.
1 Problem with 1 factor. (list # ________)
2 Problem with 2 factors. (list #s ________)
3 Problem with 3 factors. (list #s ________)
4 Problem with more than 3 factors. (list #s ________)
5 Not assessed at this time.

NONPRODUCTIVE BEHAVIOR

The following factors are involved: (1) talking to self, (2) playing with hands, (3) rocking, (4) repetitive statements, (5) preoccupied with own thoughts, (6) can't sit still.

0 No problem with any factor.
1 Problem with 1 factor. (list # ________)
2 Problem with 2 factors. (list #s ________)
3 Problem with 3 factors. (list #s ________)
4 Problem with more than 3 factors. (list #s ________)
5 Not assessed at this time.

COOPERATION

0 Cooperates fully with assessment (more than 90% of time).
1 Cooperates with assessment 75% to 90% of time.
2 Cooperates with assessment 50% to 74% of time.
3 Cooperates with assessment 25% to 49% of time.
4 Opposes assessment activities and instruction (cooperates less than 25% of time).
5 Not assessed at this time.

Section 4: Clinical Impressions

COGNITIVE/COMMUNICATION SKILLS
0 = Normal, 1 = Mild dysfunction, 2 = Moderate dysfunction, 3 = Severe dysfunction, 4 = Profound dysfunction, 5 = Not assessed

New Learning: Dominoes 3 + Follows Directions 2 * + Retention Span 2 ** = ... 7 /3 = 2.33
Organization of Time and Material: Beads 2
Follows Directions: Box 2
Old Learning: Rainy Day 1
Decision Making: Rainy Day 3
Problem Solving: Rainy Day 3
Money Management: Shopping Trip 1 + RLP 1 = ... 2 /2 = 1
Reality Orientation 0
Retention Span: Domino 2 + Box 2 + Beads 2 + RLP (1st) 2 + RLP (2nd) 2 = ... 10/5 = 2
Attention Span: RLP 1 + Domino 1 + Box 0 + Beads 0 + Sporting Goods 0 + Rainy Day 1 = ... 3 /6 = .5
Motor Performance: RLP 1 + Box 0 + Beads 0 = ... 1 /3 = .33
Verbal Communication 1
Nonverbal Communication 1

*Insert number from *Follows Directions: Box*
**Insert number from *Retention Span* total score

BEHAVIORAL SKILLS

Self-Esteem 2
Frustration Tolerance 3
Motivation 0
Nonproductive Behavior 0
Cooperation 0
Attention-Seeking Behavior 1

INTERVENTION STRATEGIES
(15 = Most Interest, 1 = Least Interest)

15 Team Sports
9 Adventure Sports
14 Individual/Dual Sports
13 Music
3 Art
12 Dance/Drama
6 Table Games
4 Solitary Games
7 Physical/Skill Games
2 Wood/Tooling Crafts
5 Clay Crafts
1 Stitchery Crafts
11 Entertainment
8 Home Activities
10 Outdoor Recreation

Additional information and/or impressions:
Client states that she would be willing to participate in speech therapy and special education to increase problem-solving skills and reduce frustration.

Section 5: Treatment Plan

Include the following: name of intervention program(s), number of times the client needs to attend the intervention program(s) per day/week, the goal or measurable objective, the prognosis, and anticipated date the goal or measurable objective will be obtained.

ST: Client will attend speech therapy to increase problem-solving ability as characterized by reducing from 4 to 3 the number of therapist assists required to solve a problem. The prognosis is good that the client will complete her objective by 9/15.

Special Education IEP: Student will attend special education to increase frustration tolerance as characterized by student reducing from 5 to 4 the number of frustrations exhi[illegible] dur[illegible] a [illegible] The [illegible]sis is good that the student will complete her objective by 9/15.

Jill Carter Speech Therapist 8/16
Therapist Date

[illegible] 8/16
Client Date

Sue Mann Special Ed. 8/16
Therapist Date

Physician Date

Recreation and Leisure Profile

The Recreation and Leisure Profile is a leisure behavior assessment designed to obtain information needed for both leisure education and recreation programming.

Example 2

Section A: General Information

Name: Jane Groves Sex: Female Age: 15

Date of: Admission n/a Referral 8/14 Assessment 8/16

Race: Caucasian Client No.: 515-64-5671 Religion: n/a

Admission diagnosis: Educable mentally retarded

Medication(s) and implications:

Other pertinent information:

Section B: Leisure Interest Chart

TOTAL SPORTS AREA	38
Team	15
Adventure	9
Individual/Dual	14

TOTAL GAMES AREA	17
Table	6
Solitary	4
Physical Skill	7

TOTAL EXPRESSION AREA	28
Music	13
Art	3
Dance	12

TOTAL CRAFTS AREA	8
Wood/Tooling	2
Clay	5
Stitchery	1

TOTAL COMMUNITY INVOLVEMENT AREA	29
Entertainment	11
Home Activities	8
Outdoor Recreation	10

Section C: Specific Leisure Activity Interest and Resource Knowledge

For each of the five boxes under the Activity category below,
write in rank order the top five specific recreation activities that you like the most.

ACTIVITY	RESOURCE PLACE
1 Soccer	1
2 Aerobics	2
3 Listen to music	3 My tape player
4 Go to the movies	4
5 Softball	5

Section D: Leisure Participation Style

For each of the paired words, circle one number that best represents the way you would like to participate in recreation activities.

While participating in my leisure/recreation activities, I like to be:

	All of the time	Most of the time	Equal amount of time	Most of the time	All of the time	
Participating	(5)	4	3	2	1	Spectating
By myself	5	4	3	(2)	1	In a group
Competitive	5	(4)	3	2	1	Noncompetitive
Not at risk	5	(4)	3	2	1	At risk

Section E: Motivational Attitudes for Leisure Participation

To what degree do you believe the following factors motivate you to engage in recreation activities?

	Not at all	Sometimes	Most of the time	Always
A. Emotional release	1	2	(3)	4
B. Physical enhancement	1	2	(3)	4
C. Self-expression	1	(2)	3	4
D. Creative enhancement	1	(2)	3	4
E. Social interaction enhancement	1	2	3	(4)
F. Sense of control	1	(2)	3	4
G. Sense of accomplishment	1	2	(3)	4
H. Intellectual enhancement	1	(2)	3	4

Section F: Leisure Barriers

To what degree do you believe the following factors prevent you from engaging in recreation activities?

	Not at all	Sometimes	Most of the time	Always
A. Lack of time	1	(2)	3	4
B. Lack of money	1	(2)	3	4
C. Fear of failure	1	2	(3)	4
D. Lack of recreation skills	1	2	(3)	4
E. Lack of transportation	1	(2)	3	4
F. Lack of motivation	(1)	2	3	4
G. Lack of social skills	1	(2)	3	4
H. Lack of decision-making skills	1	(2)	3	4
I. Lack of problem-solving skills	1	2	(3)	4
J. Lack of physical mobility	(1)	2	3	4

Section G: Leisure Awareness and Involvement

Does client believe the leisure interest chart reflects the client's leisure interest? Yes

Time client spends in leisure activities weekly: 4

Is client satisfied with current recreation activities? No

Any new recreation activities client would like to learn? No

List:

Section H: Additional Information and Impressions

Student stated she just moved into town, therefore does not know where she can engage in activities of interest to her. She would like to increase her activity level and make friends.

Section I: Facility Leisure Education and Recreation Plan

Student will attend leisure education to increase resource knowledge of the community as characterized by listing one place to engage in each of her top five interest areas. Student will complete objective by 9/15.

Section J: Community Leisure Reintegration Plan

Student will increase activity level as characterized by participating in an aerobics program at the YMCA 3 times a week. Student will complete objective by 10/15.

Jane Groves — *Client* 8/16 — *Date*

Sue Mann Special Ed. — *Staff* 8/16 — *Date*

BURLINGAME SOFTWARE SCALE

Name: burlingame software scale

Also Known As: No other name known to authors.

Author: joan burlingame

Time Needed to Administer: The burlingame software scale is a data collection system to record the client's ongoing skill levels while using a computer. No time needed to administer.

Time Needed to Score: The therapist (or direct care staff) record the client's best achieved score on each game played. The therapist will usually need to spend less than 60 seconds per game writing the required information down.

Recommended Disability Groups: Any group which can interface with a computer.

Purpose of the Assessment: The scale was developed to assist therapists in their selection of computer games and to measure the client's skills as they relate to using a computer for leisure.

What Does the Assessment Measure?: The burlingame software scale (and Individual Score Sheet) measure a client's skill level compared to the degree of difficulty of the computer game.

Supplies Needed: Computer, computer games, appropriate interface devices, assignment of a burlingame software scale score for each computer game, and an Individual Score Sheet.

Reliability/Validity: None reported.

Degree of Skill Required to Administer and Score: A recreational therapist certified at the CTRS level by the National Council for Therapeutic Recreation *and* who is knowledgeable about the use of computers should be skilled enough to administer, score, and interpret this assessment.

Comments: This assessment was first developed to have an objective measurement of the client's skills using a sip and puff or a joystick. The primary population it was used for were children and adolescents with C-1 through C-4 fractures. Psychometric testing (e.g., IQ) was usually put off until the psychologist and recreational therapist were comfortable that the testing would be measuring the client's actual IQ and not his/her ability to use the interface device.

Suggested Levels: Rancho Los Amigos Level: 5 and above. Developmental Level: 2 and above. Reality Orientation Level: Moderate and above.

Distributor: Idyll Arbor, Inc. 25119 S.E. 262 Street, PO Box 720, Ravensdale, WA 98051-0720 (206) 432-3231 (Area code 425 after April 1997.)

BURLINGAME SOFTWARE SCALE

PURPOSE: The scale was developed to assist therapists in their selection of computer games for special populations. Games may now be rated on a scale of .15 to 10.2 with .15 being the easiest. To facilitate the therapeutic usage of games, place games with similar ratings on the same disk or directory, allowing the patient easy access to multiple games. This scale may be used to rate any computer game, whether the game is played on an Apple, an Atari, an IBM (or compatible), or any other computer.

The purpose of this scale is to evaluate the relative difficulty of software games. Once the degree of difficulty is determined, the therapist can better determine the appropriate selection of software for the patient. The scale will also allow for a more accurate record of the patient's performance in a variety of functional areas.

All games should be evaluated by using their easiest level.

At this time Idyll Arbor, Inc. does not know of any formal testing to measure the statistical reliability of this assessment. The Burlingame Software Scale was first used on a pediatric rehab. unit to help determine when a patient would be ready to use a computer for psychological testing. (The Reitan-Indiana and WISC-R were converted to software programs that the patients could access through a sip and puff, a single switch, or a dual switch.) One of the jobs of the recreational therapist was to determine when the patient's competency in the use of the switch was adequate to be tested. The psychometrist wanted to be reasonably sure that she was measuring the child's I.Q. and not the child's ability to use the computer.

Another way that the burlingame software scale was used was to assist in the treatment process. If a patient showed some right sided neglect the therapist would start him/her on games that used left to right scanning to encourage the patient to attend more and more to the right. Progress could be measured by both the increase in the patient's score on the game and by the patient's ability to tackle games that required a greater skill in the area of scanning.

DEFINITION OF TERMS

SCANNING 'No scanning required' means that no visual contact with the screen is required to achieve the desired result. 'Scanning in one direction' means that the user's eyes are required to move from left to right on one single plane. 'Scanning in two directions' means that the user's eyes are required to move from left to right and back on one single plane. 'Scanning in multiple planes' means that the user's eyes are required to move through multiple planes. 'Response time' indicates the length of time the user has to make his/her motor response.

PLANNING SKILLS 'Single step planning' means that the user's performance on one step does not influence his chances on the next step. An example of single step would be CANDYLAND, a board game in which no game plan is required, the players go where the cards send them. 'Multiple stage planning' means that the user's performance on one step influences his/her chances on the next step. An example of multiple step planning would be the game of chess, where the good player plans many turns ahead to achieve his/her desired goal.

GRAPHICS 'Graphics' means pictures. The 'number of words' indicates the average number of words found on each screen.

MEMORY REQUIRED 'Memory required' means the amount of new information acquired during the game that the user must remember to continue successfully playing. This does not include the directions to the game.

MATH REQUIRED 'Simple' means numbers that have no more than two digits.

LENGTH OF GAME 'Length of game' means the average time it might take a non-impaired adult to play the game after 10 minutes of 'warm-up' time on the game.

MOTOR RESPONSE 'Single mode' means that only one button or switch is required to play the game. 'Multiple mode' means that a joy stick, a game paddle, multiple buttons, or bi-switches are required. 'Keyboard' means that the computer keyboard needs to be used to play the game. NO MOTOR RESPONSE NEEDED means that the intent of the game is to provide visual stimulation without requiring input from the user.

SCORING

Sit down and play the computer game at its slowest speed. Once you have achieved some skill, play the game at a faster speed (if it has one). Try out the various ways to interface with the computer as you play the game. When you score the degree of difficulty for any game, it is very likely that the various interfaces (e.g., joystick vs. keyboard) will have a different degree of difficulty.

Using both the scoring grid and the game table sheet as references, sit down and replay the game in its slowest mode using one of the interfaces (e.g., joystick). Assign the appropriate score to each area (e.g,, **Scanning**, **Planning Skills**, etc.).

Add up the six cognitive scores (**Total Cognitive Score = Scanning + Planning Skills + Graphics Memory + Math + Length of Game**) to find the cognitive score total.

Multiply the **Total Cognitive Score** by the **Motor Response Score** and divide by 10 to determine the **Degree of Difficulty** for the game using that specific interface.

$$\textbf{Degree of Difficulty} = \frac{\textbf{Total Cognitive Score x Motor Response}}{\textbf{10}}$$

Repeat the process for other interfaces that will be used to play the game.

Game Table Sheet for the burlingame software scale

Name of Game	Interface	Scanning	Planning Skills	Graphics	Memory	Math	Length of Game	Cognitive Score	Motor Response	Degree of Difficulty

INDIVIDUAL COMPUTER LOG
BURLINGAME SOFTWARE SCALE

Purpose: The purpose of the Individual Computer Log is to record the client's history of participation with computer games during recreational therapy.

What Does the Individual Computer Log Measure? The Individual Computer Log measures the increasing or decreasing computer skill level demonstrated by the client over a period of time.

Time Needed to Record Information: The Individual Computer Log takes under two minutes to record the necessary information for each game played.

Scoring: While the Individual Computer Log may be used with the computer games which do not have a burlingame software scale (bss) rating, the therapist will be able to obtain more information by comparing the bss rating of the game to: 1. time on game, 2. level/speed, and 3. score.

Date: Record the current date, including the year (e.g., 10/18/90).

Game Played: Write in the name of the game in this space (e.g., Myst).

Rating of Game: Use the burlingame software scale to obtain a degree of difficulty rating for the computer game. Your **Rating of Game** should be a number between .15 (easiest) to 10.2 (most difficult).

Time on Game: Place the number of minutes that the client actually played the game, (e.g., 6 minutes).

Level/Speed: Many games have multiple levels of difficulty (e.g., Nethack has 30+ levels). Indicate the greatest level achieved during the playing time. Many games may be run at different speeds. If the computer game has multiple speeds, indicate the greatest speed achieved during the playing time.

Score: Indicate the best score achieved during the playing time. If a score is not applicable, place an 'N/A' in this space.

Comments: Write down information in this space which may increase the therapist's base of knowledge on the client's demonstrated performance.

Example:
*did well with significant background noise
*switched interface device from 'joy stick' to 'sip & puff'
*significant problems with booting game; client became agitated prior to being on computer

Populations: The Individual Computer Log may be used with any population that is able to initiate a purposeful interaction with the computer.

Additional Forms: This form and instructions may be copied as long as the copyright information is included. For more information contact Idyll Arbor, Inc. 25119 S.E. 262 Street, Ravensdale, WA 98051-9763. (206) 432-3231.

Individual Computer Log

Date	Game Played	Rating of Game	Time On Game	Level/Speed	Score	Comments

Comments/Summary: ____________________

____

____

____

____

Client's Name	Physician	Admit #	Room/Bed

BOND-HOWARD ASSESSMENT ON NEGLECT IN RECREATIONAL THERAPY

Name: Bond-Howard Assessment on Neglect in Recreational Therapy

Also Known As: BANRT (Ban-art)

Author: Barbara Bond-Howard

Time Needed to Administer: 30 minutes

Time Needed to Score: Scoring takes place as the assessment is administered. The therapist should add 5 - 10 minutes to summarize and make recommendations.

Recommended Disability Groups: Clients with possible visual neglect.

Purpose of the Assessment: The purpose of the BANRT is to measure the density and scope of a client's visual neglect.

What Does the Assessment Measure?: The BANRT measures the degree to which a client demonstrates visual neglect and also measures the field (or scope) of the neglect.

Supplies Needed: All the supplies needed come in the assessment kit.

Reliability/Validity: The BANRT was developed after extensive literature searches and on-going consultation with experts in the field of visual neglect both in the United States and in the European Health Care Community. This assessment tool has been undergoing field testing with elderly patients since 1988. As a result, the BANRT has strong content validity. Reliability has not been reported.

Degree of Skill Required: Due to the degree of observational skills required to administer this assessment, the BANRT is best scored and interpreted by a recreational therapist who is certified at the CTRS level by the National Council for Therapeutic Recreation Certification.

Comments: The authors consider the BANRT one of the most exciting assessment tools to be developed by a recreational therapist. Not only does this assessment tool provide the clinical therapist with a solid basis to determine treatment, but it also meets most of the requirements to be used as both a research tool and a clinical tool.

Suggested Levels: Rancho Los Amigos Level: 5 or above. Developmental Level: 7 or above. Reality Orientation Level: Moderate and above.

Distributor: Ptarmigan West, 1061 Josh Wilson Road, Mt. Vernon, WA 98273-9619 (206) 428-9785.

BANRT

THE BOND-HOWARD ASSESSMENT ON NEGLECT IN RECREATIONAL THERAPY

PURPOSE: The purpose of the BANRT (Ban-art) is to measure the density and scope of a patient's visual neglect.

ITEMS NEEDED:
- BANRT kit which includes the appropriately-sized dart board, score sheets, and scoring instructions
- Stop Watch
- Clip Board
- Pen

TIME NEEDED:
Approximately 30 minutes for the initial assessment

TARGET POPULATION:
Patients with a right CVA who demonstrate a left neglect

LIMITATION:
The BANRT has less impact with patients who demonstrate a right sided neglect and aphasia. However, right neglect has statistically been much less of a problem with patients with a left sided CVA.

POSSIBLE SCOPE:
Patients with traumatic brain injury who demonstrate a visual neglect.

BACKGROUND INFORMATION: A major concern for many patients with a Right Cerebrovascular Accident (CVA, or stroke) is that they often fail to respond to objects or people on their left side. This is referred to as left neglect. (Also referred to as visuospatial neglect, visio-spatial perception, and visual neglect.) Visually the patient is able to see; however the brain cannot process what is seen. Consequently, a patient may eat only the food on the right side of a plate, read the right columns of a newspaper and talk to people whom s/he pass on his/her right. The patient is unaware of the left side of his/her body. The left neglect can be so strong that the patient can not even recognize that it exists. New learning is difficult and although a patient may progress in all other areas of rehabilitation, the neglect is what slows the progress. For example: A patient may have regained the skills to walk but consistently walks into objects. In the community the patient would not be able to recognize hazards in his/her left field of vision.

Patients with left neglect have difficulty enjoying leisure activities because they are unaware of half of their activity. Reading only the right half of a page is very confusing. Playing cards can be very frustrating. The patient does not understand that s/he has a left neglect problem and cannot cue himself/herself to look left toward the activity. If a patient can decrease his/her neglect in a non-threatening activity, not only can s/he increase his/her potential for leisure time enjoyment, but s/he will also become more independent in the home environment. Research and statistics show that neglect will gradually decrease without any treatment up to six (6) months after the onset of the stroke. The purpose of the Bond-Howard Assessment on Neglect in Recreational Therapy is to decrease the amount of time a patient is disabled due to this condition and to accelerate the patient's progress through rehabilitation.

There are tests available in other fields that detect neglect. Repetition or sections of a circle are often involved in these tests. By combining an easily recognized leisure activity involving a full circle and repetition the review of literature supported the hypothesis that the neglect could be decreased.

Early test trials suggest that this leisure assessment followed by treatment can greatly reduce left neglect, thus increasing rehabilitation potential.

PROCEDURE:

A. Preparing for the Assessment: The patient should be sitting with the dart board 24 inches away. Let the patient become familiar with the dart board as the therapist sets it up.

Instruct the patient to find the number on the dart board that you ask him/her to find. When s/he has found it, s/he is to tell you the numbers on each side of it. Give the example:

'If I ask you to find the number 6, when you locate number 6 you are to tell me 'number 13 and number 10'. After you have told me the two numbers, you may throw the dart'.

Throwing the dart completes the leisure activity but has no direct relationship to the assessment itself.

B. The Assessment Process: Begin with number 1. After you have said the number, begin timing the patient. Stop the watch as soon as the patient responds with the *first* correct number. Record the time in the row closest to the outer circle. Continue down the numbers in order (1 - 20) until you reach number 20. Once you have done number 20 turn backwards to number 1. End with the number 20 so that all numbers are done twice. (1, 2, 3, 4, 5, 6, 7, 8, 9, 10, 11, 12, 13, 14, 15, 16, 17, 18, 19, 20, 19, 18, 17, 16, 15, 14, 13, 12, 11, 10, 9, 8, 7, 6, 5, 4, 3, 2, 1, 20)

C. Filling Out the Clock Score Sheet: The BANRT Clock Score Sheet Target has boxes for marking times for each number. Always fill in the outer row of boxes first, then the 2nd outer row. If additional trials are run, continue to fill in the rows from the outside of the circle into the center.

Any time that is greater than four seconds indicates neglect.

D. Filling Out the BANRT Graph;
The BANRT has two different graphs. The first graph helps show the degree of density of the neglect. The graph compares the average number of seconds it takes the patient to find the numbers in his/her area of neglect to the number of treatment sessions. The numbers in the patient's area of neglect are all of the numbers that took four seconds or greater to find. The therapist should only chart on the numbers obtained during the first trial. An example would be:

Scores obtained during 1st treatment session:

#19 = 05 seconds	#14 = 11 seconds
#07 = 16 seconds	#09 = 11 seconds
#16 = 13 seconds	#12 = 08 seconds
#08 = 16 seconds	#05 = 04 seconds
#11 = 14 seconds	#20 = 03 seconds

The average number of seconds for all areas of neglect was 10.1. To help in ease of graphing, round the number to the closest whole number, in this case 10. To mark this score on the graph locate the number '10' on the left, vertical column of the density graph. Over the number '1' (indicating that this was the 1st treatment or assessment session) mark a dot across from the number 10 on the vertical column. After each therapy session place a dot on the appropriate spot on the graph. A downward line on the graph indicates an improvement, or a lightening of the degree of density of the neglect.

The second graph on the BANRT charts the scope of the patient's neglect. The numbers on the left, vertical column of the graph represent the hours on a clock. Above the appropriate treatment session number (e.g., 1st session) the therapist should place a dot parallel to all stations of the clock which had a time of four seconds or greater. This will help indicate the amount of improvement by showing the decreasing scope of the density.

E. Indications for Treatment: When all the numbers have been done twice you will see a pattern, if the patient does indeed have a neglect. If all numbers are found in four seconds or less the patient does not have a neglect and does not need further treatment. However, if some responses are greater than four seconds, locate the strongest areas of neglect. Begin with this area and counter balance with a non-neglect area. For example: number 16 takes an average of 17 seconds in the first two trials. After the patient has completed number 16 on the third trial, record the time and counter balance with number 4. Continue with all areas until the patient has continually decreased the time on the neglected side. **Be sure that you always counter with the opposite side of the neglect.**

A new assessment form should be used for each therapy session. This may be repeated daily until the neglect shows significant change at the first trial run. Charting in the patient's medical chart daily is imperative. An example may be:

S: Patient stated his day has gone well but is 'tired of everyone telling me to look left'.

O: Patient completed the Bond-Howard Assessment on Neglect in Recreational Therapy (BANRT) in 15 minutes. The assessment showed a strong left neglect with the patient taking 14 times as long to find items in the left visual field as s/he did in the right visual field. Upon repetition the patient narrowed this margin to 4 times as long.

A: Patient has the greatest neglect, in terms of a clock, between 7:00 and 11:00.

P: Continue with BANRT

Bond-Howard Assessment on Neglect in Recreational Therapy (BANRT)
DAILY SCORE SHEET

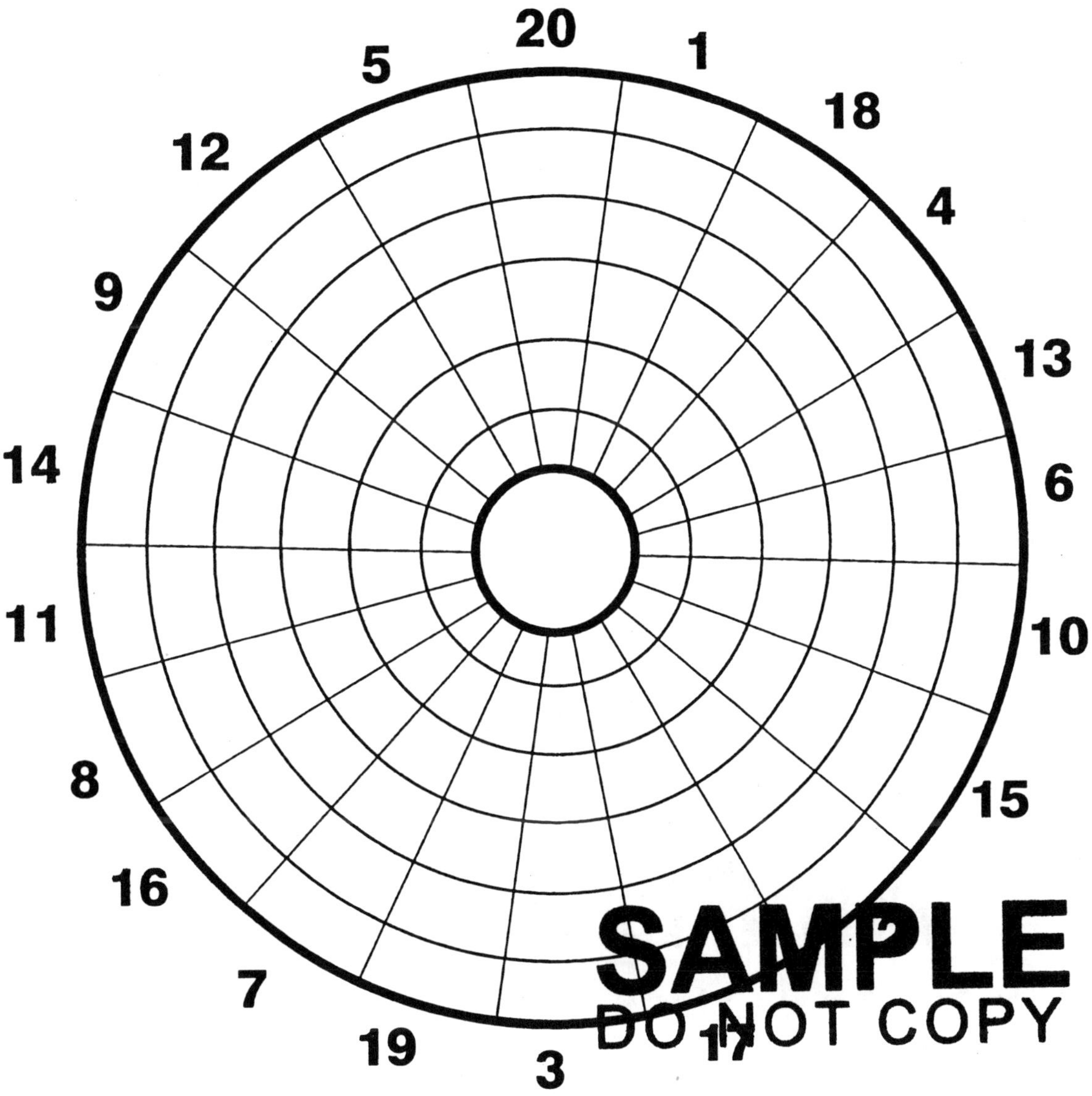

NAME____________________ TRIAL #____________

DIAGNOSIS____________________ AGE____________

ONSET____________________ TODAY'S DATE____________

ACUTE__________ CHRONIC__________

Neglect documented in any area: ☐ YES ☐ NO
(4 seconds or greater)
If yes, which #'s____________________

Density Charted____________________ Scope Charted ____________

The Bond-Howard Assessment on Neglect in Recreational Therapy (BANRT)

Density Chart

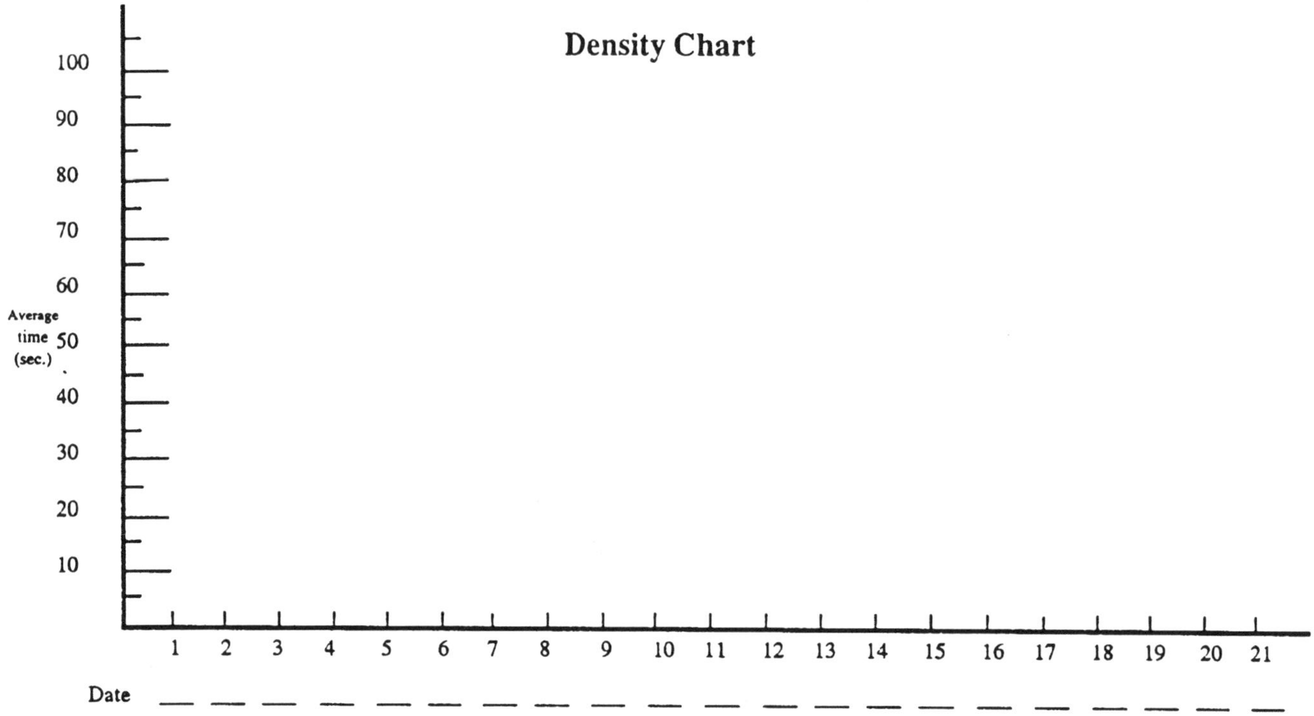

Scope Chart

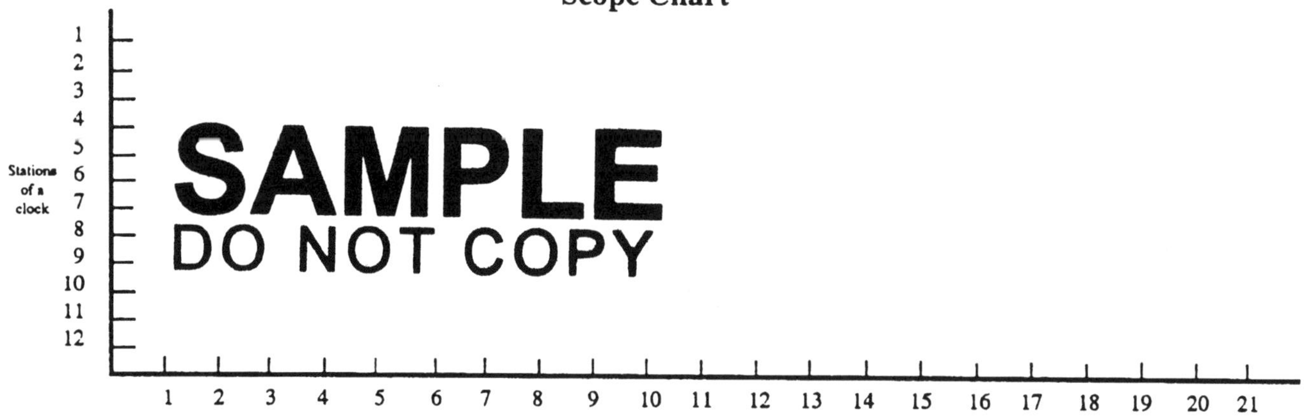

The purpose of the BANRT is to measure the scope and density of a patient's visuospatial neglect. If neglect is measured—the BANRT works to decrease the neglect. The density measures the average amount of seconds in the neglected area. The scope documents the areas of the neglect in the patient's field of vision in terms of looking at a clock.

Comments: See back.

Therapist

Date begun — Date completed

COMMUNICATION DEVICE EVALUATION

Name: Communication Device Evaluation

Also Known As: No other name known by authors

Author: joan burligame

Time Needed to Administer: 10 - 15 minutes

Time Needed to Score: Scoring takes place as the therapist administers the evaluation.

Recommended Disability Group: This evaluation tool may be used for individuals who use a communication device.

Purpose of the Assessment: The purpose of the Communication Device Evaluation is to help select the client's communication device(s) so that his/her communication needs may be met during the client's normal leisure activities.

What Does the Assessment Measure?: The Communication Device Evaluation measures the abilities (and limitations) of various communication systems. Areas evaluated include: 1) general information, 2) listener requirements, 3) message compiling time, 4) interface options, 5) process options, 6) output options, and 7) necessary qualities for use in various leisure environments.

Supplies Needed: Communication Device Evaluation Score Sheet and the client's communication device(s).

Reliability/Validity: None reported

Degree of Skill Required to Administer and Score: This evaluation may be completed by individuals familiar with communication devices and computer terminology.

Comments: This tool was developed as a graduate level project for a class in electronically adapted prosthetic devices at the University of Washington.

Suggested Levels: Suggested levels are not appropriate for this tool as it is used to evaluate equipment and not clients.

Distributor: Idyll Arbor, Inc., 25119 SE 262nd Street, PO Box 720, Ravensdale, WA 98051-0720 (206) 432-3231.

COMMUNICATION DEVICE EVALUATION

PURPOSE: The purpose of the COMMUNICATION DEVICE EVALUATION is to help evaluate a client's augmentative communication system to determine if it is compatible with his/her leisure lifestyle.

It was developed for Terry, a patient who had a complete C-1 fracture. The trach associated with his ventilator dependent lifestyle made most types of communication impossible. By working with this bright 9 year old, the recreational therapist, the speech therapist, and this form, a combination of augmentative communication systems were developed for his use.

For clients who use augmentative communication systems (e.g., word boards, autocoms, memowriters, Bliss Symbols, etc.) their leisure choices are frequently limited solely by the type of system they have. After completing a leisure interest survey and determining (with the client's input) future leisure needs, the recreational therapist and the speech therapist can work together to develop systems that will best fit the client's needs.

USE OF THIS FORM: The recreational therapist should fill out one of these forms for each type of augmentative communication system s/he comes into contact with. By developing a file of these evaluations, the therapist will have a good supplemental resource to use when assisting clients who use communication systems.

COMMUNICATION DEVICE EVALUATION

COMMUNICATION DEVICE: ______________________________
VENDOR: ______________________________
SPECIAL MODIFICATIONS ON THIS SYSTEM:

EVALUATOR: ______________________________ **DATE EVALUATED:** ______________

GENERAL INFORMATION	Yes	No
Easily Portable/Small		
Portable 3-10 Pounds		
Portable 10 Pounds +		
Battery Operated, Batteries Store Bought		
Battery Operated, Batteries Special Order		
Batteries Easily Rechargeable		
Electrical Outlet Required		
Electrical, Grounded, Meets State Institutional Standards for ICU's		
Dual Powered, Either Electrical or Battery		
May Be Used In Reclining Position		
May Be Used in Sitting Position		

LISTENER REQUIREMENTS (Skills Required to be Demonstrated by the Listener)	Yes	No
Ability to Listen		
Ability to Interpret Pictures		
Ability to Read		
Ability to Encode		

MESSAGE COMPILING TIME (Words Per Minute Capacity)	Yes	No
Short, Up to 40 Words Per Minute		
Medium, Between 15-30 Words Per Minute		
Long, Under 15 Words Per Minute		

INTERFACE OPTIONS (How the Client Uses the System)	Yes	No
Eye Gaze/Eye Pointing		
Pointing with Body Part		
Point with Device, e.g.; Head Wand		
Keyboard		
Switch		
Joystick		
Voice Generated		
Scanning		
Direct Selection		
Encoding (Type:)		

PROCESS OPTIONS (How the System Stores, Retrieves, and Puts Out Messages)	Yes	No
Direct Identification (e.g., Point to Word)		
Direct Conversation		
Storage Available (Capacity:)		
Retrieval from Code		
Compiled Messages		
Edit Messages		

OUTPUT OPTIONS (The Means by Which Messages Are Presented to the Listener)	Yes	No
Visual Display		
Printed, Ticker Tape or 3" Wide		
Printed, 8 1/2" x 11"		
Video		

LEISURE SETTINGS
(Is This Device Easily Usable in This Setting?)

STORE/RESTAURANT	Yes	No
Easily Understood by Untrained People		
Output Easily Read Under Store Lighting		
Output Easily Read Under Dimmed Lighting		
Variety of Compiled Messages in Memory		

THEATER/MOVIE HOUSE	Yes	No
Output Easily Read in Dark		
Quiet, Non-Distracting to Others		
Protected From Pop and Other Foods		
Easily Removed from W/C for Use of Restroom Facilities		
Client Able to View Stage/Screen: Device Not in the Way		

SPORTING EVENTS	Yes	No
Output Easily Read in Bright Sunlight		
Protected From the 'Elements'		
If Vocal Output, Can Be Heard Over Crowds		

TRANSPORTATION	Yes	No
Safely Secured in Case of an Accident		
Positioned so User Will Not Hurt Self on Device		
Listener Can Understand Communication While Driving		

SCHOOL/WORK	Yes	No
Ability to Prepare Messages Beforehand for Class Discussions/Meetings		
Allows Free Arm and Hand Movements for Activities		
Ability to Print Out School Work		
Quiet, Non-Distracting to Others		
Ability to Hook Into Desk Top Computer and Off-the-Shelf Software		

COMMENTS:

MALADAPTIVE SOCIAL FUNCTIONING SCALE

Name: Maladaptive Social Functioning Scale

Also Known As: MASF

Authors: The content of the MASF has been around for many years under various names. Idyll Arbor, Inc. was not able to locate the original author, and so it holds the copyright to the score sheet only.

Time Needed to Administer: Observation required during leisure activities.

Time Needed to Score: 5 minutes

Recommended Disability Groups: All groups developmentally above 4 years of age who display behaviors which are disruptive to the group process.

Purpose of the Assessment: The purpose of the MASF is to help the recreational therapist identify behaviors which are out of line, interfering with the group recreation process.

What Does the Assessment Measure?: The MASF measures the demonstrated severity of 21 specific behaviors. The 21 behaviors are: 1) somatic concern, 2) anxiety, 3) depression, 4) guilt, 5) hostility, 6) suspiciousness, 7) unusual thought content, 8) grandiosity, 9) hallucinations, 10) disorientation, 11) conceptual disorganization, 12) excitement, 13) motor retardation, 14) blunt affect, 15) tension, 16) mannerisms and posturing, 17) uncooperativeness 18) emotional withdrawal, 19) suicidal preoccupation, 20) self-neglect, and 21) bizarre behavior.

Supplies Needed: MASF Manual and Score Sheet #117.

Reliability/Validity: Unknown

Degree of Skill Required to Administer and Score: Due to the medical/psychological terms used in the descriptions, a person with formal training in recreational therapy or similar field should administer and score this assessment.

Comments: The MASF helps the recreational therapist define potential problematic behaviors using both a descripter (i.e., 'conceptual disorganization') and a numerical value (i.e., '5 = Moderately Severe').

Suggested Levels: Rancho Los Amigos Level: 5. Developmental Level: 4 years and up. Reality Orientation Level: Severe and up.

Distributor: Idyll Arbor, Inc. 25119 SE 262nd Street, PO Box 720, Ravensdale, WA 98051-0720 (206) 432-3231. (Area code 425 after April 1997.)

Maladapted Social Functioning Scale

For Recreational Therapy Programming

Purpose: The purpose of the MASF is to help the recreational therapist identify behaviors which are out of line, interfering with the group recreation process.

What Does the MASF Measure?: The MASF measures the demonstrated severity of 21 specific behaviors.

The recreational therapist may need to consult with a mental health professional when a client's behavior is disruptive to either his/her therapy and/or the group process. The MASF helps the recreational therapist define potential problematic behaviors using both a descriptor (i.e.; **conceptual disorganization)** and a numerical value (i.e.; **'5' Moderately Severe).** This information will help the recreational therapist to communicate with the mental health professional in a more meaningful manner.

The MASF presents 21 behaviors which could potentially disrupt the therapy process. While this list is fairly broad, it is not all-inclusive. There is the potential for a client to be manifesting significantly disruptive behaviors and still have a MASF score of 4 (moderate) or less.

Time Needed to Administer the MASF: Once the recreational therapist is familiar with the criteria sheet, it should take under 5 minutes to complete. The form is filled out after the therapist his observed the client in one or more group activities.

Populations: The MASF may be used with any population. The intended use of the MASF is for units that do not have a full time psychologist or psychiatrist.

The MASF should be used as a supplement to the regular recreational therapy assessment. The MASF measures some behavior patterns but does not provide the therapist with either a leisure assessment or a functional ability assessment.

Administering and Scoring: Prior to observing the client in an activity, the therapist should read the MASF Criteria Sheet. This criteria sheet defines each of the 21 assessed behaviors. Each behavior is broken down into degrees of severity. The degrees of severity are: N/A (not applicable), Not Present, Very Mild, Mild, Moderate, Moderately Severe, Severe and Extremely Severe.

The therapist will need to select the degree of severity which best describes the client's demonstrated behavior.

Twelve of the behaviors combine levels, i.e.; #18 Emotional Withdrawal. (Emotional Withdrawal lists only 4 degrees of severity; N/A, Very Mild/Mild, Moderate/Moderately Severe and Severe/Extremely Severe.) In scoring these behaviors the therapist should list the degree of severity (i.e.; 4/5 Moderate to Moderately Severe) instead of selecting just one of the numbers.

After observing the client, the therapist should fill out the MASF score sheet. Each of the 21 behaviors must be scored, even if the score is N/A (not applicable).

Note: A total score for all 21 questions has not been shown to have any clear meaning. Do not add the subscores together for a total.

The instructions suggest that the recreational therapist should initiate the appropriate referral if a change in the client's typical behavior is noted and/or if the client scores a 'five' or above in any one category. This referral criteria should be adjusted to match the specific needs of each facility.

The MASF is more accurate if it is used to measure the client's demonstrated behavior over a specific time period. The therapist should note on the score sheet if the observations cover a specific time period or are a review of the client's typically demonstrated behavior.

Example:

10/29/90 Problem: Demonstration of specific behaviors which interfere with client's ability to integrate into the community.

S: 'I'm very happy'

O: Client's verbal expression of feelings did not match observable affect. Client participated in a Halloween Party with another group home between 7 pm and 10 pm this evening. The party included such activities as a costume contest (client won 1st place for most original costume), apple dunk, Halloween stories told around a bonfire and eating pumpkin pie with hot cider. A staff was assigned 1:1 with the client to monitor the client's behavior throughout the party. The Maladaptive Social Functioning Scale (MASF) was filled out by that staff person immediately after the party.

A: The client demonstrated acceptable behavior in 20 of 21 areas of behavior measured by the MASF (degree of severity of 1 or less in all 20 areas). A score of 4/5 (Moderate/Moderately Severe) was noted in Blunted Affect. In a 3 hour period the client was observed as demonstrating:
2 smiles, 5 seconds or less in duration
0 smiles, 6-15 seconds in duration
0 smiles, 16 or more seconds in duration
0 laughs, 5 seconds or less in duration
0 laughs, 6 seconds or more in duration
0 facial expressions of surprise or fear
The client demonstrated a moderate to moderately severe blunted affect during the 3 hour period as measured by the MASF.

P: Short Term Goal: Make referral to Mental Health Specialist for further evaluation and for the development of an interdisciplinary approach to address blunted affect. Long Term Goal: Increase appropriate expression of affect.

After the therapist has marked a degree of severity for all 21 behaviors, a short summary should be written. A more detailed summary can be written in the client's chart (see the example above) or on the therapist's assessment report. The summary should give a general overview of the client's demonstrated behavior(s) **and** how those behaviors will impact the client's ability to function on a day-to-day basis:

Example:

The client has significant difficulty attending to any activity for 5 minutes or more due to his concern that others are talking about him and intend to harm him (suspiciousness: degree of severity 4/5). Because of this behavior he does not demonstrate the ability to wait for the bus, stand in line at the grocery store, work with a peer on a common goal or follow directions.

After the client's demonstrated behaviors are summarized, the therapist will need to indicate recommended interventions). In most cases the therapist will find his/her intervention to be more successful if they are discussed with, and agreed upon, by the client. In fact there should be some question as to the ethical implications of a treatment plan which is not explained to and agreed upon by the therapist and the client (and/or the client's legal guardian).

The RECOMMENDATION section should include:

1. the recommended interventions,
2. the degree to which the client participated in the development of the recommendations and
3. the degree satisfaction that the client has with the recommendations.

Referral Made: The therapist will need to indicate whether a referral was made as a result of the behaviors measured on the MASF. This boxed section should always be filled out.

If the therapist makes a referral, this section should be filled out only after the referral has actually been made. The therapist should indicate if the referral was a phone referral or a written referral and who received the referral. The time of day that the referral was received may also be written in this box.

Maladapted Social Functioning Scale

For Recreational Therapy Programming

Scoring Key	
1 = 0	Not Present
2 = VM	Very Mild
3 = M	Mild
4 = MO	Moderate
5 = MS	Moderately Severe
6 = S	Severe
7 = ES	Extremely Severe

1. **SOMATIC CONCERN**: Degree of concern over present bodily health. Degree to which physical health is perceived by the client, whether complaints have realistic basis or not.

2-3	M	Occasional complaint or expression of concern.
4-5	MO	Frequent expressions of concern or exaggerations of existing problems.
6-7	S	Preoccupied with physical complaints or somatic delusions.

2. **ANXIETY**: Reported apprehension, tension, fear, panic or worry. Rate only client's statements, not observed anxiety which is rated under TENSION (#15).

2	VM	Reports feeling worried more that usual.
3	M	Worried frequently but can turn attention to other things.
4	MO	Worried most of the time. Can't turn attention to activity or others easily. Occasional anxiety with autonomic accompaniment.
5	MS	Frequent periods of anxiety with autonomic accompaniment. Some areas of functioning are disrupted.
6	S	Anxious much of the time. Many areas of functioning are disrupted.
7	ES	Constantly anxious. Most areas of functioning are disrupted.

3. **DEPRESSION**: Includes; Moods — sadness and unhappiness. Cognition — preoccupation with depressing topics. Hopelessness — loss of self esteem, dissatisfied or disgusted with self. Do not include vegetative symptoms, e.g. motor retardation, early waking.

2	VM	Reports feeling sad/unhappy/depressed more than usual.
3	M	Same as 2, but can't snap out of it easily.
4	MO	Very sad/unhappy/depressed. Able to function, but takes much effort.
5	MS	Frequent periods of depression. Some areas of functioning are disrupted.
6	S	Depressed most of the time. Many areas of functioning are disrupted.
7	ES	Constantly depressed. Most areas of functioning are disrupted.

4. **GUILT**: Over concern or remorse for past behavior. Rate only client's statements, do not infer guilt feelings from depression, anxiety or neurotic defenses.

2-3	M	Worries about having failed someone or something, wishes to have done things differently.
4-5	MO	Preoccupied about having done wrong or injured others by doing or failing to do something.
6-7	S	Delusional guilt, obviously unreasonable self reproach.

5. **HOSTILITY**: Observed animosity, contempt, belligerence, threats, arguments, tantrums, property destruction, fights and any other expressions of hostile attitudes or actions. Do not infer hostility from neurotic defenses, anxiety or somatic complaints.

2	VM	Irritable, grumpy.
3	M	Argumentative, sarcastic.
4	MO	Angry, yells.
5	MS	Threatens, slams doors, throws things.
6	S	Has assaulted others but with no harm likely, e.g. slapped, pushed, destroyed property, knocked over furniture.
7	ES	Has attacked others with definite possibility of harming them or with actual harm, e.g. assault with hammer or weapon.

6. **SUSPICIOUSNESS**: Expressed or apparent belief that others have acted maliciously or with discriminatory intent.

2-3	M	Seems on guard. Unresponsive to personal questions. Describes incidents where others have harmed or wanted to harm him/her that sound plausible.
4-5	MO	Does not trust and says others are talking about him/her and intend to harm him/her.
6-7	S	Delusional. Speaks of Mafia plots, the FBI or someone poisoning his/her food.

7. **UNUSUAL THOUGHT CONTENT**: Unusual, odd, strange or bizarre thought content. Rate the degree of unusualness, not the degree of disorganization of speech. Delusions are illogical or clearly impossible ideas verbally expressed. Include thought insertion, withdrawal and broadcast.

2	VM	Ideas of reference (people stare/laugh at him/her). Ideas of persecution (people mistreat him/her). Unusual beliefs in psychic powers, spirits, UFOs. Not strongly held beliefs.
3	M	Same as 2 but with full conviction.
4	MO	Delusion present but not strongly held or encapsulated. Functioning not disrupted.
5	MS	Full conviction with some preoccupation and/or some areas of functioning are disrupted.
6	S	Much preoccupation and/or many areas of functioning are disrupted.
7	ES	Almost total preoccupation and/or most areas of functioning are disrupted.

8. **GRANDIOSITY**: Exaggerated, self-opinionated, conviction of special abilities or powers. Claimed identity as someone rich or famous. Rate only client's statements about self, not demeanor.

2-3	M	Exaggerates abilities, accomplishments or health.
4-5	MO	Claims to be "brilliant", a great musician, understands how "everything" works.
6-7	S	Delusional. Says he is appointed by God to run the world, has millions of dollars, can control the future of the world.

9. **HALLUCINATIONS**: Reports of perceptual experiences in the absence of external stimuli. When rating degree to which functioning is disrupted by hallucinations, do not include preoccupation with the content of the hallucinations. Consider only disruption due to the hallucinatory experience. Include thoughts aloud; "gedankenlautwerten."

2	VM	While resting or going to sleep, sees visions, hears music, whispers in absence of external stimulation.
3	M	While in clear state of consciousness, hears music or whispers. Sees illusions, e.g. faces in the shadows.
4	MO	Occasionally sees and hears things, but functioning not disrupted.
5	MS	Daily occurrences and/or functioning is disrupted.
6	S	Several daily occurrences and/or many areas of functioning are disrupted.
7	ES	Constant and/or most areas of functioning are disrupted.

10. **DISORIENTATION**: Does not comprehend situations or conversations. Confusion regarding person, place or time.

2-3	M	Occasionally seems muddled, bewildered or mildly confused.
4-5	MO	Seems confused about simple things. Has difficulty remembering things or recognizing people.
6-7	S	Grossly disoriented as to person, place and/or time.

11. **CONCEPTUAL DISORGANIZATION**: Degree to which speech is confused, disconnected or disorganized. Rate incoherence, derailment, blocking, tangentiality, neologisms and other speech disorders. Do not rate <u>content</u> of speech. Consider the first 15 minutes of the interview.

2	VM	Peculiar use of words, rambling.
3	M	Speech hard to understand or make sense of.
4	MO	Impaired verbal output on several occasions but otherwise comprehensible. Occasional sudden topic shifts, incomplete sentences or loss of direction.
5	MS	Communication is difficult for substantial portion of the interview. Occasional derailment or incoherence.
6	M	Communication is difficult most of the time or several instances of very severe impairment.
7	ES	Communication is incomprehensible. Severe disorganization of ongoing speech (word salad or severe blocking).

12. **EXCITEMENT**: Heightened emotional tone, increased reactivity, agitation, impulsivity.

2-3	M	Increased emotionality. Seems keyed up, alert.
4-5	MO	Reacts to most stimuli whether relevant or not with considerable intensity.
6-7	S	Marked overreactions to all stimuli with inappropriate intensity, restlessness or impulsiveness.

13. **MOTOR RETARDATION**: Reduction in energy level evidenced in slowed movements and speech, reduced body tone, decreased number of movements. Rate on the basis of observed behavior only. Do <u>not</u> rate on the basis of client's subjective impression of own energy level.

2-3	M	Noticeably slowed in movement or speech.
4-5	MO	Clearly retarded or seldom moves or speaks unless prodded or urged.
6-7	S	Frozen, catatonic.

14. **BLUNTED AFFECT**: Impaired in emotional expressiveness of face, voice and gestures. Marked indifference or flatness even when discussing distressing topics.

2-3	M	Client has some loss of normal emotional responsiveness.
4-5	MO	Lacks emotional expression. Doesn't laugh, smile or react emotionally when approached. Has somewhat frozen, unchanged expression.
6-7	S	Mechanical in speech and activity. Shows no feeling.

15. **TENSION**: Observable physical and motor manifestations of tension, nervousness and agitation. Self-reported experiences of tension should be rated under ANXIETY (#2).

2-3	M	Tense. Tense posture and nervous mannerisms.
4-5	MO	Anxious. Fearful expression, trembling, restlessness.
6-7	S	Continually agitated. Pacing and hand wringing.

16. **MANNERISMS AND POSTURING**: Unusual and bizarre behavior. Stylized movements, acts or any postures which are clearly uncomfortable or inappropriate, when maintained for 30 seconds or more.

2-3	M	Eccentric or odd mannerisms or activity that ordinary persons would have difficulty explaining, e.g. grimacing, picking.
4-5	MO	Does things or demonstrates mannerisms or postures that most people would regard as crazy. Behavior serving no apparent constructive purpose.
6-7	S	Posturing, smearing, intense rocking, fetal positioning, strange rituals that dominate the client's attention and behavior.

17. **UNCOOPERATIVENESS**: Resistance, unfriendliness, resentment or lack of willingness to cooperate with the interview. Rate only uncooperative behavior observed during interview.

2-3 M Gripes or tries to avoid complying but goes ahead with it without argument.
4-5 MO Verbally resists, seems defiant but eventually complies.
6-7 S Refuses to cooperate. Physically resistive.

18. **EMOTIONAL WITHDRAWAL**: Deficiency in client's ability to relate emotionally during interview situation. Objective determination of an "invisible barrier" between client and interviewer.

2-3 M Tends to not get involved.
4-5 MO Avoids emotional contact most of the interview.
6-7 S Actively avoids participation. Unresponsive. May leave when spoken to or may not respond at all.

19. **SUICIDAL PREOCCUPATION**: Expressed desire, intent or actual actions to harm or kill self.

2 VM Occasional feelings of being tired of living. No overt suicidal thoughts.
3 M Occasional suicidal thoughts without intent or specific plan.
4 MO Frequent suicidal thoughts without intent or plan. Expressed feeling of being "better off dead".
5 MS Many fantasies of suicide by various methods. May seriously consider making specific attempt but without time or developed plan. Or impulsive suicide attempt using non-lethal method or in full view of potential rescuers.
6 S Wants to kill self. Searching for appropriate means and time. Or potentially medically serious suicide attempt with knowledge of possible rescue.
7 E Specific suicidal plan and intent, e.g. "As soon as ______, I will do it by doing ______." Or suicide attempt characterized by plan thought to be lethal or in a secluded environment.

20. **SELF-NEGLECT**: Hygiene, appearance or eating behavior below usual expectations, below socially acceptable standards or life threatening.

2 VM Hygiene and appearance noticeably below usual standards, e.g. shirt out of pants, buttons unbuttoned.
3 M Much below usual standards, e.g. clothing disheveled and stained, hair not combed.
4 MO Below socially acceptable standards, e.g. large holes in clothing, bad breath, hair not combed and oily.
5 MS Highly erratic and poor, including extreme body odor. Irregular and poor eating, including convenience foods that are low in nutritional value, e.g. potato chips.
6 S Potentially life threatening, e.g. only eats and/or bathes when requested to do so.
7 ES Life threatening, e.g. does not eat or clean self.

21. **BIZARRE BEHAVIOR**: Reports of behaviors which are odd, unusual or psychotically criminal. Not limited to interview period.

2 VM Slightly odd behavior, e.g. hoarding food.
3 M Peculiar behavior done in private, e.g. collecting garbage.
4 MO Moderately unusual, e.g. bizarre dress or make-up or preaching to strangers.
5 MS Highly unusual, e.g. wandering streets aimlessly, eating non-foods, fixated staring in a socially disruptive way.
6 S Unusual petty crimes, e.g. directing traffic, public nudity, contacting authorities about imaginary crimes.
7 ES Unusual serious crimes, e.g. setting fires, associated theft, kidnapping committed in a bizarre fashion for bizarre reasons.

IA

Additional copies of this assessment may be ordered from
Idyll Arbor, Inc., 25119 SE 262 Street, PO Box 720, Ravensdale, WA, 98051-0720.

MASF
Maladaptive Social Functioning Scale
Score Sheet

The purpose of this assessment is to help the recreational therapist identify which behaviors are out of line, interfering with the group recreation process. It is adapted from the Brief Psychiatric Rating Scale

Use of the MASF Scores

When a client is exhibiting behaviors that interfere with the individual or group leisure process, the recreational therapist may use this scale to help identify the problematic behavior(s). The appropriate referral should be made if the therapist notices a change in the client's typical behavior and/or if the client scores a "five" or above in any one category.

The MASF scale helps identify behavior types and should not be used to establish a diagnosis (e.g., "the client is exhibiting somatic type behaviors," not "the client is somatic").

		Not Present	Very Mild	Mild	Moderate	Moderately Severe	Severe	Extremely Severe
1. Somatic Concern	NA	1	2	3	4	5	6	7
2. Anxiety	NA	1	2	3	4	5	6	7
3. Depression	NA	1	2	3	4	5	6	7
4. Guilt	NA	1	2	3	4	5	6	7
5. Hostility	NA	1	2	3	4	5	6	7
6. Suspiciousness	NA	1	2	3	4	5	6	7
7. Unusual Thought Content	NA	1	2	3	4	5	6	7
8. Grandiosity	NA	1	2	3	4	5	6	7
9. Hallucinations	NA	1	2	3	4	5	6	7
10. Disorientation	NA	1	2	3	4	5	6	7
11. Conceptual Disorganization	NA	1	2	3	4	5	6	7
12. Excitement	NA	1	2	3	4	5	6	7
13. Motor Retardation	NA	[illegible]	2	[illegible]	4	5	[illegible]	7
14. Blunt Affect	NA	[illegible]	[illegible]	[illegible]	4	5	[illegible]	7
15. Tension	NA	[illegible]	[illegible]	[illegible]	4	5	[illegible]	7
16. Mannerisms and Posturing	NA	1	2	3	4	5	6	7
17. Uncooperativeness	NA	1	2	[illegible]	4	5	6	7
18. Emotional Withdrawal	NA	1	2	3	4	5	6	7
19. Suicidal Preoccupation	NA	1	2	3	4	5	6	7
20. Self-neglect	NA	1	2	3	4	5	6	7
21. Bizarre Behavior	NA	1	2	3	4	5	6	7

NOTE: please refer to the MASF Criteria Sheet for the definitions of each behavior and how to determine the appropriate number score.

Summary: Recommendation:	Referral made? ❑ yes ❑ no To whom:__________ Date:__________

Name:
Date of Birth:
Unit:
Admit:

Additional Forms May Be Ordered From:
Idyll Arbor, Inc.
PO Box 720
Ravensdale, WA 98051-0720

IDYLL ARBOR REALITY ORIENTATION ASSESSMENT

Name: Idyll Arbor Reality Orientation Assessment

Also Known As: IA R/O

Author: Idyll Arbor, Inc. staff. This assessment is a combination of questions from multiple reality orientation assessment tools.

Time Needed to Administer: 20 minutes

Time Needed to Score: 10 minutes

Recommended Disability Groups: Clients in long term care or intermediate care facilities.

Purpose of Assessment: To determine the degree of cognitive orientation.

What Does the Assessment Measure?: The assessment measures the client's short and long term memory; knowledge of time of day/week/year; awareness of physical environment and residence; ability to execute basic math; and the ability to complete multi-step cognitive tasks.

Supplies Needed: Score sheet (#125) and instructions.

Reliability/Validity: Not established.

Degree of Skill Required to Administer and Score: This assessment requires some skill to administer and score. Para-professionals may be trained to administer and score this assessment.

Comments: The Idyll Arbor Reality Orientation Assessment was developed after the Idyll Arbor, Inc. staff did extensive literature searches in both the field of gerontology and in the field of cognitive measurement. Three reality orientation assessments were put together based on the research of the assessments available. These three assessments were then piloted in a variety of long term care facilities. This assessment tool was selected because the staff felt that it measured the broadest area of cognitive ability and was the easiest of the three to complete.

Suggested Levels: Rancho Los Amigos Level: 5 and up. Developmental Level: 10 and up. Reality Orientation Level: Severe and up.

Distributor: Idyll Arbor, Inc. 25119 S.E. 262 Street, PO Box 720, Ravensdale, WA 98051-0720 (206) 432-3231. (Area code 425 after April 1997.)

IDYLL ARBOR REALTY ORIENTATION ASSESSMENT

Recreational therapists and activity directors are frequently required to measure a patient's ability to think clearly and to remember past events. Extensive psychological testing is expensive and beyond the training of both the average recreational therapist and the activity director. These professionals need to have a quick and easy assessment which measures a broad area of cognitive functioning. This assessment must also be based on the extensive research already done in the area of mental ability and gerontology.

The Idyll Arbor Reality Orientation Assessment was developed after the Idyll Arbor, Inc. staff did extensive literature searches in both the field of gerontology and in the field of cognitive measurement. Three reality orientation assessments were put together based on the research of the assessments available. These three assessments were then piloted in a variety of long term care facilities. The Reality Orientation (R/O) assessment that was finally selected proved to be the one that measure the broadest area of cognitive ability and was the easiest to fill out. Please note that the assessment form itself has space for the assessment to be given three times to each patient. This makes it easier for the professional to compare the patient's scores from one assessment to the next.

The front page of the assessment contains the questions that the professional is to ask the patient. Please ask the questions just as they are written to maintain the validity of the assessment. An example would be question #20. The question states: "I bought a newspaper for 35 cents and gave the clerk 2 quarters, how much change would I get?" This question is testing the patient's ability to complete a three step command: 1) translate 2 quarters into 50 cents, 2) subtract 35 from 50, and 3) give the answer to the professional asking the question. If the professional were to ask "How much is 35 cents subtracted from 50 cents" s/he would change the question significantly. Total up the patient's score to determine which level best describes his/her cognitive ability/ orientation.

For some questions changes are required based on where the client lives. Idyll Arbor has a Canadian version of this assessment which changes a few of the questions. (one example is question 17, "Who is the current Prime Minister of Canada?")

The second page of the assessment provides the professional with a quick check list. Check the most appropriate box for each of the eight sections. Most appropriate means the statement which best describes the patient during the time period that s/he was being assessed. After both sides are completed the professional should summarize his/her findings. This summary is helpful to the other professionals who might need to use the information that you gathered during your assessment.

While reality orientation assessments are generally used on older adults, a baseline should be established for any client or patient in a intermediate or long term care setting. An example would be an adult who is diagnosed as being mentally retarded. This individual should be given an R/O assessment in his/her late teens or early twenties. The first time the assessment is given should help the professional establish a baseline of general knowledge related to orientation. A training program should then be added to the Individual Program Plan to teach him/her the information that s/he does not know. After the training program has been run, the assessment should be given a second time to establish a more realistic baseline. The R/O assessment should be readministered about every three years to help measure a change in ability.

For more information on ordering assessments from Idyll Arbor, Inc. please write the Idyll Arbor, Inc. staff at PO Box 720, Ravensdale, WA 98051-0720 or call (206) 432-3231.

IDYLL ARBOR REALITY ORIENTATION ASSESSMENT

	SCREENING DATE: ______		SCREENING DATE: ______		SCREENING DATE: ______	
Is the resident taking any medication which could affect orientation?	yes ☐	no ☐	yes ☐	no ☐	yes ☐	no ☐

SCREENING QUESTIONS

1. What is your name? (1)
2. What city are you in? (3)
3. What is the name of this place? (5)
4. What state is this? (2)
5. What is today's weather like? (1)

6. What season is it? (3)
7. What year is it? (3)
8. What month is it? (4)
9. What day of the week is it? (4)
10. What part of the day is it? (1)

11. What meal did you just eat? (2)
12. Are you married now? (1)
13. What kind of job did you have? (1)
14. How much is $7.00 + $3.00? (3)
15. Where were you born? (1)

16. How old are you? (2)
17. Who is the current president of the United States of America? (5)
18. Keep subtracting the number 3 from 20 until you can't any more. (5)
19. Professional baseball is played during what season? (2)
20. I bought a newspaper for 35 cents and gave the clerk 2 quarters, how much change would I get? (5)

21. What is your birthdate? (1)
22. What is the nation's capital? (2)
23. Please place your hand over your right eye. (2)

TOTAL

Scale	
1-15	Level 1: Severe to moderate disorientation
16-40	Level 2: Moderate to mild disorientation
41-59	Level 3: Mild disorientation to oriented

Resident's Name	Physician	Admit #	Room/Bed

IDYLL ARBOR REALITY ORIENTATION SCREENING FORM

A. APPEARANCE

- ☐☐☐ Appropriate, good hygiene
- ☐☐☐ Clothing and/or hygiene slightly dirty or smelly
- ☐☐☐ Clothing noticeably spotted and/or lack of good hygiene draws attention
- ☐☐☐ Very wrinkled and soiled clothing, poor hygiene

B. ATTENTION SPAN

- ☐☐☐ Attended to staff during complete R/O exam
- ☐☐☐ Occasionally needed to be cued to pay attention
- ☐☐☐ Frequently needed to be cued to pay attention
- ☐☐☐ Could not get attention and keep attention

C. ATTITUDE DURING R/O EXAM

- ☐☐☐ Enthusiastic and interested
- ☐☐☐ Indifferent
- ☐☐☐ Hostile but cooperative
- ☐☐☐ Hostile, uncooperative

D. BODY POSTURE

- ☐☐☐ Erect
- ☐☐☐ Rounded shoulders
- ☐☐☐ Slouched, head down
- ☐☐☐ Limp, unable to participate

E. EYE CONTACT

- ☐☐☐ Good, appropriate
- ☐☐☐ Looked away occasionally
- ☐☐☐ Looked away frequently
- ☐☐☐ Little to no eye contact

F. FRUSTRATION LEVEL

- ☐☐☐ Participated without frustration
- ☐☐☐ Occasionally frustrated
- ☐☐☐ Often frustrated
- ☐☐☐ So frustrated unable to participate

G. GENERAL AWARENESS

- ☐☐☐ Alert, aware of what was going on
- ☐☐☐ Semi-aware of reason for assessment, where s/he is, and who is giving the assessment.
- ☐☐☐ Confused, is not always aware of where s/he is, or why s/he is being tested
- ☐☐☐ No awareness of the fact s/he is being assessed

H. RESPONSE TIME

- ☐☐☐ Answered most questions immediately
- ☐☐☐ Needed some thought to come up with answer
- ☐☐☐ Needed a lot of time to respond
- ☐☐☐ Did not respond

SUMMARY #1

DATE: STAFF:

SUMMARY #2

DATE: STAFF:

SUMMARY #3

DATE: STAFF:

Resident:____________________

Chapter 6

MEASURING SPECIFIC SKILLS

Specific skills are measured using functional-environmental assessment tools. In recreational therapy, these assessments are the tools which the therapist uses to determine: 1) the client's initial skill level in a specific activity (e.g., checkers), and 2) the client's response to treatment (e.g., an increase or decrease in ability in the measured activity).

To show the differences between these assessments and the assessments in Chapter 5, we can look at two assessments which measure physical functionality. The CERT — Phys/Dis measures the client's lower extremity endurance, concentrating on the physical abilities of the client isolated from the environment. The Functional Hiking Technique measures the client's ability to perform physically, too, but it is more concerned with how the physical ability is integrated with the visual, cognitive, and endurance skills required for hiking on a trail. The first is clinical. The second is 'Real Life', based on the demonstration of dail living skills.

All the different types of assessments have a place in treatment. Health care professionals are expected to conduct an initial assessment prior to providing any treatment. The initial assessment usually is a norm-referenced assessment to determine the client's eligibility for services. It is expected that each health care professional will be able to complete his/her initial assessment in an hour or less. Most of the initial assessments are written to be administered and scored within that time limit. But the initial assessment is just that, an initial evaluation of the client's status.

Once it has been established that the client does, indeed, qualify for services, a criterion-referenced assessment is administered to determine the direction and scope of treatment services needed. A team meeting is usually held to organize an integrated approach to treatment, and then treatment begins.

The third step is to use assessments like the ones in this chapter to measure the effectiveness of the treatment plan. If the assessment shows that the treatment is effective, the treatment is continued. If not, the treatment is stopped, the outcomes evaluated (assessed) and a revised treatment plan is adapted. As the time draws near for the client to be discharged from the therapist's service, a final evaluation is completed for the discharge summary to show the level of the client's skills on discharge.

Table 6 - 1 Suggested Levels

The Idyll Arbor, Inc. staff reviewed the assessments contained in this book to *estimate* which groups the assessments may be given to. The determinations were based on their experience administering the assessments with the clients that they have worked with. (Idyll Arbor, Inc. has a general practice, admitting clients with all diagnoses except clients with a primary diagnosis of addiction). There has been no formal testing to establish these recommended guidelines. Each therapist will need to evaluate whether any specific assessment will work with the clients that s/he serves.

The shaded areas on the charts below indicate that the assessment is recommended for use with clients functioning at that level. To determine if an assessment is appropriate to use, determine the functional level of the client and then read the chart to determine if the assessment is appropriate for that client.

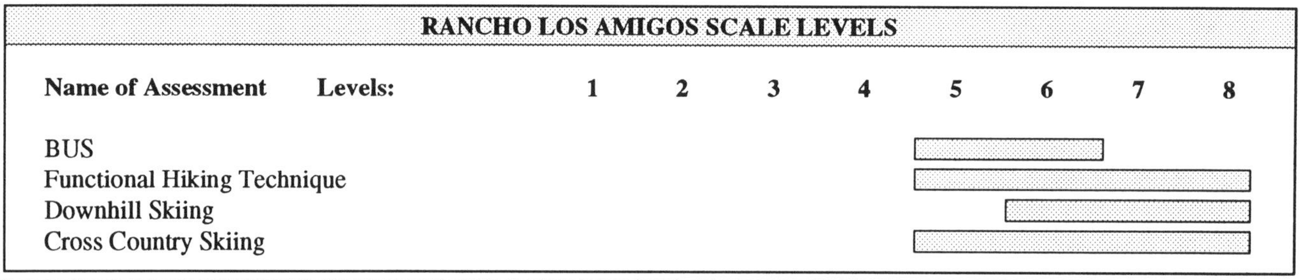

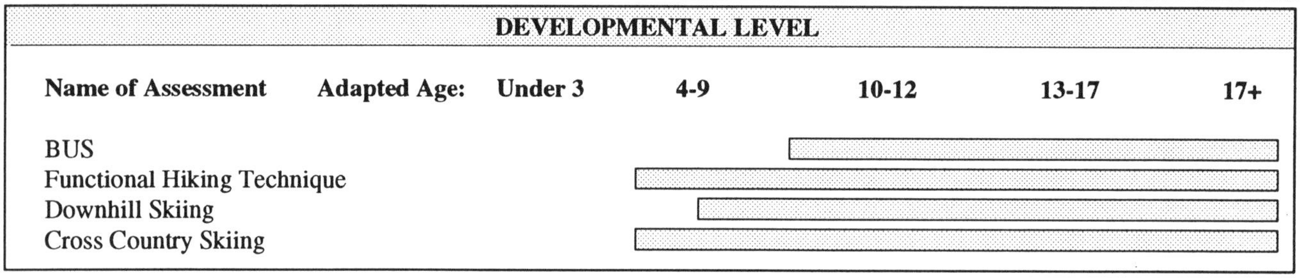

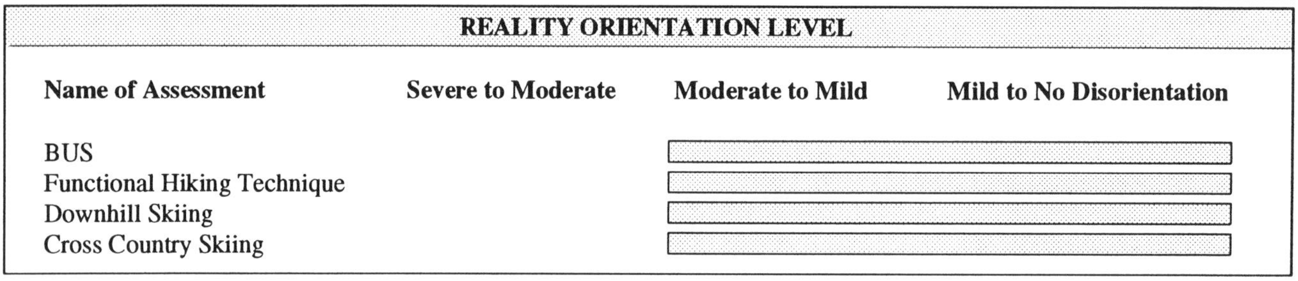

BUS UTILIZATION SKILLS ASSESSMENT

Name: Bus Utilization Skills Assessment

Also Known As: BUS

Authors: joan burlingame and Johna Peterson

Time Needed to Administer: The BUS is best administered over a period of one or two weeks. Each subsection can be used as a single therapy period.

Time Needed to Score: The scoring takes about 15 minutes.

Recommended Disability Groups: Clients with cognitive and/or physical impairment.

Purpose of the Assessment: The purpose of the BUS is to determine the breadth and depth of skills a client has related to the use of public transportation.

What Does the Assessment Measure?: The BUS is made up of two separate sections. Section One evaluates Functional Skills: 1) appearance, 2) getting ready, 3) waiting for the bus, 4) interaction with strangers, 5) pedestrian safety, 6) riding conduct, and 7) transfers. Section Two evaluates Maladaptive Behaviors: 1) anxiety, 2) depression, 3) hostility, 4) suspiciousness, 5) unusual thought content, 6) grandiosity, 7) hallucinations, 8) disorientation, 9) excitement, 10) blunted affect, 11) mannerisms and posturing, and 12) bizarre behavior.

Supplies Needed: 1) BUS Assessment Form (#126), 2) phone book and telephone, 3) paper and pen for client, 4) two dollars worth of change, 5) bus schedule, 6) some items to carry onto bus, 7) pictures for 'Interactions with Strangers' Section, and 8) transfer token.

Reliability/Validity: Initial validity studies were completed. Results may be found on the second page of the BUS instructions. Reliability not established.

Degree of Skill Required to Administer and Score: A recreational therapist certified at the CTRS level by the National Council for Therapeutic Recreation Certification has the skills to administer, score, and interpret the results of this assessment.

Comments: The BUS is a detailed checklist which provides the therapist with a clear understanding of the client's actual ability to use public transportation.

Suggested Levels: Rancho Los Amigos Level: 5-6. Developmental Level: 10 years and up. Reality Orientation Level: Moderate to No Impairment.

Distributor: Idyll Arbor, Inc. 25119 S.E. 262 Street, PO Box 720, Ravensdale, WA 98051-0720 (206) 432-3231. (Area code 425 after April 1997.)

BUS UTILIZATION SKILLS ASSESSMENT MANUAL

PURPOSE: The purpose of the Bus Utilization Skills Assessment (BUS) is to determine the breadth and depth of skills a client has related to the use of public transportation. This check list will help determine which clients are both cognitively and socially competent to use public transportation independently. Section One evaluates the cognitive and social skills of the client. Section Two is designed to check for maladaptive behaviors which may interfere with a client's ability to use public transportation even if the cognitive and social skills seem to be sufficient.

SCORING SECTION ONE: Each question in Section One is evaluated separately. If the client scores a 0 or 1 on any question, the therapist should have grave concerns about a client's ability to ride the bus independently. A passing score is achieved when the patient scores 2 or more on each question..

SCORING SECTION TWO: Most of the clients given the BUS assessment will score zero for questions 1 - 12. A score of '2' or '3' on any of the twelve questions could indicate that the client has a maladaptive behavior which should be addressed prior to training in the use of public transportation. The therapist should consider giving a more in depth assessment to determine if a client scoring a '2' or '3' needs further treatment in this area. An assessment like the CERT — Psych (Idyll Arbor, Inc. form #116) would be a good follow up assessment in this situation. Other possibilities include reviewing the client's medications with a pharmacist to see if any of the medications could be causing the maladaptive behavior. If this is the case, the therapist will need to work closely with the rest of the treatment team to develop an interdisciplinary approach to the problem.

SUPPLIES NEEDED TO GIVE THE BUS:

1. BUS Assessment Form and Pen
2. Phone Book and Telephone
3. Paper and Pen for Client
4. Two Dollars Worth of Change
5. Bus Schedule
6. Some Items to Carry Onto Bus
7. Pictures for 'Interaction with Strangers' Section (Please see comments on this section below.)
8. Transfer Token

In addition to the above listed supplies, the therapist should also plan to take the client into the community setting to field test the client's skills. The community setting should have curbs, cross walks with crossing signals, and bus stop signs.

INTERACTIONS WITH STRANGERS SECTION (AND QUESTION #29): Because so many of the clients tested using the BUS were in the 'concrete' developmental stage cognitively, significant validity problems arose with using the photos that originally came with the BUS assessment. (Police uniforms were different from city to city and county to county and the clients could not generalize.) To increase the validity, each facility should develop its own set of photos to use.

LENGTH OF TIME NEEDED TO GIVE THE BUS

The BUS is best given over a period of one or two weeks. Each subsection can be used as a single therapy period. The NOTES column on the right of each page of the assessment may be used by the therapist to make comments about a client's day-to-day progress. Each entry in the NOTES column should be dated. If more than one therapist is assessing the client's skills, the therapist making a comment should also initial the comment. Unlike such assessments as the Leisure Diagnostic Battery or the Leisurescope, the BUS is intended to be a teaching outline as well as a skills assessment. It can be used as a check list to mark off when the client achieves each skill.

DEVELOPMENT OF THE BUS

The BUS was initially developed at the request of the Camelot Society, Inc. of Seattle. Camelot Society has a set of group homes for youth and adults with a primary diagnosis of mental retardation. While some of their clients could successfully read schedules and ride the bus, they could not use public transportation because they exhibited socially inappropriate behaviors.

Idyll Arbor, Inc. staff reviewed numerous bus training systems including ones from the local school districts, the state schools for the mentally retarded, and METRO's own check list. (METRO is the name of the bus system which serves the greater Seattle area. It is one of the most extensive and most accessible bus systems in the United States.)

SECTION ONE

After the first draft was developed, Idyll Arbor, Inc. staff rode the buses for two days to observe passengers and their behavior. The initial draft was shared with the bus drivers on the routes and their suggestions were included in the second draft.

The second draft was reviewed (and in a few cases actually tested) by the Certified Therapeutic Recreation Specialists working on rehabilitation units around the greater Seattle area. This time it was tested on adults with either head injuries or spinal cord injuries.

The scoring results from both the first set of assessment (with clients who were mentally retarded) and the second set of assessments (with clients with either a head injury or a spinal cord injury) showed that:

1. The assessment was best given over a week's time period with some 'in-house' testing prior to an actual trial run on the bus.

2. The assessment had greater detail than was needed for those who were cognitively within normal ranges (and had a Rancho Los Amigos Level of at least 7).

3. The assessment was detailed enough to help the therapist isolate specific areas that needed intervention.

4. The assessment, with only sight modification, could be used to evaluate the client's ability to use other types of public transportation (e.g., trains, planes, taxis).

A third trial was run, this time using three adults who were business professionals who use the bus as their primary means of transportation. The purpose of this trial was to determine a reasonable 'baseline' score. Questions #27 and #28 were the only questions where a perfect score was not achieved by all three.

SECTION TWO

The twelve maladaptive behaviors selected for Section Two were chosen by the Idyll Arbor, Inc. staff as the most common types of maladaptive behaviors seen while evaluating why clients who appeared to have sufficient cognitive and social skills still were not able to ride public transportation. Section Two checks for these behaviors as an added assurance that there are no additional problems for the client. It is an abbreviated Maladaptive Social Functioning Scale (Idyll Arbor, Inc. form #117) which has been successfully used for three years for evaluating maladaptive behavior which can prevent a client from succeeding with normal social interactions.

Idyll Arbor, Inc. is glad to provide assessments to therapists. We request that no copies of the forms (or re-makes of the assessments) be made. Idyll Arbor, Inc. is functioning as a clearing house for assessments in the field of recreational therapy. We underwrite many of the expenses associated with this effort, and only charge the cost of sending samples, returning phone calls, developing the original art work, and the copying cost. Any actual 'profit' made goes right back into testing or developing of other materials for our field.

If you would like more information about Idyll Arbor, Inc. or the assessments we carry, please feel free to write us.
Idyll Arbor, Inc., PO Box 720, Ravensdale, WA 98051-0720.

BUS UTILIZATION SKILLS ASSESSMENT (BUS)

SECTION ONE: FUNCTIONAL SKILLS

SCORING: Each category (e.g., appropriate clothing) has 3 sets of skills or behaviors listed (a, b, and c). Each set of skills or behaviors is worth one point. (If a client or patient exhibits two of the 3 skills or behaviors (e.g., a and b) his/her score for that category would be 2 points. Mark your answers on the BUS Assessment Score Sheet.

APPEARANCE	NOTES
1. Appropriate Clothing	
☐ a. clothing is well coordinated	
☐ b. appropriate for destination	
☐ c. appropriate for weather	
2. Hygiene	
☐ a. clothing clean	
☐ b. absence of body odor (or absence of strong perfume, cologne.)	
☐ c. well groomed (hair, face, nails, etc.)	
3. Posture	
☐ a. body erect	
☐ b. head/chin up	
☐ c. shoulders appropriately back	
4. Attitude	
☐ a. neutral to positive affect of face, voice, and gestures	
☐ b. interacts purposefully with other people and objects	
☐ c. appropriately cooperative	**Subscore:** ______

GETTING READY	NOTES
5. Phone Skills	
☐ a. looks up phone number of bus information	
☐ b. can dial phone	
☐ c. knows difference between ring and busy signal	
6. Phone/Conversation Manners	
☐ a. clearly asks for information needed	
☐ b. uses friendly language (courteous)	
☐ c. refrains from frustration behaviors	
7. Ability to Record/Write Down Obtained Information	
☐ a. has pen or pencil ready prior to obtaining information	
☐ b. writes down information correctly	
☐ c. is able to read what is written down	
8. Coin Recognition	
☐ a. knows cost of fare	
☐ b. can separate required fare out of two dollars change	
☐ c. can place appropriate fare in fare box	
9. Reading Bus Schedule	
☐ a. reads bus stops correctly on schedule	
☐ b. reads time of stops correctly on schedule	
☐ c. demonstrates understanding of 50% of the symbols used on the schedule	
10. Personal Identification	
☐ a. can communicate name	
☐ b. can communicate phone number	
☐ c. can communicate location of residence	
11. Destination Information	
☐ a. knows the destination	
☐ b. can communicate destination (and be understood)	
☐ c. knows correct bus route to take to destination	**Subscore:** ______

Name:______________ Living Unit:________ Date of Assessment:________ Staff:______________

WAITING FOR THE BUS **NOTES**

12. Bus Stop
   - ☐ a. knows where bus stop is
   - ☐ b. does not try to catch the bus from a non-bus stop location
   - ☐ c. can tell if desired bus stops at bus stop
13. Safe Waiting
   - ☐ a. stands a safe distance from curb/road
   - ☐ b. does not engage in conversation with strangers
   - ☐ c. knows not to wait alone in dark or unsafe areas
14. Carry-on Items and Packages
   - ☐ a. 'packaged' so it's easy to carry
   - ☐ b. contained so that bits and pieces don't fall off
   - ☐ c. appropriate size, content for carrying on bus
15. Waiting to Get on the Bus
   - ☐ a. checks number of bus to make sure that it is the correct one
   - ☐ b. waits for the bus to stop before stepping up to edge of curb/road
   - ☐ c. waits for others to exit first

Subscore: ____________

INTERACTION WITH STRANGERS **NOTES**

16. Can Identify 'Helpers'
   - ☐ a. identifies policeman from group of six pictures
   - ☐ b. identifies fireman from group of six pictures
   - ☐ c. identifies bus driver from group of six pictures
17. Can Identify 'Strangers'
   ☐ when presented with pictures of 3 friends/family members and 3 strangers, can ID strangers (all 3 correct = 3 points, 2 correct = 2 points, 1 correct = 1 point)
18. Good Touching
   ☐ when presented with six pictures (3 good touching, 3 bad touching) can ID good touching (all 3 correct = 3 points, 2 correct = 2 points, 1 correct = 1 point)
19. Bad Touching
   ☐ when presented with six pictures (3 good touching, 3 bad touching) can ID bad touching (all 3 correct = 3 points, 2 correct = 2 points, 1 correct = 1 point)

Subscore: ____________

PEDESTRIAN SAFETY **NOTES**

20. Maneuverability — On the Ground
   ☐ can maneuver around 30 objects without hitting any within 3 minutes (3 points)
   can maneuver around 20 objects without hitting any within 3 minutes (2 points)
   can maneuver around 10 objects without hitting any within 3 minutes (1 point)
21. Cross Walks
   - ☐ a. knows correct meaning for 'Walk/Don't Walk' sign
   - ☐ b. can push cross walk button for crossing street
   - ☐ c. can maneuver ramp to cross walk
22. Crossing Safety
   - ☐ a. stays inside boundaries of cross walk when crossing
   - ☐ b. looks both ways before crossing
   - ☐ c. watches for traffic, all directions, while crossing
23. Endurance
   ☐ can maneuver sidewalk without assistance for one block (3 points)
   can maneuver sidewalk without assistance for 1/2 block (2 points)
   can maneuver sidewalk without assistance for 100 feet (1 point)

Subscore: ____________

RIDING CONDUCT **NOTES**

24. Interacting with Bus Driver
   - ☐ a. notifies bus driver of destination upon boarding (if appropriate) OR does not notify bus driver of destination upon boarding (if appropriate)
   - ☐ b. asks for driver's assistance when necessary
   - ☐ c. asks for transfer when necessary

Name:____________ Living Unit:__________ Date of Assessment:__________ Staff:____________

NOTES

25. Boarding
   - ☐ a. transports self to designated bus stop
   - ☐ b. boards correct bus
   - ☐ c. boards at designated time
26. Maneuverability — On Board
   - ☐ a. able to navigate aisles while bus is moving
   - ☐ b. does not bump into other passengers
   - ☐ c. selects appropriate place to sit
27. Personal Space
   - ☐ a. maintains reasonable distance between self and other riders
   - ☐ b. refrains from engaging in small talk with strangers
   - ☐ c. refrains from staring at strangers
28. Courtesy
   - ☐ a. offers seat to elderly rider
   - ☐ b. offers seat to (more physically) disabled
   - ☐ c. offers seat to pregnant woman (or woman carrying a small child)
29. Can ID Body Language Associated with People Desiring Privacy (given six pictures; 3 of people desiring privacy)
   - ☐ a. ID's person looking out of window
   - ☐ b. ID's person reading
   - ☐ c. ID's person turning head away
30. Stability
   - ☐ a. holds onto appropriate supports when bus is moving
   - ☐ b. able to stand without falling on moving bus
   - ☐ c. does not stand too close to doors
31. Prohibited Behaviors
   - ☐ a. refrains from smoking on board bus
   - ☐ b. refrains from littering
   - ☐ c. refrains from spitting
32. Prohibited Items
   - ☐ a. refrains from playing tape recorder/radio
   - ☐ b. does not transport flammable items
   - ☐ c. does not carry weapons or other unsafe items
33. Communication
   - ☐ a. all communication is at appropriate volume
   - ☐ b. refrains from using profanity and making degrading remarks
   - ☐ c. refrains from solicitous behaviors and co[illegible]tion
34. Preparing to Exit
   - ☐ a. knows where stop is
   - ☐ b. has all carry on items ready to be carried
   - ☐ c. pays attention so as not to miss stop
35. Exiting
   - ☐ a. pulls cord at correct stop
   - ☐ b. waits behind yellow line until bus stops and doors open
   - ☐ c. exits without problems

Subscore: ____________

TRANSFERS **NOTES**

36. Planning Transfer
   - ☐ a. reads schedules for each bus needed to get to final destination
   - ☐ b. plans a time line to meet each bus
   - ☐ c. gets transfer while paying fare on first bus
37. Transfer
   - ☐ a. gets off at designated stop to transfer to second bus
   - ☐ b. transports self to second bus stop if necessary
   - ☐ c. boards second designated bus
38. Wheelchair Only
   - ☐ a. can maneuver onto w/c lift
   - ☐ b. can maneuver to w/c area
   - ☐ c. knows correct way to be tied down
39. Emergency Situations
   - ☐ a. knows phone number to call in an emergency (911)
   - ☐ b. knows phone number of residence and/or of work site
   - ☐ c. has plan to follow if lost on bus

Subscore: ____________

Total: ____________

SECTION 2: MALADAPTIVE BEHAVIORS

This section is scored slightly differently than Section One. Select the MOST appropriate answer (a, b, or c). The behaviors listed below should be scored as follows: a = 1 point, b = 2 points, and c = 3 points. If none of the answers apply, the clients/patient's score for that questions is zero.

NOTES

1. Anxiety
   - ☐
   - a. reports feeling worried
   - b. can't turn attention to activity or other people easily due to worry
   - c. unable to perform task due to worry
2. Depression
   - ☐
   - a. reports feeling sad/unhappy/depressed, takes extra effort to perform task due to depression
   - b. performance of task delayed due to depression
   - c. unable to perform task due to depression
3. Hostility
   - ☐
   - a. irritable, grumpy
   - b. argumentative, sarcastic
   - c. throwing things, destroying property, assaulting others
4. Suspiciousness
   - ☐
   - a. describes incidents where others have harmed or want to harm him/her that sound plausible
   - b. does not trust and says others are talking about him/her with the intent to harm
   - c. delusional; speaks of Mafia or gang plots, the FBI, or other poisoning food, etc.
5. Unusual Thought Content
   - ☐
   - a. thinks that people are staring/laughing at him/her, ideas of persecution (people mistreat him/her), unusual beliefs in psychic powers, spirits, UFOs
   - b. delusions present, felt with conviction; functioning not disrupted
   - c. functioning disrupted (in part or totally) due to above listed ideas and beliefs
6. Grandiose
   - ☐
   - a. exaggerates abilities, accomplishments, or health
   - b. claims to be 'brilliant', a great musician, understands how 'everything works'
   - c. delusional; says s/he is appointed by God to run the world, has millions of dollars, can control the future of the world
7. Hallucinations
   - ☐
   - a. while in clear state of consciousness, hears music, whispers; sees illusions (faces in the shadows, etc.)
   - b. daily and/or some areas of functioning are disrupted
   - c. several times daily and/or many areas of functioning are disrupted
8. Disorientation
   - ☐
   - a. occasionally seems muddled, bewildered, or mildly confused
   - b. seems confused about simple things; has difficulty remembering things or people
   - c. grossly disoriented as to person, place, and/or time
9. Excitement
   - ☐
   - a. increased emotionality; seems keyed up, alert
   - b. reacts to most stimuli whether relevant or not with considerable intensity
   - c. marked overreaction to all stimuli with inappropriate intensity, restlessness, impulsiveness
10. Blunted Affect
    - ☐
    - a. has some loss of normal emotional responsiveness
    - b. lacks emotional expression; doesn't laugh, smile, or react emotionally when approached, has somewhat frozen, unchanging expression
    - c. seems mechanical in speech and activity; shows no feeling
11. Mannerisms and Posturing
    - ☐
    - a. eccentric or odd mannerisms or activity that ordinary people would have difficulty explaining, [illegible]
    - b. does things (postures) or has mannerisms that most people would regard [illegible] 'crazy'; [illegible] serving no apparent constructive purpose
    - c. posturing, smearing, intense rocking, fetal positioning, strange rituals that dominate client's/patient's attention and behavior
12. Bizarre Behavior
    - ☐
    - a. Slightly odd behavior, (e.g., hoarding food), peculiar behavior done in private (e.g., collecting garbage)
    - b. moderately unusual behavior (e.g., bizarre dress or make-up, 'preaching' to strangers, wandering streets aimlessly, eating non-foods, fixated staring in a socially disruptive way
    - c. unusual petty or serious crimes (e.g., directing traffic, public nudity, contacting authorities about imaginary crimes, setting fires

Score: ____________

SUMMARY AND RECOMMENDATIONS

Name:______________________ Living Unit:_________ Date of Assessment:_________ Staff:_______________

FUNCTIONAL HIKING TECHNIQUE

Name: Functional Hiking Technique

Also Known As: ICAN/Hiking

Authors: Janet A. Wessel (1979), adapted by joan burlingame (1990)

Time Needed to Administer: 3 hours or more

Time Needed to Score: 15 minutes

Recommended Disability Group: The ICAN/Hiking program was developed for individuals with MR/DD. This may also be used with any client group who is ambulatory with cognitive disabilities.

Purpose of Assessment: The purpose of the Functional Hiking Technique assessment is to determine the client's ability to demonstrate the basic skills necessary to hike independently.

What Does the Assessment Measure?: The ICAN/Hiking measures the client's ability to: 1) select the proper attire for hiking, 2) demonstrate a mature pacing pattern, 3) demonstrate a mature uphill and downhill hiking technique without assistance, 4) demonstrate mature techniques of moving under obstacles, and 5) demonstrate mature techniques of moving over obstacles.

Supplies Needed: Pictures of and actual articles needed to hike.

Reliability/Validity: None reported

Degree of Skill Required to Administer and Score: The individual administering and scoring this assessment must be: 1) able to read, 2) posses a basic knowledge of the disability group, and 3) have moderately strong skills in hiking techniques.

Comments: This assessment is a modified version of the 1979 ICAN Hiking Program. The original ICAN program was developed for classroom use and did not contain report forms appropriate for inclusion in a medical chart. The 1990 version was developed specifically for inclusion in medical charts.

Suggested Levels: Rancho Los Amigos Level: 5 and above. Developmental Level: 4 years and above. Reality Orientation Level: Moderate and above.

Distributors: 1979 version: Pro-Ed, 8700 Shoal Creek, Austin, TX 78757 (512) 451-3246

1990 version: Idyll Arbor, Inc. 25119 S.E. 262 Street, PO Box 720, Ravensdale, WA 98051 (206) 432-3231. (Area code 425 after April 1997.)

FUNCTIONAL HIKING TECHNIQUE

(Adapted from the ICAN Series, 1979)

PURPOSE: The purpose of the Functional Hiking Technique assessment is to determine the client's ability to demonstrate the basic skills necessary to hike independently.

In 1979 Janet A. Wessel, Ph.D. (Director of the Field Service Unit in Physical Education and Recreation for the Handicapped, Michigan State University) and Hubbard Press published an outstanding series of activity skills training programs and assessments. The publication states that as of January 1989 the content of the series became public domain (the copyright no longer applied). Idyll Arbor, Inc. staff have long used this series as a vital part of the recreational therapy that we provide to our clients and are excited to have the opportunity to offer the assessment forms for use by other therapists. The original assessments in the ICAN series were not formatted appropriately for inclusion in a medical chart. The forms that Idyll Arbor, Inc. has developed were formatted specifically for inclusion in medical charts. Any therapist who will be using the assessment on a regular basis should purchase the original manual from Hubbard Press, as it contains much more information than this assessment manual does.

The two primary groups that Idyll Arbor, Inc. used this series with were adults with brain injury (with a Rancho Los Amigos Scale as low as level five) and adults with developmental disabilities (with an adapted IQ as low as 35).

SKILL LEVEL: 1
SELECT PROPER ATTIRE FOR HIKING

TEACHING DIRECTIONS:

1. This skill level has six focal points. Review all points before proceeding.

2. Organize the clients into a semicircle so they can all see the therapist or aide.

3. Show and name the articles of clothing the client will need for hiking.

4. Have the client practice identifying clothes for hiking. Concentrate on focal points where the clients are having trouble.

5. Therapist or aide should teach, allow for practice of each focal point, assess, and record client's progress on score sheet.

FOCAL POINT:
a. Comfortable pair of high-topped shoes or boots.

WHAT TO DO: Show the client hiking boots. Point out features on the boots such as high-topped ankles with treaded bottoms. Have the client select hiking boots (shoes) from several pairs.
WHAT TO SAY: These are good boots (shoes) to hike in (point to). These are high-tops. They protect your ankles when you hike. These are treads. They keep you from slipping. Show me the best pair of boots (shoes) to use for hiking.
MATERIALS: High-topped hiking boots. Samples of other types of boots and shoes.

WHAT TO DO: Show the student pictures of different types of shoes. Have the student pick the best pair of hiking boots.
WHAT TO SAY: Look at the picture of boots (shoes). Point to the best boots (shoes) for hiking.
MATERIALS: Pictures of high-topped hiking boots or shoes and other types of boots and shoes.

FOCAL POINT:
b. Thick and thin pairs of socks.

WHAT TO DO: Show the client both types of socks. Have the clients identify both types of socks and indicate that thin socks should be worn under the thick ones.
WHAT TO SAY: These are socks that are worn for hiking. This is a thick sock. This is a thin sock. Put on the thin sock first (demonstrate). Put the thick sock on over the thin sock (demonstrate). Wear two pairs of socks when you go hiking.
MATERIALS: Thick and thin pairs of socks.

WHAT TO DO: Use thick socks that are all one color and thin socks that are all white.
WHAT TO SAY: The thin socks are white. This thick socks are green. Put the white thin socks on first. Put the green heavy socks on over the white socks.
MATERIALS: Green thick socks and white thin socks.

WHAT TO DO: Model identifying thick and thin pairs of socks.
WHAT TO SAY: Do this. These are thick socks. These are thin socks. Always wear two pairs of socks when you go hiking. Put the thin socks on first. Put the thick socks on over the thin socks.
MATERIALS: Thick and thin pairs of socks.

FOCAL POINT:
c. Comfortable pair of pants.

WHAT TO DO: Show the client a pair of loose fitting jeans or pants. Point out that they should fit loose rather than tight. Indicate that they should not be so long that the hem of the pants touches the ground. Show the client pictures of people wearing tight pants, pants that are too long, and comfortable pants. Have the client point to the best hiking pants.
WHAT TO SAY: There are good pants to wear hiking (point to). They are loose and the pant legs do not touch the ground. They are easy to walk in. These are pictures of people getting ready to go hiking. Point to the person whose pants are too tight. Point to the person whose pants touch the ground. Now point to the

person who is wearing good hiking pants.
MATERIALS: Picture of people wearing different types and lengths of pants. Pair of loose fitting jeans or pants.

WHAT TO DO: Show the client a picture of loose fitting shorts.
WHAT TO SAY: These are loose fitting shorts. Wear loose shorts for hiking when it is hot outside.
MATERIALS: Picture of loose fitting hiking shorts.

WHAT TO DO: Model selecting comfortable hiking pants from pictures.
WHAT TO SAY: Do this. Point to the person whose pants are loose and don't touch the ground.
MATERIALS: Pictures of people wearing different types and lengths of pants.

FOCAL POINT:
d. Suitable shirt.

WHAT TO DO: Show the client different types or pictures of shirts. Help the client point to suitable hiking shirts.
WHAT TO SAY: These are the kinds of shirts you can wear hiking. This is a T-shirt (flannel shirt, old shirt). Wear these kinds of shirts when you go hiking (point to). This is a good shirt. Do not wear good shirts when you go hiking.
MATERIALS: Pictures or a sample of a T-shirt, flannel shirt, and a good shirt.

WHAT TO DO: Have the student decide what shirt to wear.
WHAT TO SAY: Wear a T-shirt (point to) for hiking when it is hot. Wear a flannel shirt (point to) when it is cool. What is the weather like today? What shirt should you wear?
MATERIALS: Same as above.

WHAT TO DO: Model selecting a suitable shirt for hiking.
WHAT TO SAY: Do this. Point to a shirt to wear for hiking when it is hot outside. Point to a shirt to wear when it is cold.
MATERIALS: Same as above.

FOCAL POINT:
e. Suitable rain gear.

WHAT TO DO: Show the client rain gear such as raincoats, ponchos, boots, and rain hats. Discuss when the client should carry or take rain gear on a hike. Name a piece of rain gear. Have the client select the named piece of gear and put it on.
WHAT TO SAY: These are things you will need when you go hiking in the rain. This is a poncho (raincoat, boots, rain hat). Wear a poncho (raincoat, boots, rain hat) when it is raining (demonstrate). Carry a poncho with you when the weather forecast says it is going to rain. Show me a poncho (raincoat, boots, rain hat). Show me how you wear a poncho (raincoat, boots, rain hat).
MATERIALS: Pictures or samples of ponchos, raincoats, boots, rain hats, and other types of rain gear.

WHAT TO DO: Model identifying different types of rain gear from pictures or actual samples of rain gear.
WHAT TO SAY: Do this. Show me a poncho (raincoat, boots, rain hat). Show me how you wear a poncho (raincoat, boots, rain hat).
MATERIALS: Same as above.

FOCAL POINT:
f. Suitable jacket.

WHAT TO DO: Show the client a heavy jacket for cold weather hiking and light weight jacket for cool weather hiking.
WHAT TO SAY: These are the kinds of jackets that are used for hiking. This is a winter jacket (point to). Wear a winter jacket when it is cold outside. This is a spring jacket (point to). Wear a spring jacket when it is cool outside. Show me which jacket to wear when it is cool (cold) outside. You do not have to wear a jacket when it is warm outside.
MATERIALS: Pictures or samples of a heavy and light weight jacket.

WHAT TO DO: Have the client listen to the weather report and/or go outside to check the temperature and look for rain.
WHAT TO SAY: Check the weather before you go hiking. Listen to the radio for the weather report. Go outside and see how warm it is. Look up at the sky for rain clouds. Which jacket would you wear today? Which jacket would you wear if it was warm (cool, cold) outside?
MATERIALS: Pictures or samples of a heavy and light weight jacket. Radio.

WHAT TO DO: Model identifying a suitable jacket to wear in the different kinds of weather.
WHAT TO SAY: Do this. Check the weather before you go hiking. Show me which jacket to wear when it is cold outside.
MATERIALS: Pictures or samples of a heavy and lightweight jacket.

SKILL LEVEL: 2
MATURE PACING PATTERN WITHOUT ASSISTANCE

TEACHING DIRECTIONS:

1. This skill level has three focal points. Review all points before proceeding.

2. Model and practice the mature pacing pattern.

3. Organize the group into a line. Have the clients practice hiking. Concentrate on each focal point when appropriate.

4. Therapist or aide should teach, allow for practice of each focal point, assess, and record client's progress on score sheet.

FOCAL POINT:
a. Hike with steps that are a consistent distance apart and with an even pace.

WHAT TO DO: Hike beside the client. Hold the client's hand and hike at a comfortable pace that the client can keep.
WHAT TO SAY: Hold my hand. Hike with me. Take a step when I do. Take a step that is as big (small) as mine. Ready, step, step, step.
MATERIALS: None required.

WHAT TO DO: Place rubber mats or mark X's on the ground or floor twelve to eighteen inches apart. Clap (beat a drum) at an even rhythm. Have the client step on a mat with each clap (drum beat).
WHAT TO SAY: Let's practice hiking at an even pace. Listen. When I clap, step on the mat. Ready, clap, clap, clap... step on the next mat (demonstrate).
MATERIALS: Drum, mats or tape.

WHAT TO DO: Model hiking with steps that are consistent distance apart and with an even pace.
WHAT TO SAY: Do this. Hike at the same pace. Take steps that are the same size.
MATERIALS: None required.

FOCAL POINT:
b. Focus eyes ahead and frequently at feet for obstacles.

WHAT TO DO: Hike beside the client. Place your hands at the sides of the client's head. Manipulate the client's head up to look forward. Move the client's head down frequently to check feet for obstacles.
WHAT TO SAY: Look ahead as you hike (demonstrate). Watch where you are walking. Look at your feet. Check the trail for logs. Check the trail for holes.
MATERIALS: Level trail.

WHAT TO DO: Model focusing your eyes ahead and frequently at your feet for obstacles.
WHAT TO SAY: Do this. You must always watch the trail. Look ahead. There is a branch. Get ready to bend down and hike under the branch.
MATERIALS: Same as above.

FOCAL POINT:
c. Watch for fallen or low hanging obstacles.

WHAT TO DO: Hike beside the client. Manipulate the client's head so s/he can see low hanging objects such as branches. Stop the client two to three feet from the obstacle.
WHAT TO SAY: Keep your head up as you hike (demonstrate). Look ahead. Watch for branches. Get ready to bend down and hike under the branch.
MATERIALS: Level trail.

WHAT TO DO: Tie brightly colored flags around low hanging branches so they can easily be seen.
WHAT TO SAY: Look for a red flag. The flag will help you see low hanging branches. Tell me (point) when you see a flag.
MATERIALS: Level trail, red flags.

WHAT TO DO: Model watching for fallen or low hanging obstacles.
WHAT TO SAY: Do this. Look up. Look for low branches. Watch and look ahead as you hike.
MATERIALS: Level trail.

SKILL LEVEL: 3
UPHILL AND DOWNHILL HIKING TECHNIQUE

TEACHING DIRECTIONS

1. This skill level has three focal points. Review all points before proceeding.

2. Model and practice hiking uphill and downhill.

3. Organize the clients into a single file for hiking. Use physical and environmental manipulation, depending upon each client's learning style.

4. The therapist or aide should teach, allow for practice of each focal point, assess, and record client's progress on score sheet.

FOCAL POINT
a. Hike uphill with weight on the balls of the feet.

WHAT TO DO: Position yourself next to the client. Touch the front part of the client's feet. Adjust the shoulders slightly forward so the client leans toward the hill.
WHAT TO SAY: Hike uphill. Walk on the front part of your feet. Lean toward the hill (demonstrate).
MATERIALS: Trail with hills.

WHAT TO DO: Have the client practice hiking on gently rolling terrain before hiking uphill.
WHAT TO SAY: Let's practice hiking. Hike over to the hill. Hike uphill on the front part of your feet.
MATERIALS: Trail with hills.

WHAT TO DO: Model hiking uphill on the balls of the feet.
WHAT TO SAY: Do this. Hike uphill on the front part of your feet. Lean toward the hill.
MATERIALS: Same as above.

FOCAL POINT:
b. Maintain a slow, steady pace with rest intervals approximately every five to seven minutes.

WHAT TO DO: Hold the client's hand. Hike slowly and have the client step when you do. Call rest stops approximately every five to seven minutes.
WHAT TO SAY: Hike uphill slowly (demonstrate). Step with me. Ready, step, step, step. Hike until I call a rest.
MATERIALS: Trail with hills.

WHAT TO DO: Have the client sit down during rest periods. Ask the client if s/he would like a drink of water.
WHAT TO SAY: Let's take a rest. You may have a drink. Look at the wild flowers. They are pretty to look at but they should not be picked.
MATERIALS: Trail with hills, canteen.

WHAT TO DO: Model hiking uphill with a slow, steady pace and resting at intervals approximately every five to seven minutes.
WHAT TO SAY: Do this. Hike slowly uphill. Hike at the same speed. We will all rest together.
MATERIALS: Trail with hills.

FOCAL POINT:
c. Hike downhill with weight on the heels and knees bent slightly.

WHAT TO DO: Position yourself next to the client. Tap the heel of the foot to indicate where the client should step. Bend the client's knee slightly as s/he steps down.
WHAT TO SAY: Hike downhill. Watch where you are hiking. Step on your heel first (point to heel). Bend your knees as you step (demonstrate).
MATERIALS: Trail with hills.

WHAT TO DO: Have client practice on gently rolling terrain before hiking downhill.
WHAT TO SAY: Hike down the hills. Step on your heels first. Bend your knees as you step.
MATERIALS: Same as above.

WHAT TO DO: Model hiking downhill with weight on the heels and knees slightly bent.
WHAT TO SAY: Do this. Hike downhill. Watch where you are hiking. Step on your heel first. Bend your knee as you step.
MATERIALS: Same as above.

SKILL LEVEL: 4
MOVING UNDER OBSTACLES

TEACHING DIRECTIONS:

1. This skill level has three focal points. Review all points before proceeding.

2. Model and practice moving under obstacles.

3. Organize the class into a single file for hiking. As you hike down the trail, concentrate on moving under obstacles when appropriate.

4. Therapist or aide should teach, allow for practice of each focal point, assess, and record client's progress on score sheet.

FOCAL POINT:
a. Check for loose branches or rocks before proceeding under obstacles.

WHAT TO DO: Hike beside the client. As you approach an obstacle, grasp the client's shoulders to indicate that s/he should stop. Place your hands at the sides of the client's head and manipulate it so that his/her eyes can focus under the obstacle and check for hidden objects.
WHAT TO SAY: Watch for low branches. Stop. Bend down and look under the branch (demonstrate). Look for rocks (branches, puddles). Hike carefully under branches. If you see a log or rock, move it out of your way (demonstrate).
MATERIALS: Trail with obstacles.

WHAT TO DO: Place brightly colored objects on the trail. Have the client hike along and examine the area under each obstacle encountered. Have the client indicate what s/he sees before hiking under obstacles.
WHAT TO SAY: Look under branches for logs or rocks on the trail. What do you see? (Point to the logs or rocks.) Look carefully before you hike under the branch. If you see a large rock, walk around it (demonstrate).
MATERIALS: Logs and rocks marked by bright colors.

WHAT TO DO: Model visually checking under obstacles for loose branches or rocks.
WHAT TO SAY: Do this. Stop when you come to a branch. Bend and look for branches or rocks under the branch. If you see a log or a rock, walk around it.
MATERIALS: Trail with obstacles.

FOCAL POINT:
b. Check for safety on the other side of obstacle.

WHAT TO DO: Kneel next to the client near an obstacle. After the client examines the immediate trail, have the client slowly crawl toward the obstacle. At an appropriate distance from the obstacle, grasp the client's shoulders to indicate when to stop. Place your hands at the side of the client's head and manipulate it so the client can focus past the obstacle. Point from the client's eyes to the trail on the other side of the obstacle.
WHAT TO SAY: Crawl slowly toward the branch (demonstrate). Stop when you can see the trail on the other side of the branch. Look for loose branches and rocks on the other side. What do you see? Crawl under the branch where it is safe (demonstrate).
MATERIALS: Trail with obstacles.

WHAT TO DO: Mark the tail obstacles with red flags. Place rocks and branches on the other side of the obstacle. Place your hand on the client's hand and help him/her walk around any objects on the other side of the obstacle. Tell the client it is safe when no objects are in his/her way.
WHAT TO SAY: Crawl slowly toward the branch. Stop when you can see the trail on the other side. Look for loose branches and rocks on the other side of the branch. What do you see? Crawl under the branch where it is safe. Walk around any objects you see (demonstrate).
MATERIALS: Trail with obstacles, red flags to mark obstacles.

WHAT TO DO: Model hiking and visually checking for safety by examining the trail on the other side of any obstacle encountered.
WHAT TO SAY: Do this. Crawl slowly toward the branch. Stop when you can see the trail on the other side of the branch. Look for loose branches and rocks. Crawl under the branch where it is safe. Walk around any objects you can see.
MATERIALS: Trail with obstacles.

FOCAL POINT:
c. Help others behind him/her.

WHAT TO DO: Stand next to the obstacle. As the client sees the obstacle, remind him/her to tell others behind him/her about the obstacle. As the client approaches a branch, place your hand over the client's hand and guide him/her to hold the branch and walk past it until the next person can hold it. Place your hand on the following client's hand and guide that client to catch the branch.
WHAT TO SAY: Help Mary. Say 'Branch (log, puddle, hole, etc.) ahead'. Hold the branch as you walk past it. Hold the branch for Mary. Mary, reach for the branch like this (demonstrate). Say 'Branch ahead'. Hold the branch as you walk past.
MATERIALS: Trail with obstacles.

WHAT TO DO: Mark trail obstacles with red flags.
WHAT TO SAY: Look for obstacles with red flags. Walk around the log (puddle, hole, branch) with the red flag. Help Mary. Say 'Log ahead'. Mary, walk around the log.
MATERIALS: Trail with obstacles, red flags to mark obstacles.

WHAT TO DO: Model hiking and helping others by holding branches and verbally warning others of obstacles.
WHAT TO SAY: Do this. Say 'Branch ahead'. Hold the branch as you walk past. Hold the branch for Mary. Mary, reach for the branch. Hold the branch as you walk past.
MATERIALS: Trail with obstacles.

SKILL LEVEL: 5.
MOVING OVER OBSTACLES

TEACHING DIRECTIONS:

1. This skill has three focal points. Review all points before proceeding.
2. Model and practice moving over obstacles.
3. Organize the group into a single file for hiking. As you hike down the trail, concentrate on moving over obstacles when appropriate.
4. Therapist or aide should teach, allow for practice of each focal point, assess, and record client's progress on score sheet.

FOCAL POINT:
a. Check for loose branches or rocks.

WHAT TO DO: Hike next to the client. Grasp the client's shoulders to indicate that s/he should stop as s/he approaches an obstacle on the trail. Place your hands at the sides of the client's head and manipulate the head so his/her eyes can focus over the obstacle and check for loose branches, rocks, etc.
WHAT TO SAY: Hike down the trail. Stop when you see a log (rock, branch, etc.) on the trail. Look carefully over the log (rock, branch, etc.). Look for loose branches (rocks, puddles) before you step over the log (rock, branch).
MATERIALS: Trail with obstacles.

WHAT TO DO: Place loose branches (rocks or other trail hazard) near a trail obstacle. Point to the trail hazards.
WHAT TO SAY: Look closely at the trail before you step over the log (rock, branch). Here is a loose branch (rock). There is a loose branch. Do not go over the log (rock) until you find a place where it is safe to step.
MATERIALS: Same as above.

WHAT TO DO: Model checking for loose branches or rocks before proceeding over obstacles.
WHAT TO SAY: Do this. Stop when you see a log (branch, rock) on the trail. Look for loose branches (logs, puddles) before you hike on the trail. Go over the log where it is safe.
MATERIALS: Same as above.

FOCAL POINT:
b. Check safety on other side of obstacle.

WHAT TO DO: Stand next to the client. After the client examines the obstacle, hold his/her hand and walk slowly toward it. Stop at an appropriate distance from the obstacle so that other side can be examined. Place your hands at the side of the client's head and manipulate it so the client's eyes can focus on the other side of the obstacle.
WHAT TO SAY: Look at the log (rock, hole, puddle, branch, etc.) carefully. Now step slowly toward the log. Stop when you can see over the log like this (demonstrate). Check for loose branches and rocks on the other side of the log. Move your head like this (demonstrate). Look over the log. What do you see?
MATERIALS: Trail with obstacles.

WHAT TO DO: Mark obstacles on the trail with red flags.
WHAT TO SAY: Look for red flags. Step slowly toward the log with a flag. Stop when you can see over it. Check for loose branches and rocks on the other side of the log. Look over the log. What do you see?
MATERIALS: Trail with obstacles.

WHAT TO DO: Model hiking and visually checking for loose branches and rocks on the other side of an obstacle.
WHAT TO SAY: Do this. Slowly walk toward the log (rock, hole, puddle, branch). Stop when you can see over it. Look for loose branches and rocks on the other side of the log.
MATERIALS: Trail with obstacles.

FOCAL POINT:
c. Helps others behind him/her.

WHAT TO DO: Stand next to the obstacle as the client approaches the obstacle. Remind him/her to warn the others behind him/her.
WHAT TO SAY: Help Walt when you see a log (branch, hole, puddle) on the trail. Stop and say 'Log ahead'.
MATERIALS: Trail with obstacles.

WHAT TO DO: Mark trail obstacles with red flags.
WHAT TO SAY: Help Walt when you see a log (branch, hole, puddle) on the trail. Stop and say 'Log ahead'.
MATERIALS: Trail with obstacles, red flags.

WHAT TO DO: Model hiking and verbally warning other hikers about the obstacle.
WHAT TO SAY: Do this. 'Log ahead'.
MATERIALS: Trail with obstacles,

FUNCTIONAL HIKING TECHNIQUE

(Adapted from the ICAN Series, 1979)

KEY **1 = achieved skill** **2 = tried-not met** **3 = other (specify in comments)**
A skill is considered to be achieved when the client demonstrates the skill 3 out of 3 trials.

1. TO SELECT THE PROPER ATTIRE FOR HIKING
Given a verbal request, a demonstration, and pictures or selection of different clothing items, the client will identify the following clothing for hiking:

	DATE: ____	____	____	____	COMMENTS
a. Comfortable shoes or boots					
b. Thick and thin socks					
c. Comfortable pants					
d. Suitable shirt					
e. Suitable rain gear					
f. Suitable jacket					

2. TO DEMONSTRATE A MATURE PACING PATTERN
Given a verbal request and a demonstration, the client will exhibit a steady, even hiking pace for a distance of one mile on level terrain without assistance in this manner:

	DATE ____	____	____	____	COMMENTS
a. Hike with steps that are a consistent distance apart and with an even pace					
b. Focus eyes ahead and frequently at feet for obstacles					
c. Watch for falling or low hanging obstacles					

3. TO DEMONSTRATE A MATURE UPHILL AND DOWNHILL HIKING TECHNIQUE WITHOUT ASSISTANCE
Given a verbal request and a demonstration, the client will hike uphill and downhill a distance of one-half mile without assistance in this manner:

	DATE ____	____	____	____	COMMENTS
a. Hike uphill with weight on the balls of the feet					
b. Maintain a slow steady pace with rest intervals approximately every five to seven minutes					
c. Hike downhill with weight on the heels and knees bent slightly					

Client's Name	Physician	Admit #	Room/Bed

KEY	**1 = achieved skill**	**2 = tried-not met**	**3 = other (specify in comments)**
A skill is considered to be achieved when the client demonstrates the skill 3 out of 3 trials.			

4. TO DEMONSTRATE MATURE TECHNIQUES OF MOVING UNDER OBSTACLES
Given a verbal request, a demonstration, and assistance in getting down, the client will manipulate his/her body under obstacles on the trail (such as branches three to four feet from the ground) in this manner:

	DATE ____	____	____	____	COMMENTS
a. Check for loose branches or rocks before proceeding under obstacles					____
b. Check safety on other side of obstacle					____
c. Help others behind him/her					____

5. TO DEMONSTRATE MATURE TECHNIQUES OF MOVING OVER OBSTACLES
Given a verbal request, a demonstration, and assistance from another person, the client will manipulate his/her body over obstacles approximately knee high in this manner:

	DATE ____	____	____	____	COMMENTS
a. Check for loose branches or rocks					____
b. Check safety on other side of obstacle					____
c. Help others behind him/her					____

SUMMARY

RECOMMENDATIONS

Client's Name	Physician	Admit #	Room/Bed

DOWNHILL SKIING ASSESSMENT

Name: Downhill Skiing Assessment

Also Known As: No other name known.

Author: Johna Peterson

Time Needed to Administer: The administration of this assessment requires observation over a period of time: a day, a week, a ski season.

Time Needed to Score: 5 minutes, with an additional 15 minutes to formulate recommendations for the next ski season.

Recommended Disability Groups: This assessment was developed for clients with the diagnosis of MR/DD. It may be used with clients with brain injuries.

Purpose of Assessment: The purpose of the assessment is to help place clients into the appropriate class (or level). The client should be able to demonstrate 80% of the skills in each level at least 3 out of 3 times prior to being advanced to the next level.

What Does the Assessment Measure?: The assessment measures the client's ability to participate in downhill skilling. The assessment itself divides skiing capabilities into five levels: 1) beginner, 2) beginning turns, 3) improving turns, 4) versatile skiing, and 5) dynamic skiing.

Supplies Needed: The therapist and the client will need to be outfitted to participate in downhill skiing. The score sheet (#137) will also be required.

Reliability/Validity: None reported.

Degree of Skill Required to Administer and Score: The therapist should have a background in skills related to skiing, and understand the progressions associated with teaching skiing. It would also be appropriate for the therapist to have a dual certification: CTRS level from the National Council for Therapeutic Recreation Certification and Level 1, 2, or 3 Certification from the National Handicap Sports Association.

Comments: Most of the programs which offer ski instruction for individuals with disabilities rely on volunteer instructors. The instructor to client ratio is usually 1:1. The way that Idyll Arbor, Inc. worked out client coverage is that we would have 8 - 12 clients on the hill at one time. Each client had his/her own volunteer instructor. The recreational therapist rotated between each client/instructor group to help on behavior management issues, equipment/skill adaptations, and ongoing evaluations.

A book the therapist may find helpful is:

O'Leary, Hal (1987) **Bold Tracks, Skiing for the Disabled**, Evergreen, Colorado, Cordillera Press, Inc.

Suggested Levels: Rancho Los Amigos Level: 6 - 8. Developmental Level: 5 and above. Reality Orientation: Moderate and above.

Distributor: Idyll Arbor, Inc., 25119 SE 262 Street, PO Box 720, Ravensdale, WA 98051-0720 (206) 432-3231. (Area code 425 after April 1997.)

DOWNHILL SKIING ASSESSMENT

Client: ______________________ **Date Instruction Started:** ______________________

Evaluator: ______________________ **Instructor:** ______________________

Abilities:

Physical Limitations:

Ski Equipment (note if the equipment is owned by client):

PURPOSE: The purpose of this assessment is to help place students into the appropriate class (or level). The student should be able to demonstrate 80% of the skills in each level at least 3 out of 3 times prior to being advanced to the next level.

SCORING: The instructor should write in the date that each skill was demonstrated 3/3 times on the line to the left of the skill. The comments section at the end of each level is for the instructor to indicate what modifications were required for the student to achieve the skill, and to note any behavior (or other concerns or strengths) that would be important for the next instructor to know about.

Level 1 Beginner

_________ Familiar with the ski area
_________ Wears appropriate clothing for weather
_________ Familiar with the ski equipment; skis, poles, boots
_________ Assists in carrying equipment
_________ Can put equipment on with assistance
_________ Can move around on flat terrain with skis on
_________ Straight run on flat terrain w/out assistance
_________ Gliding wedge w/out assisitance
_________ Gliding wedge to a stop w/out assistance
_________ Side stepping up a small incline
_________ Can get up from a fall with assistance

Comments:

Level 2 Beginning Turns

_________ Good body position — knees bent, hands forward, head up and weight forward
_________ Terrain — able to handle gentle sloping terrain (Green Circle — Easier)
_________ Can carry own equipment
_________ Can put equipment on w/out assistance
_________ 1 wedge turn to each side, with a controlled stop
_________ 2 wedge turns linked, to a stop, w/out assistance
_________ 3 - 4 linked wedge turns, to a stop, w/out assistance
_________ Wedge change ups, to control speed and to stop
_________ Can load and unload beginning chair lift safely
_________ Can get up from a fall w/out assistance
_________ Can use poles for balance and pushing off the snow

Comments:

Client's Name	Physician	Admit #	Room/Bed

Level 3 Improving Turns

_________ Good body position — knees bent, hands forward and gripping poles, head up and weight forward
_________ Rounder, longer wedge turns on gentle terrain (Blue Square — More Difficult)
_________ 5+ linked wedge turns, in control, to a stop
_________ Can slow down and stop on command
_________ Maneuver around small moguls
_________ Traverse across the hill, watching for traffic
_________ Traverse, into turn
_________ Side step on steeper terrain
_________ Get up from a fall on steeper terrain
_________ Use poles to initiate turns
_________ Wedge christy turns

Comments:

Level 4 Versatile Skiing

_________ Advanced wedge christy, tighter, more controlled
_________ Using poles to initiate and pivot around all turns
_________ Able to handle bigger moguls
_________ Able to ski on varying terrain (Blue Square — More Difficult)
_________ Can ski at various speeds, always in control
_________ Wide tack parallel turns
_________ Uphill christy
_________ Can manage a basic racing course
_________ Increasing control of edges, pressuring on turn
_________ Independent leg action in parallel turns
_________ Using poles for rhythm and timing

Comments:

Level 5 Dynamic Skiing

_________ Can manage difficult terrain (Black Diamond — Most Difficult)
_________ Can ski in various conditions: powder, ice, moguls
_________ Good control of edges, pressure, balance, and steering
_________ Can verbally explain simple concepts about skiing
_________ Able to manage a complicated racing course
_________ Linked parallel turns, using independent leg action
_________ Skiing in control at all times
_________ Dynamic up and down rhythm while turning
_________ Using poles for rhythm, timing, and initiation

Comments:

Summary:

Recommendations:

Evaluator & Date:

Adapted from: BOLD TRACKS, SKIING FOR THE DISABLED by Hal O'Leary, Winterpark, CO; and the SNOW SKIING PROGRESSION from Skiforall, Ski Programs for the Disabled, Seattle, WA.

CROSS COUNTRY SKIING ASSESSMENT

Name: Cross County Skiing Assessment

Also Known As: No other name known.

Author: Johna Peterson

Time Needed to Administer: The administration of this assessment requires observation over a period of time: a day, a week, a ski season.

Time Needed to Score: 5 minutes, with an additional 15 minutes to formulate recommendations for the next ski season.

Purpose of Assessment: The purpose of this assessment is to help place clients into the appropriate class (or level). The student should be able to demonstrate 80% of the skills in each level at least 3 out of 3 times prior to being advanced to the next level.

What Does the Assessment Measure?: The assessment measures the client's ability to participate in cross country skiing. The assessment itself divides cross country skiing into 4 levels: 1) introduction, 2) beginner, 3) intermediate, and 4) advanced. These levels are based on the Skiforall Cross Country Ski Program Manual: **A SENSIBLE PROGRESSION**, Seattle, WA.

Supplies Needed: The therapist and the client will need to be outfitted to participate in cross country skiing. The score sheet (#138) will also be required.

Reliability/Validity: None reported.

Degree of Skill Required to Administer and Score: The therapist should have a background in skills related to skiing, and understand the progressions associated with teaching skiing. It would also be appropriate for the therapist to have a dual certification: CTRS level from the National Council for Therapeutic Recreation Certification, and Level 1, 2, or 3 Certification from the National Handicap Sports Association.

Comments: Most of the programs which offer ski instruction for individuals with disabilities rely on volunteer instructors. The instructor to client ratio is usually 1:1. The way that Idyll Arbor, Inc. worked out client coverage is that we would have 8 - 12 clients on the hill at one time. Each client had his/her own volunteer instructor. The recreational therapist rotated between each client/instructor group to help on behavior management issues, equipment/skill adaptations, and ongoing evaluations.

Suggested Levels: Rancho Los Amigos Level: 5 and above. Developmental Level: 4 and above. Reality Orientation Level: Moderate and above.

Distributor: Idyll Arbor, Inc., 25119 S.E. 262 Street, PO Box 720, Ravensdale, WA 98051 (206) 432-3231. (Area code 425 after April 1997.)

CROSS COUNTRY SKIING ASSESSMENT

Client: ______________________ **Date Instruction Started:** ______________________

Evaluator: ______________________ **Instructor:** ______________________

Abilities:

Physical Limitations:

Ski Equipment (note if the equipment is owned by client):

PURPOSE: The purpose of this assessment is to help place students into the appropriate class (or level). The student should be able to demonstrate 80% of the skills in each level at least 3 out of 3 times prior to being advanced to the next level.

SCORING: The instructor should write in the date that each skill was demonstrated 3/3 times on the line to the left of the skill. The comments section at the end of each level is for the instructor to indicate what modifications were required for the student to achieve the skill, and to note any behavior (or other concerns or strengths) that would be important for the next instructor to know about.

Level 1 Introduction

_________ Familiar with the ski area
_________ Wears appropriate clothing for weather
_________ Familiar with the ski equipment; skis, poles, boots
_________ Assists in carrying equipment
_________ Can put equipment on with assistance
_________ Actively involved in warm up and stretching exercises
_________ Can fall correctly without hurting self
_________ Gets into 'Beetle' position to get up from fall, w/ assist
_________ Gets up from fall with assistance
_________ Can move around on flat terrain w/one ski on (scooter)
_________ Balanced and controlled during scooter, w/assist

Comments:

Level 2 Beginner

_________ Body position — knees bent, eyes and head up
_________ Terrain — very flat, skiing in established 'tracks'
_________ Can carry own equipment
_________ Can put equipment on with minimal assistance
_________ 'Shuffle' with two skis on, w/ assist (walk/slide step)
_________ Beginning to let skis slide more during shuffle step
_________ Can turn skis to change directions (using a step turn)
_________ Can get up from a fall independently
_________ Ski's 100 yards or more on two skis
_________ Can use poles for balance and pushing off the snow

Comments:

Client's Name	Physician	Admit #	Room/Bed

Level 3 Intermediate

_________ Puts equipment on independently

_________ Terrain — some slight inclines/declines, not always in tracks

_________ Good body position — knees bent, hands forward and gripping poles, head up

_________ Good shuffle/glide step

_________ Using poles for balance and propulsion

_________ Beginning to go down hill using 'wedge' to slow down and stop

_________ Can slow down and stop on command

_________ Can do a 'straight run' on gentle declines

_________ Uses a herringbone to go up on steeper terrain

_________ Side step on steeper terrain

_________ Get up from a fall on steeper terrain

Comments:

Level 4 Advanced

_________ Puts equipment on independently

_________ Terrain — some slight inclines/declines, not always in tracks

_________ Good body position — knees bent, hands forward and gripping poles, head up

_________ Good shuffle/glide step

_________ Using poles for balance and propulsion

_________ Beginning to go down hill using 'wedge' to slow down and stop

_________ Can slow down and stop on command

_________ Can do a 'straight run' on gentle declines

_________ Uses a herringbone to go up on steeper terrain

_________ Side step on steeper terrain

_________ Get up from a fall on steeper terrain

Comments:

Summary:

Recommendations:

Evaluator & Date:

Adapted from: A SENSIBLE PROGRESSION by Ski Acres X-C Center, as used by the Skiforall Cross Country Ski Program, Ski Programs for the Disabled, Seattle, WA.

Chapter 7

MEASURING MULTIDIMENSIONAL ASPECTS

The assessments in this chapter are placed here because they do not easily fit into any of the other categories. The first three assessments, the Leisure Social/Sexual Assessment (LS/SA), the Idyll Arbor Activity Assessment (IA3), and the Therapeutic Recreation Index (TRI) are combination assessment tools and assessment reports. There are pros and cons to using a combination. When a combination of tool/report is used, the therapist will find it harder to include information from other criterion-referenced or norm-referenced assessment tools into the final recommendations. A benefit of using a combination tool/report is that the assessment process may flow more smoothly because a routine can be set up and the therapist does not need to spend time organizing the best combination of assessment tools to use (and still stay under one hour for the initial assessment!).

Idyll Arbor, Inc. staff seldom use a combination tool/report. Our clients are frequently better served by having a combination of assessment tools used (selected to meet individual needs) than by using one of the three tool/reports. Each department will need to make its own decision on the type and number of assessments to use.

The last assessment in this chapter is really an activity. By observing the client during the activity and asking pertinent questions, this activity provides the therapist with a quantity of subjective data. The information obtained during the use of this activity (or others like it) could provide useful information on an assessment report or a progress update.

The therapist may use the information obtained from many activities to enhance his/her functional measurements. An example would be games like **Cause and Effect Card Games.** This game provides the therapist with information about the client's abilities that is difficult to obtain just by asking questions during the assessment process. (Bradley-Richards, K. and O'Brien-Fallon, M. (1988) **Cause and Effect Card Games: Social Judgment Skills for Head-Injured Adolescents and Adults**. Ravensdale, WA: Idyll Arbor, Inc.

Table 6 - 1 Suggested Levels

The Idyll Arbor, Inc. staff reviewed the assessments contained in this book to *estimate* which groups the assessments may be given to. The determinations were based on their experience administering the assessments with the clients that they have worked with. (Idyll Arbor, Inc. has a general practice, admitting clients with all diagnoses except clients with a primary diagnosis of addiction). There has been no formal testing to establish these recommended guidelines. Each therapist will need to evaluate whether any specific assessment will work with the clients that s/he serves.

The shaded areas on the charts below indicate that the assessment is recommended for use with clients functioning at that level. To determine if an assessment is appropriate to use, determine the functional level of the client and then read the chart to determine if the assessment is appropriate for that client.

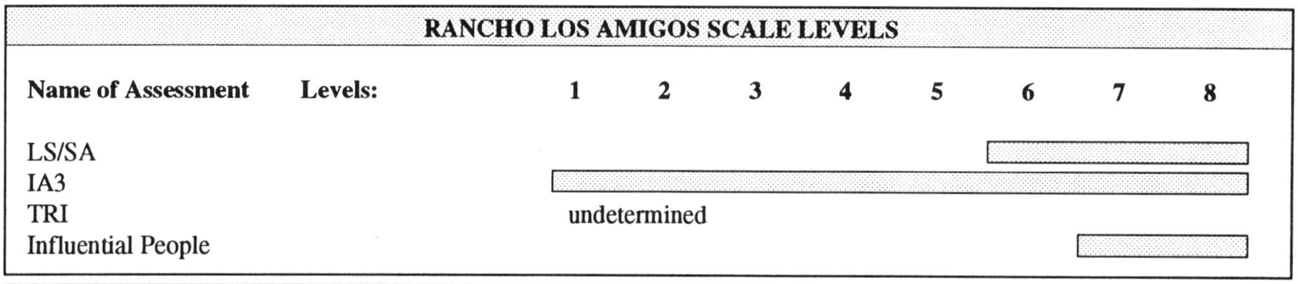

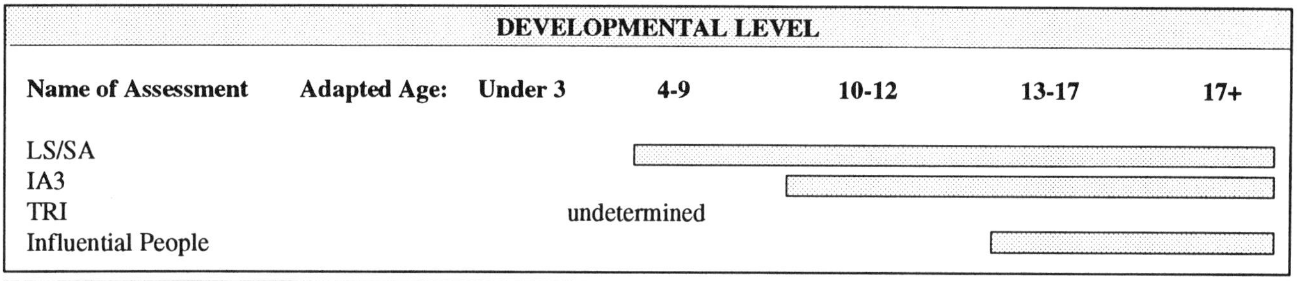

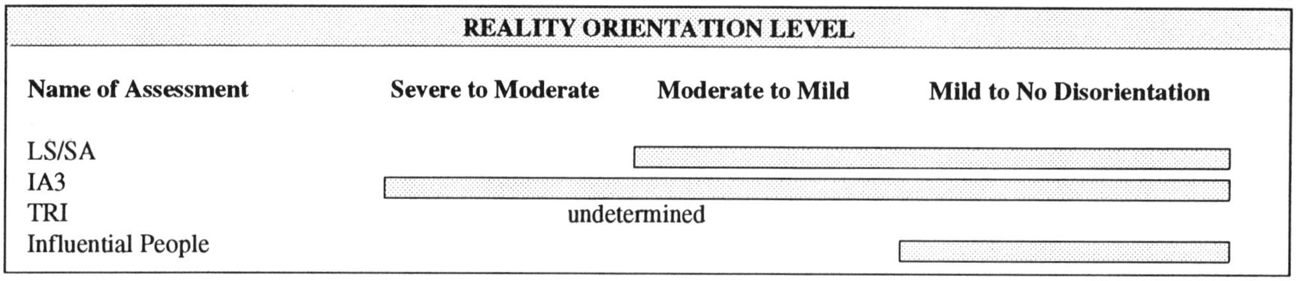

LEISURE SOCIAL/SEXUAL ASSESSMENT

Name: Leisure Social/Sexual Assessment

Also Known As: LS/SA

Author: Phyllis Coyne

Time Needed to Administer: 1 hour

Time Needed to Score: 15 - 30 minutes

Recommended Disability Groups: The LS/SA was developed specifically for clients who are diagnosed as having MR/DD. The age group that this assessment was geared toward was adolescents and young adults. The LS/SA has had limited, and successful, use with adolescents who do not have the diagnosis of MR/DD.

Purpose of the Assessment: The purpose of the LS/SA is to provide the recreational therapist with a tool to assess the breadth and depth of a client's understanding of appropriate social and sexual roles.

What Does the Assessment Measure?: The LS/SA is made up of three sections. The first section asks the client to provide the therapist with basic, personal data (e.g., name, address, phone number, sex). This section helps the therapist determine how good a historian the client is. The second section is a structured interview which explores the client's understanding of activities that cause him/her enjoyment, the client's understanding of leisure, and the client's understanding of friendship/peer interactions. The third section asks the client detailed questions about dating, marriage, and sexuality to measure his/her depth of knowledge.

Supplies Needed: The therapist will need the LS/SA manual and score sheet (#110).

Reliability/Validity: None reported.

Degree of Skill Required to Administer and Score: This assessment requires a solid understanding of leisure philosophy and theory, as well as the ability to establish a caring, non-judgmental environment to discuss issues of sexuality. It is highly recommended that the individual administering this assessment be certified at the CTRS level by the National Council for Therapeutic Recreation Certification. Some facilities have a licensed nurse administer the third section.

Comments: The LS/SA is the assessment tool which was developed as part of a complete leisure education program. Phyllis Coyne wrote two books which contain over 25 leisure education activities each. These activities help the client develop the skills necessary to successfully participate in age-appropriate peer interactions. The two books by Coyne are now out of print.

Coyne, Phyllis (1980) **Social Skills Training: A Three-Pronged Approach for Developmentally Disabled Adolescents and Young Adults.**

Coyne, Phyllis (1980) **Well-Being for Mentally Retarded Adolescents: A Social, Leisure, and Nutrition Education Program.**

Free Spirit Publishing, Inc. is a publishing company which offers many books and games which will help the therapist. Once the recreational therapist has identified areas of need by using the LS/SA, s/he will find books which offer treatment intervention strategies. Two books that the authors recommend from Free Spirit Publishing are

Fisher, G. and Cummings, R. (1990) **The Survival Guide for Kids with LD (Learning Differences)**

Kaufman, G. and Raphael, L. (1990) **Stick Up for Yourself! Every Kid's Guide to Personal Power and Positive Self-Esteem**

The address for Free Spirit Publishing is 400 First Avenue North, Suite 616, Minneapolis, MN 55401 (800) 735 -7323.

Suggested Levels: Rancho Los Amigos Level: 6 and up. Developmental Level: 7 years and up. Reality Orientation Level: Moderate to no disorientation. Reality orientation is not usually measured for developmental levels below 10 years.

Distributor: Idyll Arbor, Inc., 25119 S.E. 262 Street, PO Box 720, Ravensdale, WA 98051 (206) 432-323. (Area code 425 after April 1997.)

LEISURE AND SOCIAL/SEXUAL ASSESSMENT LS/SA

The purpose of the LS/SA is to provide the recreational therapist with a tool to assess the breadth and depth of a client's understanding of appropriate social and sexual roles.

SUPPLIES NEEDED:
Quiet room to interview client
Score sheet and pen

TIME NEEDED:
Approximately one hour

The LS/SA was written as part of a social skills training program for adolescents and young adults with developmental disabilities. This program, titled "Social Skills Training: A Three-Pronged Approach" was developed by Phyllis Coyne, CTRS,with financial support under Grant No. 50-P-50368. Although the program and assessment were first published in 1980, they fulfill a good portion of the intent of the 1988 federal legislation concerning sexuality training in ICF-MRs (Intermediate Care Facilities for the Mentally Retarded).

The new federal regulations for clients who are in ICF-MRs ask the surveyors to determine if each client's needs are being met. This is generally taken to mean that the facility has periodically evaluated a client's social/sexual understanding level. The specific section of the regulations that the LS/SA helps meet can be found under TAG NO. W223/SOCIAL DEVELOPMENT (ASSESSMENT) of Appendix J. Appendix J is the document that state and federal surveyors use to interpret the federal regulations. W223 tells the surveyors that:

> Social development refers to the formations of those self-help, recreation and leisure, and interpersonal skills that enable an individual to establish and maintain appropriate roles and fulfilling relationships with others.

Below are the instructions for the assessment from the "Three-Pronged Approach" (pages 30-32):

In the past people within the same diagnostic category have been offered the same training activities. Activities have been selected for the overall needs of that category or group rather than for specific needs of the individuals within that category. Although this model is designed for a group setting, it advocates for meeting the unique needs of individuals within the group. The key to understanding the individual's needs and unique characteristics, which will in turn lead to appropriate placement in a group, is assessment. Assessment is necessary to determine objectives, training activities and facilitation techniques.

Assessment of social skills is not a simple process. It requires a multifaceted approach characterized by pre-assessment, on-going evaluation and post-assessment. Consistent with behavioral and learning theories, this model assesses social skill functioning within a behavioral framework.

Assessment and intervention are integrally related in this model. Assessment is ongoing, so that the training changes as an individual's performance changes. The pre-assessment techniques can also be utilized to evaluate how well the objectives have been met. Progress is only measured in relation to stated objectives and specific problem areas identified in the initial assessment.

There are many ways that behaviors can be assessed within a behavioral framework. Because a participant's social functioning may differ in various situations, more than one assessment is warranted. Three effective methods used in this model include an interview to obtain information about the participant's social behavior, direct observation of the participant's behavior and behavioral checklists/rating scales that inquire into social strengths and weaknesses. This section presents an in depth examination of these assessment techniques.

THE RECREATION-SOCIAL-SEXUAL ASSESSMENT INTERVIEW

The interview is a useful pre-assessment tool for gathering information about the participant's social behavior which will aid in selection, grouping and development of objectives. In order to develop an appropriate individualized program for the development of leisure and social-sexual knowledge and skills it is necessary to obtain information about the individual's present utilization of time, knowledge, skills, and interests. If conducted by a trained person, the interview has a high degree of validity and reliability for broad assessment. "The Recreation-Social-Sexual Interview Schedule" (now called the "LS/SA") is a screening tool that has been developed for use in this model to obtain a basic recreation-social-sexual profile of adolescents and young adults with developmental disabilities (Coyne and Mock, 1979). The information needed to assess the individual and develop a profile must be kept in mind. When the necessary information cannot be gathered from the individual due to a lack of expressive language or cognitive problems, the interview can be adapted for use with a parent, teacher, or significant other. An interview with the person(s) familiar with the participant's behavior is generally necessary for supplemental information and verification of data given by the participant.

INTERVIEW TECHNIQUES

An environment characterized by privacy, freedom from interruptions and a general atmosphere of calmness and warm acceptance facilitates establishing rapport and carrying out an effective interview. The interview schedule suggests a format for collecting the necessary information during a direct interview with the individual. Generally, the nature of the interview will cause the interviewer to ask questions in a slightly different manner or different order than that presented in the interview schedule. One question may generate the answer to several others. As a general rule, open-ended questions get the most spontaneous and extensive responses. However, as cognitive levels decrease, a shift to multiple choice format may be needed. Previous information about the individual's activities can be used as a base from which to ask questions. Yes and no questions should be avoided as much as possible.

INTERVIEW SCHEDULE (THE LS/SA ASSESSMENT SCORE SHEET)

The Recreation-Social-Sexual (the LS/SA) is divided into four sections and takes approximately 60 minutes to administer. (Please refer to the LS/SA score sheet.)

SECTION I: The interview begins with structured demographic questions which require a concrete rote response. The questions provide some information about survival skills while allowing the interviewer to make some judgments about cognitive level and the best way to approach the individual. They also allow the interviewer the opportunity to get used to any unusual speech pattern.

SECTION II: This section provides a profile of the individual's recreation and social interaction pattern. To identify and assess needs, it is necessary to note deviations from an ideal pattern, which is self-initiated, balanced, has variety, and meets personal needs. Such a lifestyle is characterized by knowledge and understanding about personal and community recreation resources, skills for recreation participation, social interaction skills, personal interests and values relating to recreation, and decision-making ability. Determining what a person likes about an activity can provide information on reinforcers that might be useful in the program. It can also help avoid making erroneous assumptions about the type of activities a person enjoys. For instance, a person may like hiking and cross country skiing because it provides quality time with a special person rather than because the participant likes the outdoors or physical activity. What a person actually does in an activity is important to assess because it indicates skill level. For instance, if an individual reports that s/he plays basketball, it could mean throwing a ball in the air and catching it, bouncing it, throwing it into a basket, playing Horse with one or more peers, playing an adapted game of basketball, or playing regulation basketball. All of these represent different levels of recreation and social interaction skills. It can also indicate their role in a group (e.g., follower, aggressor, or leader). The frequency in which a person participates in an activity can suggest amount of interest, opportunity and other variables. The place where a person recreates can indicate knowledge of community and personal resources, type of program and facility preferences. For instance, it may develop that a person likes to swim only at lakes or rivers because s/he does not like chlorine, crowds, or being restricted. Identifying friends and the ages of these friends supplies further information about social interaction patterns during recreation. Some individuals do not have a concept of age comparison and do not know if a friend is younger, even if the friend is five or more years younger. How an individual gets involved in an activity helps determine self-initiation, motivation, and awareness of resources. How a person gets to an activity gives information about mobility independence. What a person feels that s/he excels in indicates perceived strengths and self-concept. Special products used for grooming can indicate basic personal hygiene practices as well as the age and cultural appropriateness of these practices. Areas of particular problems may be expressed and recorded under each boxed in question.

SECTION III: This section gives some samples of questions which are designed to assess an individual's knowledge of sexuality as well as examining personal attitudes and interests related to social-sexual behavior, such as dating, marriage, and parenting. From the affect of the individual when answering these questions the interviewer can identify overall knowledge and attitudes about sexuality and how these might affect social behavior.

When the Idyll Arbor, inc. staff re-wrote the assessment with the assistance of Phyllis Coyne, CTRS, some changes were made. The changes can be found on the summary page of this assessment. These changes are a result of years of using the assessment plus a desire to utilize some of the current language used in federal regulations for ICF - MRs.

LEISURE ACTIVITIES SUMMARY

The information for this section may come solely from the assessment, or may also include information taken from clients recreational activity participation record. The word 'Domain' means 'functional skill area'. So, 'physical domain' refers to activities that emphasize functional skill development using gross motor activities, fine motor activities, or cardiovascular activities. 'Cognitive domain' refers to activities that emphasize problem solving, memory, receptive and expressive language, and thought processing. 'Social domain' refers to activities that emphasize the ability to get along with others. 'Sensory domain' refers to activities that emphasize development of our five senses (sensory stimulation): seeing, hearing, smelling, feeling, and tasting. 'Community domain' refers to activities that emphasize specific skills required to survive and function in the community (e.g., shopping).

In theory, the community domain does not belong in this grouping, as the functional skills required to survive in the community can appropriately be listed under the other four domains. However, in reality, when the survey team arrives, they need a clear indication as to how often integration training and experiences are taking place. To help facilities avoid negative citations due to the lack of surveyor enlightenment, this area has been pulled out from the other four domains.

SOCIAL/SEXUAL SUMMARY

This section provides the recreational therapist with a quick summary of the client's social/sexual knowledge. A single check in the appropriate box and a one or two sentence summary is all that is expected for the four knowledge areas.

SUMMARY

This space is provided for the recreational therapist to compile the information from both the Leisure Activities Summary and the Social/Sexual Summary. It is extremely important to remember that the federal regulations require that the therapist both report the findings *and* clearly state in a measurable and meaningful way how the findings will impact the client's ability to perform. An example might be:

Charlie Doe does not demonstrate an understanding of even the most basic of knowledge related to sexuality. He does not understand the concept of 'private parts'. This leaves him at high risk for uninvited sexual advances. Close supervision is required in the community, especially since he is ambulatory. Specific training in this area should be tried but, due to his low cognitive abilities, it is not likely that he will ever be independently safe in this area.

RECOMMENDATIONS

The intent of the federal regulations concerning clients in ICF - MRs is that no training objectives are to be developed until the interdisciplinary team can discuss (and approve) them at the annual IPP. This section should list one to three possible program (training) ideas for the next 1 to 3 years. An example might be:

1. Continued 1:3 supervision in the community
2. Training in the concept of 'private parts'
3. Training in the concept of 'free time'

Leisure and Social/Sexual Assessment

Name:______________________ Date of Birth:______________ Staff:______________

Unit: ______________ Admit: __________ Sex: ❑Male ❑Female Date of Assessment: ______

Section I

Question	Summary of Answer		Correct Answer	No Answer	Tried but Incorrect Answer	Does Not Understand Concept
1. What is your name?		1.	❑	❑	❑	❑
2. What's your address or Where do you live?		2.	❑	❑	❑	❑
3. What's your phone number?		3.	❑	❑	❑	❑
4. Where were you born?		4.	❑	❑	❑	❑
5. What day is it today?		5.	❑	❑	❑	❑
6. Are you a male or female?		6.	❑	❑	❑	❑

Section II

1. What is your favorite part of school/work? ❑client works ❑client unemployed ❑does not understand concept

Answer:		How often do you work? How long have you worked?	Where do you work?	Who do you do work with? How old are they?	How do you get involved in doing work? How do you get there?
What do you enjoy about work?	What do you do in work?				

2. What is your favorite part of free time? ❑does not understand concept

Answer:		How often do you ____? How long have you ____?	Where do you ____?	Who do you do ____ with? How old are they?	How do you get involved in doing ____? How do you get there?
What do you enjoy about ____?	What do you do in ____?				

3. What sports, games, and other activities have you engaged in? ❑answers generally correct ❑listed activities not involved in ❑does not understand concept

Answer:		How often do you ____? How long have you ____?	Where do you ____?	Who do you do ____ with? How old are they?	How do you get involved in doing ____? How do you get there?
What do you enjoy about ____?	What do you do in ____?				

Section II (continued)

4. What do you enjoy the most outside of school/work?		❑answers generally correct ❑does not understand concept		❑listed activities not involved in	
Answer:					
What do you enjoy about ____?	What do you do in ____?	How often do you ____? How long have you ____?	Where do you ____?	Who do you do ____ with? How old are they?	How do you get involved in doing ____? How do you get there?

5. What other things do you do with friends or people you live with?		❑answers generally correct ❑does not understand concept		❑listed activities not involved in	
Answer:					
What do you enjoy about ____?	What do you do in ____?	How often do you ____? How long have you ____?	Where do you ____?	Who do you do ____ with? How old are they?	How do you get involved in doing ____? How do you get there?

6. What other things do you do when you are alone?		❑answers generally correct ❑does not understand concept		❑listed activities not involved in	
Answer:					
What do you enjoy about ____?	What do you do in ____?	How often do you ____? How long have you ____?	Where do you ____?	Who do you do ____ with? How old are they?	How do you get involved in doing ____? How do you get there?

7. What are you good at?		❑answers generally correct ❑does not understand concept		❑listed activities not involved in	
Answer:					
What do you enjoy about ____?	What do you do in ____?	How often do you ____? How long have you ____?	Where do you ____?	Who do you do ____ with? How old are they?	How do you get involved in doing ____? How do you get there?

Section II (continued)

Question	Summary of Answer	Correct Answer	No Answer	Tried but Incorrect Answer	Does Not Understand Concept
8.. How do you feel when you lose a game or do not do something well?		8. ❑	❑	❑	❑
9. How much money do you have to spend a week?		9. ❑	❑	❑	❑
10. What do you spend it on?		10. ❑	❑	❑	❑
11. You have just won $10,000 in the lottery. How would you spend it?		11. ❑	❑	❑	❑

Section III

Question	Summary of Answer	Correct Answer	No Answer	Tried but Incorrect Answer	Does Not Understand Concept
1. Do you have a boyfriend/girlfriend?		1. ❑	❑	❑	❑
2. What activity do you do with him/her/them?		2. ❑	❑	❑	❑
3. What does it mean to go on a date?		3. ❑	❑	❑	❑
4. What do people do on dates?		4. ❑	❑	❑	❑
5. Who goes on dates?		5. ❑	❑	❑	❑
6. Would you like to go on a date someday?		6. ❑	❑	❑	❑
7. Would you like to get married someday?		7. ❑	❑	❑	❑
8. If Yes, when would you like to get married?		8. ❑	❑	❑	❑
9. What does it mean to be married?		9. ❑	❑	❑	❑
10. Would you like to have children?		10. ❑	❑	❑	❑
11. Do all married people have children? How many?		11. ❑	❑	❑	❑
12. Does the mother or the father take care of the children?		12. ❑	❑	❑	❑
13. Where do babies come from?		13. ❑	❑	❑	❑
14. How does a woman get pregnant?		14. ❑	❑	❑	❑
15. Where do the babies grow in the mother?		15. ❑	❑	❑	❑
16. Has anyone ever talked to you about sex? If Yes, who?		16. ❑	❑	❑	❑
17. If Yes, what did they tell you?		❑	❑	❑	❑
18. Do you have any problems with sex?		18. ❑	❑	❑	❑
Women Only					
19. What is menstruation?		19. ❑	❑	❑	❑
20. How often do women have periods?		20. ❑	❑	❑	❑
21. Do you menstruate or have a period every month?		21. ❑	❑	❑	❑
22. Do you have a problem with your period?		22. ❑	❑	❑	❑
23. Who should be told if someone misses their periods?		23. ❑	❑	❑	❑

Leisure and Social/Sexual Assessment Summary

Leisure Activities	Physical Domain	Cognitive Domain	Social Domain	Sensory Domain	Community Domain
How many different activities per category?					
How often (range of times per month)?					
How many activities done in the community?					
Any discrepancies with activities of others in household?					

Social/Sexual	Correct Answer	No Answer	Tried but Incorrect Answer	Does Not Understand Concept	Comments
Knowledge of Dating					
Knowledge of Marriage					
Knowledge of Sex					
Safety and Mobility					

Summary:

Recomendations:

Therapist Signature: ____________________

Date: ____________________

Therapist Signature: ____________________

Date: ____________________

Name:

Birthdate:

Unit:

Admit:

Additional forms may be ordered from:

Idyll Arbor, Inc.
PO Box 720
Ravensdale, WA 98051
(206) 432-3231

IDYLL ARBOR ACTIVITY ASSESSMENT

Name: Idyll Arbor Activity Assessment

Also Known As: IA3, Form #124

Author: joan burlingame

Time Needed to Administer: The IA3 is meant to be used up to three times on each client (e.g., admission, 90 day review, 180 day review). The first assessment takes about one hour, including the time needed to read the medical chart. The therapist will want to schedule 15 minutes for the second and third time the assessment is administered.

Time Needed to Score: The administration and scoring of the IA3 happen simultaneously.

Recommended Disability Group: The IA3 was written specifically to meet the OBRA regulations (Health Care Finance Administration — Long Term Care Regulations). It is best suited for clients who live in a nursing home or other long term care facility. The content allows it to cover both physical medicine and psychiatric long term care assessment needs.

Purpose of the Assessment: The purpose of the IA3 is to obtain enough information about a client, in a reasonable amount of time, to be able to develop a treatment plan.

What Does the Assessment Measure?: The IA3 assessment report form has five sections: 1) personal and medical history, 2) leisure interests, 3) leisure history, 4) individual performance/social strengths, and 5) maladaptive behaviors.

Supplies Needed: IA3 Manual and score sheets.

Reliability/Validity: Initial validity was tested by comparing the assessment questions to required assessment content (OBRA) and by submitting the assessment to a peer review process. The IA3 was first submitted to and comments received from three individuals who held CTRS certifications and to five individuals who held jobs as Activity Directors and who were not CTRSs. Next, the assessment was submitted to and comments received from three individuals (one RN and two MSWs) who had previously been Health Care Finance Administration Surveyors. The comments of the reviewers were integrated into the assessment form. Over the next six months the IA3 was used in four long term care facilities (three for clients with medical diagnoses, one for clients with mental illness diagnoses). Final revisions were made.

After six months of use, 15% of the IA3 forms completed in the 4 facilities were reviewed to note problems with administering the assessment. A log had also been kept of the questions concerning the administration of the assessment. This information was reviewed, trends were noted, and the IA3 Assessment Manual was written.

Degree of Skill Required to Administer and Score: The IA3 was written to allow an individual with limited training in activities or recreational therapy to fill out the assessment report form.

Comments: One of the most important aspects of the IA3 is the leisure history grid. The grid allows the recreational therapist to graphically chart the client's normal leisure patterns. This, in turn, can protect the client's rights by documenting that large group activities may be very inappropriate for him/her. (Many recreational therapists are pressured into 'serving many people at one time', regardless of whether it is a positive experience for the individual.)

Suggested Levels: Rancho Los Amigos Level: All. Developmental Level: 10 and up. Reality Orientation Level: All.

Distributor: Idyll Arbor, Inc., 25119 S.E. 262 Street, PO Box 720, Ravensdale, WA 98051 (206) 432-3231. (Area code 425 after April 1997.)

IDYLL ARBOR ACTIVITY ASSESSMENT

POLICY: **Each resident will be given an activity assessment within 14 days of admission. The assessment will clearly state the resident's likes and skills. This assessment will be filled out completely.**

WHEN TO GIVE ASSESSMENT

1. The assessment will be given no more than 14 days after admission.

2. At least once every year ***or*** within 14 days of a major change in health or ability, whichever comes first.

NOTE: The Idyll Arbor Activity Assessment Form allows for three consecutive assessments on the same form. This makes it easy to see changes.

The Idyll Arbor Activity Assessment has two places to record the date of the assessment: 1) at the top right of the first page and 2) on the fourth page in each summary section. Remember to date both places.

WHEN TO REVIEW ASSESSMENT

1. Re-read the assessment 7 - 10 days before the resident's care conference.

2. If no changes are needed write in the top right section of the page:

   (date)-NC-(initials)

3. If minor changes are needed:

   a. yellow out information that needs to be changed
   b. place the date next to the yellowed out information
   c. write in updated information and date entry

4. If major changes are needed, re-give the assessment.

TIME NEEDED TO GIVE ASSESSMENT

1. The first assessment should take about one hour.

2. The second and third assessments using the same form should take 15-30 minutes each, depending on the depth of chart review.

REALITY ORIENTATION ASSESSMENT

1. In addition to the Idyll Arbor Activity Assessment the resident will be given a reality orientation assessment.

2. Reality orientation assessments which may be given are listed at the end of this document.

FILLING OUT THE FIRST PAGE

The purpose of the first page of the Idyll Arbor Activity Assessment is to help gather the information necessary for the activity staff to safely and meaningfully interact with the resident.

1. **NAME:** Include the resident's full name and any appropriate 'nick-names'.

2. **DATE OF BIRTH:** Give the resident's date of birth (important information to have when giving a reality orientation assessment).

3. **DATE OF ADMISSION:** Write in the current admission date. If the resident is being re-admitted one of two options may be used:
   a. Fill out a new assessment form and in the DATE OF ADMISSION space write Re-Adm (date).
   b. Obtain a copy of the last Idyll Arbor Activity Assessment given to the resident. Yellow out the date of admission and write in the new admission date.

4. **EDUCATION:** Include information on formal training and degrees or certificates. Many times this information is important to the resident. It also helps the staff anticipate the resident's ability to understand new and/or complicated information.

5. **DATE OF ASSESSMENT**
   a. If the resident is being assessed for the first time and a blank score sheet is being used, place the date in the box that says FIRST ASSESSMENT.
   b. If the resident is being assessed and the score sheet has been used once already for the resident, place the date in the box that says SECOND ASSESSMENT.
   c. If the resident is being assessed and the score sheet has been used twice already for the resident, place the date in the box that says THIRD ASSESSMENT.

6. **REVIEW DATES:** Please see 'WHEN TO REVIEW ASSESSMENT' at the beginning of this procedure.

7. **OCCUPATION:** Include information on the resident's primary occupation(s). This information could be important to the resident, as much of his/her identity may have been related to the occupation (e.g., housewife/mother, farmer, minister, corporate manager, etc.).

8. **RETIREMENT DATE:** Place date of retirement (if appropriate) here. This is important because it lets the staff know how long the resident has had to adjust to a schedule free of work commitments. If the resident is newly retired, it is likely that s/he has not 'settled' into a comfortable pattern of free-time activities. S/he may also not have adjusted to not being 'needed' at work.

   POTENTIAL CARE PLAN GOALS related to a recent retirement date:
   Problem: Lack of adjustment to increase in free-time due to recent retirement.
   Goal: Resident will be able to identify and will have the skills to do 5 activities that s/he is interested in to help fill day by (date).

   Problem: Decreased opportunity to 'take control' and be 'responsible' for well-being of self and others due to recent retirement and recent admission.
   Goal: Resident will be responsible for the care of the plants in the activity room.

9. **MARITAL STATUS:** Check the appropriate box.

   a. M = married, S = single, W = widowed/widower, D = divorced
   b. If the marital status changes during the admission the staff should yellow out the old response and check the new response. Place the date above the new response.

10. **NAME OF SPOUSE:** Write in the name of the most recent spouse.

11. **CHILDREN:** Write in the name(s) of the children.

12. **SIGNIFICANT OTHERS:** Write in the name(s) of the people who are important to the resident other than his/her spouse and children.

    POTENTIAL CARE PLAN GOALS related to family and significant others:
    Frequently a move out of his/her home makes it harder for a resident to keep in touch, especially if no telephone is in the resident's room.
    Problem: Barriers to maintaining long term social contacts.
    Goal: Resident will be able to have a minimum of 4 contacts per week with old friends through letter writing.

13. **RELIGION:** List the resident's religious preferences (if any).

14. **PREVIOUSLY ACTIVE?**
    a. Check 'yes' if resident participated at least 2x/month in religious activity.
    b. Check 'no' if resident participated less than 2x/month in religious activity.

15. **RESIDENCE HISTORY:** List primary residential locations for resident.

    POTENTIAL CARE PLAN GOALS related to residence history:
    Problem: Lack of skills in adjusting to new residence due to previous length of time in last home (45 years).
    Goal: Have the resident decorate room as closely as possible to favorite location in old residence.

16. **PHOTO RELEASE:**
    a. If the resident (or his/her legal guardian) has signed a release to have his/her photo taken, *and* that release is in the chart, mark 'Y' for yes.
    b. If the resident's chart does not have a signed release for the resident to have his/her photo taken, mark 'N' for no.
    c. If the resident did not have a written release in the chart then obtains one, yellow out the 'N' and mark the 'Y'. Place the date of the change next to that section.

17. **OUTING RELEASE:**
    a. If the resident (or his/her legal guardian) has signed a release for an outing, *and* that release is in the chart, mark 'Y' for yes.
    b. If the resident does not have a signed release for an outing in the chart, mark 'N' for no.
    c. If the resident did not have a written release in the chart then obtains one, yellow out the 'N' and mark the 'Y'. Place the date of the change next to that section.
    d. Place physician's order for outings under the section titled 'PHYSICIAN'S ORDER FOR ACTIVITY'.

18. **IS THE RESIDENT A SMOKER?:**
    a. If the resident currently smokes, mark 'Y' for yes.
    b. If you marked 'Y', fill in the 'NUMBER OF CIGARETTES A DAY' box.
    c. If the resident currently does not smoke, mark the 'N' for no.
    d. If there are any special comments about the smoking place that information under the 'UPDATE' section on the next line. Date your entry.
    e. If the resident uses a pipe or chews tobacco write a comment about that in the blank space to the right of 'NUMBER OF CIGARETTES A DAY'. Date your entry.

19. **UPDATE:** The primary purpose for this section is to make comments about changes from one assessment to the next. Remember to date all entries. Yellow out any comments that no longer apply.

20. **DIAGNOSES:**
    a. List each diagnosis that could impact the resident's ability to do things.
    b. If a diagnosis has been dropped by the second or third assessment yellow it out.
    c. If a diagnosis has been added between assessments, add it to the assessment. Place the date that you wrote in the change after the new diagnosis.

21. **PHYSICIAN'S ORDER FOR ACTIVITY:** Place the physician's order for activity, order for outings, and order for beer and wine here. If the orders change, yellow out the old orders and write in the new orders. Date your entry.

22. **VISION:** Check the appropriate box. 'Correctable' means that the resident has good enough vision to function on a day to day basis with the aid of glasses. Just because a resident has glasses does not mean that s/he uses them. If the resident's vision is correctable and s/he usually wears his/her glasses, also check the box that says 'Uses Correction'.

23. **AUDITORY:** Check the appropriate box. 'Correctable' means that the resident has good enough hearing to function on a day-to-day basis with the help of a hearing aid. Just because a resident has a hearing aid does not mean that s/he usually wears his/her hearing aid. If the resident's hearing is correctable and s/he usually wears his/her hearing aid, be sure to also check the box that says 'Uses Correction'.

24. **DIETARY:** This section has three separate groupings. The first grouping (the left column) indicates the consistency of the food as prescribed by the resident's physician. Check the appropriate box. This information will be found in the physician's orders section of the chart.

    The second grouping (the middle column) lists three common control problems related to eating. Many residents have one or more of these problems. Each of them is potentially life threatening if due caution is not taken. Review the nursing assessment to see if any of the three problems exist. If they do not, check 'No Problem'.

    The third grouping (the right column) lists three levels of independence related to eating. Please check the correct level.

    Food and beverages are often served during recreational activities. This is a normal pastime, both in a nursing home and in a person's own home. Unlike the residents, the activity staff needs to look upon food as if it were a prescription which needs to be delivered in the correct manner with the right precautions.

25. **MAN:** The purpose of the picture is to allow the activity director to quickly review the resident's physical disabilities.

    a. **x = total paralysis**. This means that the resident is not able to move that part of the body at all.
    b. **/ = partial paralysis**. This means that the resident has only partial strength in that part of the body.
    c. **0 = contracture**. This means that the resident is not able to fully extend (or bend) a joint because of tightening or shortening of a muscle or group of muscles. Contractures may be caused by a resident staying in one position for a long time, by paralysis, or from spasms which cause a reduction in normal range of motion.

    Review the information in the chart and get to know the resident. Indicate what, if any, physical disabilities the resident has using the 'x' or '/' or '0'.

    If the activity director is working with a population that tends to have changes in physical ability, a different color ink should be used for each assessment. If different color inks are used, indicate on the sheet which color is used for the different assessments.

    1st assessment = black ink 9/12/88
    2nd assessment = red ink 12/1/88
    3rd assessment = green ink 8/12/89

NOTE: The activity director can show other disabilities easily. Idyll Arbor, Inc. staff draw a circle around the head with a line to a statement about cognitive ability.

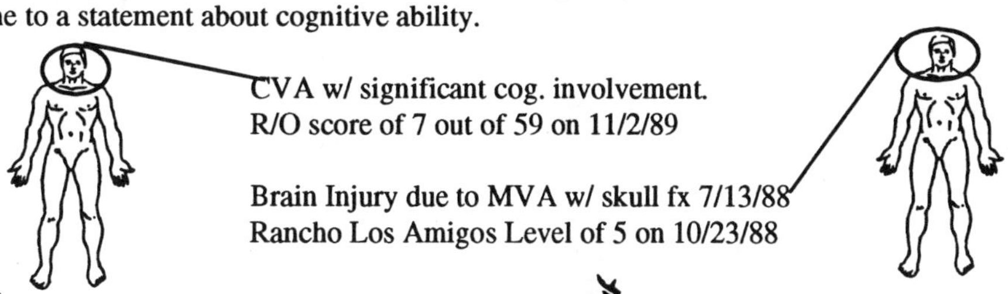

OTHER USES:

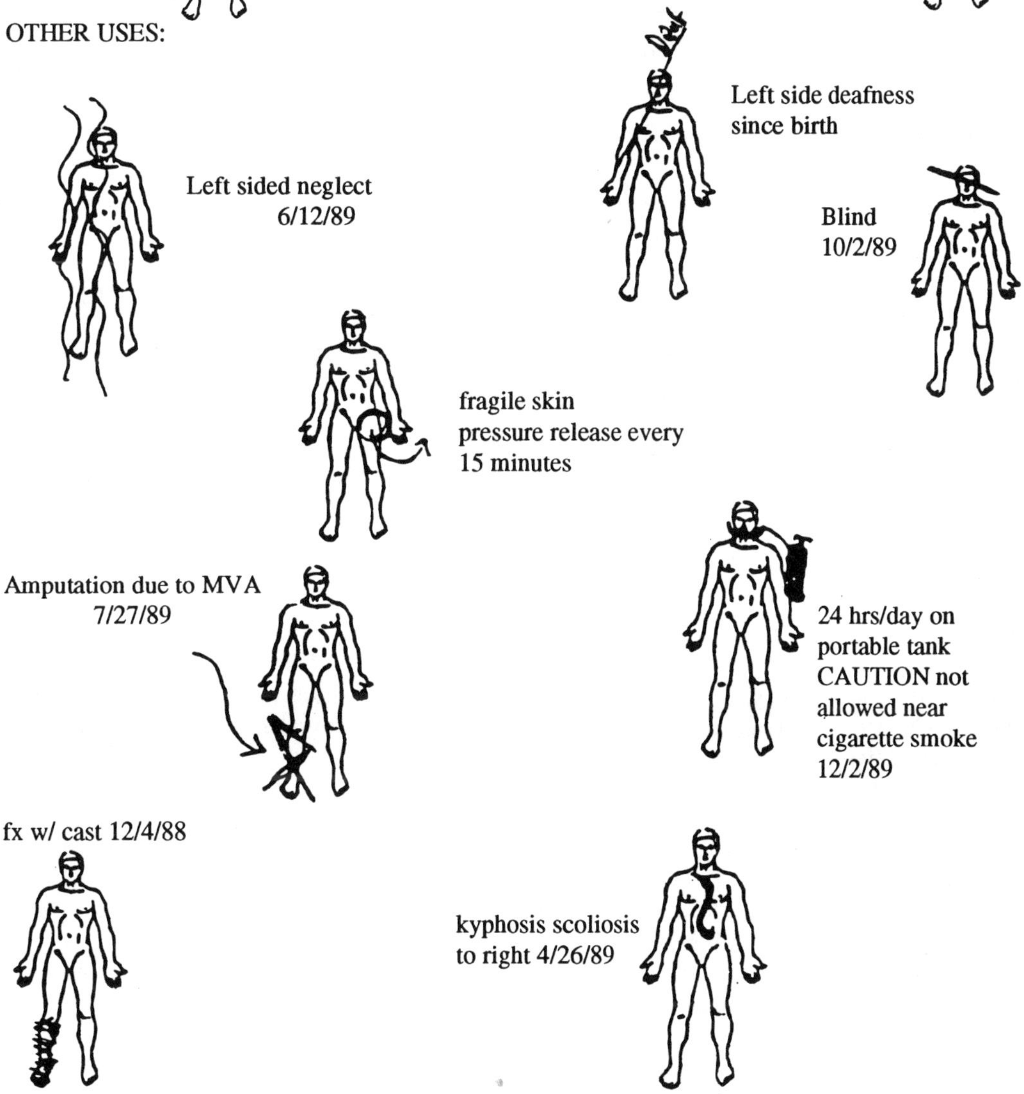

26. **MEDICATIONS**: The purpose of this section is to write down the medications the resident is taking that might affect their ability to participate in a safe and meaningful way. The activity director does not have to be an expert in the area of medications. Asking the nursing staff if any medications could affect the resident should be enough.

Below is a short list of medications that could affect the resident's ability to safety and meaningfully participate. The information was found in **Improving Mobility in Older Persons** by Carole B. Lewis (Aspen Publishers, Inc. 1989). This book would be a good addition to every activity department's resource library. Each activity department should have its agency's pharmacist make a similar list specifically for your facility.

SELECTED DRUGS ASSOCIATED WITH DEPRESSIVE REACTIONS IN THE ELDERLY:

Alcohol	Cogenitin	Neptazane	Symmetrel	Tagamet
Aldomet	Naprosyn	Prednisone	Sinemet	

NOTE: How many times have you seen staff write 'depression' or 'social isolation' as a problem in the nursing care plan? The staff then try to overcome the depression by having the resident go to activities when, in reality, depression may be drug induced!

DRUGS ASSOCIATED WITH WITHDRAWAL REACTIONS OF WHICH DEPRESSION OR CONFUSION MAY BE AN IMPORTANT COMPONENT:

Alcohol	Baclofen	Codeine	Demerol	Morphine	Ritalin
Artane	Barbiturates	Cogentin	Methadone	Oxymorphone	Talwin

DRUGS ASSOCIATED WITH CONFUSIONAL REACTIONS IN THE ELDERLY (These drugs may lower a resident's Reality Orientation score):

Artane	Cogentin	Demerol	Lithium	Sinemet	Tagamet
Barbiturates	Darvon	Digitoxin	Parlodel	Symmetrel	Talwin

DRUGS THAT MAY CAUSE DIZZINESS AND VERTIGO BY A TOXIC EFFECT ON THE VESTIBULAR SYSTEM:

Amikin	Ibuprofen	Motrin	Quinaglute	Tolectin
Clinoril	Meclomen	Nalfon	Streptomycin	

More and more activity directors are being asked to give input on how medication changes are affecting the resident's ability to function. For those activity directors who want to give more objective answers, the reality orientation assessments listed at the end of this document will be helpful.

27. **ALLERGIES**: List any allergies.

28. **ADAPTED EQUIPMENT**: This section has 2 parts:

The first part consists of a list of w/c, cane, and walker, each with 3 boxes in front. The reason that these 3 ambulation devices are already written out for the activity director is to save him/her time. (R. Weg in **The Aged: Who, Where, How Well?** 1979 indicates that 15% of the non-institutionalized elderly over 65 have mobility problems, over 80% of the elderly in nursing homes have mobility problems.)

a. If the resident uses either a w/c, a cane, or a walker at the time of the FIRST assessment, place an 'x' over the appropriate box in the left column.
b. If the resident uses either a w/c, a cane. or a walker at the time of the SECOND assessment, place a 'x' over the appropriate box in the middle column.
c. If the resident uses either a w/c, a cane, or a walker at the time of the THIRD assessment, place an 'x' over the appropriate box in the right column.

The second section consists of three lines. The activity director should write in any other adapted equipment that the resident might use during activities.

Example: Rt hand splint for PROM may be taken off during activities 6/7/88.

29. **UPDATE**: The primary purpose of this section is to make comments about changes from one assessment time to the next. Remember to date all entries. Yellow out any comments that no longer apply.

30. **OTHER**: The purpose of this sections is to write in important information not found on the first page which should be noted. Examples:
Resident is a victim of spousal abuse. Do not leave her alone with her husband. 3/15/89
Resident has received numerous awards for being a community leader. Was head of United Way for King County from 1957-1963.

FILLING OUT THE SECOND PAGE

The purpose of the second page of the Idyll Arbor Activity Assessment is to help determine the resident's leisure interests *and* leisure/social patterns. The activity director needs to find out what kind of activities the resident used to like, and those that s/he still likes. The activity director also needs to find out:

When/How Often?
With Whom?
At What Time of Life? (Youth, Middle Age, Retirement)

As of 1990 the activity director in skilled nursing facilities and intermediate care facilities must provide the resident with activities of his/her choice that are similar to those prior to admission.

LEISURE INTERESTS AND LEISURE HISTORY

The pattern of leisure activities that a person has found enjoyable over his/her lifetime will probably not change greatly upon admission to a nursing home. In fact, with the resident having just experienced a change of health and a change of residence, a change in his/her leisure patterns can be too much to ask.

Such a change may lead to depression and/or learned helplessness in addition to causing undue stress. The activity department needs to structure the resident's leisure activities inside the nursing home as close to his/her past patterns as possible.

The three sections on this page are used together to provide information on the resident's past history. The activity director uses each item in the Leisure Interests section to fill out information in the top two sections.

Example:
The activity director asks the resident 'Do you like to play cards?' The resident answers 'yes'.
Activity Director: 'What kind? Bridge, Poker, ...'
Resident: 'Bridge. I was part of a bridge club. The other ladies in my church circle would get together every Wednesday at 2 pm for 15 years. I stopped going 2 years ago when I moved. '
Activity Director: 'How did playing bridge make you feel? Did you find it relaxing, exhilarating, or just plain fun?'
Resident: 'Oh, just plain fun.'

The activity director then puts a '+' by cards. Then s/he finds 'That were just plain fun' in the Leisure History section and goes across to the small group column and writes in that box: 'Bridge 1x wk/15 yrs until 2 yrs ago.'

After the activity director has asked the resident about his/her leisure interests and filled out the Leisure History, a pattern should be found. With a yellow marker, draw a box around the squares listing the most activities.

The average resident will have 3 or 4 boxes outlined. Please review the examples included with this manual. Below are expanded descriptions of the three sections on this page:

1. **LEISURE INTERESTS:** This section is a basic 'check list' of activities. Use the appropriate mark from the key to indicate the resident's attitude about the activity. Other leisure interest inventories may be used and the information added here.

2. **LEISURE HISTORY**: This section helps the activity director determine what leisure patterns the resident had prior to being admitted. The activity director should look for three basic patterns: 1) What kind of activities (e.g., nature, sports, crafts), 2) What size of group (e.g., solitary activities, large group activities), and 3) What kind of feelings did the resident experience during those activities?

The job of the activity director is to duplicate at least the typical type of activity, group size, and feelings even if s/he cannot offer the exact activity the resident used to enjoy. Many times the resident cannot participate in a long-enjoyed activity due to a new disability, not just because the activity department cannot offer the past activity.

3. **LEISURE SUMMARY**: This section should be used to summarize both the leisure interests and leisure history sections using just two or three sentences.

   Example: Mrs. Black's past and current leisure pastimes tend to be those activities that involve arts and crafts or nature in small groups or just by herself. She seemed to prefer activities that promoted relaxing or creative feelings and seldom took great risks in her leisure activities.

If the resident's Leisure History indicated that s/he had preferred 1:1 or solitary activities for the last 30 years, it would be inappropriate to expect that resident to feel comfortable in large groups. A resident just admitted experiences the stress of a move and the stress of a change in health status. It does not make sense to also change the resident's leisure patterns.

LEISURE HISTORY				
ACTIVITIES	**ALONE**	**1:1**	**SMALL GROUP 3-5 PEOPLE**	**LARGE GROUP 6 OR MORE**
THAT WERE EXHILARATING, ACTIVE	Walking 3x wk / 30 min Gardening, depending on season			
THAT WERE CALMING, RELAXING	Reading Paper 1 x day, book 1 a week Listening to radio	Watching TV with husband daily, 2 hrs	Having friends over for dinner	
THAT ALLOWED ME TO BE CREATIVE	Needle Point, 1x month writing column for church newsletter, 1 x week			
THAT MET MY SPIRITUAL NEEDS	Church, 1 x week Reading Bible, 1 x week			Church on Sunday
THAT WERE JUST PLAIN FUN	Crossword puzzles, 2 x day			Vacations with 2 sons and their families
OTHERS:				

LEISURE SUMMARY Mrs. Smith's past leisure history consisted of mostly solitary, peaceful activities. A few times a week she would meet with some friends whom she had known since high school.

FILLING OUT THE THIRD PAGE

The third page is divided into two sections:

1. Individual Performance and Social Strengths
2. Maladaptive Behaviors

Both sections are best filled out after the activity director has observed the resident in at least four activities.

INDIVIDUAL PERFORMANCE AND SOCIAL STRENGTHS

The purpose of 'Individual Performance and Social Strengths' is to rate the resident's ability in six areas. Just as with the first page of this assessment, the boxes in the left column are to be used for the first assessment. The boxes in the middle column are to be used for the second time the assessment is given to the resident. The boxes in the right column are to be used for the third time the assessment is given.

1. **READING ABILITY**: The basic ability to read important signs, activity calendars, and books (letters, etc.) is so often taken for granted. Even prior to being admitted into the skilled nursing facilities between 11 to 20% of the people in the United States are non-functional readers. (Based on studies listed in the World Book Encyclopedia, 1989.) In this assessment 'READING' means not only being able to read the words out loud but also the ability to remember the basic point of what's read five minutes later. This criteria would mean that many individuals who are moderately to severely impaired on their R/O assessment would be rated as 'non-readers'.

2. **ABILITY TO FORM NEW RELATIONSHIPS**: The ability to form new relationships means that the resident has the skills to develop and nurture a relationship with another person or persons. If the resident has a mental illness diagnosis or an dementia that makes it impossible to develop new friendships (let alone maintain old ones), check 'Unable Due to Diagnoses'. If the resident is cognitively healthy but on bedrest due to physical disabilities, s/he should be able to make new friends. In this case, check one of the other choices.

3. **FAMILY/FRIENDS SUPPORT**: Family/Friends Support means that the resident either sees, talks to, or receives letters from family and/or friends. The resident who has very good support from family and friends (on an almost daily basis) and who does not attend the facility's activities should not be considered socially isolated.

   There are four quick assessments which would give the activity director a more in depth understanding of the resident's perceived satisfaction with his/her relationships with family and/or friends. All four can be found in the **Handbook of Geriatric Assessment** by Gallo, Reichel, Anderson published by Aspen Publications, 1988.

   The four assessments are

   a. The **FAMILY APGAR SCALE**. This assessment asks five questions to help assess social functioning with family members.

   b. The **FRIENDS APGAR SCALE**. This assessment asks five questions to help assess social functioning with friends.

   c. The **SOCIAL DYSFUNCTION RATING SCALE**. This somewhat subjective assessment uses 21 questions to rate the resident's self-esteem, interpersonal systems, and performance. While this assessment's scoring is subjective in nature, Gallo et al. reports that it helped 'to correctly categorize 92% of patients when applied to a group of 80 psychiatric and non-psychiatric outpatients as compared to the judgments of clinicians unaware of the scale.' (page 101)

   d. The **SOCIAL RESOURCES SECTION of the OARS Multidimensional Functional Assessment Questionnaire**. This 9 question assessment (which is only slightly longer than its title!) is a short questionnaire which gives the activity director a lot of information about the resident's perceived support from family and friends.

The next 3 categories are often mixed up by therapists. They are very different from each other and the activity director needs to be sure that s/he is measuring the correct skill for each section.

4. **INITIATION LEVEL:** Initiation level means that the resident takes responsibility for taking part in an activity. The resident's inability to participate due to physical disabilities should not be counted in this section. Only assess the resident's general willingness to engage in activities.

5. **INDEPENDENCE LEVEL:** Independence level means that the resident is physically able to engage in activities, even if it means using adapted devices. Do not measure a resident's willingness to engage in activities in this section.

6. **PARTICIPATION LEVEL:** Participation level means the amount of involvement the resident usually demonstrates in activities. PLEASE NOTE: Active participation should not be considered the most desirable answer. The activity director should go back to the resident's leisure history to determine if the resident's past leisure patterns included being an active participant in recreation, or if they *normally* needed encouragement to engage in activities. A football fan who spends Sundays and Mondays watching football games is a passive participant. That level of participation is *normal.* The objective for the activity director's intervention should be to promote normalization in a non-normalizing environment.

MALADAPTIVE BEHAVIORS

The purpose of this section is to list ten common maladaptive behaviors that *may* be found when working with residents who are physically or cognitively impaired. The way to score this section is to place a number between zero and three in each box. Zero indicates that the listed behavior is seldom to never a problem. One indicates that the listed behavior occurs a few times a week during activities. Two indicates that the listed behavior occurs frequently during activities. Three indicates that the behavior is severe enough to significantly limit participation. Most of the residents in nursing homes should score a zero in every one of the behaviors listed.

The law governing the delivery of service to residents in long term care facilities has some specific guidelines concerning the identification and treatment of residents with maladaptive behaviors. The activity director can obtain a copy of the law from his/her administrator.

MEASURING MENTAL STATUS (REALITY ORIENTATION)

Mental State Questionaire (MSQ): From an article by Kahn, et al, in the American Journal of Psychiatry 117 (1960b): 326-328. The MSQ has 10 questions and a key for scoring.

Philadelphia Geriatric Center Mental Status Questionaire: This R/O assessment was written by D.B. Fishback and published in the Journal of the American Geriatric Society 25(1977):167-170. This assessment has 35 questions and a key for scoring.

Short Portable Mental Status Questionaire: Adapted from the Multidimensional Functional Assessment: the OARS Methodology, this assessment consists of 10 questions and includes a key for scoring.

Viro Orientation Scale: A scale for assessing the interview behavior of elderly people. This assessment is easy to give, but has no key to indicate the degree of impairment.

The four R/O assessments listed above can be found in **Assessing the Elderly** by Kane and Kane published by Lexington Books in 1981. Idyll Arbor, Inc. also has a Reality Orientation assessment (#125) which is professionally formatted and ready to be placed in a chart.

MEASURING OVERALL PSYCHOSOCIAL ABILITY:

CERT — Psych.: This assessment has 25 different questions for the activity director to answer after observing the resident during activities. It tends to be sensitive enough to indicate behavior changes due to medications. The assessment can be found in the *Therapeutic Recreation Journal* of the National Therapeutic Recreation Association (1975) or ordered from Idyll Arbor, Inc. (form #116).

Idyll Arbor, Inc.'s version is professionally formatted and ready for inclusion in the medical chart. The Idyll Arbor, Inc. version has 5 spaces to mark down behavior prior to the medicine change and 5 spaces to mark down behavior after the medicine change. A comparison of the scores pre and post should be able to indicate measurable change in behavior. This assessment may be used on residents who score down to Severely Impaired on R/O assessments.

Philadelphai Geriatric Center Morale Scale (Lawton, 1972) The 22 questions are asked during an interview or the resident may fill out the questionnaire themselves.

Contenement Index (Bloom and Blenkner, 1970) This assessment has ten questions. The staff asking the questions scores the answer as either 'favorable' or 'not scorable'. One point is given for each favorable score.

The last two assessments listed need to be given at least twice each: once before the medication change and once after. They should not be used on residents who score as moderately impaired to severely impaired on R/O assessments.

The two assessments listed above may be found in **Assessing the Elderly** by Kane and Kane published by Lexington Books in 1981.

Life Satisfaction Scale: (Lohmann, 1976) This is a 20 questions scale which is in this book. This assessment helps measure the resident's change in contentment with his/her life before and after the medication change. The Life Satisfaction Scale should only be given to residents who are at most moderately cognitively impaired.

Idyll Arbor, Inc. is glad to provide assessments to therapists. We request that no copies of the forms (or remakes of the assessments) be made. Idyll Arbor, Inc. is functioning as a clearing house for assessments in the field of recreational therapy. We underwrite many of the expenses associated with this effort, and only charge the cost of sending samples, returning phone calls, developing the original art work, and the copying cost. Any actual 'profit' made goes right back into testing or developing of other materials for our field.

If you would like more information about Idyll Arbor, Inc. or the assessments we carry, please feel free to write us.

Idyll Arbor, Inc., PO Box 720, Ravensdale, WA 98051.

Idyll Arbor Activity Assessment

DATE: FIRST ASSESSMENT	☐	SECOND ASSESSMENT	☐	THIRD ASSESSMENT	☐
REVIEW DATES:					

NAME ______________________

DATE OF BIRTH __________ DATE OF ADMISSION __________

EDUCATION ______________________

OCCUPATION ______________________ RETIREMENT DATE __________

MARITAL STATUS ☐ M ☐ S ☐ W ☐ D NAME OF SPOUSE __________

CHILDREN ______________________

SIGNIFICANT OTHERS ______________________

RELIGION ______________________ PREVIOUSLY ACTIVE? ☐ Y ☐ N

RESIDENCE HISTORY ______________________

PHOTO RELEASE? ☐ Y ☐ N OUTING RELEASE: ☐ Y ☐ N

IS RESIDENT A SMOKER? ☐ Y ☐ N NUMBER OF CIGARETTES A DAY ☐ ☐ ☐

UPDATE ______________________

DIAGNOSES ______________________

PHYSICIAN'S ORDERS FOR ACTIVITY ______________________

VISION		AUDITORY	
☐ ☐ ☐	Normal	☐ ☐ ☐	Normal
☐ ☐ ☐	Correctable	☐ ☐ ☐	Correctable
☐ ☐ ☐	Limited w/ Correction	☐ ☐ ☐	Limited w/ Correction
☐ ☐ ☐	Blind ☐ L ☐ R	☐ ☐ ☐	Deaf ☐ L ☐ R
☐ ☐ ☐	Uses Correction	☐ ☐ ☐	Uses Correction

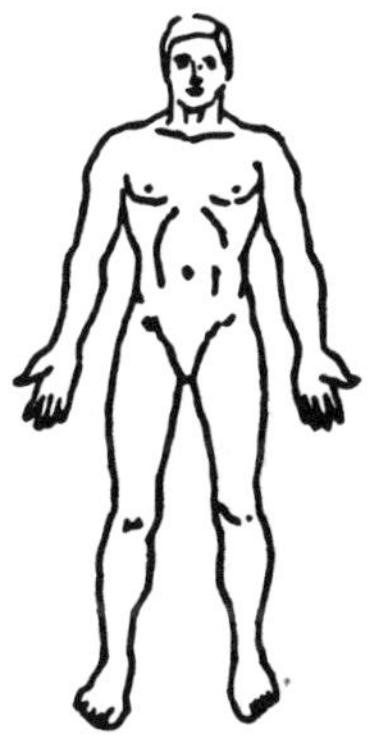

DIETARY

☐ ☐ ☐	Regular	☐ ☐ ☐	Pocketing	☐ ☐ ☐	Self Feeder
☐ ☐ ☐	Mech Soft/Regular	☐ ☐ ☐	Head Control	☐ ☐ ☐	Moderate Assist
☐ ☐ ☐	Mech Soft/Fork Mash	☐ ☐ ☐	Jaw Control	☐ ☐ ☐	Full Assist
☐ ☐ ☐	Pureed	☐ ☐ ☐	No Problem		

X = total paralysis
/ = partail paralysis
0 = contracture

MEDICATIONS ______________________

ALLERGIES ______________________

ADAPTED EQUIPMENT ______________________

☐ ☐ ☐ w/c ______________________

☐ ☐ ☐ cane ______________________

☐ ☐ ☐ walker ______________________

UPDATE ______________________

OTHER ______________________

LEISURE INTERESTS

GAME
_____ Board Games
_____ Cross Word Puzzles
_____ Cards
_____ Bingo
_____ Lawn Games
_____ Pool/Billiards
_____ Darts
_____ Other

SPORTS
_____ Swimming
_____ Golf
_____ Baseball
_____ Boating
_____ Winter Sports
_____ Bowling
_____ Racket Sports
_____ Walking/Jogging
_____ Other

NATURE
_____ Gardening
_____ Reading About
_____ Bird Watching
_____ Fishing
_____ Camping/Hiking
_____ Barbecues
_____ Horseback Riding
_____ Other

COLLECTING
_____ Stamps
_____ Coins
_____ Antiques
_____ Rocks
_____ Baseball Cards
_____ Other

CRAFTS
_____ Knitting
_____ Painting/Drawing
_____ Ceramics
_____ Woodwork
_____ Models
_____ Other

MUSIC AND ART
_____ Radio/Tapes
_____ Dancing
_____ Photography
_____ Museums
_____ Playing Instrument
_____ Concert
_____ Other

OTHER____

LEISURE HISTORY

ACTIVITIES	ALONE	1:1	SMALL GROUP 3-5 PEOPLE	LARGE GROUP 6 OR MORE
THAT WERE EXHILARATING, ACTIVE				
THAT WERE CALMING, RELAXING				
THAT ALLOWED ME TO BE CREATIVE				
THAT MET MY SPIRITUAL NEEDS				
THAT WERE JUST PLAIN FUN				
OTHERS:				

LEISURE SUMMARY ____

INDIVIDUAL PERFORMANCE AND SOCIAL STRENGTHS

READING ABILITY

- ☐☐☐ able to read any book; able to learn new skills just by reading instructions
- ☐☐☐ able to read most books, able to learn some new skills just by reading instructions
- ☐☐☐ limited reading ability
- ☐☐☐ non-reader

ABILITY TO FORM NEW RELATIONSHIPS

- ☐☐☐ relates readily to many people; finds making new friends a pleasant pastime
- ☐☐☐ hesitant at first to meet new people; is somewhat open to developing new friendships
- ☐☐☐ reluctant to be put in the position of having to meet new people, uncertain that it's a good idea to develop new friends at his/her age
- ☐☐☐ refuses to develop new relationships with peers
- ☐☐☐ unable due to diagnosis

FAMILY/FRIENDS SUPPORT

- ☐☐☐ broad support for leisure activities (at least 2x week)
- ☐☐☐ support of leisure activities moderate (4-7x month)
- ☐☐☐ family/friendship relations strained; some effort made
- ☐☐☐ isolated; no family or friends make contact with resident

INITIATION LEVEL

- ☐☐☐ independently initiates activity without cueing from staff
- ☐☐☐ initiates activity after being cued by "Would you like to do _____ now?" or "What activity would you like to do now?"
- ☐☐☐ requires staff assistance to participate in activity
- ☐☐☐ does not indicate desire to participate and/or initiate activity

INDEPENDENCE LEVEL

- ☐☐☐ independently participates — does not require physical support from staff or peers to participate in the activity. No special adaptations required of equipment or activity
- ☐☐☐ semi-independently participates — requires little modification to activity or equipment to be able to successfully, physically take part in the activity
- ☐☐☐ semi-dependently participates — requires special adaptation of activity or equipment, or needs specially ordered equipment to successfully, physically take part in the activity. Requires occasional physical assistance from staff or peers.
- ☐☐☐ dependent — requires special adaptation of activity and/ or specially ordered equipment *and* requires physical assistance from staff or peers even with the equipment to take part in the activity

PARTICIPATION LEVEL

- ☐☐☐ active — actively participates, responsive/eye contact, alert, enthusiastic, willingly participates, engrossed in activity
- ☐☐☐ semi-active — participates with encouragement, needs staff assistance but does not necessarily require it, needs cues to willingly participate, needs staff encouragement
- ☐☐☐ passive — fringe participant; prefers to observe only, requires staff encouragement
- ☐☐☐ refuses/does not participate — resistive, noncooperative, [illegible] inappropriate [illegible], disrupti[illegible]

MALADAPTIVE BEHAVIORS

KEY:
- 0 = seldom to never a problem
- 1 = occurs a couple times a week during activity
- 2 = frequently occurs during activities
- 3 = severe enough to significantly limit participation

- ☐☐☐ EMOTIONAL WITHDRAWL: The resident appears to have an "invisible wall" between himself/herself and others. An inability to emotionally relate to others.
- ☐☐☐ INAPPROPRIATE VERBALIZATIONS: The resident exhibits verbal behaviors that are usually considered socially inappropriate: e.g., foul language, volume too loud or soft, perseveration, containing sexual overtones, etc.
- ☐☐☐ INJURIOUS TO OTHERS: Actions or threats that could cause others physical or psychological harm.
- ☐☐☐ PICA: Pica is the compulsive eating or mouthing of non-food items.
- ☐☐☐ PICKING BEHAVIORS: Picking behaviors are those actions where the resident uses his/her hands to scratch, rub, or otherwise compromise his/her skin integrity.
- ☐☐☐ SELF-NEGLECT: The resident's hygiene, appearance, or eating behaviors are below his/her normal level and are below socially acceptable standards, or iare life threatening.
- ☐☐☐ SIB (Self Injurious Behavior): SIB is any action that causes personal harm and is self-inflicted (whether it's premeditated or not).
- ☐☐☐ STEREOTYPIC BEHAVIORS: The persistent repetition of seemingly useless actions e.g., rocking back and forth, tapping finger on chin, etc.
- ☐☐☐ SUICIDAL PREOCCUPATION: The resident expresses the desire (verbally or through actions) to significantly harm or kill himself/ herself.
- ☐☐☐ WANDERING OR ELOPEMENT: The resident has the tendency to leave the activity or facility without proper authority to do so.

FIRST ASSESSMENT
SUMMARY
RECOMMENDATIONS
STAFF
SECOND ASSESSMENT
SUMMARY
RECOMMENDATIONS
STAFF
THIRD ASSESSMENT
SUMMARY
RECOMMENDATIONS
STAFF

Information on obtaining additional copies of this or other forms may be obtained from
Idyll Arbor, Inc., PO Box 720, Ravensdale, WA 98051-0720 (206) 432-3231

THERAPEUTIC RECREATION INDEX

Name: Therapeutic Recreation Index (no longer available)

Also Known As: TRI, the TRI System

Author: Rozanne W. Faulkner

Time Needed to Administer: One hour

Time Needed to Score: 30 minutes

Recommended Disability Group: The TRI has 3 scales, each one developed for a different population: 1) substance abuse, 2) physical rehabilitation, and 3) intermediate care.

Purpose of the Assessment: The purpose of the TRI is to identify a starting point for recreational therapy services, to define parameters within which recreational therapy services must function, and to identify specific programs which will meet the needs of the client.

What Does the Assessment Measure?:

Substance Abuse Scale	Physical Rehabilitation Scale	Intermediate Care Scale
1. Physical	1. Endurance and Medical Stability	1. Endurance and Medical Stability
2. Educational	2. Conversive Skills	2. Conversive Skills
3. Transportation	3. Leisure Attunement	3. Leisure Attunement
4. Economic	4. Leisure Function	4. Leisure Function
5. Family Support	5. Leisure Access	5. Leisure Access
6. Stress	6. Leisure Retention	6. Leisure Retention
7. Play Status	7. Interaction Skills	7. Interactive Skills
8. Problem Solving	8. Problem Solving	8. Leisure Support
9. Leisure Skills	9. Leisure Skills	9. Education
10. Leisure Awareness	10. Leisure Awareness	10. Activity Skills

Supplies Needed: Paper version: TRI Manual and Score sheet
Computer version: TRI Manual, disk, appropriate hardware

Reliability/Validity: Not reported.

Degree of Skill Required to Administer and Score: A recreational therapist certified at the CTRS level by the National Council for Therapeutic Recreation Certification should be able to administer, score, and interpret the results.

Comments: The TRI assessment report was an example of a testing tool developed to meet the assessment needs of clients going into a specific 'canned' program. The treatment interventions available through recreational therapy departments are well-defined. The TRI was a precursor to the treatment protocols of today.

This tool is no longer available.

Suggested Levels: The authors have not had enough experience administering the three versions of this assessment to make a recommendation as to appropriate levels.

Distributor: No longer available. Historical significance because of its style as one component of an overall, 'canned' program.

THERAPEUTIC RECREATION INDEX
THE TRI SYSTEM

NOTE TO READERS: The following provides information on the Therapeutic Recreation Index (TRI) and ***is not*** the complete assessment. Like the LDB, Leisurescope, and the CERT, the TRI had different versions of the assessment which were developed for specific populations. The assessment itself and the treatment that went along with it are no longer available.

Purpose: The purpose of the TRI was to identify a starting point for recreational therapy services, to define parameters within which recreational therapy services must function, and to identify specific programs which met the needs of the client.

The TRI did not seek to know all there was to know about a client. It only sought to identify enough information to get started. Sometimes, the TRI indicated that the starting point was to re-evaluate the client with a more in depth assessment tool. For most clients, the TRI provided enough information to plan a program of care.

CONTENT

The TRI had three 'scales' or sets of questions for three different populations. Many recreational therapists combined questions from different scales to create new scales which more specifically addressed the needs of the population they served. Each 'scale' had ten 'items' or major areas of consideration. (See Table #1)

Each item addressed a need as it related to provision of recreational therapy. For example, the 'Education Item' did not ask if the client had completed high school; for knowing that a person has a diploma says little about his/her ability to read a hobby instruction manual, or to use reading as a leisure pursuit. The 'Educational Item' asked if the client read well enough to perform the tasks required during recreational therapy involvement. If not, then the recreational therapist knew that leisure information must be presented verbally, experientially, or by assigning a volunteer to read information to the client.

SAMPLE ITEM From the Substance Abuse Scale:

ITEM 2. EDUCATION:
4. INDEPENDENT: Able to read any book of choice without regard to complexity. Client reports ability to learn new skills through reading instructional materials.
3. SEMI-INDEPENDENT: Average educational level permits reading most books of choice. Able to learn new skills from reading instructional materials but often requires instructor to interpret and assist in the learning of new skills.
2. DEPENDENT: Limited reading ability. Primary choice of reading materials is newspapers and magazines. Prefers not to learn new skills through reading.
1. AT RISK: Non-reader.
0. UNKNOWN

SCORING

Each item had five possible levels of response. In the 'Education Item' the client who was unlimited in reading ability was scored as 'Independent' and given a raw score of four (4). If able to read, yet had some limitations, then the client was scored as 'Semi-Independent' and given a raw score of three (3). If some assistance in reading was required, then the client was placed at the 'Dependent' level and given a raw score of two (2). If the client was a non-reader, then the client was placed 'At Risk' and given a raw score of one (1) for the item. If there was insufficient data to make a determination, then the client was scored 'Unknown' and given a zero (0). Scoring of each item followed the same system.

Raw scores for the ten items were weighted, permitting those items for which there was greatest potential for improvement through participation in recreational therapy programs to receive greater weight than those items which were more likely to block leisure progress. For example there was a high potential that an adult who scores 'At Risk' on the Leisure Awareness would increase his/her score if involved in appropriate recreational

Table 1: TRI Scales

Substance Abuse Scale		Physical Rehabilitation Scale		Intermediate Care Scale	
1.	Physical	1.	Endurance and Medical Stability	1.	Endurance and Medical Stability
2.	Education	2.	Conversive Skills	2.	Conversive Skills
3.	Transportation	3.	Leisure Attunement	3.	Leisure Attunement
4.	Economic	4.	Leisure Function	4.	Leisure Function
5.	Family Support	5.	Leisure Access	5.	Leisure Access
6.	Stress	6.	Leisure Retention	6.	Leisure Retention
7.	Play Status	7.	Interaction Skills	7.	Interactive Skills
8.	Problem Solving	8.	Problem Solving	8.	Leisure Support
9.	Leisure Skills	9.	Leisure Skills	9.	Education
10.	Leisure Awareness	10.	Leisure Awareness	10.	Activity Skills

therapy programming. On the other hand, an adult who scored at risk on the education item, probably would not learn to read well enough to increase his/her score through participation in therapeutic recreation programming.

The best course of action for the client at risk in leisure awareness is to create a treatment plan which includes leisure education, while the best course of action for the client at risk in education is to refer the client to an education specialist and encourage participation in Adult Basic Education classes as a leisure pursuit post discharge. Weighting reflected the differences between items in potential benefits to be derived from involvement in recreational therapy programming. Where there were two to or more items showing need for improvement, and not enough time available to work on all of them, then the recreational therapist selected the item with the greatest weight. (Would it make sense to read a discharge summary that indicated client was involved in recreational therapy programs and, as a result, had improved reading skills but not improved awareness of leisure needs? The weighting system simply coded in a priority system.)

The weighted scores from each item were added together to provide an overall description of leisure functioning. It was assumed that a person receiving a score of 100 on the TRI was able to meet his/her leisure needs without assistance from another. A person receiving a score of '75', is able to meet his/her needs with only minor assistance. A score of 50 indicated that the person needed assistance to meet his/her leisure needs. A score of '25' assumed that a person would not be able to meet his/her leisure needs. A score of '0' indicated that in depth evaluation must occur before any determination could be made.

Repeated administration of the TRI provided a method of tracking client progress. Usually changes in item scores were used for treatment planning, progress notes, and treatment revisions. The overall score (sum of item scores) was used for discharge summary, quality assurance and for determining how well the recreational therapy service was meeting clients needs.

CODING AND WEIGHTING SYSTEM

The TRI was developed to be just one part of a comprehensive recreational therapy service. The manual that accompanied the TRI assessment explained how to organize the services delivered by the recreational therapy department so that the therapist could integrate the client into the appropriate programs easily.

Prior to client's assessment, all programs and activities being offered by the service were evaluated. The program or activity's primary purpose was assigned a code number which indicated the purpose, and which correlated to the TRI assessment item number and score. Activity codes beginning with a one (1) indicated that the activity was provided for the purpose of leisure education. Activity codes beginning with a two (2) indicated that the activity taught skills required to perform a specific activity. Activity codes beginning with a three (3) indicated that the purpose was to permit a client to experience the intrinsic value of leisure participation. A four (4) indicated that the primary function is to provide therapy.

The second digit in the code often reflected the interest category (social, creative, intellectual, competitive, etc.). The third digit indicated the TRI assessment item number, followed by a decimal point and then the level for that item was indicated. So an activity named 'Horrible Hannah' with a code of '262.1' would tell the recreational therapist that 'Horrible Hannah' was an activity which developed skills, using creative interests, for clients that on item two (education) scored at risk. Horrible Hannah could have been an art project, or a skit production, but the recreational therapist knew that the client's non-reading would be dealt with in a healthy way.

RELIABILITY AND VALIDITY

Reliability and validity data is unavailable for the TRI. Interrater reliability has been investigated for previous versions, but content changes made past reliability ratings unreliable.

THE TRI MANUAL

The TRI manual provided an item by item, level by level, discussion for each scale. The discussion included the purpose of each item, the intent of each item, how to score the each item, and what to do to verify the answer that the client gave. There were also descriptive titles of activities which might meet the needs identified by the item and also space for the user to record actual activities being used which met the identified need.

Leisure Enrichment Service is no longer providing services or supplies related to recreational therapy.

INFLUENTIAL PEOPLE WHO HAVE MADE AN IMPRINT ON MY LIFE!

Name: Influential People Who Have Made An Imprint on My Life!

Also Known As: The authors do not know of another name.

Authors: Kathy L. Korb, Stacey Azok, and Estelle A. Leutenberg

Time Needed to Administer: The form is filled out by the client. Allow 20 - 40 minutes for filling out the form.

Time Needed to Score: This assessment is not 'scored'. The therapist gleans information about the client from the form. This is an example of an activity which can be used to find out more about the client as well as providing therapy.

Recommended Disability Group: Clients with little to no cognitive disability.

Purpose of the Activity: The purpose of this activity is to increase the client's self-awareness by recognizing how people have influenced his/her life.

What Does the Activity Measure?: This activity helps the therapist measure 1) the client's awareness of how others have influenced his/her life, 2) the client's ability to put his/her thoughts into writing, and 3) the client's definition of who has been important in his/her life.

Supplies Needed: Activity book: Korb, K., Azok, S., and Leutenberg, E. (1989) **Life Management Skills I: Reproducible Activity Handouts Created for Facilitators,** Beachwood, Ohio, Wellness Reproductions (800) 669-9208.

Reliability/Validity: None reported.

Degree of Skill Required to Administer and Score: Due to the subjective nature of this activity, the services of a recreational therapist certified at the CTRS level by the National Council for Therapeutic Recreation Certification should be utilized.

Comments: By observing the client participate in the activities in **Life Management Skills** or other, similar, books, the therapist will develop a greater understanding of the client's functional skills. There are now four books for adults in the **Life Management Skills** series and two books for adolescents in the **SEALS** series.

Suggested Levels: Rancho Los Amigos Level: 7 and above. Developmental Level: 13 and above. Reality Orientation: Mild to No Disorientation.

Distributor: Wellness Reproductions, Incorporated, 23945 Mercantile Rd., Beachwood, OH 44122 (800) 669-9208.

INFLUENTIAL PEOPLE WHO HAVE MADE AN IMPRINT ON MY LIFE

This activity is just one of the fifty similar exercises in a book called **Life Management Skills I: Reproducible Activity Handouts Created for Facilitators** by Korb, Azok, and Leutenberg (1989). This book is published by Wellness Reproductions, Inc., 23945 Mercantile Road, Beachwood, OH, 44122, 1-800-669-9208, FAX 216-831-1355.

Activities like this one serve a dual role. The first role is to help the client (with the therapist's help) identify his/her attitudes and frames-of-reference. The knowledge in turn can be built upon to help the client achieve a more healthy, satisfying leisure lifestyle. The second role is to provide the therapist with additional material with which to assess the client.

This type of activity is extremely difficult to test for reliability. The therapist should use caution in interpreting the results.

DOCUMENTATION ACCOMPANING THIS ASSESSMENT
WHEN IT IS USED AS A GROUP ACTIVITY

I. PURPOSE
To increase self-awareness by recognizing how people have influenced one's life.

II. GENERAL COMMENTS:
Many factors influence who we are today, e.g., education, money, values, religion, jobs, and people. This handout encourages one to look at the positive and/or negative influences people have had on his/her life.

III. POSSIBLE ACTIVITIES:

A. 1. Use the examples below to explain activity.
2. Encourage group members to complete handout.
3. Facilitate discussion.
4. Process feelings experienced as a result of doing this activity.

	Influential people...	What about...	How did/or...
Fictional Characters	Wicked Witch of the west	she was evil and intentionally hurt people	allows me to be more sensitive to my children's fears
Family	Grandfather	taking me to the circus	I love the circus and the memories it binds

B. 1. Write several examples of each category on separate index cards:
a. FAMILY MEMBERS (father, sister, aunt, grandfather)
b. PEOPLE IN HISTORY (J.F.K., Jonas Salk, Harriet Beecher Stowe)
2. Instruct group member to choose one.
3. If this person has had an 'imprint' on his/her life, s/he can share 'What about them influenced me' and 'How did or does that influence my behavior'. If this person had no 'imprint', the individual can pass the card to the right until someone can contribute or until the card goes back to the beginning. Encourage the next group member to choose a new card and the game continues.
4. Process feelings experienced as a result of doing this activity.

Influential people who have made an *imprint* on my life!

	Influential people in my life.	What about them influenced/influences me?	How did/or does that influence my behavior?
FAMILY MEMBERS			
FRIENDS			
TEACHERS			
PUBLIC FIGURES			
FICTIONAL CHARACTERS			
LOVES			
PEOPLE IN HISTORY			
CELEBRITIES			
CLERGY			
OTHER			

Chapter 8

SAMPLE ASSESSMENT REPORTS

The purpose of this chapter is to provide the reader with some samples of assessment reports. An assessment report is the summary of the assessments which the therapist completed plus some basic background information on the client. Idyll Arbor, Inc. staff have five guidelines that they follow to determine if an assessment report is acceptable:

1) Does the outcome of the assessment report address the client's actual needs?

2) Does the material presented in the assessment report meet the standards of the accrediting agency?

3) Does the material presented in the assessment report meet the standards of practice for the field of recreational therapy?

4) Does the material presented in the assessment report make sense to the other team members?

5) After reading the assessment report, could another recreational therapist select the client out of a group of 10 clients just by using observational skills?

ACTUAL NEED

There will always be times when, no matter how careful the therapist is when s/he selects the assessment tools, the results obtained will not *really* identify the client's greatest need. After completing the assessment process the therapist needs to take a moment to look at the client again and ask: 'Is this really what the client needs, or have I really identified a service that is easy for me to deliver, or have I identified a service convenient for the facility to provide?'. At times the therapist will need to make a tough decision. Some examples of actual need versus assessed need are:

*A 32 year old male with a diagnosis of MR/DD in the moderate range. He was assessed as having few leisure skills and only 30 minutes a day of discretionary time between 6:00am and 9:30 pm. Between his slowness in movement, ADL training programs for self-care (bathing, dressing), a long ride each way to work (90 minutes), and an 8 1/2 hour work day he had neither the time nor energy to engage in a leisure training program. It was actually in his best interest to have his leisure training program put off for 4 weeks while his team leader and the recreational therapist worked on finding him a job-training program closer to home.

*A 27 year old female, living in the community, with a primary diagnosis of an intermittent explosive disorder was assessed as having poor cardiovascular endurance, obesity, and (due to advanced scoliosis) restrictions for using the facility's exercise equipment. She enjoyed taking walks and needed the exercise. However, she also had the history of unpredictable, violent attacks on toddlers and young children. Until the team was able to work through the red tape and have her placed in a 'locked' program, her assessed need for outdoor exercise could not be met. The team's decision to restrict the client's treatment program was not well received by the local mental health agency, which put pressure on the team to meet the client's assessed functional needs — even if it meant exposing her, and the community, to probable danger.

In both of the situations listed above, the client's assessment report provided the results of the assessment tools administered, listing the areas of greatest need. However, in the recommendation section, the recreational therapist wrote that, due to a greater, temporary need, the assessed needs would not be addressed immediately.

ACCREDITING AGENCIES

Whether the therapist works in an acute care hospital, a mental health facility, an intermediate care facility for the mentally retarded, a long term care facility, or in-home health care, s/he will have guidelines for the assessment process. To help all of the recreational therapy staff in the department, the department director may want to summarize the criteria, interpreting how it affects the recreational therapy assessment process. This summary could be in the form of a departmental policy and procedure and added as a specific item in the department's quality assurance review. The therapist then can check his/her assessment report against the accrediting agency's guidelines.

STANDARDS OF PRACTICE

The field of recreational therapy has formal (written) as well as informal (unwritten) standards of recreational therapy practice. In addition, the recreational therapist will be expected to comply with the standards of practice for the entire health care team. The quality of work that the therapist provides will be compared against the quality of work in other facilities. (The typical surveyor may survey 20 different facilities a year, and will have many samples of recreational therapy assessments and services to compare against each other.)

The recreational therapy department may want to develop a 'peer review' agreement with another facility in the area. This outside input may be able to increase the quality of services provided to clients and not have the threat of a possible citation (as a survey would).

MEANINGFUL TO OTHER TEAM MEMBERS

The recreational therapy assessment should not be filled with 'leisure jargon'. The other team members will be relying on the recreational therapy assessment to help them make decisions about their own treatment goals. One of the sample assessment reports in this chapter has a manual which outlines a reporting format for recreation assessments (page 293). By following the format, the recreational therapist's assessment reports should be able to be understood by the other team members.

At times compromises will need to be made in the reporting process. An example of a compromise requested by the other team members can be found on the Leisure Diagnostic Batter - Scale H summary on page 301. The team members asked the Idyll Arbor, Inc. staff to report the LDB scores in percentages, not by a number correct score. This seemed to make the team feel better, and the final summary and recommendations were not compromised (the conversion of the number score to the percentage correct score did not change the recreational therapist's summary or recommendations).

CLIENT SPECIFIC

One way that the Idyll Arbor, Inc. staff check the quality of the recreational therapy assessment is to show the results (without the name or diagnoses evident) to a nurse or an aide and ask them to guess whose assessment it is. It is amazing how this test helps the recreational therapist 'fine-tune' his/her assessment reports so that the report *really* reflects the client's demonstrated functional skill level.

PROGRESS NOTES ASSESSMENT REPORT FORMS

The first three assessment report forms are blank reports used by the recreational therapy staff at Harborview Medical Center in Seattle, Washington. These are not assessments. The recreational therapy department has developed a community integration assessment manual which contains specific questions (Missy Armstrong and Sara Lauzen, 1994, **Community Integration Program, 2nd Edition**, Idyll Arbor, Inc., Ravensdale, WA). After administering all appropriate questions from the community integration manual, the therapist summarizes the client's demonstrated functional ability on the Progress Notes Assessment Report Form. This report form goes right into the chart. The recreational therapy department at Harborview has a Progress Note Assessment Report Form for most of the treatment protocols they implement. Harborview staff modify the forms as needed to neet current reporting needs.

STANDARDIZED REPORT FORMS

A report form is standardized if:

1) the information which is expected to be entered onto the form comes from objective assessment tools,

2) the information obtained encompasses a predetermined set of skills and/or domains,

3) the criteria for filling out the form is well defined,

4) the form is used by multiple agencies to enhance communication between professionals, and

5) the form facilities the comparison of recommended treatment strategies to listed diagnoses and assessed skills across facilities.

There are many examples of standardized assessment report forms outside the field of recreational therapy. Two of the better known standardized assessment report forms are

1) the MDS developed by the Health Care Finance Administration for use in Long Term Care Facilities

2) the OARS (Older American Resources and Services Group) developed by the Duke Center for the Study of Aging and Human Development for use in case management.

There are also standardized rating scales. The best known is the FIM (Functional Independence Measure) which was developed jointly by the American Congress of Rehabilitation Medicine and the American Academy of Physical Medicine and Rehabilitation for use on rehabilitation units. (Please see Table 8-1 for a Description of the Levels of Function and Their Scores.)

Idyll Arbor, Inc. developed a standardized assessment report form for use in Intermediate Care Facilities for Mentally Retarded (ICF-MRs). The reader will find the manual for the assessment report form and the form itself following the three report forms from Harborview.

NARRATIVE ASSESSMENT REPORTS

Many of the assessment reports written by health care professionals are in the 'Narrative' style. The Narrative style is a report which follows a pre-established outline to present the information gathered.

The last two assessment report forms were pulled right from the Idyll Arbor, Inc. client files. (Except for changing the client's identifications, no changes were made to the assessment reports.)

The first narrative report is an example of a multi-year narrative assessment. Because Idyll Arbor, Inc. uses computers to store client information, it is very easy for the therapist to update the client's assessment report.

The second narrative report is both an assessment of the client's functional skills and a discharge summary.

CONCLUSION

The assessment report is the written document which summarizes the client's strengths and areas of need based on the review of the medical chart, the interview with the client (and significant others), and the use of assessment tools. This report addresses the client's actual needs, meets the requirements of the accrediting agency, meets professional standards of practice, is easily understood by the other team members, and clearly outlines the client's functional ability. Quality assurance and risk management reviews are aided when multiple agencies use a standardized assessment report.

Table 8 - 1 DESCRIPTION OF THE LEVELS OF FUNCTION AND THEIR SCORES

Functional Independence Measure (FIM)

INDEPENDENT — Another person is not required for the activity (NO HELPER).

7 COMPLETE INDEPENDENCE All of the tasks described as making up the activity are typically performed safely without modification, assistive devices, or aids, and within reasonable time.

6 MODIFIED INDEPENDENCE Activity requires any one or more than one of the following: an assistive device, more than reasonable time, or there are safety (risk) considerations.

DEPENDENT — Another person is required for either supervision or physical assistance in order for the activity to be performed, or it is not performed (REQUIRES HELPER).

MODIFIED DEPENDENCE The subject expends half (50%) or more of the effort. The levels of assistance required are

5 SUPERVISION OR SETUP Subject requires no more help than standby, cueing or coaxing, without physical contact. Or, helper sets up needed items or applies orthoses.

4 MINIMAL CONTACT ASSISTANCE With physical contact the subject requires no more help than touching, and subject expends 75% or more of the effort.

3 MODERATE ASSISTANCE Subject requires more help than touching, or expends half (50%) or more (up to 75%) of the effort.

COMPLETE DEPENDENCE The subject expends less than half (less than 50%) of the effort. Maximal or total assistance is required, or the activity is not performed. The level of assistance required are

2 MAXIMAL ASSISTANCE Subject expends less than 50% of the effort, but at least 25%.

1 TOTAL ASSISTANCE Subject expends less than 25% of the effort.

INSTRUCTIONS: Complete in black ink only, because other colors do not reproduce on Microfilm well.
Notes: Each entry should note month/day/year; time, problem number and title; writer's name, title, and department, e.g. John Doe, Resident, Cardiology, or Staff Nurse, 5N, or student.

DATE AND HOUR	PROB. NO.	NOTES

RECREATIONAL THERAPY: COMMUNITY INTEGRATION EVALUATION
Assessment of Environmental Awareness Skills - Rehab.

KEY: (+) = independent function, affirmative response, or demonstrated appropriate knowledge
(-) = patient needs assistance, negative response, or lack of appropriate knowledge
(N/A) = not applicable
(N/T) = not tested

Patient is a__________________ with a diagnosis of ___________________________
seen on________________________________ to assess the following skills:

I. Pre-plan phase

A. Demonstrates orientation /knowledge or memory of:
___purpose of evaluation
___date and time of evaluation
___appropriate dress and grooming needed for weather
Comments:

II. Future Leisure Phase

___Demonstrates knowledge of accessible recreation/leisure or facilities appropriate to discharge site
Comments:

III. Management Phase

A. Functional Behaviors: Demonstrates:
___ability to negotiate architectural barriers, curbs, curb cuts, ramps and doorways (mobility/wheelchair skills)
___ability to tolerate activity
___speed adequate to safely cross street, monitor traffic
___ability to scan or locate road signs, curb cuts
Comments:

UNIVERSITY OF WASHINGTON HOSPITALS
HARBORVIEW MEDICAL CENTER
UNIVERSITY HOSPITAL
SEATTLE, WASHINGTON

PROGRESS NOTES
UH 0142 REV AUG 76

DATE AND HOUR	PROB. NO.	NOTES

B. Cognitive Behaviors: Demonstrates ability to:
___pathfind selected spots
___remain task oriented
___monitor traffic, use signals for safe crossing
___read maps, directions
___remembers destination, medical needs, information
Comments:

C. Social Behaviors: Demonstrates:
___consistently positive social interactions
___appropriate and realistic comfort level in community setting
___appropriate response to authority or conflict
Comments:

Assessment:

Recommendations:

Therapist ______________________________ **Date**__________ **Time Spent** __________

303.02

INSTRUCTIONS: Complete in black ink only, because other colors do not reproduce on Microfilm well.
Notes: Each entry should note month/day/year; time, problem number and title; writer's name, title, and department, e.g. John Doe, Resident, Cardiology, or Staff Nurse, 5N, or student.

DATE AND HOUR	PROB. NO.	NOTES

RECREATIONAL THERAPY: AQUATICS PROGRAM COMMUNITY INTEGRATION EVALUATION

KEY: (+) = indicates independent functioning, affirmative response, or appropriate knowledge
(-) = indicates patients needs assistance, negative response, or lack of appropriate knowledge. All (-) will be clarified in comment section
(N/A) = not applicable
(N/T) = not tested

Patient is a ______________________________ with a diagnosis of __________________
seen on _________________ to assess the following skills.

I. Pre-planning

A. Demonstrates orientation/knowledge or memory of:
___ commitment
___ timeliness
____ appropriate dress/equipment/medical needs
Comments:

II. Clinical ADL Carryover

A. Demonstrates ability to carry over:
___ dressing
___ LE
___ UE
___ safety/judgement
Comments:

III. Community Skills

A. Demonstrates knowledge/ability regarding:
___w/c mobility
___architectural barriers: doors, rough ground, level surfaces
___enter/exit pool
___follows directions
___general pathfinding
___safety/judgment
Comments:

UNIVERSITY OF WASHINGTON MEDICAL CENTERS
HARBORVIEW MEDICAL CENTER
UNIVERSITY OF WASHINGTON MEDICAL CENTER
SEATTLE, WASHINGTON

PROGRESS NOTES
UH 0142 REV JUN 89

DATE AND HOUR	PROB. NO.	NOTES

IV. Adaptive Aquatics/Technique

A. Demonstrates ability of:

___flotation

___ROM

___balance/ambulation

___adaptive technique

___back float

___safety/judgment

Comments:

V. Family Education

A. Investment/knowledge

___family involvement

___continued involvement

Comments:

Previous Swimming Ability:___participated___did not participate

Assessment:

Recommendation/Plan:

Therapist ______________________ **Date** __________ **Time Spent** __________________

303.26

INSTRUCTIONS: Complete in black ink only, because other colors do not reproduce on Microfilm well.
Notes: Each entry should note month/day/year; time, problem number and title; writer's name, title, and department, e.g. John Doe, Resident, Cardiology, or Staff Nurse, 5N, or student.

DATE AND HOUR	PROB. NO.	NOTES

RECREATION THERAPY: COMMUNITY INTEGRATION EVALUATION
Assessment of Environmental Awareness and Skills to a Grocery Store

KEY: (+) = indicates independent function, affirmative response, or appropriate knowledge
(-) = indicates patients needs assistance, negative response, or lack of appropriate knowledge. All (-) will be clarified in comment section
(N/A) = not applicable
(N/T) = not tested

Patient is a ____________________________ with a diagnosis of ________________________
seen on _______________ to assess the following skills

I. Pre-plan phase

A. Demonstrates orientation/knowledge or memory of:

___ date and time of evaluation
___ appropriate dress and grooming needed for weather
___ purpose of evaluation
___ items necessary (list, cart, etc.)
___ money needed
___ medical necessities (i.e., pressure releases, meds, splints, braces)

Comments:

II. Future leisure phase

A. Demonstrates orientation to:

___ shopping available at d/c site
___ transportation available to shopping at d/c site
___ leisure options with food/cooking (i.e., entertaining, gourmet or holiday cooking, family responsibilities)
___ demonstrate knowledge of accessible recreation sites or facilities appropriate to discharge site

Comments:

UNIVERSITY OF WASHINGTON MEDICAL CENTERS
HARBORVIEW MEDICAL CENTER
UNIVERSITY OF WASHINGTON MEDICAL CENTER
SEATTLE, WASHINGTON

PROGRESS NOTES

UH 0142 REV JUN 89

DATE AND HOUR	PROB. NO.	NOTES

III. Management phase

A. Functional behaviors: demonstrates ability to:
___negotiate architectural barriers
___speed adequate to safely cross street, monitor traffic
___ability to scan or locate road signs, signals, curb cuts
___grasp, hold, and carry items
___reach and lift
___scan and locate items in store
___tolerate activity
Comments:

B. Cognitive behaviors: demonstrates ability to:
___pathfind to/from grocery store
___monitor traffic, use of signals for safe crossing
___read maps, directions
___remember destination, medical needs, information
___locate all areas requested in store
___sequence/categorize items
___count back correct change
___allow directions
___identify/discriminate (of items on list)
___remain task oriented
___appropriate time to complete task
Comments:

C. Social behaviors: demonstrates
___consistently positive social interactions
___appropriate and realistic comfort level in community setting
___appropriate response to authority or conflict
Comments:

Assessment:

Recommendations:

Therapist ________________________________ **Date** __________ **Time Spent**____________

303.16

THERAPEUTIC RECREATION ASSESSMENT REPORT INSTRUCTION MANUAL

The purpose of this manual is to help the assessment report user to understand both how to fill out the Therapeutic Recreation Assessment Report and how to comply with the federal regulations concerning the assessment of individuals in ICF-MR's (Intermediate Care Facilities for the Mental Retarded). This assessment report was developed specifically for use with clients in ICF-MRs.

The T.R. Assessment Form user should be clear that an assessment (e.g., CERT, GRST, LDB) is not the same as an assessment report. Both are required. The assessment is a tool which evaluates the client's skill. The report is a tool which the therapist uses to interpret the findings of the assessment for others (usually outside of the field of recreation).

INTRODUCTION

Recreation (or play) is an important component of every person's life. While most recreational activities should be undertaken just because they are fun and help maintain health, for clients in ICF-MRs, some of their recreation also needs to be geared toward acquiring new skills through specific training programs. To be able to accurately determine which area(s) need intervention via training programs, assessments (testing devices) and ongoing documentation need to be done.

Assessments help determine baseline and new acquisition of skills as they relate to recreation. Because it is impossible (or impractical) to have just one assessment that meets everyone's assessment needs, the recreational therapist should have between five and ten different assessments to select from. Each assessment allows the recreational therapist to see the client from a slightly different perspective.

A minimum of one assessment should be administered to each client each year. This not only helps the recreational therapist know more about the client's functional skill, it also provides a means to validate the results. The ICF-MR system had been structured so that each client received a complete assessment at least once a year. A complete assessment in recreation should usually involve the use of four or more testing tools. The assessments given should cover the following areas: 1) functional skills (e.g., fine motor skills), 2) leisure interests (e.g., likes basketball), 3) activity skills (e.g., beginner swimmer), and 4) actual participation patterns (and to check for a balanced leisure lifestyle). To help ensure accurate, healthful programming in recreation for the client, and because most clients recreate every day, the recreational therapist should monitor closely both the client's functional skill and activity patterns. The results of this monitoring will help the client achieve a healthy leisure balance.

Just as the recreational therapist who work in ICF-MRs need to have more than one assessment to determine the client's need, they also need more than one kind of documentation to record a client's leisure status. The scoring sheets from the assessments are just one way to pinpoint skill acquisition or loss.

A second kind of documentation is used to record a client's specific performance on his/her training objective. When a client has a specific training goal in the area of recreation and leisure, data must be kept to determine if and when the client is able to meet the objective. Occasionally this data can be kept on the recreation participation data sheet.

The last major means to document a client's leisure health is the recreation participation data sheet. The purpose of this data sheet is to document participation trends and to monitor for a healthy balance in leisure. The type of activities recorded on the recreation participation data sheet are primarily 'every day recreation' (or recreation for fun, not training). This type of recreation is a very important part of a normalized living experience.

Any of the above types of documentation may be used as the mode to document the client's status on the recreation/leisure training objective on the client's IPP (Individual Program Plan). The recreational therapist should select the format that provides the most efficient means of documenting the required information.

SUGGESTED POLICY ON CONDUCTING INDIVIDUAL PROGRAM PLAN ASSESSMENTS

POLICY: All Individual Program Plan (IPP) assessments done by the recreation staff will be comprehensive and complete. A minimum of one assessment will be used on each client each year.

PROCEDURE:

1. Review last year's IPP Recreation Evaluation. Note past year's recreation concerns.
2. Review the psychological report for general developmental function. Note scores.
3. Review PT/OT reports (note date of last evaluation) to note recorded physical limitations.
4. Review speech and nursing reports (note date of last evaluation) to note information that indicates limitation related to any of the domains used by recreation (physical, cognitive, affective, sensory, community).
5. Review reports from other professionals which might provide useful information for your evaluation.
6. Review monthly/quarterly summaries from the recreation participation flow sheets. What trends can be noted over the last 12 months (or the last 36 months)?

7. Administer the appropriate assessments (e.g., REDS, GRST, Leisure Interest Inventory, LS/SA, etc.)
8. Review results from recreation assessment(s) and data collected over the past year.
9. Summarize the data by:
   a. listing the noted areas of strength and weakness
   b. noting primary area of concern(s)
   c. deciding if concern(s) are due to the lack of client skill and participation or due to staff and resource limitations.

   If due to lack of client skill/participation, decide if a training objective is needed.
   If due to the need to inservice attendant care staff, write up guidelines for staff to help alleviate the problem.
   If due to resource limitations, explore ways to re-allocate resources.

THERAPEUTIC RECREATION ASSESSMENT FORM GUIDELINES

HISTORY: Histories usually start out: "(Client's name) is a (number) year old (male/female) with the following diagnoses..."

A more detailed discussion about the onset of the various diagnoses could follow; do not include such information on this form unless it has a direct impact on treatment.

Placement history has a large impact on this population. Give a one sentence history of placement.

COGNITIVE: Check the box that best describes the client's cognitive/MR classification. Note: Often the IQ score will vary from year to year. This does not usually reflect an acquisition or loss of ability as much as insensitivities of the various IQ tests.

VISION: Check the box that best describes the client's visual abilities. If vision is impaired, describe impairment in the 'OTHER' section (e.g., tunnel vision, left/right neglect).

AUDITORY: Check the box that best describes the client's auditory abilities. If hearing is impaired, describe impairment in the 'OTHER' section (e.g., low frequency loss in left ear).

OTHER: Place other information of note in this space.

PICTURE: This section is for a quick reference to visually depict paralysis, contractures, etc.

GENERAL INFORMATION: This section is meant to be used to record significant information from the other professional's assessments in addition to allergies, photosensitivity, etc.

RECREATION ASSESSMENT RESULTS: This section should be used to record scores from the GRST, CERT-Phys/Dis, CERT-Psych, FOX, REDS, MASF, or other functional skill assessments. (See the section on 'Reporting Format for Recreation Assessments' below.)

LEISURE INTERESTS: This section should contain information about what activities the client enjoys during his/her leisure time. Whenever possible this information should be obtained through a formal leisure interest assessment tool like the Leisure Step Up or Leisurescope.

This section should also be used to record: 1) results from skill acquisition tests (e.g., swimming and other pool checklists), 2) a summary of the client's recreation participation gleaned from the monthly/quarterly recreation notes, and 3) the progress (or regress) on any recreation training objectives. List both strengths and weakness.

ADAPTED EQUIPMENT: List adapted equipment that would be used during recreational activities and leisure time (e.g., w/c with quad peds, special w/c tray, communication board).

RECOMMENDED SUPERVISION RATIO: List the recommended staff to client ratio for supervision in each of the five categories. This ratio (one staff/# clients) should reflect the recreation staff's professional judgment after they took into account safety issues (being somewhat conservative) as well as the client's learning/cognitive processing capabilities.

BEHAVIOR PROGRAMS/INTERVENTIONS OF NOTE: List appropriate interventions for known behaviors and/or formal behavior programs. It is important to list any restraints used on the resident, *including chemical restraints* and how these chemical restraints impact leisure safety.

RECOMMENDATIONS — GENERAL (FUNCTIONAL SKILLS): List any recommendations based on data found in this report (e.g., increased ability to recognize/distinguish 5 simple toys/objects and their use in play).

RECOMMENDATIONS — RECREATIONAL PROGRAMS: (Activity/Participation) List any recommendations for change in the client's leisure participation patterns. For example:
1) use of pool to 4x/month to decrease contracture development/hypertonis; increase physical fitness, and
2) increase activities that promote the development of various senses (Start by using smells kit to help the client learn to distinguish various smells (minimum 10).

REPORTING FORMAT FOR RECREATION ASSESSMENTS

1. Report name of assessment and (if any) the abbreviation for the assessment (e.g., Comprehensive Evaluation in Recreational Therapy Scale (CERT)).
2. Provide a one or two sentence overview of the purpose of the assessment (e.g., The CERT evaluates twenty five behaviors associated with successful participation in group leisure activities. Lower scores indicate fewer problems. The functional threshold is 5 for GENERAL and 10 for INDIVIDUAL and GROUP.)

3. Report Score(s).

GENERAL = 15/20	INDIVIDUAL = 21/40
GROUP = 25/40	OVERALL = 61/100

4. Report specific individual scores from the assessment that indicate an extreme. List no more than five if possible. Select the five you feel are of the greatest concern or categorize the areas of concern (e.g., The main areas of concern brought out in this assessment are: decision making ability, performance in organized activities, leadership ability in groups, and competition in groups.)
5. Provide some interpretation of the scores (e.g., Charlie demonstrates significant difficulty in successfully and purposely interacting with peers. Given his overall developmental level (3 years) one would expect him to be able to improve his skills in this area with appropriate training and staff support.). The federal regulations require that the therapist clearly spell out how the client's ability will impact his/her everyday life.
6. List some recommendations based on the assessed results.
   Recommendations:
   1. Provide formal training in making choices
   2. Provide inservice for staff on various ways to nurture Charlie Brown's interactions with peers

EXAMPLE:

Charlie was given the Comprehensive Evaluation in Recreational Therapy Scale (CERT). The CERT evaluates twenty five behaviors associated with successful participation in group leisure activities. Lower scores indicate fewer problems. The functional threshold is 5 for GENERAL and 10 for INDIVIDUAL and GROUP. His scores were: GENERAL = 15/20, INDIVIDUAL = 21/40, GROUP = 25/40 and OVERALL = 61/100. The main areas of concern brought out in this assessment are: decision making ability, performance in organized activities, leadership ability in groups, and competition in groups. Charlie demonstrates significant difficulty in successfully and purposefully interacting with his peers. Given his overall developmental level (3 years) one would expect him to be able to improve his skills in this area with appropriate training and staff support. Recommendations: 1) Provide formal training in making choices, and 2) Provide inservice for staff on various ways to nurture Charley's interactions with peers.

EXAMPLE:

Lucy was given the General Recreation Screening Tool (GRST). The purpose of this assessment is to give a very general overview of the client's functional developmental level as it relates to recreation. Her overall score was 12 months with some scattering to 3 years.

Physical: solid to 12 months; scattered to 3 years in the area of gross motor.

Cognitive: solid to 12 months (with the exception of expressive language being 6 months); problem solving and language comprehension scattered to 3 years.
Affective: solid to 12 months (with the exception of emotional control being 6 months) scattered to 3 years in imitation play, people skills, story/drama, and music.

The two scores of greatest concern are expressive language and emotional control (exhibited by aggression toward others).

Recommendations:
1. Work with speech to increase Lucy's ability to express her thoughts, concerns, and desires.
2. Support behavior program developed by psychologist to decrease outburst behavior.
3. Continue to monitor Lucy's balance of leisure activities. Participation data over the last year indicated a need to increase cardiovascular activity. Appropriate level maintained for the last 3 months.

EXAMPLE:

Shawn was given the Functional Assessment of Characteristics for Therapeutic Recreation (FACTR). The FACTR does not measure the areas of greatest disability but indicates the area that recreation resources could have the greatest impact. The lower the score, the greater the impact of recreational therapy intervention. His scores were: PHYSICAL = 9/11, COGNITIVE = 9/11, and SOCIAL/EMOTIONAL = 2/11. Shawn's Social/Emotional score was low primarily due to his difficulty in asserting himself. Specific areas of concern were: 1) overly passive in competitive behavior, 2) doesn't initiate, but doesn't avoid social contacts/ situations, and 3) passively submits in argument/conflict situations. Recommendations: 1) Provide formal training in basic, appropriate competitive behavior and 2) Provide inserve for staff on various ways to encourage assertiveness.

NOTES ON ASSESSMENTS FOR ICF/MR FUNDED CLIENTS

The following notes are part of the standard presentation that Idyll Arbor, Inc. staff give on the specific requirements for all assessments as outlined in Appendix 'J'. (Some of the material also came from inservices given by Federal Surveyors.) Appendix 'J' is the document that interprets the 1988 regulations concerning the delivery of services for clients in ICF-MRs.

1. Assessments must be 'accurate'. Accurate means that the assessments contain current, relevant and valid data (data from standardized assessments is nice, but not necessarily required). Assessments must list abilities (measurable) and training needs.

2. Assessments used must be sensitive to the client's developmental status — youth, middle-aged, elderly.

3. Does the assessment reflect how a person actually functions in a living, learning, and working environment?

4. When statements are made indicating a diagnosis or a 'label' of any kind, the assessment data backing up that label must be included.

5. Diagnoses or imprecise terms and phrases (including, but not limited to; 'grade level', 'age appropriate', 'age level', 'good attending skills', and 'poor motor ability') in the absence of specific terms, are not acceptable.

6. Assessment of the behavior assumed to be maladaptive will include analyses of the potential causes, such as lack of exposure to positive models and teaching strategies, lack of ability to communicate needs and desires, lack of success experiences, a history of punishing experiences, or presence of a physiological condition.

7. Each discipline will list specific 'developmental' strengths and needs describing what the client 'can' and 'cannot' do.

8. If any professional group determines that the client does not need their service, in addition to stating that direct intervention by (let's say) PT is not needed at this time, the following must also be included:

a. The assessment must identify the course of specific interventions recommended to meet the client's needs in lieu of direct professional therapy, and

b. Information about when the profession should be contacted again, and under what conditions?

9. Not only does each professional need to list specific data, but the significance of the results in terms of the client's functional daily life needs must be included.

10. The full name of each testing tool must be written out in full at least once in each assessment report.

11. Just listing clinical impressions without clearly explaining the resulting implications on the client's ability to do everyday tasks is not acceptable.

12. The assessment should reflect how the environment could be changed to support the client.

13. Does the assessment clearly state whether or not 'hands-on' therapy conducted by professionals is indicated?

14. Every training objective written will have an identifiable and direct link to specific functional assessment findings.

15. The old regulations required a complete assessment every three years with just an updated assessment the two years in between. The new regulations require a complete reassessment and IPP every year.

SUMMARY

The staff at Idyll Arbor, Inc. have prepared both the Therapeutic Recreation Assessment Report Form and this instruction manual. We hope that the clients who live in ICF-MRs will be better able to receive the kind of training in leisure that they need as a result. We also are available, by phone, to try to answer questions that might arise in the delivery of recreation services to this population. Please feel free to call us at: (206) 432-3231.

Therapeutic Recreation Assessment Report

History: ____

____

____

____

____

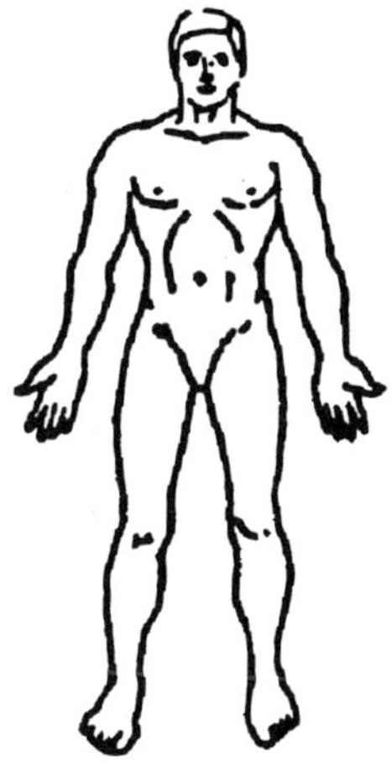

Cognitive	**Vision**	**Auditory**
o Borderline	o Normal	o Normal
o Mild	o Correctable	o Correctable
o Moderate	o Limited w/ Correction	o Limited w/ Correction
o Severe	o Blind o L o R	o Deaf o L o R
o Profound	o Uses Correction	o Uses Correction

Other ____

____

____

X= total paralysis

/= partial paralysis

O= Contracture

General Information: ____

____

____

____

Recreation Assessment Results: ____

____

____

____

____

____

____

____

Leisure Interests: ____

____

____

____

Addressograph #	Therapeutic Recreation Assessment Report
Name Living Unit Birthdate Admission Date	

Therapeutic Recreation Assessment Report
Page 2

Adapted Equipment: ____

____

____

____

Recommended Supervision Ratio:

On campus escort _____ In leisure activity _____ In leisure training _____

In aquatics program _____ Off campus _____ Off grounds never leaving vehicle _____

Precautions/Reasons: ____

____

____

Behaviour Programs, Interventions of Note: ______________________________

____

____

Recommendations - General (Functional Skills): ______________________________

____

____

____

____

____

____

Recommendations - Recreational Programs (Activity, Participation): ______________

____

____

____

____

Recreation Participation Data Results: ______________________________

____

____

____

____

Addressograph #	Therapeutic Recreation Assessment Report
Name Living Unit Birthdate Admission Date	

SAMPLE ASSESSMENT REPORT

Narrative Combining Data From Multiple Years With Selected Score Sheets

ASSESSMENT SUMMARY -- RECREATIONAL THERAPY

NAME: Jenny Doe
DATE: 8/5/89
DOB: 11/10/89

LOCATION: Snowmeadows Group Home
THERAPIST: joan burlingame, CTRS
SS#: 000-00-0000

HISTORY:

Jenny is a 28 year old female with the primary diagnosis of Prader-Willi Syndrome. Jenny functions independently in living skills, but often operates very slowly. She is on the token economy reinforcement system which has aided in controlling previous problems with stealing, hoarding, assault, and destruction of property. Jenny often looses points due to her slowness. Jenny continues to need assistance in the areas of self-control, weight control, interpersonal/social relationships, rectal digging, verbal aggression, lying, yelling, stealing, and passive non-compliance.

LEISURE DEVELOPMENT LEVEL AND APTITUDES:

(Assessment tool(s) used: interview, chart, GRST (1988), and LDB (1989))

Information was obtained via chart records, activity data sheet, interview with staff member, Colleen, and interview and administration of the following assessments with the client:

GENERAL RECREATION SCREENING TOOL (GRST): The purpose of the GRST is to give a very general overview of the client's functional developmental level as it relates to recreation. Jenny's scores were at the high end of this scale, functioning at 10+ years in most areas of cognitive, physical, and affective functioning. Scores indicating a functional level of 6 years in the areas of problem solving, emotional control, and people skills were noted.

LEISURE DIAGNOSTIC BATTERY, SCALE 'H': The LDB-H is a kind of reality orientation test related to leisure. Jenny scored low to moderate in her knowledge of the ins and outs of utilizing recreational opportunities. This will have an impact on her if she moves into a less restrictive living situation, as she will be at risk to become isolated due to her lack of general knowledge. Please see the attached summary for further detail.

LEISURE INTERESTS AND ATTITUDES:

(Assessment tool(s) used: interview, LeisureScope (1988), and LDB-G (1989)

LEISURESCOPE (1988): Jenny appeared to be most interested in games and nature, with some interest in crafts and music. She was the least interested in sports.

LEISURE DIAGNOSTIC BATTERY - SCALE G: The LDB-G indicated that Jenny prefers activities related to nature and the out of doors as well as those activities that involve mental and linguistical skills. Sports increased in desirability while arts and crafts activities decreased. The LDB-G also measures personal preference for risk/non-risk, active/passive, and group/individual activities. Jenny's profile placed her in the Non-Risk, Passive, Group categories. This means that she will tend to find activities that fall into this profile more enjoyable, no matter what type of activity it is (e.g., sporting, arts and crafts, drama, etc.).

Often when clients in ICF-MR settings receive structured recreational activities a change in actual interest can be measured as they learn new skills in the different areas. Jenny was exposed to a variety of normal outdoor/sporting leisure activities over the last year as part of her IPP (Individual Program Plan). Her preference for normal outdoor/sporting activities has increased, probably as a direct result of this exposure.

RECREATION PARTICIPATION:
Over the last 12 months Jenny has demonstrated the ability to manage her own money on outings 96% of the time. She has been averaging 9.3 hours of physical activity (Levels 1 or 2) per month, with a range of 5.3 hours to 11.5 hours.

Over the last three months Jenny has averaged a 97% in three areas related to her leisure activities: active participation (Levels One and Two), independence (Level One), and initiative (Level One).

Eleven months ago her lithium was d/c'd. Since that time she has shown increases in the following behaviors during leisure activities:

stealing: up 150% from an average of 4 x month to 6 x month
hoarding: up 110% from an average of 3.3 x a month to 4 x m.
assault: up 133% from an average of 3 x month to 4 x month
lying: up 200% from an average of 1.5 x month to 3 x m.

SOCIO-ECONOMIC SITUATION:
Jenny visits her mother in Kansas once a year. She also talks with her sister in Seattle on the phone approximately three times a month. Jenny is working with her case worker to find a residential facility in Kansas so that she could live closer to her mother.

Jenny has an average of $37.00 discretionary money each month to spend on her leisure activities and clothing. This amount significantly handicaps her ability to participate in recreational activities offered by the community. Over the past year scholarships have been obtained for her to participate in her local parks department and to go skiing one time a week during the winter. The group home is providing an instructor in hiking and camping skills under the direction of the recreational therapist.

STRENGTHS:
Without cuing Jenny will exercise by using the stationary bike or by going for a walk. She reports that she enjoys these two activities. Jenny averages 9.3 hours of physical activity a month at Levels One or Two.

She participates actively, independently, and takes the initiative an average of 97% of the time.

Jenny responds well to her new token program.

OVERALL SUMMARY:
Jenny's leisure tends to be somewhat self-directed. She prefers activities that revolve around nature and/or the out-of-doors. For in-house activities she prefers activities that challenge her mind. Generally she will be most happy in non-risk activities where she can be a passive member of the group. She does not have enough of the general knowledge related to recreational opportunities to be truly independent in the community.

RECOMMENDATIONS:
1. Staff should provide Jenny with opportunities at home and in the community to increase her problem solving and people skills. Do not rush her; let her work out solutions to problems.

2. Jenny needs to be an active participant in planning and implementing her leisure activities. She needs to gain the knowledge of how much things cost and where you find out about leisure activities.

LEISURE DIAGNOSTIC BATTERY - SCALE H
KNOWLEDGE OF LEISURE OPPORTUNITIES

The LDB-H is used to determine the individual's knowledge of specific information concerning leisure opportunities. It measures knowledge in the following areas related to recreation: 1) cost, 2) who can participate, 3) where, 4)when, and 5) what. Low scores indicate little knowledge of leisure opportunities in the listed sub-areas.

A. WHAT refers to knowledge of which thing or things, events, or conditions are happening or exist. An example is: 'For which art project do you need paper? a) felt-decorating, b) painting on ceramics, c) collage-making, and d) pottery making'.

SCORE FOR 'A. WHAT': 63%

B. WHO refers to what person or persons can participate in an activity or go to a specific place. An example is: 'Visiting art galleries and museums are limited: a) to persons 18 and over, b) to persons under 16, c) to students during field trips, and d) to persons who are interested'.

SCORE FOR 'B. WHO': 75%

C. WHERE refers to the place or location at which an event will take place. An example is: 'Professional football is usually played at: a) a college campus, b) a stadium, c) a high school, and d) word games.

SCORE FOR 'C. WHERE': 75%

D. COST refers to the price paid to enable an individual to do something. An example is; 'Which of the materials used in an arts and crafts class costs the most to buy?: a) water-colors, b) clay, c) paintbrush, and d) paste.

SCORE FOR 'D. COST': 75%

E. WHEN refers to during or at what time period something takes place. It also refers to upon what occasion a piece of equipment should be worn. An example is: 'A playing board for the game is needed for: a) bridge, b) charades, c) parchesi, and d) old maid'.

SCORE FOR 'E. WHEN': 33%

Note: The treatment team which received this report requested that the LDB scores be reported in a % correct format instead of the standard LDB reporting format.

LEISURE DIAGNOSTIC BATTERY - SCALE G
LEISURE PREFERENCES

The LDB-G is used to determine the individual's patterns of selection among activities. In addition, this scale measures preference for mode or style of involvement.

The Activity Domains assessed are: 1) Outdoors/Nature, 2) Music/Dance/Drama, 3) Sports, 4) Arts/Crafts/Hobbies, and 5) Mental Linguistics.

Jenny's preference fell within the domains of Outdoor/Nature and Mental Linguistics. A preference for Sports increased while Arts/Crafts/Hobbies decreased over the last year.

The Style Domains assessed are: 1) Individual vs. Group, 2) Risk vs. Non-Risk, and 3) Active vs. Passive. Jenny's profile placed her in the Non-Risk, Passive, Group categories. This means that she will tend to find activities that fall into this profile more enjoyable, no matter what type of activity domain they are in (eg; sporting, arts and crafts, drama, etc.).

GRST: General Recreation Screening Tool (Score Sheet)

Name Jenny Doe Date of Birth 11/10/89 Staff joan burlingame

Unit Snowmeadows Date of Assessment 8/5/88

The purpose of this screening tool is to provide the therapist with a general assessment which helps determine the strengths and weaknesses of the resident. The results also provide a developmental level for each assessed functional skill that relates to the resident's leisure capabilities. Please note that the skills listed within each category may not be in exact developmental order. — **Scoring:** Read the developmental skills listed in each age group for each functional leisure skill category. If the resident is able to demonstrate between 50% to 75% of the skills listed within the age group, draw a dashed line through that age group. If the resident is able to demonstrate 75% or more of the skills listed within the age group, draw a solid line through that age group.

Example:

	0-6 mos.	6-12 mos.	1-3 yrs.	3-6 yrs.	7-10 yrs.
Fine Motor					

DEVELOPMENTAL GROUPS

	Functional Leisure Skills	0-6 mos.	6-12 mos.	1-3 yrs.	3-6 yrs.	7-10 yrs.	10+
Physical	Gross Motor						
	Fine Motor						
	Eye-Hand						
Cognitive	Play Behavior		6mos.-9mos.	9mos.-3yrs.	3-4yrs. / 4-5yrs.	5-10yrs.	
	Play Structure			1-3 yrs.		5-10yrs.	10+
	Language Use						
	Language Compr.						
	Numbers						
	Object Use						
	Follow-Directions						
	Problem Solving						
	Attending Behavior						
Affective	Possessions						
	Emotional Control						
	Imitation Play						
	People Skills						
	Music						
	Stories/Drama						

[illegible signature] CTRS

Summary / Recommendations:

Jenny's scores are at the high end of this scale, functioning at 10+ years in most areas of cognitive, physical, and affective functioning. Scores indicating a functional level of 6 years in the areas of problem solving, emotional control, and people skills were noted. Please refer to the Recreational Therapy Report for recommendations.

LEISURESCOPE

a leisure interest assessment

Name Jenny Doe
Unit Snowmeadows Group Home
Birthdate 11/10/59
Admission Date 10/4/80
Therapist joan burlingame
Assessment Date 8/3/88

step 1:

COMPARE COLLAGE #1 WITH COLLAGE #2. DECIDE WHICH COLLAGE YOU LIKE BEST. **(DO NOT SPEND A GREAT DEAL OF TIME DECIDING WHICH COLLAGE YOU PREFER. RESULTS WILL BE MORE ACCURATE IF YOU RELY ON YOUR FIRST IMPRESSION.)** NOW DETERMINE HOW MUCH BETTER YOU LIKE YOUR FAVORITE, EITHER JUST **SLIGHTLY** BETTER, **MODERATELY** BETTER OR **EXTREMELY** BETTER. WHEN YOU HAVE MADE THE DECISION AS TO THE DEGREE OF YOUR PREFERENCE, USE THE INFORMATION BELOW TO MARK YOUR ANSWER.

SLIGHTLY MORE INTEREST → **SHADE 1 SQUARE**
MODERATELY MORE INTEREST → **SHADE 2 SQUARES**
EXTREMELY MORE INTEREST → **SHADE 3 SQUARES**

IN THE ROW OF YOUR PREFERRED COLLAGE, BEGINNING AT THE **LEFT SIDE** OF THE CHART, SHADE THE NUMBER OF SQUARES THAT INDICATE YOUR PREFERENCE (SLIGHT, MODERATE, EXTREME). FOR EXAMPLE, IF YOU PREFERRED COLLAGE #2 MODERATELY MORE THAN COLLAGE #1, YOU WOULD SHADE 2 SQUARES IN ROW #2. **YOU ALWAYS SHADE IN THE ROW OF THE ONE YOU LIKE BEST.**

LEISURE CATEGORIES CHART

Begin here

1. Games
2. Sports
3. Nature
4. Collection
5. Crafts
6. Music & Art
7. Education, Entertainment, and Cultural
8. Volunteerism
9. Organizational

step 2:

NOW CONSIDER WHAT YOUR **PRIMARY FEELING** IS THAT YOU ASSOCIATE WITH THE ACTIVITIES PICTURED IN THE PREFERRED COLLAGE **(ONE FEELING ONLY). BEGINNING AT THE LEFT,** PLACE AN X IN THE FIRST SQUARE OF THE ROW THAT DESCRIBES HOW YOU FEEL ABOUT THE COLLAGE. IF NONE OF THE WORDS DESCRIBE YOUR PRIMARY FEELING, YOU MAY WRITE IN A WORD IN ONE OF THE BLANK SPACES PROVIDED.

FEELINGS CHART

Begin here

- RELAXATIONAL
- HEALTHY
- EXCITEMENT
- ACCOMPLISHMENT
- FUN
- RELIEF
- SATISFACTION
- ESCAPE
- COMPANIONSHIP
- CONTENTMENT
- REJUVENATION
- PHYSICAL
- PLEASURE
- Social
- Happy

step 3:

PLACE A CHECK MARK NEXT TO THE COMPARISON YOU HAVE JUST COMPLETED. NOW PROCEED WITH THE NEXT COMPARISON, 1 & 3, THEN 1 & 4, 1 & 5, ETC.

COLLAGE COMPARISONS

vs # ✓

1 vs 2, 1 vs 3, 1 vs 4, 1 vs 5, 1 vs 6, 1 vs 7, 1 vs 8, 1 vs 9, 2 vs 3, 2 vs 4, 2 vs 5, 2 vs 6, 2 vs 7, 2 vs 8, 2 vs 9, 3 vs 4, 3 vs 5, 3 vs 6, 3 vs 7, 3 vs 8, 3 vs 9, 4 vs 5, 4 vs 6, 4 vs 7, 4 vs 8, 4 vs 9, 5 vs 6, 5 vs 7, 5 vs 8, 5 vs 9, 6 vs 7, 6 vs 8, 6 vs 9, 7 vs 8, 7 vs 9, 8 vs 9

SAMPLE ASSESSMENT REPORT

Narrative Style

NAME: Lance Terry
PATIENT NUMBER: 000-00-000
DATE ADMITTED TO IA SERVICE: 12/12/86
DATE DISCHARGED FROM IA SERVICE: 1/5/87

LOCATION: Home Health Care
HARBORVIEW #: H0-00-00-00

PUBLIC TRANSPORTATION ASSESSMENT

This assessment was generated by a prescription from Shawn Baley, M.D. to supplement the assessment completed by the Certified Therapeutic Recreation Specialist on staff at Haborview Medical Center. The purpose was to determine if Mr. Terry would be able to attend outpatient therapy instead of remaining an inpatient. At this point independent transportation from his home to the outpatient head injury program at Virginia Mason Hospital is the only element that is holding up his discharge. The funding for this assessment was approved through Labor and Industry.

The administration of this assessment took place over four different sessions. The results from each session were reported back to his therapist, some adjustments were made to his program, and he was then re-assessed.

HISTORY: The patient is a 33 year old white male who fell 50 feet from a loading dock sustaining a right temporal contusion on 8/12/86. He is anticipating discharge soon from Harborview. Upon discharge he will start an outpatient program at Virginia Mason.

PROBLEMS ASSESSED BY RECREATIONAL THERAPY:

1. Decreased Short Term Memory. The patient scored poorly on a reality orientation assessment given on 12/29/86 (18 points out of a possible 59 placing him in the Moderate to Mild Disorientation category). Retention of new information is extremely limited. The patient requires the use of a memory book to complete normal day to day activities. There is now a section in his memory book which addresses the basic personal history information that he needs. Using his memory book as an adaptive device the patient was re-tested on 1/5/87. With the use of his book he scored 43 out of 59 points; enough of an improvement to move him into the Mild to Oriented category. At this level he should be able to survive if lost in the city when given moderate to mild challenges.

2. Decreased Mobility. The patient's path finding skills are not functional at this point and he requires the use of maps and his memory book to find locations. Mr. Terry demonstrates above average physical endurance, being able to walk at a brisk pace from 1st Ave. up to 3rd Ave. with little noted shortness of breath. He does not demonstrate the concentration necessary to notice if the 'walk sign' says 'walk' or 'don't walk'. This, and other cognitive disorders, impede his mobility more than his physical disability (slight left-sided weakness).

3. Decreased Cognitive Function. The patient does not demonstrate functional problem solving and flexibility of thought at this time. Specific areas of cognitive functioning that proved to be a limitation to his independence were: a) personal information (phone number, location of residence), b) destination information, c) ability to identity 'good touching' versus 'bad touching', d) recognition of frequently seen locations (e.g.; the bus stop where he is to get off), e) simple problem solving (e.g.; how to get the bus driver to stop the bus because he wants to get off), and f) the ability to recognize coins and add them up to the correct amount for his bus fare.

After an initial assessment a special chapter in his memory book was developed to assist him in achieving this treatment goal. In addition, a Metro Discount Pass was obtained for him. Not only will this pass allow him to ride the bus for a whole year for just $40.00, but it will allow the therapists to work on money recognition at a later date. He was able to demonstrate the ability to show the pass to the driver 4 out of 5 times with just one cue from the driver each time. (Each trial he had a different bus driver to interact with. The recreational therapist had no interaction with the bus drivers to help duplicate a solo ride by Mr. Terry.)

Upon completion of the assessment it became obvious that while Mr. Terry frequently had difficulties of one kind or another, he could ride the bus with some degree of independence from hospital staff. His primary problem was that he would either forget to check his memory book for the next step or he would lose his place and start reading the wrong section of the instructions. With some change in the wording of the bus section of his memory book and additional pictures, he was able to make it to Virginia Mason with the therapist only shadowing him.

Mr. Terry's functional ability dropped drastically (to the point of being non-functional in the community) when he was presented with a large amount of information. (An example would be if he asked the person sitting next to him a question about how to locate his stop and that person then gave him a lot of detail.) His dysfunction becomes so overwhelming that he becomes almost incoherent and trembles. During the two times this happened it took ten minutes of sitting in a quiet place for him to calm down enough to continue with his bus ride evaluation. Both his in-house recreational therapist and I worked on this problem. It really needs to be addressed in his new out-patient program.

Summary: During the three weeks that I saw the patient I noticed a significant increase in his ability to retain new information. While he is still far from normal in this area, it is encouraging to note the change.

Mr. Terry should be able to independently ride the bus 80% of the time without significant difficulty. Given the speed in which he is regaining cognitive ability and his improved skill in using his memory book this percentage should increase to over 95% by mid-February. Because his skills decrease when he is tired or sick (i.e.; a cold), Mr. Terry's family should call a cab for him on these occasions until the outpatient therapists feel that this problem is resolved. When Mr. Terry's functional ability drops he is more apt to exhibit inappropriate touching and inappropriate language. During the first two therapy sessions Mr. Terry upset two women bus riders. While this problem decreased as his functional ability increased, a public complaint to the police or the bus company would be a set-back for him. There are strong therapeutic reasons (tied directly to his diagnosis) for Labor and Industry to reimburse the family for the cab expense.

Idyll Arbor, Inc. staff do not plan to continue seeing Mr. Terry, as the services prescribed have been delivered. If the staff at either Harborview or Virginia Mason wish to refer Mr. Terry for additional recreational therapy services, we would be glad to take the referral.